THANK GOD
WE KEPT THE FLAG
FLYING

THANK GOD
WE KEPT THE FLAG
FLYING

The Siege and Relief of Ladysmith
1899-1900

KENNETH GRIFFITH

THE VIKING PRESS / NEW YORK

Published in 1975 by The Viking Press, Inc.
625 Madison Avenue, New York, N.Y. 10022

LIBRARY OF CONGRESS CATALOGING IN PUBLICATION DATA
Griffith, Kenneth, 1921-
Thank God we kept the flag flying.
Bibliography: p.
Includes index.
1. Ladysmith, Natal—Siege, 1899.   I. Title
DT934.L2G74   1975   968'.4   74-23751
ISBN 0-670-69756-7

Printed in U.S.A.

CONTENTS

	Acknowledgements	vi
	Illustrations	vii
	Preface	xi
	Introduction	xv
1.	The Eve of War	1
2.	The War Begins	21
3.	The Battle of Elandslaagte	41
4.	The Retreat to Ladysmith	58
5.	The Boers Close In	74
6.	The Siege of Ladysmith: *November 1899*	96
7.	The Relieving Force: *November 1899*	123
8.	The Siege of Ladysmith: *December 1899*	145
9.	The Relieving Force: *December 1899*	174
10.	The Siege of Ladysmith: *January 1900*	210
11.	The Relieving Force: *January 1900*	237
12.	The Siege of Ladysmith: *February 1900*	285
13.	The Relieving Force: *February 1900*	300
14.	The Relief of Ladysmith	354
	Epilogue	371
	Bibliography	379
	Index	383

ACKNOWLEDGEMENTS

Thanks are due to John Murray Ltd, for permission to quote from *Rifleman and Hussar* by Sir Percival Marling (John Murray 1931), to William Blackwood and Sons for quotations from *A Soldier's Saga* by General Sir Aylmer Haldane (William Blackwood 1948), to Arthur Barker & Co., for quotations from *Soldiering On* by General Sir Hubert Gough (Arthur Barker 1954), to Faber and Faber Ltd for quotations from *Commando* by Deneys Reitz (Faber 1929), and to Shuter and Shooter Pty Ltd, for quotations from *Besieged in Ladysmith* by H. Watkins Pitchford (Shuter and Shooter 1964). Every effort has been made to trace holders of copyright material, and the author apologizes for any inadvertent omissions.

ILLUSTRATIONS

Frontispiece: 'Le lion Anglais et le taureau Boer' – from a French satirical magazine

Between pages 94 and 95

THE BOERS

President Paul Johannes Kruger – a signed photograph
General Schalk Burger
General Christian De Wet – a signed photograph
General Lucas Meyer
General Louis Botha
President Martinus Steyn – a signed photograph

THE BRITISH

General Sir George White
General Sir Redvers Buller – a signed photograph
General Buller with Bennet Burleigh
General Sir Charles Warren
British prisoners captured at Colenso, with their Boer guards

Between pages 190 and 191

THE RELIEVING FORCE

Winston Churchill at the wreck of the armoured train
Field artillery cross the Tugela River
General Clery at the Battle of Colenso
The Battle of Spion Kop
The dead on Spion Kop
A shell explodes in a Boer gun emplacement
British troops advance on the Tugela Heights

LADYSMITH BESIEGED

Major R. Bowen, with an extract from his last letter
A civilian shelter at Ladysmith
The British Naval Brigade in Ladysmith
A map of Ladysmith, used by the Boers
The Base Hospital Camp
British troops after the Relief
The first and last shells – from *The Leaguer of Ladysmith* by Captain
  Clive Dixon

Between pages 286 and 287

SOUVENIRS FROM THE WAR

The 'Gentleman in Kharki' – a bronze statue by Caton Woodville
Medals for the Relief of Ladysmith
The Queen's chocolate box
'Bobs' – a Boer War game
A khaki valentine from a British soldier
A commemorative handkerchief
Generals Buller and White on contemporary jugs
A china money-box, caricaturing President Kruger

CARTOONS FROM THE WAR

Warren bathes on Hussar Hill – from a French journal
Queen Victoria is spanked by Kruger – from a French journal
Three contemporary anti-British postcards
A cartoon panorama emphasizing the Siege of Ladysmith

MAPS

Map of Ladysmith, drawn with features in relief   ix
South Africa   xiv
Northern Natal   xviii
The Tugela Heights   15
Talana Hill   33
Elandslaagte   45
Rietfontein   69
Colenso   179
Taba Nyama   251
Vaal Krantz   303
Pieter's Hill   345

This sketch of Ladysmith and its surrounding hills, seen from the south, is an accurate reproduction of a contemporary British map. The massive hill in the right foreground is Umbulwana, on which the Boers positioned their 'Long Tom.' Pepworth Hill, another Boer position unmarked on the map, is to the left of Long Hill, and Surprise Hill is in the distance beyond Observation Hill.

Rifleman's Ridge

Telegraph Hill

Wagon Hill

Rifleman's Post
Range Post

Highlander's Post
King's Post
Observation Hill

Caesar's Camp

Convent Hill
Intombi Camp
LADYSMITH
Gordon Hill
Junction Hill
Dummy Gun

Cemetery Hill

Long Hill
Flag Hill

Gun Hill

Lombard's Kop

PREFACE

In 1952 I went to South Africa for the first time. I travelled to that land as a member of the Old Vic Theatre Company and I am proud of the fact that my job there was to play Oberon in a Tyrone Guthrie production of *A Midsummer Night's Dream* – proud because Tyrone Guthrie was, I believe, the greatest theatre man of my time.

One night, after a performance of the play at His Majesty's Theatre, Johannesburg, a visitor came to my dressing room. As the man limped through the doorway and I looked at his heavily moustached face, I slowly recognized an old friend from my boyhood. The man's name was Peter Strong and he was a remarkable spirit. After sustaining serious injuries in his Royal Air Force fighter aircraft during the Second World War and after surviving a long period of military hospitalization, he garnered his 'gratuity' and what private funds he could scrape together and journeyed to southern Africa, where he bought a single-engined aircraft with which he planned to earn his living. After various struggles to sustain this idea, Peter Strong hit upon the idea of opening up the interior of Basutoland (today's Lesotho) with his flying skill and courage. It should be understood that Lesotho is a mountain mass and until the arrival of Peter was inaccessible except on foot or on horse. It is an epic story; he cut down the time of carrying some of the Royal Mail out of Basutoland to a Union of South Africa railhead from about two weeks to fifty minutes. Peter Strong had made his headquarters at Ladysmith in Natal, and he urged me to visit his house there – which I did.

Peter Strong walked me for many miles around the defences of the old garrison town. The atmosphere of the siege that began on 2 November 1899 still pervades the place. We climbed onto the tops of kopjes (hills) and I looked at the graves of British soldiers from Devon and Manchester and from other places six and a half thousand miles away. From that time I became deeply interested in what the hell were the poor dead soldiers doing there. It has never seemed quite so questionable to me why South African farmers – known as Boers – were also buried in that vicinity. It did suggest to me that it was a simple matter of attack and defence. And my subsequent obsession with the story has confirmed my initial instinct.

Peter Strong walked me around the little town – still strangely British in atmosphere. He showed me the Town Hall with its clock-tower which during the siege had been pierced by a Boer shell. I believe this shell-hole remained for a long time as a proud souvenir, till it was decided to repair it to appease latter-day Boer and British animosity. Personally I am sorry that we have now lost the historic hole; there are better ways of forgiving – without forgetting.

I was shown Sir George White's headquarters during the siege. Sir George commanded Ladysmith during the investment. The house is, like much of Ladysmith, totally unchanged. It just stands there, lived in, no plaque of commemoration and totally unpretentious.

Close to the Town Hall, on the other side of the street, is the Royal Hotel where the most privileged of the besieged lived. I felt the presence of ghosts most strongly. Outside the hotel, set into the pavement, is one of the few self-conscious memorials to that strange Victorian drama: it is a small brass plate registering the death of Dr Starke on that very spot, as he hurried to a place of shelter under the banks of the old Klip River.

Indeed every square foot of that town and the country around is pulsating with that terrible and brave time.

Peter Strong took me to the southern defences of Ladysmith, where the Boers heroically attacked on 6 January 1900 and the British with equal courage threw them back. If you know the details of the battle and the summer grass is burnt away, you can stoop down and pick up little batches of British .303 ammunition, and then, pursuing your knowledge of the old Boer tactics, you can move to the perimeter of Caesar's Camp or Wagon Hill and there, behind protective boulders, pick up Boer ammunition – usually mauser – dated 1898. And if you care to notice, there is shrapnel under your feet.

I have often thought that Peter Strong was a little disappointed with me because I did not – perhaps – appear to share the same degree of interest that he had. Well, he was wrong; because of his kindness I have returned and returned to South Africa and have made five films about the Boer War – and now I have written this book.

Where I have quoted the words of those present at the time, I have kept the wording and spelling of the original.

I dedicate the book to his memory and to the old gentlemen, both Boer and British, who fought the story with their lives. And also I dedicate the book to my editor, Anthony Whittome, who gently nagged and nursed me through the reliving of the siege and relief of Ladysmith.

KENNETH GRIFFITH

SOUTH AFRICA
1899

0   100
miles

—— railways
----- state borders

RHODESIA

PORTUGUESE TERRITORY

TRANSVAAL

Pretoria
Mafeking   Johannesburg

ORANGE
FREE STATE
                Ladysmith
Orange River   Kimberley   Tugela River
                Bloemfontein

                Pietermaritzburg   Durban

CAPE COLONY

                                East London
Cape Town
                Port Elizabeth

INTRODUCTION

*They have asked for my trousers, and I have given
them; then for my coat, I have given that also; now
they want my life, and that I cannot give.*

PRESIDENT KRUGER

The Second Boer War, which did not officially begin until 11 October
1899, became inevitable much earlier in 1886 when gold was discovered
some thirty miles south of Pretoria, the capital of the Transvaal Republic.
The actual area of the discovery was called the Witwatersrand or, in English,
the Ridge of the White Waters, and a city was to evolve there called Johannesburg, named after Paul Johannes Kruger, the sometime President of
the Transvaal Republic.

Of course the discovery of gold does not always cause a war; the trouble
with this gold was that there was more of it in one place than the world had
ever known. And Britain already had a long record of dabbling in the
Transvaal's affairs; indeed, since the time the country was established by
trekking Boers, back in the 1830s. However in 1852 the Transvaalers
secured a categorical promise of freedom from English interference at the
Sand River Convention. Britain stuck to her promise when it suited her
and broke her promise when it did not. On 12 April 1877, with a Tory
Government in Britain, the Transvaal was annexed into the British Empire. On 15 December 1880, the Boers rose in rebellion against the British
army of occupation and quickly inflicted defeats on them at Bronkhorst
Spruit, Laing's Nek, Ingogo and finally, crushingly, at the battle of Majuba
Hill. By this time, Mr Gladstone and his Liberals had come to power in
England and they decided to come to terms with the Transvaalers; the
British soldiers marched out of the country. But now, with this massive
gold discovery around Johannesburg, it was only a matter of how and when
England would return.

Cecil Rhodes, the English imperialist businessman personified, made the first move. Into Johannesburg, to mine the gold and do the business, came a great concourse of foreigners, and a considerable proportion of them were British. These foreigners or Uitlanders, as the Boers called them, finally outnumbered the entire Boer electorate of the Transvaal. President Kruger saw the danger to his country of giving an easy franchise to the Uitlanders; he took measures to make it increasingly difficult for them to achieve the vote - indeed they had to prove that their commitment was to the Transvaal Republic, and to no other country, before they got it. Rhodes saw in this issue his chance to undermine the authority of Kruger's Government. He pointed out that the Uitlanders were providing wealth for the Transvaal but were not enfranchised. The fact that the Uitlanders were there to become wealthy themselves and that few of them would swear loyalty to the Transvaal State was not mentioned.

Rhodes, using this franchise issue, fomented a rebellion of the Uitlanders in Johannesburg and, in collusion with it, organized his private army to invade the Transvaal; and this wretched chicanery ended in the abortive Jameson Raid of 1896. A renegade Scottish doctor named Leander Starr Jameson led the invasion. Back in England, the sly, arrogant Tory Colonial Secretary, Joseph Chamberlain, had given a wink of approval. Kruger's Boers met Jameson and his raiders west of Johannesburg and smashed them. President Kruger prevented his Boers from hanging the leaders of the plot and eventually they were sent back to England on condition that they were tried at the Old Bailey; but with such elevated collusion that they only received sentences varying from six to eighteen months. Leander Starr Jameson was released before his sentence was completed.

This then was the plot, and the stage on which the Second Boer War was to be fought. After the Jameson Raid, Joseph Chamberlain showed his colours more honestly and sent as England's representative to South Africa Alfred Milner, a cold, ruthless fish who determined, come what may, that England should be paramount in the Transvaal and thereby control everything the Transvaal might contain.

President Kruger met the British High Commissioner, Sir Alfred Milner, at the Bloemfontein Conference in the Orange Free State Republic on 31 May 1899. Kruger made desperate concessions; Milner hardened his demands and finally old President Kruger said, 'I am not ready to hand over my country to strangers . . .' The Conference was at an end and Milner was a great step closer to his goal.

Whatever concessions were made in the few months that followed, Milner, with hair-raising certainty, crushed. Chamberlain, back home in Old England, followed as best he dared - but not with the same naked determination.

Of course, Kruger and his Boers had expected this confrontation since the Jameson Raid of 1896. From that date, they had been arming themselves formidably.

On 7 September President Kruger said in the Raad, the Parliament in Pretoria, 'They have asked for my trousers, and I have given them; then for my coat, I have given that also; now they want my life, and that I cannot give.'

The old man then gave the British Empire a hard look and turned to his people and said: 'The republics are determined, if they must belong to England, that a price will have to be paid which will stagger humanity.'

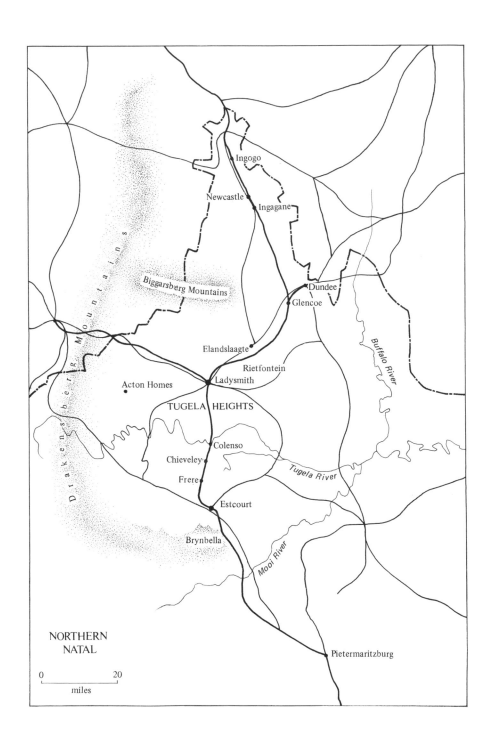

Ingogo

Newcastle •Ingagane

Biggarsberg Mountains

•Dundee
•Glencoe

Elandslaagte•

Rietfontein
Acton Homes •Ladysmith

TUGELA HEIGHTS

Colenso
Chieveley•
Frere•
•Estcourt

Brynbella

Buffalo River

Tugela River

Mooi River

Drakensberg Mountains

NORTHERN
NATAL

0   20
    miles

•Pietermaritzburg

I

THE EVE OF WAR

*The supremacy of England in South Africa is no
doubt in state.*

GENERAL PENN-SYMONS

IT is a recurring theme in Britain's imperial story that its politicians make
wars inevitable whilst overlooking adequate military preparations. Who were
those two cartoon generals during the 1939–45 war? Generals Too Little
and Too Late, I think . . . The Second Boer War was no exception to that
rule. High Commissioner Milner, while working himself into his bureaucratic ground, did manage to give the military problem a little thought and
was horrified to realize that the commander-in-chief of the British forces in
South Africa, Lieutenant-General Sir William Butler, was deeply sympathetic to the Boer predicament. And what was even more embarrassing, the
General appeared, by his words and actions, to be so naive that he could not
believe that a British Government would play a dirty trick on anyone – or on
any country. General Butler viewed the machinations of the Uitlander
business element at Johannesburg, and as Acting High Commissioner –
because Milner was in England – sent a warning despatch to the Colonial
Secretary, Chamberlain. One can imagine what Milner and Chamberlain thought when they saw that! They, more than any others now that
Rhodes had been disgraced into the background, were the chief movers of
what Butler was complaining about.

At the conclusion of the Bloemfontein Conference, Milner wrote his
report of the bullying negotiations for Chamberlain's perusal and added a
coup de grâce for innocent General Butler:

> The General. He is too awful. He has, I believe, made his military preparations
> all right, but beyond that I cannot get him to make the least move or take the
> slightest interest . . . His sympathy is wholly with the other side. At the same time
> there is nothing to lay hold of. He never interferes with my business and is perfectly

polite. But he is absolutely no use, unless indeed we mean to knuckle down, in which case he had better be made High Commissioner.

Well, a nod was as good as a wink and General Butler was out on his ear.

At this juncture there were between nine and ten thousand imperial troops in South Africa. They were divided between the two British colonies of southern Africa. In the Cape there were three and a half battalions of infantry, two companies of garrison artillery, plus a few Engineers, etc. In Natal there were three infantry battalions, two cavalry regiments, three batteries of Royal Field Artillery and a mountain battery – and it is this Natal situation that our story is about. Slap in the middle of Natal is the town of Ladysmith, known to old soldiers as 'the Aldershot of South Africa' – the garrison for the whole colony.

Commanding this Natal force was Major-General Sir William Penn-Symons, aged fifty-six, who had seen considerable service in South Africa, including the Zulu War of 1879 and, latterly, away from Africa, on the Indian Frontier.

On 25 May 1899, Milner, realizing that the British colonists in Natal were getting uneasy about his impending war, wildly telegraphed to that colony:

> You can tell Minister from me that it is out of the question that any invasion of Natal should be tolerated by Her Majesty's Government. Such an event is highly improbable, I think; but Natal would be defended with the whole force of the Empire if it occurred, and redress would be exacted for any injury to her.

So the Natal Government asked Sir Walter Hely-Hutchinson, Governor of Natal, to ask General Penn-Symons how things stood militarily, if the Boers decided to hit first. The reply was not cheering: 'I consider the force now in Natal, even aided by the Natal Volunteer forces, insufficient to do more than to hold the colony up to the Dundee [Natal] mines and to secure Ingagane railway bridge, leaving Newcastle and the northern apex of Natal to the Boers.' And again on 21 July 1899, General Symons calculated that to hold all of Natal he would require another 5600 soldiers. On 3 August, Chamberlain telegraphed from London that arrangements were being made to add at least another 2000 men to the Natal garrison – which was far from being 'the whole force of the Empire'.

The above estimation was extremely ominous, because General Symons was not a cautious soldier. His two guiding principles were: 'To do my duty and to do it in the spirit of a high minded chivalrous gentleman.' Without a few definitions, this could cause military problems. Governor Hely-Hutchinson had described Penn-Symons as having 'lots of energy and was as keen as mustard'. The best person to know him was his old boss from Asia days, General Sir George White VC, and he held Symons in high regard, having described him as 'the most competent man in India – to command an infantry division'. Of course he was being called upon to do more than command an infantry division in the late summer of 1899.

At about this time Symons wrote to Sir George White back in London:

> The situation is as critical as it can be, and I am ready to move troops into their positions, to do their best to protect Natal, in two hours . . . I respect our maybe enemy for his love of independence, for his power of mobility, and for his marksmanship. I think also that he has generally behaved fairly well in previous wars. His rule, however, is abominably bad and corrupt. The supremacy of England in South Africa is no doubt at stake.

That letter is quite shrewd before the event. General Symons picks out the salient qualities of the Boers: independence, mobility and marksmanship, and when he emphasizes – unkindly in my book – their corruptibility . . . well, that was another of the English jingo's propaganda cards, heavily played back home in 1899's equivalent of the Monday Club and again ruthlessly dealt by the business boys of Johannesburg. Not that Boers were incapable of behind-the-back payments – as long as these did not transgress one psalm in the Old Testament. Yes, some Boers were certainly capable of making a quick Kruger pound, but their methods were less sophisticated than those used in the City of London.

Colonel Rawlinson, another of General White's protégés, saw it all differently. Referring to Penn-Symons and his military staff's attitude, he said: 'They . . . speak of a British brigade being able to take on five times their number in Boers which is silly rot.' And Colonel Ian Hamilton, another White man, wrote: 'A great deal of the old contempt for the Boer is still existing. Symons is very boastful and bad in this way.' Ian Hamilton had no contempt, military or otherwise, for the Boer. He had been run off the top of Majuba Hill by the Boers in 1881.

Of all the assessments of the potential of Penn-Symons, who would have to face any initial assault from fighting Boers, I think my favourite comes from Major Marling, who won his VC at Tamai in the Suakin Campaign of 1884. Major Marling had arrived in Natal for military duty accompanied by his new wife 'B' and he inscribed in his entertaining diary:

> September [1899]: To Government House to stay with Sir Walter [Hely-Hutchinson], and found the General, Sir Penn-Symons, there, who was command-

ing the troops in Natal and who was one of the most charming people I have ever met. We got back to Ladysmith on September 11th, and on the 16th Sir Penn-Symons had a big Field Day of all the troops, and we practised taking Boer positions, which in view of what happened afterwards were rather weird.

So much for Penn-Symons' attitude towards the Boers. Overconfidence is a dangerous chink in anyone's armour – but on the Republican side of the Natal border, the amateur soldiers, the Boers, were not timid as they viewed England's quality. Bennet Burleigh, a famed newspaper correspondent, travelled to Pretoria to interview President Kruger and recounted a conversation between a Boer and a Britisher. Said the Boer: 'I suppose the English can send an army of 20 000 soldiers against us?' 'Oh yes; 500 000 troops, if necessary,' answered the Englishman. '*Verdompt!*' rejoined the Boer. 'It would take us three months to kill them all.' Strangely enough that Boer was a justified optimist in one way: England did have to send nearly 500 000 soldiers before the Boers surrendered.

And what of the ordinary British 'Tommies' at this time? Generally they shared Penn-Symons' blind confidence. Their wives and children, back in Old England or elsewhere, might be worried where the next decent meal was coming from, but that, astoundingly, did not prevent most of them from standing squarely with Britannia, the Queen and the Union Jack. On 6 September 1899, Private Oliver Kimpsey of the 5th Lancers wrote from Ladysmith camp: 'I think Mr Kruger will find his master this time, and Majuba Hill will be avenged by the British army ... They have been threatening to come over the border to attack this place, and cut us off from the troops up at Glencoe; but if they did, not many of them would reach the Transvaal again.' On 20 October 1899, at the battle of Elandslaagte, Private Kimpsey of the 'Dandy Fifth' was killed trying to prevent the Boers from carrying out this very threat.

On 2 October 1899, a private in the 18th Hussars wrote home to his mother in Blakeney:

Dear Mother, – After getting your letter, which I received quite safe, I can't stop to say much, as I am at last up to the front facing Kruger. I can tell you it is an awful hard life; I never thought it was like this. I can't say whether I shall come home again, but, if not, you can say your son died a soldier, with his face to the foe, revenging Majuba Hill. But, dear mother, I hope to come home safe and sound, because there is not a Boer living to shoot me, your son. I write in haste. Don't get down-hearted, mother dear. Tell dear little C— his brother is fighting for home, sweet home. Good-bye, and God bless you. From the base of operations, with Boers all round.

'Where duty calls I must obey,
I stand between love and duty'

The letter from the private from Blakeney was laying it on a bit thick, in the classic Victorian spirit. The war had not then started – and though he was right that 'there is not a Boer living to shoot me', in the very first fight in Natal, he was taken prisoner and carted off to Pretoria.

By Monday 25 September, the Right Reverend Arthur Hamilton Baynes, Bishop of Natal, was seeing troops off up northwards from Pietermaritzburg station:

I went to the station to see the 60th Rifles and part of the 5th Lancers entrained. The men were carried in open trucks, which had been fitted up with benches and a sort of scaffolding round the sides, with a beam for a back to the seats – not a very comfortable method of spending the night in the train, but fortunately the weather was fine. These troops were going to take the place at Ladysmith of those who, the night before, had been quietly and swiftly moved from Ladysmith to Glencoe. The order for this move was only given at 8 on Sunday night, and the troops were in the train by 2 a.m., and in their new camp by 6 on Monday morning. These consist of battalions of the Leicestershire Regiment, the Dublin Fusiliers, and the 18th Hussars, besides one or two batteries of artillery, and some engineers.

Joseph Chamberlain, England's Colonial Secretary, behaved as if he were Prime Minister. The actual Prime Minister was one of those Lord Salisburys who have left their mark on millions of lives, white and black, south of the Zambesi river. But Joseph Chamberlain, known popularly as Pushful Jo, did most of the scheming. He hoped to frighten the Transvaal so much that it would give way to his power designs without fighting and thereby save England the cost of a distant war. It was a calculated gambit, with the resident British military garrison as a potentially expendable pawn.

Nevertheless, military calculations were made by the Tory Cabinet and Lord Wolseley, the commander-in-chief. It was estimated that the Boers could put into the field of war at least 40 000 men, in less than two weeks. Wolseley therefore advised that an additional 10 000 British soldiers should be despatched at once. The trouble was that this military force would take thirteen weeks before it could arrive in South Africa and be ready to fight. The uncomfortable question was: would the Boers be wise enough to strike before they landed? It was becoming quite clear that President Kruger and his people were not going to climb down because the British Empire threatened them. The rest of the world looked on and wished the Transvaalers luck.

The other Boer republic, the Orange Free State, led by a wise and courageous leader, President Steyn, was also making its responsible position clear. President Steyn did everything humanly possible to create a peaceful solution, but was stating that if war came, his country would fight with the Transvaal. Though this area of the impending war is outside the scope of our story, it is worth remarking that the Orange Free State was prepared to go to war on simple principle. Countries have often claimed 'principle' as their motive for fighting. Analysis rarely confirms this; the Orange Free State is a proud exception.

And so, with imperial fingers crossed, the 10 000 embarked and were on the high seas. Because of the complicated military system of linked battalions operating in Britain and because it would save perhaps a vital week of travel time, it was decided to draw the soldiers from the British garrison in India and the Mediterranean stations. The first military transport 'set sail' on 17 September 1899. From Bombay and Calcutta came the 5th Dragoon Guards, 9th Lancers and 19th Hussars; four infantry battalions; the 1st battalion Gloucestershire Regiment, the 2nd battalion Gordon Highlanders, the 2nd battalion King's Royal Rifles and the 1st battalion Devonshire Regiment; the 21st, 42nd and 53rd Field Batteries with an ammunition column and ammunition park, and a field hospital.

From Gibraltar came the 1st Manchesters, and from Fermoy in Ireland the 1st Munster Fusiliers. And following, during the next few weeks, came the 1st Northumberland Fusiliers from Aldershot, the 1st Border Regiment from Malta, half of the Yorkshire Light Infantry from Mauritius, the 18th, 62nd and 75th Field Batteries, and detachments of Engineers and Army Service Corps. From Egypt came the 1st Royal Irish Fusiliers and the 2nd Rifle Brigade from Crete. A telegraph division and balloon section of engineers, and detachments of Army Service Corps and Ordnance Corps. Oh, you men of Britain's counties! They were all on South African soil before the end of October 1899.

As the Boers made their steadfastness more clear and England prepared to despatch these additional soldiers, it was also decided to appoint a more senior officer than Penn-Symons to command in Natal, and Sir George White was selected. Sir George had been commander-in-chief in India and now, in September 1899, was Quartermaster General at the War Office in London.

General White, aged sixty-three years, was not happy at the War Office. Shortly before leaving India he had been thrown from his horse and had badly smashed a leg and now he felt that his active days as a soldier were

A WAS AN **A**RMY
THAT SAILED
To THE CAPE

B WERE THE
BOERS
THAT IT LICKED
INTo SHAPE

From An Active Army Alphabet *by John Hassall (Sands and Co., 1900), a patriotic children's book on the Boer War*

over. And they had been active: the Indian Mutiny, the Afghanistan War of 1879 – where he won his Victoria Cross – command of the 92nd Highlanders, the Sudan War of 1885, the Burmese War of 1885, and pacification of the North West Frontier of India – not that the North West Frontier ever was pacified . . .

On 12 July 1899, the commander-in-chief, Lord Wolseley, sensing Sir George's unease, offered him the governorship of Gibraltar, which he readily accepted – but there was a time-lag before he could take up the appointment. On 6 September, while still waiting, Lord Wolseley communicated with him again, tipping him off 'that matters are in a very critical state in South Africa, and that you must be prepared to start almost immediately for Natal.' Lord Wolseley emphasized that his job was simply to organize the 14 000 soldiers that would be in Natal with him in such a military way that if the Boers attacked, Natal would be protected. No further instructions were given; he was to decide what to do when he got there.

However, before the deal was finally clinched, Lord Wolseley raised the subject of Sir George's battered leg. The leg was in a bad state. A little while before, Sir George had occasion to address a meeting of Irish doctors – he himself belonged to that strange breed of 'Irishmen' who are more English than any man of Sussex – and to that meeting he said: 'I landed in England with a leg so broken up that a very high authority described it, I believe, as "a bag of bones" . . . The fact, gentlemen, that I can get on my legs and address you tonight . . . is due to the skill of your profession, and I think I ought to express gratitude to your profession for such a leg-asy.'

But now, with Lord Wolseley thinking of the defence of Natal and at the same time casting uneasy glances at the gammy leg, Sir George White VC, quickly responded: 'My leg is good enough for anything except running away.' Sir George got the job and limped out of the commander-in-chief's office towards unexpected active service.

The truth is that at this juncture Sir George didn't really expect fighting in South Africa. He was surprisingly shrewd about extra-military matters, for a soldier, when he wrote to Field-Marshal Lord Roberts of Kandahar: 'The big financiers remain confident in the preservation of peace and they watch the pulse of such affairs more closely and with better information than any other body.' Now, I find that paragraph very interesting. One of my personal angers has been that imperial big business has not only exploited the indigenous population of conquered colonies, but has conned the soldiers to die and be wounded in carrying out their business designs. This letter from White to Roberts states clearly that White knew what was afoot at Johannesburg and in the City of London.

Sir George received a message from Her Majesty Queen Victoria, summoning him to visit her at Osborne as she '. . . could not let him go without saying good-bye to him'. This was typical of the very old Queen. She was bemused by the ways of the new world, personified by the small-arms manufacturer from Birmingham, her Colonial Secretary, 'Pushful Jo' Chamberlain. 'The Old Widow', as late Victorians called her, focused more and more on the human tragedy. She looked at her soldiers and conveyed womanly support and sympathy.

On 16 September 1899, Sir George travelled to Southampton with his wife and eldest daughter. There they said good-bye to him and on that day he wrote a letter to his brother: 'Good-bye, my dear J. I have much on me. If anything happens to me, look after those that remain behind me. I will try to keep the name up. You have been the closest affection and the longest of my life.' Well, there writes the simple good man and soldier.

But in the nucleus of British imperial aggression, the Tory party, there were other confidential military chats going on. As early as mid-June 1899, the Marquis of Lansdowne, Secretary of State for War, sent for General Sir Redvers Buller VC. The meeting was so private that it took place at the Marquis's home residence. Sir Redvers recorded the conversation:

Lord Lansdowne told me that the Government had reason to fear that a war in South Africa was in certain circumstances probable, and that, should the war occur, I had been selected as the best officer to hold the chief command. I said that I had never actually held an independent command, that a war in South Africa, if one really occurred, would be a big thing, and that I could only say with regard to the command of it what I had said to Mr Campbell-Bannerman when he proposed that I should be Commander-in-Chief of the Army. I then told Mr Campbell-Bannerman that I thought a stronger combination, and a better one for the Army, than myself as Commander-in-Chief with any other officer as Adjutant-General, would be Lord Wolseley as Commander-in-Chief and myself as Adjutant-General, and I thought the same combination, namely, Lord Wolseley as Commander-in-Chief and myself as Chief of the Staff, was the best that I could recommend for the war in South Africa. I said that I always considered that I was better as second in a complex military affair than as the officer in chief command.

General Buller had successfully argued himself out of the ultimate in British military honour, the commander-in-chiefship, and now he was attempting to bow himself away from the paramount position on active service. One cannot help respecting his honesty and sense of responsibility.

Of course, it is true that he was past his virile prime – with what dash and humanity he had won his Victoria Cross, saving a brother officer in the Zulu War of 1879 – and he was now addicted to rich food and copious champagne – but few of us can say 'no' to the dizzy heights. Sir Redvers tried to.

Then he argued his proper merit to the Marquis:

So far as knowledge of detail, power of organisation, tactical knowledge, and capacity for handling the three arms, and for getting men to fight for me in the field, I thought I could fairly say that I could hold my own with any officer in the Army; but . . . I had never been in a position where the whole load of responsibility fell upon me, alone, in the manner it would were I in command of such an expedition 6000 miles away from home. That I was combatant by nature, and that, if difficulties arose, I should, I knew, be apt to plunge into the actual struggle with those difficulties, and thus possibly affect my power of discrimination and magnify, because of its difficulty, a point of minor into one of supreme importance.

Well, Sir Redvers knew his strength and suspected his weakness, but he was a professional soldier and conditioned to obey, if the request came from 'above'.

Of Sir Redvers' argument against his appointment:

Lord Lansdowne demurred to this, and said that I could have his support, that everybody had agreed in recommending me: the consensus of opinion, he said, was remarkable. I said: 'Well, no man should decline to try what he is worth. I will do my best.'

Examining this conversation further, the critical bit lies between Sir Redvers' very clearly spelt-out doubts about his own ability to command an overall complex military strategy and 'Well, no man should decline to try what he is worth.' If General Buller was correct on the first point, in exercising the second, a lot of British soldiers could get messed up. I cannot help pitying the General's predicament.

General Buller had thought about strategy in South Africa before his meeting with Lord Lansdowne. Indeed he had been in the disastrous First Boer War of 1881 and the Zulu War of 1879. So he was able to raise strategic problems immediately with Lord Lansdowne and his reasonings proved him to be no military fool: 'A desultory conversation ensued, in which we discussed the best route [for the invasion of the Transvaal] to be followed.' He is against Natal, considering 'that by Durban objectionable, on account of the very difficult country . . .' He plumps for '. . . the route via Bloemfontein [as] the route, and the only route, by which an English Expeditionary force could, with fair prospects of success, attack Pretoria.'

The trouble with this 'route' was that Bloemfontein was the capital of the other Boer republic, the Orange Free State, and the Free Staters were making it increasingly clear that if it came to the crunch, they would fight with the Transvaal. Therefore Lord Lansdowne, being a politician, did not like this practical question being raised. Though Secretary of State for War, he was simply asking General Buller to prepare himself to fight an attacking war, which the General was not all that keen about, without wanting the General to discuss the practical feasibility. How I wish General Buller had had a brainstorm and had simply said to Lord Lansdowne: 'Look here, if you want to paint the Transvaal red, and get our hands on all that gold in Jo'burg, I must take the poor bloody British Army through the Orange Free State.' Unfortunately Buller did not say this or anything like it. But how sickening politicians almost invariably are. That awful impulse: never speak the whole truth.

What Lord Lansdowne did say was ' . . . that at the time, an advance through the Free State at all was out of the question'. Buller's reply had to be pretty forthright – political tact or no political tact – and he said: 'Well, before we go to war with the Transvaal, the Government must consider this point. The Government of the Orange Free State must be compelled to declare itself actively on one side or the other: it is *impossible* to allow it, as in 1881, the advantages of a belligerent, and the comforts of a neutral.' For Buller, so far, so good.

The trouble about this Orange Free State business was that they had nothing in the way of hard cash that the British wanted. Years before, Britain had deprived them of an area of land to which they laid claim which contained the biggest diamond deposits that the world has ever known, around Kimberley. Britain had cooked and was eating that goose. Now she didn't want to hustle the Orange Free Staters into an armed alliance with the Transvaal. She would rather just fight the Transvaal on its own – naturally.

But Lansdowne was prepared to discuss how many soldier souls were required to conquer the Transvaal. He and Buller arrived at an agreed army corps, a cavalry division, and seven battalions for the lines of communications. That is, some 48 000 soldiers in addition to those who were already there or already thinking about embarking.

Nothing more was said to Sir Redvers, though his appointment was leaked to the press. Then on 3 July 1899 he was again summoned to Lansdowne's presence, though this time in London. Much the same politically careful demands were made and Sir Redvers sent a memorandum of his reactions to the meeting to Lord Wolseley at the War Office: ' . . . Secondly our relation to the Orange Free State should, if possible, be definitely put upon a known basis before any invasion of the Transvaal is attempted. A hostile friend is worse than a declared enemy; and the route to be adopted in operations against Pretoria must chiefly be decided on with regard to our relations with the Orange Free State.' Sir Redvers was absolutely right. He was understandably worried because the Government were asking him to prepare for an event which they were preventing him from preparing. His continuing dilemma was: until the Government knew whom they were going to fight, where should he put his vast military stores and lethal magazines? If he had to move them on a sudden decision as to who was fighting whom, great distances were involved, ' . . . and then if I have to move to another theatre of war (and the theatre of war in South Africa is immense, while the lines of intercommunication are not good) I should probably have to commence military operations by the abandonment of important magazines . . .' And so he had to sweat out an unnerving prospect.

At last the Cabinet met on 29 September and afterwards Buller was told by Lansdowne that the route for attacking the Transvaal was to be through the Orange Free State and that he, Buller, was 'to proceed with all military preparations excepting the mobilization of the men.' Buller replied to this: 'I think that if they delay the dispatch of troops, the Government will be incurring a very grave responsibility.' Lord Lansdowne then confessed that he was 'unable to call out the Reserves, or in other words to mobilize, before the 7th of October'. The Government was hanging on until the last moment, not in the hope of simply averting war but in the hope of getting what they wanted without fighting – which is a very different matter. It was a cowardly period and at risk were the British military garrison and to a lesser extent the British citizens of the Cape and Natal colonies. But money interests always come first; this is the curse of our system and our conditioned mentality.

Buller calculated that if 7 October was the date of mobilization, the army corps could not embark before 22 October and that they could therefore hope to be assembled at the Cape by 22 December. He was now frantically juggling with time. He asked if he could leave by the first steamer bound for southern Africa on 7 October, but 14 October was arranged for his departure. On 9 October he was gazetted commander-in-chief of the expedition. Buller's die was cast.

On 3 October, Sir Redvers received his first telegram from Sir George White in Natal. It begged Sir Redvers not to allow any weakening of the force in Natal – Sir George quite rightly believed that the Boers would choose Natal's vulnerability for their prime onslaught – particularly if the Orange Free State were with them. Look at the map facing page 1, and consider the Orange Free State on Natal's western border and the Transvaal to the north and north-east.

Sir George White also suggested that a British cavalry force could be sent through the Drakensberg Mountains at Van Reenan's Pass on the north-western border of Natal with the object of threatening particularly the Orange Free State Boers. Buller must have lost his ruddy Devonshire complexion at least momentarily. He certainly discouraged the idea: prancing cavalry overlooked by probably the finest marksmen in the world. Boers could knock springbok over when they were leaping at thirty miles an hour!

Buller also warned White about the dangers of occupying the northern apex of the Natal triangle. He wrote that Glencoe, guarding the coalfields at Dundee, was too exposed for the force then at White's disposal, and though he did not actually inscribe it, I presume he meant that this also applied to exposed Ladysmith.

The great strategic question that was now facing thinly-held Natal was the deeply-etched defensive line of the west–east flow of the Tugela river, with the high jagged hills along its northern bank and the flat, though sometimes undulating, terrain south of that river. Understand that geographical fact and you will begin to understand the whole strategic problem of this story. Ladysmith is some nine miles north of this river. Look at page 15. The Tugela, with those cruel hills on its northern bank, is the clear, unarguable line of demarcation between Briton and Boer – if the Briton has to be on the defensive; and every Britisher in Natal, militarily speaking, was about to go on the defensive at least until the arrival of that army corps.

Most of us, I am sure, are used to occasional bouts of impertinence from people with power. Poor Buller was no exception and how strange and dangerous was the inexplicable treatment meted out to him during this period. Sir Redvers noted, on his visits to the War Office, that such instructions as were sent to the military in South Africa by different branches of the service were often contradictory. He therefore suggested that it would be advantageous if periodic meetings were held for all the military heads of departments and that they should be presided over by the commander-in-chief, Lord Wolseley. This arrangement was instituted during the latter part of July 1899, but to Buller's dismay, he was never invited. The explanation may lie in the fact that Lansdowne didn't like him – but that seems an awkward reason, in view of what duty was pending for Buller. Sir Redvers claimed that he did not insist on being invited for reasons of personal tact.

But again it is unfortunate that the lives of men were not put before the tact of English gentlemen.

Sir Redvers described his relationship with Lord Lansdowne: 'We did not agree. He found it difficult to work with me, and I with him, though I can truly say that I never worked harder for anyone. In the end he told me, what no one had ever said before, that I was disagreeable to work with.' Poor old Buller! The whole wretched enterprise seemed doomed with rottenness from the word go. Perhaps even more astounding than Buller's exclusion from those War Office conferences was the fact that Buller and Sir George White were never brought together before the latter's departure for South Africa – though both appointments were at that time settled. What unbelievably dangerous stupidity!

However, in all fairness to Lansdowne, he did not see Buller's grievances in quite the same light. The Secretary of State for War replied that ' ... there was not a room in the War Office that Sir Redvers Buller could not have walked into whenever he pleased, with the certainty that whatever assistance he called for in that room would be given to him without demur. I have known Sir Redvers Buller for some time and it never occurred to me that he was a particularly diffident person, or very easily intimidated, especially by civilians.' Well, he may not have been either diffident or easily intimidated – but he was not gregarious and if a person such as Lansdowne didn't strike a compatible note, Sir Redvers was likely to withdraw and glower, like an introspective bull.

During the second half of September 1899, General Sir George White and his staff were steaming southward on the *Tantallon Castle*. With him were his military secretaries, the gallant Ian Hamilton and Beauchamp Duff; his Director of Supplies, Colonel Ward, and other officers. Sir George, having no instructions whatsoever, except to defend Natal, avidly read books about the country. The ship called at the island of Madeira on 20 September and he eagerly asked for telegraphic messages from the War Office. There were none, no news whatsoever; and since wireless telegraphy had not been invented, this was his last chance to receive information for two weeks, when they would dock at Cape Town.

Ahead in Africa, the British were already taking some action. On Sunday 1 October the Bishop of Natal held a church parade for General Sir William Penn-Symons and his soldiers. The text was 'Stand fast in the Lord, my dearly beloved'.

Early in the morning of 3 October 1899, the *Tantallon Castle* reached Cape Town 'in drizzling rain and very cold'. Immediately General Forestier

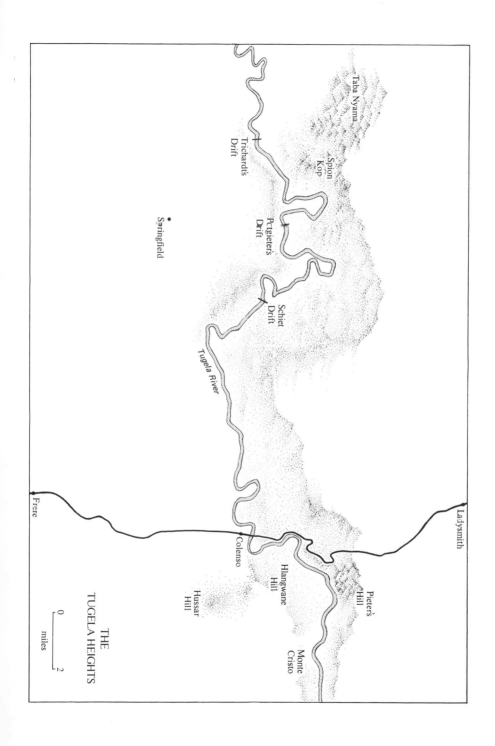

THE
TUGELA HEIGHTS

0   2
miles

Taba Nyama

Trichardt's
Drift

Spion
Kop

Springfield

Potgieter's
Drift

Schiet
Drift

Tugela River

Frere

Ladysmith

Colenso

Hlangwane
Hill

Hussar
Hill

Pieter's
Hill

Monte
Cristo

Walker, the officer commanding British troops in the Cape Colony, came aboard and hurried Sir George White to the presence of High Commissioner Milner. White noted that he looked 'worked and worried'. Good; the ball that Milner had started was now rolling steadily. War had not been declared but no one could now see how it could be averted. On 26 September, President Steyn had intimated to Milner that the Orange Free State would fight with the Transvaal – if war came.

There is a note in Sir Alfred Milner's diary at this time: 'A fresh scare this evening . . . Late, and very uneasy, to bed.' And so he should have been! He could not believe that these small republics would actually fight the arrogance of the British Empire. He telegraphed to President Steyn:

The question is whether the burgher forces will invade British territory, thus closing the door to any possibility of a pacific solution. I cannot believe that the South African Republic [Transvaal] will take such aggressive action, or that Your Honour would countenance such a course, which there is nothing to justify. Prolonged negotiations have hitherto failed to bring about a satisfactory understanding . . . but till the threatened act of aggression is committed, I shall not despair of peace, and I feel sure that any reasonable proposal from whatever quarter proceeding, would be favourably considered by Her Majesty's Government, if it offered an immediate termination of present tension and a prospect of permanent tranquillity.

This was a time, as far as I can tell, unique for Milner. Neither before nor afterwards was there to be another note of courteous human communication – with the Boers. Of course his trouble – his 'very uneasy, to bed' – was not only the realization that Britain would have to fight for power over the Transvaal, but the fact that those troops from India and the Mediterranean garrisons were still on the high seas. Ouch!

Sir George White digested this unnerving news about the troops, and decided to hasten towards Natal, not by the *Tantallon Castle* waiting for him at the dockside, but across to Port Elizabeth by train, where he would catch another boat, the SS *Scot*, bound for Durban. He described what he saw from the train in a letter to his wife:

At nearly every station the people appeared to be divided into two camps, one English and one Dutch. The railway is manned chiefly by Englishmen [I think if he had got out and inquired more closely, he would have found them to be mainly Scots] Station Masters, Guards, Conductors, etc; but grouped by themselves at most stations were parties of Boers, bearded, with slouched hats, looking physically, I thought, above the standard of the English, but intellectually much below them. At some stations the Dutch were travelling from our Colony with arms in their hands, presumably to join their Countrymen across the border. We constantly passed bands of refugees or persons that had been ordered out of the Transvaal and Orange Free State. I had not before realized what a large proportion of Dutch there are in the Cape Colony and how sharp-edged is the antagonism between the races . . .

This was Sir George White's first sight of South Africa. He wrote to his wife on his pressing problem: 'For the next three months the Dutch have the best of us as regards armed strength and position. A little success might give them enormous advantage . . . ' Here he was calculating the arrival and assembly of the great army corps, which he now knew would arrive in due course, to be commanded by Sir Redvers Buller. His problem was how to hold on for three months . . .

Sir George continued, to his wife:

If I am to have a look-in in this campaign important events will probably take place before this reaches you. If the Boers take the initiative and I can beat them heavily, I believe the war will be practically over. If they gain the first successes the consequences may be very far reaching. The telegraph will have told you before this reaches you. Every day we can put off the Boer advance the better for us. The Indian troops are landing at Durban and are well up to time, but I would like to have another fortnight to organize them and their transport before the storm breaks. It is all most interesting, and I have charming men to work with . . .

This is my lucky day, 6th October, Charasia day. May it be a date of good omen for us all. Your most affectionate George.

'Charasia' was the name of the village around which a battle was fought by Sir George White and his 92nd Highlanders on 4 October 1879, during the Afghan War.

The SS *Scot* steamed into Durban harbour, the picturesque port of Natal, on 7 October 1899. Sir George spent exactly one day there anxiously asking about the 'Indian' contingent. The news was remarkably good in this respect. The Government of India had received the telegram requesting the nearly 6000 'white' troops on 8 September; by 2 October they were beginning to land at Durban. By 9 October they were almost all there. The reinforcements from the European garrisons (Crete, Malta and Ireland) and from Egypt were slower; but all had arrived before October was out. Sir George, with his sentimental attachment to the Indian Army, began to feel that the Indian contingent might very easily become the saviours of Natal.

Sir George, having made hasty arrangements for the movement up-country of the arriving troops, then travelled the three-hour train journey to Pietermaritzburg, the colonial capital, to meet the Governor of Natal, Sir

Walter Hely-Hutchinson. Major-General Sir William Penn-Symons had travelled down-line to be present and report.

The three men looked at very simple statistics. If the Boers invaded Natal they would probably send about 30 000 men. The British, with the arriving reinforcements, would have about 15 000 men. Could these Britishers hold Natal, or some part of it, until the arrival of the great army corps towards the end of December? On the day of this meeting, the British force already assembled were divided into two main groups: 8000 men at Ladysmith and 4000 at Glencoe, forty-two miles north of Ladysmith, on the main railway running up to the Transvaal and guarding, as it were, the branch line to the coalfields at Dundee. Incidentally you can see from these Scottish place-names why I wrote that the railway officials whom Sir George White saw were probably Scots rather than English.

Running east and west, in the vicinity of Dundee and Glencoe, are the Biggarsberg Mountains. Sir George White, studying his rather poor maps – British responsibility had been parsimonious about 'intelligence' – had originally thought that his soldiers should hold this line of mountains as their forward defence. But he discovered in time that there were inadequate watering facilities in these mountains, so that was out. And he also felt that Glencoe and Dundee were too far north and exposed to potential flanking attacks from the Orange Free State in the west and from the Transvaal in the east – let alone from both countries on his front. Glencoe and Dundee, he felt, would be wide open to a giant pincer movement from the two republican forces. He therefore wanted to withdraw the 4000 soldiers back to join the 8000 at Ladysmith – the military supply centre.

But on this argument of falling back to Ladysmith, he was forcefully opposed by Hely-Hutchinson, the Governor of Natal, and by General Penn-Symons. The Governor's argument was, of course, political. He argued that if the British soldiers withdrew as far south as Ladysmith it would be disastrous, psychologically, to the British colonists, particularly those who would be left in the northern apex of Natal to be overrun by the Boer forces. He also argued that such an initial occupation of British territory would encourage the Boers living in Natal to revolt. And, of course, he did not fail to remind Sir George White about the 750 000 black Africans who would view the British retreat with some delight – and 'blacks' on the rampage were mentioned. Not that the Zulus preferred the Boers to the British. They had no reason to love any white men. They were naturally looking for any signs of white disintegration.

Then General Penn-Symons threw in his argument. He was, as noted earlier, a very optimistic soldier and didn't think very highly of the military potential of the Boers when they might have to face British regular professional soldiers. General Penn-Symons couldn't have dwelt keenly on the military facts of the short but decisive First Boer War. By and large, the British Army in 1881 hadn't known whether it was coming or going, and many red coats were left on the veldt.

General Penn-Symons said that from Glencoe with his 4000 soldiers he could strike effectively at any gathering Boer armies – particularly with the support of the 8000 soldiers with Sir George White at Ladysmith.

Sir George was new to Africa. Governor Hely-Hutchinson spoke the wish of the Natal Government, and Penn-Symons was the soldier already on the potential battle-spot. It would have required a very adamant character to overrule these two wishes almost as soon as he had stepped ashore. Therefore with some uneasiness Sir George permitted Penn-Symons to stand at Glencoe.

In Pretoria, the capital of the Transvaal, President Kruger, ably advised by the young State Attorney, Jan Smuts, noted Queen Victoria's proclamation summoning the British Parliament and calling out the British Army's reserves. They noted also the order for the mobilization of an army corps for South Africa. Smuts personally made the last gesture for peace: he offered the British representative in Pretoria, Conyngham Greene, a new deal on the franchise argument. It was a concession which would have met the original British demands: a five-year retrospective franchise. From the Boer point of view it was an offer of some desperation; it did invite national suicide. But it was not enough for Jo Chamberlain and the Tory Government. They had set their hearts on control of the Transvaal and now that at last they had set the wheels of massive military preparation in motion, they preferred not to stop them.

So, on 9 October 1899, the Boers, noting that the grass was already beginning to sprout for the horses of their mounted armies – their commandos – issued an unequivocal ultimatum to the British Government. The ultimatum demanded:

1. That all points of mutual difference shall be regulated by the friendly course of arbitration or by whatever amicable way may be agreed upon by this Government with Her Majesty's Government.

2. That the troops on the borders of this Republic shall be instantly withdrawn.

3. That all reinforcements of troops which have arrived in South Africa since the 1st of June, 1899, shall be removed from South Africa within a reasonable time, to be agreed upon with this Government and with a mutual assurance and guarantee

on the part of this Government that no attack upon or hostilities against any portion of the possessions of the British Government shall be made by the Republic during further negotiations within a period of time to be subsequently agreed upon between the Governments, and this Government will on compliance therewith be prepared to withdraw the armed Burghers of this Republic from the borders.

4. That Her Majesty's troops which are now on the high seas shall not be landed in any port of South Africa.

The ultimatum went on to express that if there was no affirmative answer to these four questions before 5 p.m., on 11 October 1899, the Transvaal Government would 'with great regret be compelled to regard the action of Her Majesty's Government as a formal declaration of war . . .'

Well, Britannia wasn't accustomed to being spoken to like this! Germany, France, indeed the whole world would have liked to, but no country had yet summoned up sufficient nerve – except, now, seventy-four-year-old President Kruger and his farmers. Therefore, Britannia, in the person of Conyngham Greene, the British representative at Pretoria, replied that the conditions demanded by the Transvaal '. . . were such as Her Majesty's Government deemed it impossible to discuss . . .' and he asked for his passport and hurried away.

On 10 October the Right Reverend A. H. Baynes, Bishop of Natal, saw Sir George White and his 'illustrious group of officers' off up north to Ladysmith. The Bishop wrote: 'As I said "Good-bye" to General White on the station platform [Pietermaritzburg], I knew from both his manner and his words, more than I had realized before, how grave was the task which lay before him . . .'

2

THE WAR BEGINS

War declared. This place is full of Boer spies, but
apparently nothing is done to clear them out, and
they come and look at the camp and spy out
everything. All our men had their swords sharpened
yesterday . . .
Diary of MAJOR MARLING

As Conyngham Greene was packing his bags in Pretoria, Sir George White was arriving in Ladysmith, for the first time in his life. It was 11 October 1899, the very day the Second Boer War broke out. On that day he wrote a letter to his brother:

The Boers are certain to declare war tonight, and I am far from being confident in the military position here.

I found troops at Glencoe Junction, and also of course at Ladysmith. The Governor thinks it absolutely necessary politically to hold Glencoe, and I had hoped to have had sufficient force to hold both it and Ladysmith sufficiently strongly, but the authorities at home have diverted the 9th Lancers to the Cape Colony, where they are also very short of troops, and the 5th Dragoon Guards, the Border Regiment, the Gloucester Regiment, and the Royal Irish Fusiliers are still at sea. This makes the present military position much weaker than I could wish, and when the ultimatum was reported I considered it would be a wise military measure to withdraw from Glencoe and concentrate on Ladysmith. The Governor, who is a very good fellow, and helpful, however said that he considered to withdraw from Glencoe would involve a grave risk of the natives rising against us. I therefore told him I would hold on to both Glencoe and Ladysmith.

I think it possible that with their great numbers and mobility the Boers may isolate us even at Ladysmith . . . It is hard not having been able to get a line from any of you, but I have travelled very fast, and am where I ought to be, in the front. – Ever yours, George.

Sir Redvers Buller was still in England – though having his gear packed. He visited Queen Victoria but had to puff all the way up to Balmoral to see her. Her Majesty liked the old warhorse; after all, he was not unlike Devonshire's answer to Scotland's John Brown. In her latter days, the Queen's taste in men tended towards bluffness. She wrote after Buller's visit that he had 'much that was interesting to say in his blunt, straightforward way'. The old General appeared very optimistic about the outcome of the war, in the presence of his Queen. A responsible old squire, unsubtly cheering up an old lady who was, after all, lonely and worried.

Came 14 October and General Buller was at Waterloo station, bound for Southampton and thence to the southern tip of Africa. An attempt had been made to keep secret the precise time of the departure of his special train, but somehow a great crowd had assembled and we are assured that they gave the old hero a rousing cheer. Sir Redvers wore a blue overcoat and his customary rather square-shaped bowler hat. He was nobly escorted down the platform by none less than the Prince of Wales, the Duke of Cambridge, Lord Lansdowne, Lord Wolseley and the distinguished soldier, Field-Marshal Sir Evelyn Wood. And of course Lady Buller was there. They all assembled in his special silk-lined saloon where presumably a noble chat took place. But Waterloo was the end of social involvement for Sir Redvers. At Waterloo station, like so many other soldiers before that day and since, he kissed his Lady good-bye. He shook hands with the bigwigs. A high-ranking railway official waved a flag, and as the conveyance eased south, the assembled citizens of London sang 'Rule Britannia'.

Sir Redvers probably hoped that south of Waterloo station he was on active service and could begin to put his mind entirely to the strife ahead. But he was not yet free of England. Right down the railway track, to the sea, people waited for Buller's Special to pass, and as it did so, they cheered formidable John Bull on his military way. At Southampton a vast crowd waited and the Mayor and Corporation urged him to share a civic lunch but the General refused and boarded the SS *Dunottar Castle*. The Mayor pursued his civic duties and said his farewell on the ship. The last that England saw of General Buller, for the time being, was as he walked towards the bridge with the ship's captain, Mr Rigby.

As the *Dunottar Castle* moved into the Solent, voices rose over the water, singing 'God Save the Queen'. It is reported that women's voices predominated.

An astonishing side to Sir Redvers' character is that he was given to philosophical musings – and these, of course, often applied to hard military problems. He looked at the approaching conflict in South Africa in this abstract way:

In the first place, it was evident that the war would be of the kind which is described by General Jomini as a national war. . . . Moreover, time had not yet glorified the seat of Government with a halo of sentiment. To every man his home is the capital. Hence there is no commanding centre by the occupation of which the whole country, or even a whole district, can be brought in subjection; no vital spot at which a single blow can be struck that will paralyse every member of the body.

And then he moved into realms which must have left his staff aghast:

There are living organisms which can be divided into a multitude of fragments without destroying the individual life of each fragment . . .

Yes, he was still discussing the Boer military problem. He proceeded to an analogy of the coming war with the American War of Independence, and here he philosophized like a prophet new inspired:

. . . shows that the mere occupation of provincial capitals in such a country is of little furtherance to the work of conquest.

Looking back at the end of the Second Boer War, this was shrewd.

He saw the coming British military problem 'like a man who tries to arrest the flow of a river by walking through it. Such a man may indeed stem its force where he stands, but let him move where he will, the waters always close before and behind and around him.' Field-Marshal Lord Kitchener of Khartoum was still trying to comprehend that problem in South Africa two and a half years later. And here was old Buller, steaming south in 1899, throwing the problem around like a brilliant juggler. He finally analysed the Boer people and proposed psychological warfare.

On 17 October 1899, the *Dunottar Castle* arrived at the Portuguese island of Madeira. Most of the travellers went ashore but not Sir Redvers. On board he received two telegrams. The first, dated 15 October, was from Sir George White in Ladysmith. It read: 'Transvaal and Orange Free State forces are converging towards Dundee and Ladysmith, and are in strength inside Natal border . . .' The second telegram came from General Sir F. Forestier Walker, the officer commanding British forces in Cape Colony. That message informed Buller that Mafeking and Kimberley were besieged by Boer forces.

On board the *Dunottar Castle* was young Winston Churchill travelling to the war as newspaper correspondent for the *Morning Post*. Sir Redvers, like so many other senior soldiers, didn't like journalists and a young Marlborough cut no special ice with him. There was no interview given for any newspaper on that ship. But Winston, though expressing terrible boredom with the voyage, kept his eyes open – from afar. He wrote:

On the 23rd we sighted a sail – or rather the smoke of another steamer. As the comparatively speedy *Dunottar Castle* overtook the stranger everybody's interest was aroused. Under the scrutiny of many brand-new telescopes and field glasses – for all want to see as much of a war as possible – she developed into the *Nineveh*, hired transport carrying the Australian Lancers to the Cape. Signals were exchanged. The vessels drew together, and after an hour's steaming we passed her almost within speaking distance. The General went up to the bridge. The Lancers crowded the bulwarks and rigging of the *Nineveh* and one of them waggled a flag violently. An officer on our ship replied with a pocket-handkerchief. The Australians asked questions: 'Is Sir Redvers Buller on Board?' The answer 'Yes' was signalled back, and immediately the Lancers gave three tremendous cheers waving their broad-brimmed hats and gesticulating with energy while the steam siren emitted a frantic whoop of salutation. Then the speed of the larger vessel told, and we drew ahead of the transport until her continued cheers died away. She signalled again: 'What won the Cesarewitch?' But the distance was now too great for us to learn whether the answer gave satisfaction or not.

What a graphic description of the Empire meeting on the high seas, which that Empire ruled with ships of steel. Winston Churchill, Sir Redvers Buller, the Australian volunteers and the result of an English horse-race. There it all is, in a nutshell!

Also on board was Earl de la Warr and his letters home appeared in *The Globe*. He wrote on 17 October: 'Approaching Madeira. . . . By the way, Sir Redvers hopes to be back in time to see the Derby, which is something. The General is naturally very reticent, and those who have been bold enough to try and ascertain his movements in the near future have not learned much; and the members of his staff are not very communicative.'

Then the weather deteriorated and Winston Churchill duly reported on that: 'But whatever the cause may be, the fall in temperature produces a rise in spirits, and under greyer skies everyone develops activity. The consequence of this is the organisation of athletic sports. A committee is appointed, Sir Redvers Buller becomes President.'

Earl de la Warr looked as close as he could at Buller:

The General himself is an extremely interesting character. He speaks mostly to the members of his Staff. He is reported to have snubbed politely a venturesome correspondent [this must be Winston] who addressed him soon after our departure from Southampton. His subordinates are said to stand in terror of him. They say he is uncompromisingly stern. To an observer he appears as a man entirely without nerves. That alone would make him fearless, and no one disputes his fearlessness. He appears to be shrewd, observant, impassive. The officers who have served under him declare that he is the greatest General now on the Active List of the Army.

Winston Churchill recorded: 'We have a party of cinematographers on board . . .' which demonstrated that the British film industry had initiative in 1899. The leader of this 'Biograph' expedition was W. K. Dickson, who afterwards wrote a book entitled *The Biograph in Battle – its Story in the South African War*. W. K. Dickson focused on General Buller as often as he could:

I made an interesting sketch of General Buller scrambling up on to the skylight to avoid the deluge, where most of us perched, to be shortly afterwards ousted by the sailors who wished to wash down the skylights. When the sailor requested the General to get down he laughingly remarked, 'Now then, you wouldn't wash me off, would you?' and nimbly jumped down. Catching his eye, I could not help laughing outright as his kindly and intelligent face depicted the liveliest humour.

W. K. Dickson had all sorts of ideas for the use of the Biograph. One of them was to approach Cecil Rhodes and persuade him that moving pictures could help 'in the matter of opening up South Africa'. Mr Dickson discovered that Cecil's brother, Major Frank Rhodes, was on board and he tackled him on the subject. But Frank was pessimistic about any early help in this matter; he knew Cecil was trapped in Kimberley with his diamonds.

Mr Dickson, ever observant, noted General Buller's eating habits on board: 'The bugle echoes through the ship, announcing lunch, and immediately the General, a true soldier, is on time and takes his place at table. Never have I seen him late for any meal.'

He also observed the preparations for General Buller to have his hair cut on ship, and after the event the excited barber reported what took place: '. . . the General is a gentleman, sir, and as kind as he can be. Just think how easily he talked to me, yes, he did, all the time he was having his hair cut; and when a man came in for a pipe, and I told him to come later, the General up and said, "Why, give him his pipe, I am in no hurry" – and I did.'

Earl de la Warr wrote about the film-unit: 'I must not forget to mention that we have a cinematograph on board; an enormous machine which has to be present at any cost at all the actions. Those are the orders, but I think it is doubtful whether they will be carried out. The gentlemen in charge of it are not very military in appearance, and are, I believe, quite new to this kind of work.'

On Sunday, 29 October, General Buller had retired to his cabin with a book, when he was informed that a ship had hove in sight, bound for London. She was the *Australasia* of the White Star Line and was now 535 miles distant from her last port of call, Cape Town. Sir Redvers hurried from his cabin and puffed up to Captain Rigby on the bridge. Was there any hope of news from the battlefields of South Africa? Captain Rigby brought the *Dunottar Castle* closer to the course of the approaching ship. He sent a brief signal: 'What news?' The *Australasia* steered very close and from the side was hanging an enormous blackboard; on it were words. She came within three hundred yards of the *Dunottar*. All peered at the inscription – not least the General – and everyone read 'Boers Defeated – Three Battles – Penn-Symons Killed'.

This news was received in disconcerted silence. Winston Churchill asked, 'What does it mean – this scrap of intelligence which tells so much and leaves so much untold?' Steaming southwards, there could not have been a soul on board who did not analyse each word. 'Boers Defeated – Three Battles – Penn-Symons Killed.' Were the Boers defeated in all three battles? If so how did General Penn-Symons manage to get himself killed? Well, they would have to wait until they reached Cape Town before the words could be explained. It was not to be long. The *Dunottar Castle* reached her berth at Cape Town on 31 October 1899.

As soon as General Sir George White arrived in Ladysmith on 11 October 1899 – the day war officially commenced – he proceeded to decide on the specific perimeter of defence. He knew that the Boers had long-range guns and therefore he wished to push his defence line as far away from the town as possible, but had to consider the number of men at his disposal to hold safely these outer entrenched positions. Sir George believed from the beginning that there was a strong probability that the Boers would reach the approaches to the town, and the first determination was that they should not actually capture the place. A committee was formed to decide on the line of the defence perimeter. When it was finally settled, Sir George rode around the great circle; it was a fourteen-mile ride. His other top priority was to hurry into the town an additional supply of food. Everything confirmed his fear that a siege could happen. Ladysmith is often described as lying in a shallow saucer, an impression created by the surrounding hills. It can be a very hot and dusty place and it was, at the time of the Second Boer War, a very unhealthy one. It is situated on the railway line 189½ miles from the port of Durban, and Johannesburg lies some 290 miles to the north-west. The border with the Orange Free State is 36 miles away westward at Van

Reenen. The township of Ladysmith was first established in 1851 by the then Governor, Sir B. C. C. Pine. The Zulu War of 1879 and the Transvaal War (the First Boer War) of 1881 gave the place a significant prominence, but it was the construction of the Government railway that made it the third largest place in the Colony of Natal. The population, excluding the military, at the outbreak of the war comprised 2200 Europeans, about 1500 Africans and about 1200 Indians. A map of the town and its surrounds appears on page x.

On that hectic 11 October, Major Marling was at Dundee and so was his wife 'B.', staying at the Royal Hotel. The Major wrote in his diary:

War declared. This place is full of Boer spies, but apparently nothing is done to clear them out, and they come and look at the camp and spy out everything.

All our men had their swords sharpened yesterday. Our position here is the worst possible. From the surrounding hills the Boers can count every man, horse and gun in the camp. Of course the force never ought to have been sent to Dundee at all. . . . I was told that Lord Wolseley, on being asked his advice, had written to Sir George White to say he should withdraw the whole of his troops south of the Mooi River, and hold that line, but he also added that, of course, the man on the spot must be the best judge.

The poor man on the spot! Incidentally, the Mooi river is well south of even the Tugela river – and I suppose that if one casts all political expedience away, and considers only the hard military facts, this line of defence might have been the safest – until the arrival of the army corps and General Buller. But the truth is, it would have taken a Napoleon to have been as over-ridingly positive as that.

But Sir George White was definitely committed to Ladysmith, though with continuing uneasy doubts about Penn-Symons up around the area of Glencoe and Dundee. His whole hope now was to strike somewhere, somehow, at the Boers. But where would they come from? If only he had those 4000 soldiers who were now up there with Penn-Symons! He vacillated from day to day on these hopes and doubts.

The Boers did not hesitate at this time; by 12 October, only one day after poor Sir George arrived in Ladysmith, they were pouring on to Natal territory. On that date Sir George telegraphed to the War Office in London:

Four thousand Boers with 18 guns have invaded Natal from Free State via Tintwa Pass. They are probably encamped tonight ten miles west of Acton Homes. I move out to meet them at 3 a.m. tomorrow with 5th Lancers, three field batteries, one Mountain Battery, Liverpools, Gordons, Manchesters, and one other Battalion which comes from Glencoe by train tonight. Also with 250 Natal Carbineers and a

Colonial Battery. No occasion for public alarm. I believe myself stronger than the enemy. Spirit of the troops excellent.

If there was no cause for 'public alarm', Sir George must have suffered a twinge of private alarm. Tintwa Pass was pretty well due west of Ladysmith and therefore the Boers were not only threatening the Dundee–Glencoe soldiers in their rear – but Sir George and his lads in Ladysmith as well. The situation was quick confirmation of his dread: from where and when? His quick reaction to go out and meet and fight the Boers proved an intimation of what difficult men he was facing. When the British force arrived in the Acton Homes area, the Boers had disappeared. It was believed that like Glencoe and Dundee, Ladysmith also was strong in Boer spies. But the unnerving aspect was Boer mobility. Self-sufficient men, only loaded with a mauser and bandoliers of ammunition, plus probably a formidable supply of home-dried biltong – and that was all. Here we are – and now we're gone. Even the dust from the 5th Lancers was warning enough, let alone those batteries of Royal Field Artillery.

Reports arrived nonstop at Sir George's headquarters. The Boers were invading Natal in formidable numbers. They were coming through every possible pass in the Drakensberg Mountains; from the Orange Free State and from the north the Transvaal Boers were joining the flood of invasion.

Down south, at Durban, the troopship *Avoca* docked and the soldiers were hustled to Ladysmith. An officer who disembarked from this described the emotional atmosphere:

We passed through the town, which was in a state of wild enthusiasm, and our men returned the cheers; indeed, although they were packed sixty in an open truck without any protection, and it poured with rain nearly the whole night, they never stopped cheering. At one small station some ladies had come miles to get tea ready for us, which was very acceptable, as it was cold . . . We got to Ladysmith early on the morning of the 13th, and had a very cold reception, nearly all the troops having gone to meet the Boers, and the camp, which was some distance from the town, expected to be attacked . . .

As each day fell away, Sir George fretted more and more about Penn-Symons, stuck out at Dundee. From the time of Sir George's unhappy agreement to hold Dundee, he had ordered Penn-Symons to do what he had done in Ladysmith – to decide on the best defensible positions and entrench them effectively and also to ensure the Dundee soldiers an adequate water supply. But the truth is that General Penn-Symons hadn't fully carried out these stipulations. He was so confident that his regular British soldiers could outmanoeuvre the Boers that he did not even look for a defensive position. Penn-Symons saw himself up there to attack and nothing else.

When Sir George White learnt that defensive preparations had not been carried out with enthusiasm at Dundee – and as the Boers threatened further south – he telegraphed to Penn-Symons on 18 October 1899:

I have been in communication with Governor, and he thinks the political importance of your force remaining at Dundee has already greatly decreased. Maritzburg [the capital, Pietermaritzburg] is now threatened, and I have to reinforce it heavily. If, therefore, you are not absolutely confident of being able to entrench yourself strongly, with an assured water supply within your position, fall back on Ladysmith at once. Reply as quickly as possible.

Now that telegram was a polite method of overruling Penn-Symons' wish to stay put and out-box Johnny Boer. But Penn-Symons wasn't beaten. Two hours later his reply arrived at Ladysmith:

133 urgent. Clear the line. I cannot fulfil the conditions you impose, namely to strongly entrench myself here with an assured water supply within my position. I must therefore comply with your order to retire. Please to send trains to remove civilians that still remain in Dundee, our stores, and sick. I must give out that I am moving stores and camp to Glencoe junction in view of attacking Newcastle at once.

This telegram was an attempt at checkmate and certainly hit back at Sir George's wishes. Rolling stock at Ladysmith railhead was in short supply and what if it were captured? And Sir George did not want the civilian population of Dundee and elsewhere moving into Ladysmith. Indeed he was already encouraging civilians in that town to move south themselves. Faced with this embarrassing prospect, he immediately replied to Penn-Symons, passing the buck without reserve:

Sent at 3.30 a.m. on 18th October 1889. With regard to water, are you confident you can supply your camp for an indefinite period? The difficulties and risk of withdrawing civil population and military stores are great, and railway may be cut any day. Do you yourself, after considering these difficulties, think it better to remain at Dundee and prefer it?

Penn-Symons replied like lightning:

Glencoe Camp. 18th October. 134. Clear the line. We can and must stay here. I have no doubt whatever that this is the proper course. I have cancelled all orders for moving.

This appeared to be game and set to Penn-Symons and Sir George White compounded this appearance by replying:

Sent at 6 a.m., 18th October. Your 134 to clear line. I fully support you. Make particulars referred to by me as safe as possible. Difficulties and disadvantages of other course have decided me to support your views.

To stay up there in Dundee or not to stay? Well, that game of military tennis was not finally over, not by a long chalk!

The following day, 19 October, General White learnt that rail communication with Glencoe and Dundee was interrupted. The Boers advanced south through the Biggarsberg Mountains and captured a goods train at Elandslaagte station, only seventeen miles north of Ladysmith. Sir George immediately moved his military camp to a position covering Ladysmith – but the Boers came no further south, at least not in force.

Major Marling had sent his new wife 'B.' south to Ladysmith two days before, and also recorded a few other unhappy facts:

Poor B. left for Ladysmith, much against her will. We have done nothing to strengthen our position here, which is very bad. We ought to occupy Impati and hold Talana and the other little hill. We are very short of gun ammunition. Apparently none of the authorities estimate the Boers at their proper value. What fools our War Office are. B.'s train was fired on for 4 miles.

Major Marling is an enigma of his time. There he was, one of England's patricians, elegant man-about-town – plus the Victoria Cross – and now showing positive military common sense, yet merely a major. I suppose he must gaily have criticized the War Office at supper parties and what-have-you, and for that reason was left behind in the military promotion race. Anyway he was demonstrating more foresight than General Penn-Symons . . .

When General White learnt about the capture of that goods train at Elandslaagte, he must have regretted giving way to Penn-Symons. Was the capture of the train an audacious raid by the Boers only seventeen miles north of the Aldershot of South Africa, or was it something worse? He quickly learnt that it was something worse.

Joubert, the Transvaal commandant-general, had crossed the northern Natal border with his army on 12 October 1899. But being of the old conservative school – he had successfully led the Transvaalers against the British in 1881 – he did not exactly pound southward. By 16 October, facing virtually no opposition, he had only penetrated thirty miles, as far as Newcastle. And there, once he was reassured that the British were not going to attack him, he devised a simple but effective piece of strategy for the further move south. There were to be three columns. One, under General Lucas Meyer, with between four and five thousand mounted men, would move down the eastern border of Natal until it reached a point due east of Dundee. A centre column, under General Erasmus, with five thousand mounted men, would push southward to Dundee and would occupy Impati Hill – the same Impati Hill that Major Marling regretted General Penn-Symons had rejected. And thirdly a smaller column, under General Kock (indeed less than a thousand burghers), would sweep in a wide arc reaching westward, there to join an Orange Free State force, before swinging back eastward to cut the railway line south of Dundee, thereby isolating General Penn-Symons and his force in the Dundee–Glencoe area. And, of course, simultaneously Lucas Meyer and his men would press on Dundee from the east. Penn-Symons with 3280 infantry, 497 cavalry and eighteen field guns was about to find himself outnumbered more than two to one. And if Kock could successfully cross south of Dundee in strength, help from Sir George White could be prevented.

Before 19 October was over, all three Boer columns had successfully reached their strategic goals. Penn-Symons was not astonished at their arrival. He was standing on British territory and therefore he was well informed about these encroaching movements. He was apparently totally confident. He held his force in their British camp, and waited like some Douglas Fairbanks Senior for one or all three of the Boer columns to appear, when he could dart forward and destroy them. Of course the Boer operation at this final point was not easy. Three separate columns from three points of the compass planned to converge on an enemy force at the same time, and in the darkness.

The British camp selected by Penn-Symons was between Glencoe and Dundee and was in a valley almost completely surrounded by hills. It would not seem to be an ideal place to select if a fight were in the offing, but Penn-Symons selected it. The principal hills dominating the British camp were Impati Hill, some 5000 yards northward, and Talana Hill, about 4000 yards to the east. As Major Marling recorded, Penn-Symons did not bother to occupy Impati in any way. Neither did he occupy Talana Hill but he did send a mounted infantry picket about two miles east of the British camp and therefore east of Talana.

General Lucas Meyer on the evening of 19 October 1899 moved between 3500 and 4000 of his mounted men, together with six heavy guns, westward towards Talana Hill. They rode through the night. Eventually, the Boer force reached the British mounted infantry picket, which retreated to a break in the Talana Hill – a break called Smith's Nek. Here the picket sent back to General Penn-Symons a report about Lucas Meyer's approach. Penn-Symons didn't turn a hair. Before dawn broke, Meyer's force had reached Talana Hill, climbed to the top and succeeded in dragging some of their guns with them. As the African sun rose, the Boers were in a position to shell the British camp – though the range was considerable.

Lieutenant R. G. Stirling, of the 1st King's Royal Rifles, wrote about that early morning:

> We paraded as usual in the morning, 4.30. We had dismissed the men, and went back for a cup of tea, when one of our fellows said: 'There they are!' Of course we all laughed, went and got our glasses, and saw them all on two hills, two or three miles away. We were so amazed we must have stood for nearly quarter of an hour, when suddenly a shell brought us to our senses.

I have an old friend, Mr George Hall of Newcastle, England, who, as a Royal Engineer, was there that morning. Mr Hall, or Private Hall, on 20 October 1899 was constructing a dam for a military water supply. He has told me: '. . . we were damming this river for a water supply for horses. All of a sudden there was all hell up in the camp – and then a shell came amongst us – the poor horses – they were hurried back to the guns . . .'

A non-commissioned officer from Rochdale, Lancashire, also in the King's Royal Rifles recorded that early morning:

> At about 3 a.m. [it was later] on Monday we were surprised to hear a shell come whistling over the camp – our first intimation of their possession of guns . . . The camp, composed of Rifles, Dublins, Royal Irish Fusiliers, 5th Royal Lancers, and Artillery, was soon astir . . . The Artillery at once answered, and shell after shell struck in the camp, not exploding. Then the Cavalry trotted away through the town, and took up a position on the right. Then our Mounted Infantry left us with our cheers, laughing and singing as they went, anxious to get a smack at the Boers . . . Presently up dashed some cavalry scouts. Then came the order: Dublins first line, Rifles second, Fusiliers third. And our Colonel, poor old Bobby Gunning, said, as he called together the non-commissioned officers, 'Now quietly lads. Remember Majuba, God, and our country.' I cried like a kid as I walked quietly to my company and passed word on to the men. You do not half realize at home what war is. When we got the order and extra ammunition, we marched through the town. Some were blustering and joking, some were smiling, and others were trembling; and the civilians, both men and women, caught us by the hand. One woman whom I never saw before or since caught me by the neck and kissed me as I marched along by the Company and said, 'God bless you, lad.' Do you know I've

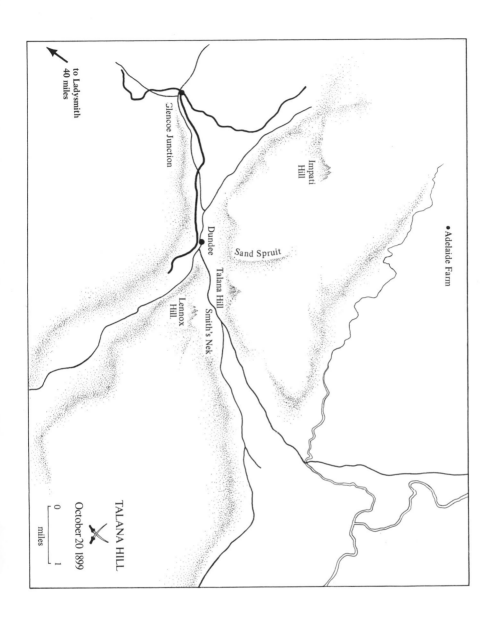

to Ladysmith
40 miles

Glencoe Junction

Impati
Hill

Dundee

Sand Spruit

Talana Hill

Lennox
Hill

Smith's Nek

• Adelaide Farm

TALANA HILL

October 20 1899

0

miles

1

laughed since at it; but at the time I only saw the pathetic side, and I did some more choking and swallowing.

Once the Boers started firing at the British camp, General Penn-Symons took action. He ordered one battalion of infantry plus a company from each of the other three battalions at his disposal, plus a battery of artillery to do what they could about Impati Hill – but that thought was too late: General Erasmus was already on top, with guns. And General Symons ordered his main force, the Dublin Fusiliers, with the King's Royal Rifles in support, and in reserve the Royal Irish Fusiliers, to assault the Boers on Talana Hill. In command of this attack was Brigadier-General Yule.

The British now moved quickly. By 7 a.m. these three battalions were assembled in the bed of a watercourse, called Sand Spruit. The camp was now more than a mile west of them and the Boers on the crest of Talana Hill were about a mile to the east. By 7.20 a.m. the Dublin Fusiliers were advancing towards Talana Hill and immediately came under a heavy fire – not only from Talana but also from Lennox Hill, which is immediately south of Smith's Nek.

Lieutenant Stirling with the King's Royal Rifles wrote:

> When we got the order to advance my heart was rather in my mouth, as I knew then we were under fire, and in a minute or two I might be a corpse, or rather cold. However, up I had to get and give my men a lead. They all behaved splendidly. Bullets came whizzing past rather unpleasantly. I was dying to run to get to the wood. However, I got so excited I forgot everything. In the wood . . . poor Hambro was shot through the jaw but would take no notice.

The first assault by the Dublins was stopped by the Boers, about 550 yards from the crest of Talana Hill. The King's Royal Rifles in support reached the Dublins, but were also held – not only from the rifle fire to their front but from Lennox Hill on their right flank. General Penn-Symons, seeing the attack being so cruelly pinned down, rode forward into the bloody wood and there dismounted and urged his soldiers to advance into the mauser fire. Sergeant J. Freeman of the King's Royal Rifles recorded what happened then: '. . . The order was given by General Symons to storm the hill. He called out, "Forward, the Rifles, the gallant 60th, and take that hill!" . . . He turned and led the way, and in a minute or so he was shot . . .'

General Penn-Symons had been struck in the stomach by a Boer bullet. *The Official History of the War* states: 'Directing Brigadier-General Yule to proceed with the attack, he turned and walked calmly to the rear. Then,

meeting his horse, he mounted and not until he had passed entirely through
the troops was any sign of suffering allowed to escape him . . . and was
carried to the dressing-station . . . Five minutes later, at 9.35 a.m. the surgeon
pronounced his wound to be fatal, and the news was telegraphed to Ladysmith.'

Back on the side of Talana Hill, the battle continued to rage. Colonel
Bobby Gunning of the King's Royal Rifles stood in this rain of bullets and
tried to rally his men. Private Down of that regiment wrote: 'Our men were
dropping down wounded, and our Colonel thought they were retiring. He
turned round, revolver in hand, and said that any man retiring under the
Boer fire he would shoot, and he immediately received a bullet in his heart,
and fell to get up no more. He was in charge of my company at the time.'

Lieutenant Stirling was also there on that terrible hillside:

When I got half-way up the hill I found myself next to Hambro, who had been
wounded twice; we lay down under the rocks as the firing was very heavy. Hambro
and I had to retire. I had my helmet knocked off with a piece of rock the shell hit.
When I went up the hill a second time, Hambro was lying almost dead, with his legs
reduced to pulp. Too terrible! . . . Colonel Sherston was dying, his groans were awful.
Then an awful part happened – our artillery mistaking us for Boers, began firing
on us. Colonel Gunning, who was just below me, stood up and yelled out, 'Stop
that Firing!' These were the last words I heard him speak, but I believe his last
words were, 'Remember you are Riflemen.' . . . When we got over the wall the
scene was terrible. Three of our officers shot within five yards of one another, Pechell
and Taylor dead, Boulthee wounded in the groin . . .

Private L. Thompson, again of the Royal Rifles, wrote home:

One man next to me was hit by a shell, and I was almost blinded by his blood.
It was awful. Our advance had now lasted five and a half hours, and we were about
one hundred yards from the top when came that order which put new life into us –
'Fix bayonets'. As he gave this order our Colonel fell, shot dead. We then closed
in and with levelled bayonets went at them for all we were worth. With a wild
cheer we were amongst them. The bayonets went to work, and heads were smashed
like pumpkins . . . You will be cut up to hear that poor Ford is among the killed,
but he sent four Boers to 'Kingdom come' with a bayonet before he fell dead in my
arms . . . But he died like a British soldier, and I hope he has gone to a better world.

The Irish were present at the battle of Talana Hill and they were perhaps
the most vehement. Private Francis Burns of the Royal Irish Fusiliers wrote:
'The papers say the Dublins were first on the hill, but it was the Royal Irish.
It does not matter anyhow, for we were all Irish. Tell my mother England's
first battle was won by the Irish Brigade.'

When one considers that Ireland was under British military occupation at that time and when one considers the destitution of the Irish people as a result of England's policy on that island, a letter from an Irishman in the the Dublin Fusiliers, to his mother, takes the biscuit:

I needn't start praising my regiment, for every one in Ireland has heard of their deeds of daring – both my regiment and the Royal Irish Fusiliers. You can tell any one in Newry [presumably the writer's home town] who has a son in the Royal Irish Fusiliers that the hills which we took with our splendid charge are going to be called the Irish Mountains. I was reading in the papers where the Irish people were subscribing for the Boers, and are backing them up; but the Irish people will want to be careful of themselves, or we will do the same with them as we are doing with the Boers.

This jingoistic feeling was common amongst many Irishmen – right up to the Easter Rebellion in Ireland in 1916. And even then, it was not until the English executed the leaders of that rebellion that the Irish people became united against England and most things that England stood for.

The State Secretary of the Transvaal Republic, F. W. Reitz, composed a poem about this military Irish mystery, known as 'The Wearing of the Green':

> They tell me that good honest Pat,
>> By favour of the Queen,
> Has got the right – as well he might –
>> To wearing of the Green.
> Ah, Patrick Atkins, how your breast
>> Must swell with pride and joy
> To think that Mr Chamberlain
>> Has found his Irish boy!
>
> Did we not hear, only last year,
>> That on St Patrick's Day
> Denis Malone in 'gaol' was thrown,
>> And docked of all his pay,
> Because – oh dreadful to relate –
>> This 'Soldier of the Queen'
> Had with unblushing impudence
>> Been wearing of the Green?
>
> Now this great change is very strange,
>> And sure it's puzzling quite,
> That was wrong for centuries long
>> Should now at last be right!

And that the Dublin Fusiliers
By all may now be seen
Without the fear of punishment
A-wearing of the Green.

But if you say, now tell me pray,
What may this difference 'mane'?
Listen to me and you will see
The matter is quite plain.
It means that Paddy now has got
This 'favour' from the Queen,
Because – and that's a fact – because
He is – so very green!

Whatever the mysteries of imperial brainwashing may have been, the poor bloody British soldiers were on top of Talana Hill, and General Lucas Meyer's Boers were tearing pell-mell down the other side to safety. The Boers on Lennox Hill, adjacent and south, were doing the same. This was obviously the moment for British cavalry.

Mounted troops at the battle of Talana Hill consisted of three squadrons of the 18th Hussars and some mounted infantry; in command was Colonel Möller. The Colonel, sensing that the Boers might be wavering on Talana's crest, ordered Major Knox with two squadrons and a troop round the northern end of Talana and round to the back of the Boer position on the hill, until they were out on the veldt, well behind the back of Lennox Hill. Colonel Möller presumed that if the Boers retreated, they would depart in that direction. He posted himself with the remaining 250 mounted men directly behind Talana. The time was 10 a.m.

When the mass of Boers came tumbling down the rear of Talana and leapt into their saddles and beat a retreat, there was nothing Colonel Möller could do to stop them. Indeed all he could do was to order his men to about face and ride like hell – northward. Apparently he had hopes of riding a wide circle to the north and west, round the back to Impati Hill – to safety. But old General Erasmus on Impati, who incidentally had done nothing much to support his Boer comrades on Talana, saw Möller's horsemen and now every Boer seemed to be chasing them. The proposed pursuers were being pursued.

The young Boer, Deneys Reitz, son of F. W. Reitz, the sometime President of the Orange Free State, wrote: 'How this handful of men came to be right in the rear of the whole Boer Army I never heard but they were on a desperate errand, for between them and their main body lay nearly 15000 horsemen . . .' What were they doing there? Still hoping to cut off the Boer retreat? If Colonel Möller's end had not been so tragic, it would have been very funny. The British retreat ran out of steam and out of horses at Adelaide's Farm, about eight miles north-north-west of Talana. An English officer wrote from his place of captivity in Pretoria:

Our position, selected by the Colonel, was a farm with a wall in front, behind which we took shelter. We took the position at about 12.15 [p.m.] and for three hours we resisted overwhelming forces . . . we suffered heavily. We replied to the enemy's fire, but at length our ammunition began to run short, and the enemy began to surround us. A poor fellow beside me was killed and wounded . . . and when heavy guns were brought into position against us I thought our last hour had come. The shells killed many horses and several men; nearly all the remaining horses stampeded. The enemy promptly found the range, and they handled their guns admirably. I remember taking out my cigarette case and putting it in a breast-pocket to cover the heart. When the Colonel ordered the white flag to be hoisted a man ran into the farm, brought out half a sheet and tying it to a stick, waved it over the wall. Instantly the firing ceased on both sides. The Boers galloped up and we surrendered . . . We were very well treated, and were allowed to visit the wounded. We had eight wounded and two killed, and the mounted infantry with us the same number. We were altogether nine officers, thirty-two men of the 18th Hussars, eighty men of the Dublin Fusiliers and fourteen of the 60th Rifles . . .

Now apparently Möller's force was actually captured by the Irish-American brigade, volunteers fighting for the Boers. They were commanded by a swashbuckling Irish soldier-of-fortune, a Colonel Blake. An Irish-American, a Mr Dunn, reported what he remembered and considering the low casualty figures and the fact that the British were not without ammunition (though it was low) Mr Dunn's version probably tells the interesting truth:

The Irish Fusiliers we captured . . . didn't seem to be very sorry they were taken, and were sort of tickled when they saw our brigade had them. They retreated into a cattle pen – they call them kraals here – on the side of a hill, and were going to put up a fight when they saw our flag [the Irish-American flag]. Colonel Blake sent out Major O'Hara and Captain Pollard . . . with a flag of truce and demanded their surrender, and they came out and laid down their arms. They are a good-looking lot of chaps, but they ought to be on our side.

Yes, I rather agree with Mr Dunn about that, but needless to say, Englishmen and Irishmen were wheeled off to Pretoria – nine officers and over 200 men. The young Boer Deneys Reitz wrote:

Their leader, Colonel Möller, stood on the stoep looking pretty crestfallen, but the private soldiers seemed to take the turn of events more cheerfully. Officers and men were dressed in drab khaki uniforms, instead of the scarlet I had seen in England, and this somewhat disappointed me as it seemed to detract from the glamour of war; but worse still was the sight of the dead soldiers. These were the first men I had seen killed in anger, and their ashen faces and staring eye-balls came as a great shock, for I had pictured the dignity of death in battle, but I now saw that it was horrible to look upon . . .

And what of the cavalry under Major Knox? Well, our happy and shrewd Major Marling went with this group. Before the mounted force was divided, they were in a strong position to make life difficult for the Boers as they climbed down the rear of Talana to get to their horses. Major Marling wrote in his diary: 'I begged him [Möller] to let us open fire on the Boer led horses with the machine gun . . . but he wouldn't hear of it, and told me when he wanted my advice he would ask for it.' It seems a pity that Colonel Möller hadn't wanted Major Marling's advice, very early in the action.

Majors Knox and Marling with their two squadrons and a company of mounted infantry became hard pressed in their new position behind Lennox Hill. Major Marling with only one troop was attacked by Boers who got within 300 yards. Two men were hit and three horses. Major Marling rejoined Knox and temporarily lost his own horse, but 'Knox said I had done very well to get the men off so cheaply. I know I was very glad to get my horse again, as I hate walking, and running even more.' Under pressure Knox and Marling withdrew their men and horses back to camp.

And again, what of the British artillery, once the infantry had taken the tops of Talana and Lennox Hills? British guns were hastily hauled to the summit of Smith's Nek, the pass which separated the two hills – but, to the anger of the sweating infantry, they failed to fire on the retreating Boers, massed on the plains below them. The story is that at the critical moment a message from the Boers reached the commander of the British artillery, asking for an armistice to collect the wounded and the British commander held his fire.

The bloodied infantry could not understand these apparent short-comings of cavalry and artillery. A Welsh Hussar wrote:

As they were crossing the open, we could have cut them to pieces, but the officers in command would not give the order, saying this is a poor way of retaliating . . . It is sad to see our own men being butchered by them, and when we have a few prisoners we have to take tea with them. Our officers sympathize with them in a marked degree, begging us not to cut them down, but to disarm them and take them prisoners.

Perhaps the better educated officers were beginning to feel twinges of unease about the rights of these fighting farmers.

And so ended the first battle. The battle of Talana Hill. Who won? The Boers had been driven from Talana Hill. But we must remember that it was almost invariably their military policy to fight as long as their casualties were low, then exercise a highly mobile withdrawal and then select their next field of action. The Boer republics had small populations; they could not afford high casualties. In this battle they lost 150 men; the British lost over 500. Conan Doyle wrote: 'The battle of Talana Hill was a tactical victory [for the British] but a strategic defeat.'

And the epitaph? Both sides had underrated each other and now both sides were taken aback by the other's fighting qualities. Neither Boer nor Briton would look down their respective noses at each other again – at least in Natal. And poor old brave General Penn-Symons? Mr H. H. Paris, the postmaster at Dundee, reported:

I saw General Penn-Symons brought in mortally wounded in the stomach. He was suffering intense agony, and said, Oh, tell me, have they taken the hill yet? That was at 10.20 a.m., and the hill was not taken for hours later. After the doctors had injected morphine his pain was easier and he said he would be with the columns on the following day.

The Right Reverend Baynes, Bishop of Natal, wrote in his diary:

Poor General Symons! We were told at first that the wound was in the thigh and was slight, but we hear now that it is in the stomach and that it is feared that it is fatal. Still he lives, and they say is brighter this morning . . . A lot of the officers of the 60th are killed. Poor Barnet, my partner at golf! When I went to see them off for the front I said, 'We must play our return match when you come back,' – for he and I had won one and lost one match against the Governor and Blore.

3

THE BATTLE OF ELANDSLAAGTE

*Until that moment I never thought how horrible war
is   And when I looked round again the old Boer
was dead, clasping the cold hand of his dead boy.*

AMBULANCE BEARER AT ELANDSLAAGTE

ON the morning of the battle of Talana Hill, 20 October 1899, General White was busying himself with the defences of Ladysmith – indeed it was on the previous day that he had ridden round the entire fourteen-mile perimeter – when he received a telegram from General Penn-Symons' headquarters, forty miles up the line between Dundee and Glencoe: 'Boers shelling camp with big guns. Troops moving out.'

That very morning Major-General French (who in the First World War became Field-Marshal Sir John French, commander of the British Expeditionary Force in Flanders) arrived in Ladysmith, and was immediately ordered northward to investigate the severance of communication with Penn-Symons' force. This had been caused by General Kock and his Boers swinging in from the west and cutting the railway line at Elandslaagte, well south of Glencoe and only seventeen miles north of Ladysmith. General Kock was too far south to co-operate with General Lucas Meyer at the battle of Talana Hill. But he was well content to be in a position either to oppose the Talana Hill British retreating down to Ladysmith or to face General White's soldiers coming up to their support.

The arrival of the Boers at Elandslaagte station was full of dramatic incident and not without comic overtones. On the morning of 19 October – that is, the day before the battle of Talana Hill – two trains of 'military stores' arrived from Ladysmith at Elandslaagte station en route for Penn-Symons' soldiers at Glencoe and Dundee. As the first train steamed in, the Boer advance guard arrived. Fortunately the station-master, a Britisher, wrote an account of that memorable time, which was printed in England's *Daily News*:

'Pick up the mails and go for all you're worth,' I said to the driver. There was hardly time, however. Loud cries, rattling hoofs, crackling reports from Mauser rifles, and the pattering of bullets all round – the Boers were upon us. Driver Cutbush did not wait. He put on full steam and amid a shower of bullets the train went ahead. At the moment the van passed me several Boers rode on to the platform and fired over our heads at the train. Others dismounted and took steady aim at the driver.

As the train rattled north, two shots came from it, killing a horse and wounding a Boer. A Boer officer got very angry with the station-master, despite being compensated with capturing the second train, but having taken the station-master prisoner, he relented:

Field-Cornet Pienaar addressed me in the following terms: 'I'm very sorry, old man, that I said to you what I did when I first came. I said too much. You can understand my feelings. Seeing the train escape was bad enough, because you could have stopped it, and did not. As I rode up I saw one of my poor men fall, wounded by a shot from the train, and this made my blood boil. I spoke in the heat of passion. However it is all over now. Here's my hand. We will have a drink!

During that day, the Boers interested themselves by unloading the captured train, which was meant to be hurrying to aid Penn-Symons' critically-placed soldiers. As the Boers progressed with the unpacking they became more and more astonished at England's mentality. There were supplies of polo sticks, tennis rackets and chessboards and – unbelievably – a whole truckful of whisky. This the supervising Boer officers destroyed immediately.

Then some 300 German volunteers, fighting for the Boers under Lieutenant-Colonel Schiel, arrived at Elandslaagte. Incidentally, most 'western' countries were represented on the Boer side by such high-principled volunteers. And that evening Field-Cornet Pienaar organized a smoking concert for all who were free to attend, Boers, Germans and British. Again our station-master recorded the strange event, pressed, as it were, between manoeuvring armies:

The concert was opened by a comic song, rendered by a refugee from Newcastle [British Natal], whose musical abilities proved of great service. He and I then rendered the old duet, 'All's Well', and on being encored responded with the 'Army and Navy' duet. A Transvaal burgher sang an Irish song as only an Irishman can. He told us afterwards that this was his eighth campaign, but he did not know then that it was his last. Next day he was dead. A German sergeant then sat down to the piano. Sir Joseph Barnaby's glee, 'Sweet and Low', was sung to his accompaniment, and when I say that it was a success vocally and instrumentally, and add that we all had to trust to memory, it goes to show how wide is the popularity the little composition enjoys. The Boer sergeant then played a series of National Anthems, including both 'God Save the Queen' and the 'Transvaal Volkslied'. They were all played with great taste, and I certainly never expect to hear our National Anthem played or sung again under such apparently impossible conditions.

While we English prisoners sang our National Anthem the Dutch present joined in; but as they sang in the Taal I could not make out what they were singing, but they were all acquainted with the air, and sang it freely. 'God bless the Prince of Wales' was also played by the German, both English and Dutch singing in their respective tongues.

What a generous and astounding concert! Even if one wonders what exactly were the words the Boers were singing. My own bet, knowing the Boers pretty well, is that they sang 'God save our gracious Queen . . .' etc., word for accurate word. At eleven o'clock Field-Cornet Pienaar left for outpost duty and most of the others went to sleep – on the floor.

Meanwhile, back at Ladysmith, Major-General French started to ride towards Elandslaagte with mounted troops and a battery of artillery. In support came Colonel Ian Hamilton with a brigade of infantry. General French rode within sight of the Boer army – but was immediately ordered back by General White because Orange Free State Boers began to assemble west of Ladysmith and it was feared the place might be attacked. French and Hamilton were back in Ladysmith that night (20 October).

Then General White received the news of the outcome of the battle of Talana Hill, and since it emphasized the withdrawal of the Boer force, the report looked more like a sweeping victory for the British than it really was. But it was sufficient inspiration for General White to jump to the idea of an attack. And so, very early on the morning of 21 October 1899, at 4 a.m. to be exact, General French was moving towards the Boer General Kock and his men at Elandslaagte. This time French had with him half a battalion of the Manchester Regiment (though they followed at 6 a.m.), five squadrons of the cream of the South African volunteers, the Imperial Light Horse under Colonel Scott-Chisholme, and the Natal Volunteers Field Battery. Railway and Telegraph companies of the Royal Engineers puffed less spectacularly behind by train. By 7 a.m. General French and his imperial lads reached the Boers at Elandslaagte.

Our station-master at Elandslaagte remembered the moment well:

About 9.30 [a.m.], bang, shriek, crash, and a shell burst in the goods shed not fifty yards from where we were. Consternation is a mild term to apply to the feelings which prevailed. When I got into the open air, and found the English artillery pounding away in our direction, such a scene of confusion met the eye as is seldom witnessed.

This bit of gun-play was a tentative effort to open the proceedings. General French skirmished a little closer and the Boers replied with their artillery. French sensed that the Boers were outranging his heavy guns to the extent of about 500 yards.

The famed war-correspondent and war-artist, Melton Prior, arrived on the scene. He recalls that General French, estimating that the Boers numbered 'about a thousand men', tapped the railway telegraph wires and sent a message to Sir George White in Ladysmith asking for reinforcements to the extent of three battalions, two batteries of artillery and some cavalry. Sir George White replied: 'Am sending reinforcements, and coming out in person.' Sir George appointed his Chief of Staff, Sir Archibald Hunter, to command Ladysmith during his absence and moved towards Elandslaagte with a squadron of the 5th Lancers, one squadron of the 5th Dragoon Guards, the 21st and 42nd batteries of Field Artillery, seven companies of the 1st battalion Devonshire Regiment under Major Park – of whom we shall hear again – and five companies of the 2nd battalion Gordon Highlanders, under dashing Colonel Dick-Cunyngham. With General French's original force this made the British 3500 in number. The Boers were not 1000 strong as French had calculated; they were about 750 men.

Boer General Kock had an additional problem on his hands, apart from being gravely outnumbered. His force consisted mainly of foreigners: 300 Germans under Colonel Schiel, 250 Hollanders and 200 burghers from degenerate Johannesburg. It is said that the Boers themselves refused to join this small army under Kock because they sang 'comic songs in camp' – and no doubt dirty ones as well – instead of joining the religious Boers in psalm singing.

While General French waited for the arrival of formidable reinforcements, the Boers continued to bombard the British with their 15-pounders. Melton Prior, the war-correspondent, had brought with him to the scene of battle a fledgling journalist named Ernest Smith. Mr Prior wrote: 'While waiting for the correspondents and a fresh supply of troops I might tell you that I had noticed little Ernest Smith had behaved with remarkable coolness under his first fire, and I was perfectly satisfied that I had not done wrong in allowing him to join my show.'

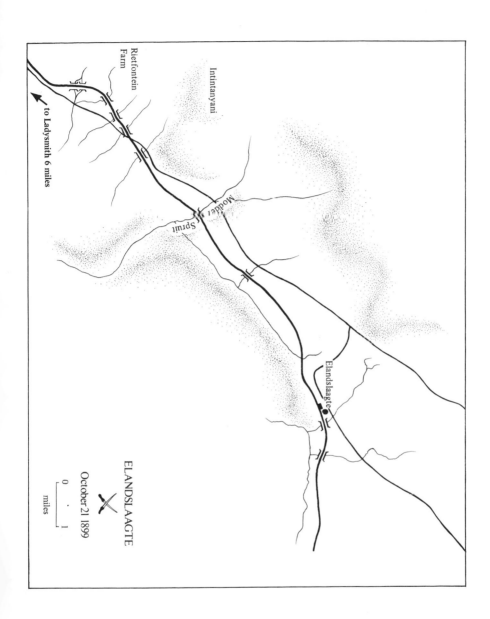

to Ladysmith 6 miles

Rietfontein
Farm

Intintanyani

Modder Spruit

Elandslaagte

ELANDSLAAGTE

October 21 1899

0   1
miles

For the record, Melton Prior had reported on the Ashanti War 1873–4, the campaign in Herzegovina 1875, the Turkish War 1877, the Kaffir War 1878, the Zulu War 1879–80, the First Boer War 1881, the Egyptian Campaign 1882, El Teb 1883, the Nile Expedition 1884, the Burmese Campaign 1887, the Jameson Raid 1895, the Matabele War 1896, the Afridi Campaign 1897, Crete 1897 and now the Second Boer War. He was entitled to be patronizing to 'little Ernest Smith'.

Mr Prior continued:

Sooner than I expected I found carts and carriages turning up with correspondents, and in the van was my dear old friend Bennet Burleigh [another distinguished war-correspondent] who, I am happy to say, had brought out food as well as drink, which I was mighty pleased to see. Then soon the troops began to arrive, the infantry regiments by train . . . and Sir George White then met General French. During their consultation as to the position of affairs I heard General French say, 'I hand over the command of this to you, sir', but General Sir George White, with his usual charming manner, replied 'Oh no! You commenced the show, you carry on.'

The Boers, though primarily foreign volunteers in this case, chose for their position a line of rugged hills, about 300 feet above the veldt, and approximately a mile and a half to the south-east of Elandslaagte railway station. It was well selected; the rocky top gave cover to the defenders and the attackers would have to advance across exposed and difficult terrain.

The 'Fighting Commandant' of the questionable Johannesburg Commando was Ben Viljoen, who represented Johannesburg in the Volksraad, the Boer parliament. He stood next to old General Kock as the British massed to the south-west. Ben Viljoen pleaded with General Kock to open fire with their artillery on the parading British but the General refused. These Boers of the old hierarchy had rigid principles, rooted in their awe of God. Ben Viljoen commented: 'Possibly if we younger commanders had had more authority in the earlier stages of the war, and had had less to deal with arrogant and stupid old men, we should have reached Durban and Cape Town.' The question was to be raised again and again by the younger Boer. It was the beginning of a new materialistic toughness in the Afrikaner.

The British reinforcements were in battle order by 3 p.m. and General French moved swiftly. The tactics were simple, indeed obvious. The Devons, under Major Park, were to advance in extended order directly on to the Boer front. The half-battalion of the Manchesters, with the Gordon Highlanders in support, were to turn the Boers' left flank. The Devons were directed to hold their position, once they had reached effective rifle range, while the

Manchesters and Gordons developed their flanking movement. The artillery were to support the advance of the infantry and move in closer as soon as that infantry had achieved their initial objectives.

The mounted men, of course, were to edge towards the rear of the Boer position, in readiness to deal with the enemy's retreat. A squadron of the 5th Dragoon Guards, commanded by Major St J. C. Gore and later supported by a squadron of the 5th Lancers, moved round the right flank of the Boer position and a mixed detachment of 5th Lancers and Imperial Light Horse moved on the right of the Manchesters and Gordons. It is interesting to consider that the Imperial Light Horse were mainly recruited from the privileged English refugees from Johannesburg and the Boer Johannesburg Commando on top of the defensive position were mainly the conscripted layabouts from that gold-inspired city. Between these two groups was a nasty class war, among other differences.

The Devons reached their allotted place and held it, threatening the Boers' front. The Manchesters and Gordons pressed forward their flanking movement which was to develop into the main assault. An officer of the Manchester Regiment wrote a letter which was eventually published in the London *Times* on 9 December:

Our attack was to become the main attack, and we, supported by the Gordons, were ordered to assault the position. Thus, the regiment had the place of honour! . . . At about 3.30 p.m. we came under the fire of the Boer guns and the rifle fire from his first infantry position. When this happened we were crossing an open grass slope where there was no cover. We were in three lines at the time. We were ordered to lie down, and our firing line opened fire. The first volley made the Boers open a tremendous fire on us; then ensued what I consider the worst seventeen minutes of the day. We were lying in the open under a terrific fire and could do nothing but lie still. The bullets simply whistled over our heads and struck the ground all round us. One struck the ground between my legs and several threw the earth over me. A man quite close to me was shot through the stomach, the poor chap made the most pitiful noises. I am bound to acknowledge I was very glad when I saw the Boers beginning to retire, and I dashed up to the firing line to tell them to advance . . .

A Gordon Highlander wrote after the battle to his parents in Leigh, Scotland:

It was here our first man fell – Bobbie Hall, of B Company. A shell knocked his head off – he went down very quickly . . . The men began to fall. We started to run short distances, then we threw ourselves flat on the ground behind stones, and fired at the enemy. I could not tell you how they fell, but it was awful. Our Colonel and every one of our soldiers behaved splendidly. Just about this time the Colonel, who was on the right of the line from me, got hit, and I heard someone say, 'The Colonel is down', but when I glanced to the right I saw him rise, with his jacket-arm covered with blood. He shouted 'Go on, my lads!' and waved his helmet in his right hand.

The next time I stopped, a man tried to step over me to get in front. He only got one foot over, and saved me from being shot in the left side by receiving the bullet in the side of his left foot. He told me he was hit when I asked him why he sat down on top of me. I told him to shift, and I would dress it the best way I could . . . Before I could get away again I had to wrap up three others . . . God alone knows how I escaped without a scratch. After I had bandaged up the last one I saw the Colonel being led by Sergeant Forbes. I shouted to him 'Do you want assistance, sir?' and he replied, 'Thank you, my lad, get to the front again.'

The officer of the Manchester Regiment continued:

As we crossed the skyline we were met by a perfect hail of bullets, and the Gordons began to reinforce us . . . The Imperial Light Horse [dismounted] now prolonged the line to the right of the Gordons . . . Our losses began to increase as we got down into the dip, the Colonel, M. and P. were all hit here.

Mr H. W. Nevinson, war-correspondent for the London *Daily Chronicle*, viewed the battle from 'a heap of loose stones a little to the right of the Devons . . .' He watched the effect of the British artillery on top of the Boer position:

The ordinary Boers – the armed and mounted peasants – still clung to their rocks as though nothing could drive them out. One big man in black I watched for what seemed a very long time. He was standing right against the sky line, sometimes waving his arm, apparently to give directions. Shells burst over his head, and bullets must have been thick around him. Once or twice he fell, as though slipping on the rocks, for the rain had begun again. But he always reappeared, till at last shrapnel exploded right in his face, and he sank together like a dropped rag.

Now the rain increased till it was a blinding tropical storm. The shells exploded and the men of Manchester and Scotland pressed forward. The Devons also began to assault the front of the hills. The Boers held on grimly.

Melton Prior, representing the *Illustrated London News* and recording the battle from the vicinity of the British military command, was also in the thick of it:

I saw a shell burst by the side of General White's horse, and as for me, I had a very bad time too. I could not make it out how all the shells seemed to come in my direction as well as the bullets, and never could I get anybody to come near me. If I advanced on one of the correspondents he ran away as though I were stricken with plague. At last Burleigh [Bennet Burleigh, the distinguished war-correspondent] said, 'Confound your white helmet, Prior; you are drawing all the fire!' It had never occurred to me that my white helmet with the sun on it was a magnificent target. I realised that if I took it off, my bald head would act like a heliograph to them. What was I to do? Fortunately I had a waterproof cloak, so I took my helmet off, carried it under my arm, and flung the coat over my head; then crouched as low as I could, like the rest were doing, by the side of ant-heaps. This certainly had the right effect, for the shells left me and chose another objective.

This story only goes to show how slow in the uptake humans can be in the heat of battle. But I do wonder how Mr Prior survived all those campaigns. But he, apparently, was more careful than his friend Bennet Burleigh for 'the bullets were whizzing about like hail. I crouched behind the wall, but Burleigh, with that devil-may-care manner of his, leant up against the wall and with binoculars watched the enemy's little tactics. I begged him to come down, for I felt certain he would be hit.'

By this time the Gordons, the Manchesters and the dismounted Imperial Light Horse on their right had reached about 1200 yards from the Boer camp – and directly in front of them was a flat area devoid of cover. Beyond, where the Boers lay, was ample rocky protection. And, to make the situation even less attractive for the British, the German contingent arrived on the scene to reinforce the Boer line. Previously they had been raiding the railway line. At least that is what Sir George White's official despatch claims.

The officer of the Manchester Regiment continued his letter:

The men had all got their blood thoroughly up by this time, and they went at the last hill in splendid style. It was very steep and broken and covered with rocks and stones. As we went up it we saw the Boers gradually begin to leave their sangars [rough man-made stone protections] and retire. Then our drums sounded the 'Charge', it was taken up by the Gordons' pipers, and we dashed in with a tremendous cheer.

The Boer General, Ben Viljoen, was amongst the Boers who faced this murderous attack:

Then the Gordon Highlanders and the other infantry detachments commenced to storm our positions. We got them well within the range of our rifle fire, and made our presence felt; but they kept pushing on with splendid determination and indomitable pluck, though their ranks were being decimated before our very eyes. This was the first, as it was the last, time in the War that I heard a British band playing to cheer attacking 'Tommies' . . . About half an hour before sunset, the enemy had come up close to our positions and on all sides a terrible battle raged. To keep them back was now completely out of the question . . . my rifle was smashed by a bullet. A wounded burgher handed me his . . . We poured a heavy fire into the British, but they were not to be shaken off. Again and again they rushed up in irresistible strength, gallantly encouraged by their brave officers. Poor Field-Cornet Joubert perished at this point.

The Manchester Regiment's officer continued:

I jumped a sangar wall, and I believe I was the first man into their main position [this is probably claimed by at least a dozen others]. Very few of them waited for the bayonet, the remainder retired about 200 yards and opened fire again . . . As we got over the highest part of the hill we saw one of their guns in front of us; it had been abandoned, but was still under a heavy fire. I went for the gun as hard as ever I could split, and had a great race with the Sergeant Drummer of the Gordons, whom I beat by a short head. I then sat on the gun and waited for some of our men to come up and take possession. I now saw that the position was practically taken.

At this point occurred one of the many unfortunate incidents which punctuate the story of the Second Boer War – incidents which were inevitable between an army of trained professional soldiers and a part-time army of rugged individualists such as the Boers. Our Manchester officer was caught at the centre:

Behind the gun the ground dropped steeply to the rear, where the Boer camp was in the valley below. I could see dozens of Boers mounting and galloping off, but considerable numbers were still firing from behind the camp, and a certain number were still under cover on the steep slope behind the gun. It was now pouring with rain [which began about 4.45] and was rapidly getting dark.

At this moment our Brigadier, Colonel Ian Hamilton, who had just joined us, saw a white flag hoisted in the Boer camp, and, thinking they wanted to surrender, ordered the 'Cease fire' to be sounded. Just after this a Boer appeared from behind a rock about twenty-five yards in front of me and held up his hands. Some of our men and some of the Gordons rushed towards him, so, thinking they were going to bayonet him, I ran up, made him give me his rifle, and turned to face our men, when I was struck on the back of the left shoulder with such force that I reeled for about ten yards before I fell. The whole of my left arm and side seemed to be paralysed by the force of the blow, and I was faint and sick with pain. At this moment the Boers on the steep slope dashed up the hill towards us, a tremendous fire was poured into us from the hill above the camp, and the whole line, not understanding why the 'Cease fire' was sounded, wavered for a moment and then retired about 40 yards. I was left lying on the ground between the two forces. Seeing this, one Sergeant Murphy, of my old company, ran back, held me up, and shouted to the men not to retire. (The Colonel has sent on a report I made out about this incident, and I hope Murphy will get something out of it: it was a very plucky act.) The panic was only momentary; the officers rallied their men, and the whole line dashed back to the edge of the slope and poured a heavy fire into the retreating Boers.

This sort of incident was snatched upon by the newspapers in England and used as violent anti-Boer propaganda. Of course, not only were many of the Boers totally unsophisticated about the usages of war, but also the terrain was usually rocky and many things were obscured from men only a short distance away. As that white flag was being 'abused' the Boers were suffering a similar 'wrong' in the Elandslaagte station area. The Boers had placed their three ambulance wagons in the vicinity of the railway station. From each wagon they had hoisted a Red Cross flag. There was no wind blowing so the flags were not distinct. Working with the Boer medical staff was a Mr Walter Herald, a chemist from Manchester who had been commandeered as an ambulance assistant, and he reported what happened:

Suddenly there appeared on the hill opposite, a lot of British troops, with a battery of guns . . . Within five minutes of the battery appearing the first shot (shrapnel) was fired . . . The next shot struck one of our mules, and took half its head away. The third shell burst close by, and part of it went bang through the waggon in which I was dressing, and was within a foot of finishing my little career.

I very much doubt whether either the firing after the white flag had been raised or the shelling of the Red Cross emblem was a deliberately evil act.

Meanwhile the 1st Devonshire Regiment had pressed from their front-holding position to within 350 yards of the Boers, and then after a short breather, no doubt lying very close to the African earth, they fixed bayonets and charged.

G. W. Steevens, the London *Daily Mail* war-correspondent, saw the final charge:

The pipes shrieked of blood and the lust of glorious death. Fix bayonets! Staff officers rushed shouting from the rear, imploring, cajoling, cursing, slamming every man who could move into the line . . . It was a surging wave of men – Devons and Gordons, Manchesters and Light Horse all mixed, inextricably; subalterns commanding regiments, soldiers yelling advice, officers firing carbines, stumbling, leaping, killing, falling, all drunk with battle, shoving through hell to the throat of the enemy.

A Hollander volunteer fighting with the Boers wrote:

At this moment the majority of the Johannesburgers gave way, in spite of the encouragements of our commander, who cried: 'Stand firm! All my Dutchmen are here yet.' The advancing infantry kept a terrible fusillade on our 300 men . . .

Except the dead I saw nothing. The other had gone without my perceiving the movement on account of the infernal noise of the shells. A few, however, still remained a little behind me. I waited, still lying down, a couple of shells covering me with dirt, while the little leaden bullets fell, without exaggeration, on my back and beside me.

The battle seemed to be over. The surviving Boers and their volunteer foreign allies tumbled down the rear, eastern, side of the two hills and raced for their horses. Away in a north-eastward direction they went. And that was the beginning of the most terrible episode of the battle of Elandslaagte. At about 5.45 p.m., through the gathering darkness, from the west rode the 5th Royal Irish Lancers. And they caught the fleeing Boers.

An American newspaper, the *Cincinnati Enquirer*, published a letter written by an eighteen-year-old American boy, fighting with the Boers:

As the Lancers charged, some of our men fled, a few hid. I am very small, as you remember, so I crept into a hole under a rock about big enough for a dog. Our men – about seventy of them – who could not escape threw down their guns and cried out, 'Surrendered!' From where I lay I could see those brave soldiers of the Queen, who want to civilize Africa, with shouts of glee thrust their lances through men on their knees. It was awful!

One woman, the wife of a burgher, was with her husband at the time. He might have escaped and left her, but turned, threw down his gun, and, taking her hand, shouted, 'We surrender!' A bold, brave Lancer shouted, 'Stick those pigs!' and thrust first through the man and then the woman. When the slaughter was over an officer rode up, who shouted 'Stick the pigs, boys!' When he saw the woman he ordered some of them to dig a hole with their lances and they thrust her into it. The man who killed them took the ring off her finger as booty. She lies there today, and when the man and woman were killed three lives were given. Now you know why I will aim true.

Unfortunately, that is not an isolated, prejudiced report. British infantry viewed the terrible spectacle and reported. A private of the 1st King's Royal Rifles wrote to a friend in Preston, Lancashire:

It was a great but a terrible sight to see those horsemen hew their way through the Boers. Three times they rode right through the Boers, hacking, cutting, slashing. We had suffered pretty severely, and I suppose we got our backs up a bit. Anyhow, we got even with Joubert's men . . . Some of the Boers had died in praying attitudes. Many, I was told by a friend in the 5th Lancers, flung down their arms as soon as they saw the flash of the lances, and, clasping their hands above their heads, begged for mercy. But they had shown no mercy to our men . . . and this was our revenge.

The British Army's sport of pig-sticking had certainly conditioned the

5th Lancers. A British officer had a letter quoted in the London *Times* – which, after all, usually tried to make Old England look clean:

One of our squadrons (not mine) pursued, and got right in among them in the twilight and the most excellent pig-sticking ensued for about ten minutes, the bag being about sixty. One of our men, seeing two Boers riding away on a horse, stuck his lance through the two, killing both with one thrust. Had it not been getting dark we should have killed many more.

A Mr W. Williams, who I believe was a British gunner, wrote to his father:

I got hold of one Boer, and I was mad. He did not know what I meant when I spoke, so I made motions for him to run for his life. So he went, and I galloped after him with the Sergeant's sword, and cut his head right off his body.

On 15 December 1899 a letter was quoted in the London *Evening News* which confessed to a pious atrocity:

It was a sad sight to see the Boers when our Lancers charged. They knelt down crying and saying, 'Please, sir, don't kill me!' some taking off their rings and the money from their pockets. We ran amongst them and shot them with our revolvers, while the Lancers charged with lances. It was a mix up, some of us nearly shooting our own men.

Well, the Boer General, Ben Viljoen, rode for his life from the battlefield of Elandslaagte:

Revolvers were being promiscuously fired at us, and at times the distance between us and our pursuers grew smaller. We could plainly hear their shouting 'Stop, or I'll shoot you', or 'Halt, you damned Boer, or I'll run my lance through your blessed body.'

We really had no time to take much notice of these pretty compliments. It was a race for life and freedom. Looking round furtively once more I could distinguish my pursuers; I could see their long assegais [lances]; I could hear the snorting of their unwieldy horses, the clattering of their swords. These unpleasant combinations were enough to strike terror into the heart of any ordinary man.

General Viljoen escaped, but when he came to reform his broken Johannesburg Commando a few days later, he found some of them in a sorry state.

The shock of Elandslaagte had been too much for the weaker brethren, who seemed deaf to every argument, and only wanted to go home. I gave each of these a pass to proceed by rail to Johannesburg, which read as follows:

'Permit —— to go to Johannesburg on account of cowardice, at Government's expense.'

They put the permit in their pockets without suspecting its contents, and departed with their kit to the station to catch the first available train.

With European and American volunteers present at this battle of Elandslaagte, the brutality of the British was advertised widely over the two continents, but in Britain it was accepted as a glorious and devastating victory. An Irish-American, J. G. Dunn from Lowell, Massachusetts, fighting with the Irish Brigade against the British, wrote on 29 November 1899:

The Lancers acted as if fighting Indians, and gave no quarter, stabbing and murdering prisoners and wounded in a horrible fashion, just like a lot of Sioux. It is said that officers are responsible for this dastardly work, but it makes little difference to us. That lot of gentry are down in our black book, and if the opportunity presents itself . . .

Darkness settled over the battlefield and with it came a bitter cold rain. Melton Prior, the war-correspondent, investigated as best he could.

Wet mud and rocks – great Scot! I slipped any number of times, but eventually reached the light, which turned out to be two candles in bottles, with two surgeons hard at work with the wounded. What a sight! The battle is bad enough, but this hasty, improvised field-hospital in pouring rain – no chloroform and not enough surgeons – was simply very dreadful. Of course we had not expected such a heavy loss (or butcher's bill as it is called) . . . For about two hours I helped as far as I could in collecting the wounded, and holding men while they had wounds dressed.

H. W. Nevinson, war-correspondent for the *Daily Chronicle*, also stumbled through the darkness looking for the wounded.

I was nearly two hours on the ground moving about. The wounded lay very thick, groaning and appealing for help. In coming down I nearly trod on the upturned white face of an old white-bearded man. He was lying quite silent, with a kind of dignity. We asked who he was. He said: 'I am Kock, the father of the commandant.' But the old man was wrong. He himself had been in command, though instead of fighting, he had read the Bible and prayed. One bullet had passed through his shoulder, another through his groin. So he lay still and read no more. Near him was a boy with a hand just a mixture of shreds and bones and blood. But he too was very quiet, and only asked for a handkerchief to bind it together. Others were gradually dying. Many were not found till daylight. The dead of both sides lay unburied till Monday.

A cover addressed and decorated by a soldier in the 2nd King's Own Regiment with the Natal Field Force

There were sinister rumours about General Kock. A private correspondent, writing from Pretoria to a friend in England, wrote:

Our wounded were robbed and murdered by the Lancers. General Kock had his money, rings, and watch stolen from him. He was stripped of his clothes, all but his trousers; and thus, wounded as he was, he had to lie out in the cold all night, half naked.

But of course, there were many acts of kindness performed during that awful night. Battlefields like Elandslaagte were not large areas and they therefore were strangely personal. An officer of the 1st Manchester Regiment, who had been shot through the leg and lay out in the open unable to move, wrote:

I am glad my Tommy – a private in my own company, called Rogers – stayed with me, for he wrapped me in his own great-coat, and lay with his arms round me all the night to try and keep me warm. If he hadn't I am afraid I should have pegged out, for it was bitterly cold and I couldn't move at all. Search parties were out all night, of course, looking for us, and four men tried to carry me in their arms, but it was too frightful, as they kept falling amongst the rocks and dropping me, till I had to cry off.

Some Britishers showed compassion towards the Boers. An ambulance bearer described an incident:

We were out looking after the wounded at night when the fight was over, when I came across an old, white-bearded Boer. He was lying behind a bit of rock supporting himself on his elbows.

When I got near I saw that he was too far gone to raise his rifle. He was gasping hard for breath, and I saw he was not long for this world. He motioned to me to go and find his son, a boy of thirteen who had been fighting by his side when he fell.

Well, I did as he asked me, and under a heap of wounded I found the poor lad, stone dead and I carried him back to his father. Well, you know I'm not a chicken hearted sort of a fellow. I have seen a bit of fighting in my time and that sort of thing knocks all the soft out of a chap. But I had to turn away when the old Boer saw his dead lad. He hugged the body to him and moaned over it, and carried on in a way that fetched a big lump in my throat. Until that very moment I never thought how horrible war is. I never wanted to see another shot fired. And when I looked round again the old Boer was dead, clasping the cold hand of his dead boy.

The battle of Elandslaagte was summed up by various war-correspondents. Mr George Lynch in his *The Impressions of a War-Correspondent* wrote that 'my heart goes out to Tommy Atkins – sweating, swearing, grimy, dirty, fearless, and generous – Tommy is a bit of "all right"!' From Bennet Burleigh of the London *Daily Telegraph* came the comment that 'given a fair field, man to man, Tommy is more than a match for the Boer, even at the latter's own game – and the Boer now knows the fact'. Lastly Melton Prior of the *Illustrated London News* reported that 'General French was very satisfied with his day's work, as he thought he had taught the Boers a salutary lesson; but they, I fear, thought differently.'

The Times History of the War in South Africa gives casualty figures for the British as 5 officers and 50 men killed, 30 officers and 175 men wounded; and for the Boers as 'at least 60 killed, 120–150 wounded and nearly 200 prisoners' (out of a total force of under 800). The Boers lost the leaders of the Hollander Volunteer Contingent, for Count Zeppelin was killed, and Colonel Schiel and Captain De Witt Hamer were wounded and taken prisoner. Also Field-Cornet Pienaar, the jolly Boer who organized the Anglo-Boer concert at Elandslaagte, died that day.

The Boer prisoners of war were removed to Cape Town and then on board the ship *Penelope* were finally sailed to imprisonment on the island of St Helena in the South Atlantic.

One of General White's personal escort at the battle of Elandslaagte was a Mr G. J. Golding, probably a Natal Volunteer, and I have a letter from him written two days later to a friend in Durban, Natal.

Ladysmith, 23rd Oct. 99.

Dear Taft,

It strikes me that it were about time I sent you a line or two. I was in the engagement at Elands Laagte on Saturday but was not injured in any way, though we were in the thick of the fight. The Boer fire (Artillery) was excellent, and did a lot of damage amongst our poor fellows. The Devons and Gordons, also the Imperial Light Horse did splendid service. We lost about 120 men altogether. The General – Sir G. White – is a regular old fire eater and refused to get out of danger. We were on two occasions all but wiped out en masse, i.e. the General and Escort. Two shells – fired bang at us failed to burst – thank God – but mowed down two of our horses under us.

The General says we are to breakfast in Pretoria with him, if all goes well. He also has remarked that he intends to let us have a real good smack at the Boers soon to revenge ourselves for the loss of our horses etc. Good-bye old boy and kindest regards to all. In great haste. I am,

Ever yours, G. J. L. GOLDING. Write us a line soon.

4

THE RETREAT TO LADYSMITH

*We left all our wounded, tents, and a lot of stores
at Dundee ... Also band instruments of four
infantry regiments, so that old Kruger is now
probably playing the soft trombone to his old
Dutch at Pretoria.*

MAJOR MARLING

DURING the evening of the day before the battle of Elandslaagte (20 October) Brigadier General Yule marched his troops away from the battle-field of Talana Hill to their camp at Dundee. Though the British felt that they had been victorious, the General was too sensible to feel confident about his strategic predicament. He had reason to believe that the Boer army's eastern flank had been driven back at Talana Hill, though at that time he was unaware that Colonel Möller's cavalry had been destroyed, but he knew that the Boer centre under General Erasmus on and around Impati Hill was intact and he knew that the Boer western flank had swung down south and cut off his railway retreat at Elandslaagte. Perhaps his only comfort was that the Boers, in unknown strength on Impati Hill, were timid. Why had they not attacked his rear or his camp while he was bloodily engaged at Talana? And to add to his problems he was feeling very ill.

But General Yule dreaded evacuating Dundee. Since he could not use the railway he would be faced with a cruel forced march which would mean the abandoning of the wounded, including General Penn-Symons, and the considerable stores – and of course it meant the loss of the coalfields, upon which the colony of Natal depended.

Therefore, the next morning (21 October) General Yule withdrew his camp a little further to the south and hopefully out of range of the Boer guns in the vicinity of Impati. Within an hour of the British settling down they were shelled from the north and suffered a few casualties in the camp. General Yule then telegraphed to Sir George White, supposedly in Ladysmith, explaining his situation and asking for reinforcements. The reply came that Sir George was at Elandslaagte with the Ladysmith troops, fighting a battle, but that the request for reinforcements would be put to General White as soon as possible.

During that night and the early morning of 22 October, in heavy rain, General Yule pulled back his camp another two miles to the south, hoping for some peace at base. A few hours after they arrived there the psychological pressure was eased by the news of the apparent victory at Elandslaagte. Immediately General Yule marched his force eastward towards Glencoe Junction in the hope of cutting off Boers in flight from Elandslaagte. Well, if the Boers were still fleeing, they were not riding in that direction and all the British got for their soldierly instinct was another pounding from the Boer long-range guns that now had moved just north of Glencoe.

Our Major Marling VC was on this expedition and he wrote:

A message came in from Ladysmith saying the Boers had been beaten the day before at Elandslaagte, and were retreating up Glencoe Pass, and we all bucked up wonderfully. So we [18th Hussars] and one battery started off for the pass, only however to find two Boers – one of them was wounded, and the other said he was on our side. We had a fight of sorts all day with a fresh lot of Boers who had arrived from Newcastle. At 5 p.m. it was decided to withdraw the whole force . . .

General Yule marched his men back to their camp and he must have thought very hard every step of the way. He was outgunned, outnumbered and stuck up northward on a ridiculous limb, as it were. It began to dawn on him that if he was going to save his force he had better hurry. In fact, General Yule was teetering on the edge of disaster. Major Marling was there and he gives a hair-raising account of conditions at that juncture:

It was now getting dark, and there was the most awful confusion: regiments without their commanding officers, and commanding officers without their regiments. No one knew where the General was, and all the Staff but two had been knocked over. The Headquarters telegraph clerk came and asked me where the General was, as he had been hunting for him with a most important message for an hour. It was to this effect: 'From G.O.C. Ladysmith. I cannot reinforce you without sacrificing Ladysmith and the Colony behind. You must try and fall back on Ladysmith. I will do what I may to help you when nearer.' Cheery under the circumstances. I couldn't find General Yule so gave it to old Pickwood in the R.A., the next senior officer, who nearly fell off his horse when he read it. It had been drizzling since 5 p.m., and now rained in a steady downpour. We had no tents or covering, and held on to our horses all night. We got no orders at all, and none of us had any idea what we were to do in the morning.

When the message finally got to poor old General Yule, ill in the teeming rain, it settled everything. It was now simply a matter of how the hell to get his men back to Ladysmith. First he would have to send a body of men back to the old Dundee camp to grab sufficient stores to feed his retreating force and this being successful he would embark his force southward to Ladysmith along the Helpmakaar till they reached a place called Beith and then strike a more westerly route for Ladysmith. It was something of a wild gamble. Heads down and hope for the best. They had to pass through the eastern end of the Biggarsberg mountains and cross the unpredictable Waschbank river. It could be assumed that Generals Lucas Meyer and Erasmus would pursue, and why could not General Kock's force attack their right side as they stumbled southward in a long, long column?

A Major Wickham was selected to steal their own stores from under the noses of the Boers. Sir Frederick Maurice in the *History of the War in South Africa* describes this initial operation:

No sooner had darkness fallen [the night of 22 October] than Major Wickham of the Indian Commissariat, taking with him thirty-three waggons guarded by two companies of the Leicestershire Regiment, left the hill and moved with great precaution into the deserted camp. The convoy performed its short but dangerous journey without attracting the attention of the enemy, and the waggons, after being quickly loaded with as many stores as the darkness, the confusion of the levelled tents, and limited time made possible, were drawn up on the outskirts to await the passage of the column.

Now the entire force had to march gingerly three miles or so northward to the outskirts of Dundee, reach the Helpmakaar road and turn sharply southward. It was a delicate operation for a tired cumbersome column. Private Allen of the Leicestershire Regiment described the move off: 'General Yule sent men down to the camp to light candles in tents to make believe that they had retired into camp, and while this was going on we were on the move.'

The retreat began at 9.30 p.m. Only senior officers and Colonel Dartnell, commanding the Natal Police, who was to lead and be guide to the enterprise knew the real purpose of the march. A manager of one of the coalmines who was with the column wrote:

We were under the impression we were going to take up a fresh position ready for the morning. We marched for hours and hours, passed quietly through Dundee under the Boer guns, and found ourselves on the road out of Dundee. We were dead tired, hungry, and footsore, but on we went until four o'clock in the morning, and then we knew that we were retreating on Ladysmith.

The postmaster of Dundee, Mr H. H. Paris, was asked by General Yule, early that evening, to return to his post office in the town and destroy all military messages that had been sent. Mr Paris recalled what happened:

As we could not get horses we walked into the town, and we did as requested. At 11.30 p.m. a friend, who is a guide to the military, rode up very excitedly, saying he had come to inform us that the troops had gone, and that their last waggon was then moving down the street. The General had forgotten all about us!

Needless to say, we soon had our lights out, and after cramming the registered letters into the safe, and carrying away what office cash and stamps we could, amounting to £200, we soon caught up the last waggon, and walked throughout the night, toiling through slush, mud, and rain, over a very bad, hilly road.

As a matter of ephemeral fact, I am now holding in my left hand one of those very letters left behind in Dundee. It was written on 19 October by Private W. Ball of G Company 1st Leicestershire Regiment, Natal Force, Dundee, to a Miss M. Walker, who ran the Soldiers' Institute in Pietermaritzburg. He wrote: 'We have not commenced operations yet but we expect it at any time. We shall have enough when we do start. I have heard they are doing good work at Mafeking . . . we are all well and in good hopes of victory and my chum has come up to the Regiment so I am all right now . . .' By 2 November this letter was in Pretoria and was censored by the Boers, but by January 1900 it had been returned to the British and delivered to Miss Walker. The Boers always tried to keep things civilized.

General Yule's idea was to get his force as far away from the Boers as possible before they even realized that he was retreating. He was therefore forced to desert every person in Dundee without even telling them. For this action he was criticized by many Natalians, but from a military point of view he did the only thing possible.

The Natal point of view about the desertion of Dundee was expressed by H. Watkins-Pitchford, who was I believe a volunteer Natal Carabineer, in a letter to his wife:

The town is left to its fate, is sacked, and the inhabitants, many of them, reported shot in defending their own homes. This place having fallen the enemy is marching on Ladysmith, distant only 45 miles, with the object of laying siege to it and wiping us out. Whether, when the war comes to be quietly thought out, the abandonment of Dundee, with its dying General, its full hospitals, and its large reserves of stores, will be found to be justifiable I do not know, but I 'has my doubts'.

Through the black night Colonel Dartnell led the troops. The rain poured down and the mud got deeper but the column pressed on relentlessly.

By 4.30 a.m. 23 October, they had marched fourteen miles and General Yule
called a halt. They rested for three to four hours and then off again. Ahead lay
Van Tonders Pass, the deep defile through the Biggarsberg mountains, six
miles long. Would the Boers be waiting? The truth is that Yule's column
had put twenty miles between themselves and Dundee before the Boers
realized they were gone. And their General Lucas Meyer of Talana Hill
pursued slowly and General Erasmus of Impati Hill criminally failed to move
till 24 October.

Almost twenty-four hours after Yule's force had begun their hazardous
retreat from Dundee, the Boer General, Lucas Meyer, composed the following telegram:

T.D. ZAR 23.10.1899. From Assistant-General Lucas Meyer via Vryheid

To State Secretary, Pretoria, begins:

9.20 p.m. Ever since yesterday morning I have been all set to attack Dundee
with my burghers. But as a result of rain and cold, Generals Erasmus and Trichardt
have not completed their preparations. I now await their report and the possible
arrival here this evening of General Schalk Burger with four guns before moving
on . . . Am in the field with just mounted men, thus have no suitable writing
materials. Tell this to the General – ends.

Commandant-General Joubert addressed the tardy Lucas Meyer:

T.D. ZAR 24.10.1899. From Commandant-General, Dannhauser

To Assistant-General Meyer, Vryheid, begins:

10 a.m. I have telegraphed and written to you so often that I really think it
useless to persevere. I hear of your readiness, I hear of your coming but I see
nothing. You are no longer needed for an attack on Dundee but for a combined
attack on the enemy. What hinders you? In heaven's name let at least Schalk
Burger come up. In my name call up all tardy burghers to report here immediately.
If you fail to do so, you yourself will be responsible for the demoralization of our
gallant army and indeed for the loss of our land. The troops have fled from Dundee
it is true, but only to gather strength for a counter attack. Come then without
any delay at all. Your immediate answer please. Punish all laggards according to
martial law – ends.

Nine and a half hours later poor Commandant-General Joubert was still
wrestling with General Lucas Meyer by telegram:

T.D. ZAR 24.10.1899. From Commandant-General, Dannhauser

To General Meyer, Vryheid, begins:

7.30 p.m. I saw today the telegram sent by you to the Government wherein you state that you have been all set to attack Dundee as from noon yesterday; but since Trichardt and Erasmus's men have already occupied Dundee and been in it since yesterday morning, there are no longer troops there to attack. No one quite knows where they are now, but it is reported today that they have fled past Helpmakaar with their guns, leaving behind large tents, fodder for horses and enough food for our men . . . At Dundee there is nothing to do for the present. We must get moving or great harm will ensue. So hurry forward all of you – ends.

Lucas Meyer and some of his conservative Boers prove that England did not have a monopoly of dangerously stupid leaders.

As Mr J. C. Dunn, fighting for the Boers with the Irish Brigade, said, 'Had the Boer contingent had more experience in military matters we could have got the whole of Yule's bunch, horse, foot, and waggons, for I never saw a worse beaten, demoralized crowd than that same British army.' The colliery manager, quoted earlier, continued his story of the struggle back to Ladysmith: 'I cannot go into the awful hardships we encountered, walking seventy miles in horrible storms of rain and thunder. Suffice it to say, we walked for five days with not a dry thread on us, and nothing to eat except hard biscuits and bully-beef. The last mile I walked without boots: they had fallen off my feet.'

General Yule's force therefore got through Van Tonders Pass and on the morning of 24 October, they had reached the Waschbank river. Here they heard the sound of heavy gunfire, far away to the west. It was presumed that General White was fighting somewhere along the railway and although everyone was thoroughly worn out, mounted men rode westward to co-operate. But during the afternoon the gunfire died away and they returned to their main force.

On the next morning the column marched again for twelve miles and then, in desperate condition, prepared to rest during the night. At this point an order arrived from Sir George White for them to press on through the night and get into Ladysmith with all haste. The rain came down in torrents. The soldiers struggled on and fortunately reached Ladysmith by 26 October. The very day that General Erasmus, for all his slowness, would have gained their right flank.

Corporal Hallahan of the 2nd battalion Irish Fusiliers wrote about the last night's march:

So we packed up again, this time putting our great-coats on the transport, and we were ordered to form the rear guard. It started raining again . . . When we would halt some of the men would fall asleep on their feet in the mud. There was a young officer standing beside me where we halted once, and he was asleep on his feet, with his hands out groping for my rifle. I had to rouse him. He told me afterwards that he was going mad that night. We arrived at Ladysmith about 11 a.m. on Thursday.

Major Marling gave his account of the final effort:

We halted every minute, as the wagons got stuck, and the track was up to the horses' hocks with slush and mud, and a few huge boulders thrown in just to break the monotony. About 9 p.m. half the wagons got stuck, and although we had sixteen mules to each wagon, they could hardly move. At 10 p.m. I went up with the General [Yule] and the A.D.C. [Murray] to see what could be done, and presently we started them on the right track, which a lot of them had lost. Into Ladysmith by 11 a.m, everyone soaked to the skin, and more or less covered with black slush. Distance from Glencoe to Ladysmith the way we came, 64 miles. Our horses ate their last forage Thursday morning.

Major Marling was being discreet in this account of the end of the retreat. The truth is that General Yule was broken by the event and the column was safely brought back by Major Murray and Colonel Dartnell of the Natal Police, and, of course, by officers such as Major Marling.

The British soldiers now congregating in the town of Ladysmith were generally confused by their situation. For long they had been conditioned to believe that they were 'God's Almighty' as an old veteran of the Second Boer War once said to me. Now it was clear that they had been forced back by rough-looking foreign farmers. It was difficult for ordinary gulled Tommy Atkins to understand.

I now hold in my hand a letter from a Mr H. Edwards who took part in the retreat from Dundee. He was with the 1st Leicestershire Regiment but what rank I know not, and he writes from Ladysmith on 20 October to, again, Miss Walker of the Soldiers' Institute, Pietermaritzburg. Incidentally, the envelope is postmarked 'Ladysmith November the 2nd, 1899', the day the famous siege commenced, and therefore was not delivered to Miss Walker till 3 March 1900. The gentleman writes:

I daresay you heard of our safe arrival [the Dundee column] at Ladysmith last Thursday morning. Although we had to leave Dundee owing to strength of the Boers, yet it seemed too much like running away to go down very well with the lads who were on the column. We had a very arduous march on short rations and no shelter from the rain which was very bad. It is a great wonder to me that so few were knocked up by the constant wetting and chills, but to the utter astonishment of the Boers, who kept in touch with us all the way, we proved that Englishmen (Rooineks) were as good for hardships on the veldt as themselves, to the manner born. They can't beat the Britishers at all can they Miss Mabel?

And the Natal Volunteers' feelings were expressed by Mr Watkins-Pitchford in his long letter-diary to his wife:

One of the 'Dubs', a captain, came to borrow a handkerchief and a pair of socks, and a drink. His feet were like underdone meat. We cannot despair while we have such stuff to work with. If only we could get rid of the Staff-College element we should walk through the whole country from end to end, but at present all our checks and reverses – of which you have not heard at home – are due to a miserable adherence to existing regulations and an absence of any flexibility or adaptability to South African conditions.

It is the same dreary old game, and our people are again committing the same blunders and adopting the same haw-haw eye-glass tactics which led us into such horrors as Isandhlwana [Zulu War] and Majuba [First Boer War], and many other defeats.

On 23 October, the day after the British marched away from Dundee, General Penn-Symons died there, a prisoner of the Boers. His body was sewn in a Union Jack and was carried by the non-commissioned officers and men of the British Hospital staff who had remained behind to look after the wounded. As the body was carried to the Church of England cemetery every wounded soldier capable stood to attention, and the Boers raised their great slouch hats. Many Boers attended the burial service and, as was their custom, behaved with great reverence. The Commandant-General of the Boer forces wrote a letter to General White. A kindly letter – but one that also carried his outrage:

Must express my sympathy. Symons, unfortunately badly wounded, died, buried yesterday. I trust great God will speedily bring to close this unfortunate state of affairs, brought about by unscrupulous speculators and capitalists, who went to Transvaal to obtain wealth, and, in order to further their own interests, misled others and brought about this shameful state of warfare all over South Africa, in which so many valuable lives have been and are being sacrificed, as, for instance, Symons and others. I express my sympathy to Lady Symons at loss of her husband.

General Yule's departure from Dundee was such a last-minute affair and then under such schemes of secrecy that there was no opportunity to destroy stores that were not carried with the column. When the Boers entered the British camp they inherited provisions of every conceivable description. The Boers valued the haul at £350000, enough to supply 10000 men with rations for two months.

Major Marling, as always giving good value, notes this serious loss in his diary:

We left all our wounded, tents, and a lot of stores at Dundee, as, now the railway is cut, we had no transport to carry it away. Also band instruments of four infantry regiments, so that old Kruger is now probably playing the soft trombone to his old Dutch at Pretoria.

And then top secret documents were discovered in the British camp. One must presume that General Yule was ignorant of their existence, at least in the camp, otherwise he would have ordered their removal as he had ordered the destruction of the military telegrams at the post office. A special correspondent of Reuters News Agency telegraphed from Glencoe Junction on 28 October the following report. To the world in general it spilled out more shame on John Bull's bandaged head:

The papers captured at Dundee camp from the British unveil a thoroughly worked out scheme to attack the independence of both Republics as far back as 1896, notwithstanding constant assurances of amity towards the Free State. Among these papers there are portfolios of military sketches of various routes of invasion from Natal into the Transvaal and Free State, prepared by Major Grant, Captain Melvill, and Captain Gale, immediately after the Jameson Raid.

A further portfolio marked secret, styled *Reconnaissance Reports of Lines of Advance through the Free State*, was prepared by Captain Wolley, on the Intelligence Division of the War Office in 1897, and is accompanied by a special memorandum, signed by Sir Redvers Buller, to keep it secret . . . Further, there is a short military report on the Transvaal, printed in India in August last, which was found most interesting. The white population is given as 288 000 of whom the Outlanders [foreigners around Johannesburg's goldfields] number 80 000, and of the Outlanders 30 000 are given as of British descent, which figures the authorities regard as much nearer the truth than Mr Chamberlain's statements made in the House of Commons . . .

The Free State burghers are now more than ever convinced that it was the right policy for them to fight along with the Transvaal and they say, since they have seen the reports, that they will fight with, if possible, more determination than ever.

This Reuters news-cast was more than even England could manage to suppress. Unfortunately few nations go to war for moral reasons and though world outrage against England swelled, there was pitifully little hope of help for the Boer republics from the major powers of that 1899 world.

An American war-correspondent, Mr C. Easton, working for the *New York Journalist*, reported the events directly to his newspaper:

Regiment after regiment at Dundee fled through the fog before the merest handful of Boer farmers. The disorder was indescribable. The British there deserted two trainloads of provisions and one of ammunition. The officers left even their secret documents and plan of campaign. These I have seen, and they show that the English had been preparing for the war ever since the Jameson Raid . . .

Of course the first sentence was untrue; although the British were potentially ounumbered and outflanked, and conceivably outwitted, fleeing before a merest handful was angry propaganda. And the second sentence was also untrue. Indeed the British achieved a near miracle of extrication.

I have been unable to discover whether the British officer or officers responsible for the embarrassing blunder of losing these incriminating documents were ever court-martialled. Anyway, searching British popular journals of the time, I can find no mention of the exposure of such British intentions and since the British Government's main concern was to convince the British people that their cause was just, if not holy, no real damage was done to the John Bull image – in British eyes. And what of the rest of the world? Well, we were powerful enough then to imply a rude salute.

As the Boers observed the British hurry into Ladysmith, they issued the following proclamation:

Praise the Lord and ask His protection and assistance, as our troops have had heavy losses, as also have the enemy. Pray the Lord, all ye Burghers, for our success and victory, which, with the Lord's assistance, we shall gain, ever praising and blessing the Lord and a just cause.

Though the Boers were very religious, if not sometimes sanctimonious, this side of their character can be exaggerated, as the Boer General Ben Viljoen explained:

Our spiritual welfare was being looked after by the Reverends Nel and Martins, but not for long, as both these gentlemen quickly found that commando life was unpleasant and left us spiritually to ourselves, even as the European Powers left us politically. But I venture to state that no member of my commando really felt acutely the loss of the theological gentlemen who primarily accompanied us.

That gunfire which General Yule's column heard on the morning of 24 October and which he bravely but abortively went out to investigate is known as the battle of Rietfontein and it still carries with it an air of contradiction, if not obscurity.

On the day before General White (in Ladysmith) knew that General Yule was in retreat down the Helpmakaar road, he had learnt that an army of 9000 Orange Free State Boers, under Chief-Commandant Marthinus Prinsloo, had approached from the west, had reoccupied Elandslaagte and were probably only about seven miles north of Ladysmith but west of the railway line, inhe vicinity of a farm called Rietfontein.

Now General White longed to clout the Boers good and hard and he also wisely thought that it would be best if he hit the Transvaalers and Free Staters separately, before they joined hands. This news of the arrival of the Free Staters could be his last chance. The Transvaalers under slow General Erasmus couldn't be far up the line . . . The British had hit the Transvaalers twice, at Talana Hill and at Elandslaagte, but had never met the Free Staters. Of course Sir George White, like every other Britisher, still dreamed of a crushing blow against these humiliating farmers, though the hope was fast dimming.

But the immediate desperate need was to protect General Yule's right flank as the column trudged and stumbled towards Ladysmith. So at 5 a.m. on 24 October 1899, General White led a force out of Ladysmith, 5000 strong. They were composed of the 5th Lancers, 19th Hussars, Imperial Light Horse, Natal Mounted Rifles, three batteries of artillery, and four battalions of infantry (the 1st Liverpools, 1st Devonshires, 1st Gloucestershires and the 2nd King's Royal Rifle Corps). This force was the biggest yet to meet the Boers (Yule's column being about 4000 strong) and it was approximately half of General White's command; the other half remained to hold Lady-smith.

General White threw out in front of his force a wide screen of mounted men. About six miles from Ladysmith and holding to the railway line, they met the Boers. Under General Cronje, 6000 Boers were placed along a rugged and broken line of hills running roughly parallel to the railway. The Boer centre was on the highest of these hills, a place called Intintanyani, 400 feet high.

Midway between Intintanyani and the railway was a low bridge called the Rietfontein Ridge and it was from this forward position that the British mounted force came under fire. Shortly after 7 a.m. these Hussars, Lancers and Imperial Light Horse had driven the Boer outposts from the Rietfontein Ridge and were therefore successfully covering the main British force.

The British infantry and artillery then pushed forward to Rietfontein and just before 8 a.m. two Boer heavy guns on Intintanyani opened fire on them and the British artillery sparkled in reply. Indeed, in this battle, it was the British artillery which shone brightest.

Mr Donald Macdonald of the *Melbourne Argus*, Australia, was present and was impressed by the Pommie gunners:

The British artillery swung their guns into action with the splendid prompti-tude of the highly-trained Indian troops, but before they could do so three or four

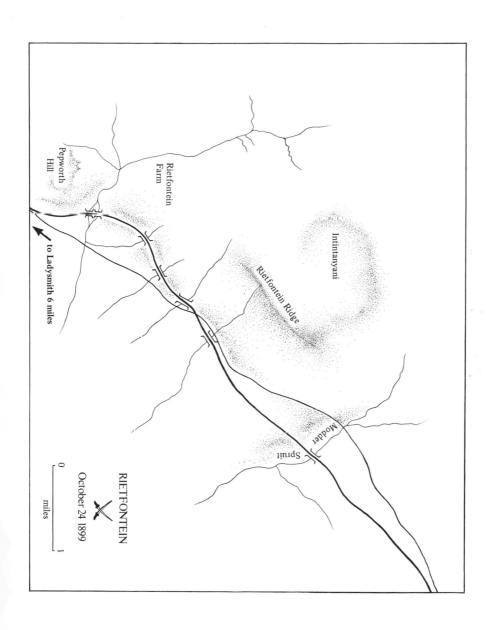

RIETFONTEIN

October 24 1899

to Ladysmith 6 miles

Pepworth Hill

Rietfontein Farm

Rietfontein Ridge

Intintanyani

Modder

Spruit

0 miles 1

of the gun horses were hit, and a couple of gunners wounded. One thick-set Tommy, as he ran past with a couple of brass-capped shells, cried out, 'This is the medicine for 'em, Beecham's pills – a 'ole box-full given away' and he affectionately kissed the shell, which the next instant was bursting over the heads of the crouching Boers on the hill-top. As he ran from the limber with the next charge he suddenly said 'Oh!' and fell – the red, white, and blue shell he carried rolling away down the slope – the one spot of colour in the green landscape. The gunner was dead with a Mauser bullet through his mouth.

George Steevens, the distinguished journalist, described the 10th Mountain Battery of the Royal Garrison Artillery go into action on the Rietfontein Ridge:

The mountain guns came up on their mules – a drove of stupid, uncontrolled creatures, you would have said, lumbered up with the odds and ends of an ironworks and a waggon factory. [Mountain batteries were carried in separate parts by mules and had to be assembled on the field of action.] But the moment they were in position the gunners swarmed upon them and till you have seen the garrison gunners working you do not know what work means. In a minute the scrap-heaps had flown together into little guns, hugging the stones with their low bellies, jumping at the enemy as the men lay on to the ropes. The detachments all cuddled down to their guns; a man knelt by the ammunition twenty paces in rear; the mules by now were snug under cover. 'Two thousand,' sang out the major. The No. 1 of each gun held up something like a cross, as if he were going through a religious rite, altered the elevation delicately, then flung up his hand and head stiffly, like a dog pointing. 'Number 4' – and Number 4 gun hurled out fire and filmy smoke, then leaped back, half frightened at its own fury, half anxious to get a better view of what it had done. It was a little over. 'Nineteen hundred' cried the major. Same ritual, only a little short. 'Nineteen fifty' – and it was just right. Therewith field and mountain guns, yard by yard, up and down, right and left, carefully, methodically, though roughly, sowed the whole [Boer area] with bullets.

The Boer guns were quickly silenced by this British efficiency.

This artillery duel together with the infantry's long-distance fire was really the full extent of this unconventional confrontation. Between the British-held Rietfontein Ridge and the Boer centre on Intintanyani was a totally exposed area of about 1000 yards. It is true that the British cavalry, guarding the right flank, were ordered by General White to try and turn the Boers' left wing and thereby get behind their positions and threaten their laagers, but it was quickly discovered that the Boers were widely extended and strongly held in that direction so that vague hope was dropped.

Some Natal volunteers (the Natal Mounted Rifles) held the British left, then slightly back were half a battalion of the King's Royal Rifles, then forward and centre the 1st Gloucesters, the 1st Devons and the 1st Liverpools. The mounted troops held the British right.

Shortly before midday an event took place certainly contrary to General White's wishes, which to this day remains a tragic mystery.

Without warning Colonel E. P. Wilford, commanding the 1st Gloucestershires, charged over the Rietfontein Ridge with a company of his men and they carried their regimental Maxim gun. A second half-company dashed ahead to cut wire fences obstructing their progress. What they could have achieved – a small group charging across 1000 yards of exposed veldt towards the massed Boer mausers – it is impossible to imagine, except perhaps a mad, proud impulse to demonstrate the vaunted British Lion was not dead. What happened George Steevens saw:

> At a quarter-past eleven the Gloucesters pushed a little too far between the two hills, and learned that the Boers, if their bark was silent for the moment, could still bite. Suddenly there shot into them a cross-fire at a few hundred yards. [I suspect more than that.] Down went the colonel dead; down went fifty men.
>
> For a second a few of the rawer hands in the regiment wavered; it might have been serious. But the rest clung doggedly to their position under cover; the officers brought the flurried men up to the bit again.

It was a quick and horrifying reminder of what the modern rifle could do at long range, in competent hands.

The Australian, Donald Macdonald, saw one British soldier 'strolling out of the din, both hands held helplessly before him, and the front of his brown tunic smeared with blood from the neck down. I asked him where he was hit, and he held out his hands with a Mauser bullet-hole through each palm. "One were damn bad," he said, "but it were dog's luck to ha' both hit!" '

As in most of these battles, a remarkable amount of personal observation took place. Mr H. W. Nevinson, the London *Daily Chronicle* correspondent, saw:

> [One Boer was] near the top of Intintanyani, who evidently had an old Martini [rifle] which he valued much more than new-fangled things. Whenever he fired a little puff of grey smoke followed, and I always thought I heard the growl of the bullet particularly close, as though he steadily aimed at some officer near by. He sat under a bush, and had built himself a little wall of rocks in front. Shell after shell was showered upon that rocky hillside, for it concealed many other sharpshooters besides. But at each flash he must have thrown himself behind the stones, and when the shower of lead was over up he got, and again I saw the little puff of grey smoke and heard the growl of a bullet close by.

Lieutenant Tringham, of the West Surrey Regiment, wrote:

There was a very curious thing at the fight at Rietfontein. Several ladies turned up on bicycles. Of course they kept a long distance off, but one of the enemy's shells pitched fairly close to them, which sent them pedalling off to a safer position, where they took cover behind rocks, as if they were born to it. Very plucky of them, though they were rather in the way.

During the early afternoon the Boer fire died away almost completely along their whole line and General White gave the order for a general retirement. This was carried out with little difficulty and the British force marched back to Ladysmith.

The battle of Rietfontein did the Free Staters some good psychologically. It is doubtful whether they knew where General Yule was at that time. It is very doubtful whether they had plans to attack his column. What they did see was a formidable force of British regular soldiers come out to meet them and apparently be held by their long-range rifle fire. They observed the quixotic charge of Colonel Wilford and his Gloucesters and probably assumed that they had quickly checked a general advance. They then witnessed General White and half his army withdraw into Ladysmith.

Of course by fighting the battle of Rietfontein, the General had guaranteed the safe passage of General Yule's column – a vital 4000 men for the coming showdown at Ladysmith.

General White was still being pestered by the civil authority of Natal to release troops to guard the capital, Pietermaritzburg. He got off a letter to his wife on 25 October 1899:

I try to point out that we have but one chance, and that is to give me sufficient troops with which to strike out boldly. If they have two or three regiments to guard Maritzburg they will not save it if I am beaten, but they might enable me to give the enemy a hard, or even decisive blow. While I can go out and fight the colony remains unconquered. If I am held in or beaten in the field England will have to reconquer Natal from the sea. The consequences of this would be most lamentable even after the reconquest.

Oh yes, Sir George was desperate to save the Dundee column!

His official despatch on the battle of Rietfontein is simple and might be taken at face value.

Reverting to my action at Rietfontein on October 24th, I may mention in general terms that my object was not to drive the enemy out of any positions, but simply to prevent him crossing the Newcastle road from west to east, and so falling on General Yule's flank. This object was attained with entire success, the enemy suffering severely from our shrapnel fire, which was very successful in searching the reverse slopes of the hills on which he was posted. Our own loss amounted to 1 officer and 11 men killed, 6 officers and 97 men wounded, and 2 missing. The details of this action, as well as the various plans and returns, which should accompany a despatch will be forwarded later; but I am anxious that this report should be sent off at once, as it is very doubtful whether any communications by rail with Pietermaritzburg will remain open after today.

For the same reason I have omitted all personal mention of the very many officers and men who have performed services of the utmost gallantry and distinction. In a further despatch I hope to bring those services prominently to your notice.

Incidentally, for all General White's words about Boer casualties from shell fire, it is unlikely that they sustained losses anywhere near as high as the British. The British would expose themselves; the Boers tried not to.

5

THE BOERS CLOSE IN

We shall all be locked up in Ladysmith!
BENNET BURLEIGH

LADYSMITH was now beginning to look like crisis-town. Donald Macdonald wrote:

No conception of war is complete until one has watched its painful sequel – the bringing in of the wounded and the burial of the dead. The central British field hospital was the Town-hall Ladysmith, where the Red Cross, the emblem of all that is beautiful and beneficent in warfare, floated from the tower. All round there was the reek of iodoform, and as the first of the wounded were brought in one heard the groans of a Boer, who had three shots in the thigh, and was having the bullets extracted. There was no other sound as the sisters and white-aproned dressers moved from bed to bed. The wounded were brought in dhoolies or stretchers, hooded over with green canvas, to keep off sun and rain, and suspended from a bamboo pole carried on the shoulders of four black bearers, who, taking short, quick steps, did their work with wonderful gentleness, and scarcely any oscillation of the cot. As the wounded arrived a dapper, thick-set surgeon lifted the hood of each dhoolie, with a cheery, 'Well, my lad, what's the matter with you?'

That historic Town Hall stands today, as it did on that 24 October 1899. I was in it most recently about six years ago and I had paid to get in. There was a party in progress in support of Ian Smith and his white supremacy policies in Rhodesia. No Boer spy could have felt more uneasy than I did that evening!

After the battle of Rietfontein the Boer forces from the Orange Free State, to the north-west, and the Transvaalers from the north and north-east, at last joined hands. At the same time General White combined his entire army; the Dundee column was now part of his command in Ladysmith.

The British had been driven back to this Aldershot of South Africa.

74

Every single soldier must have realized by this time that they were facing a formidable and generally successful enemy. What else could Sir George do to help Ladysmith fight? There were no more troops available. He had been advised that the Boers were bringing with them heavy guns, which, it was said, outranged the British artillery. So, on 25 October he telegraphed a surprising and vital request to Admiral Sir R. Harris, commanding the British Royal Navy in South Africa. Sir George White asked Admiral Harris if he could, somehow, send heavy ships' guns to help him fight from Ladysmith. The question was, even if the audacious idea could be achieved, would the naval guns arrive in time?

The Bishop of Natal sat and considered the British retreat and began to fret about a peculiarly white South African problem: 'I am a good deal afraid of what the effect may be on the natives all over South Africa. They will certainly say: "It is no good your talking of victories. Who is master of the country? Have not the Boers actually got half Natal?" '

Sir George White could not bear to accept a defensive mentality. Though the Orange Free Staters and the Transvaalers were touching hands they were still moving as two separate armies, with little, apparently, in the way of a joint command. Sir George felt that he could still decisively clout the Transvaalers, before the Free Staters fully reacted. On 27 October, the day following the arrival of the Dundee column, he wrote to his wife in England:

The English mail goes today, and I must send you one line to say that the enemy is appearing in great numbers on the east and north-east of Ladysmith. I have been receiving reports all night, and before this reaches you there will be important events. I hope we may come well through it. I will try to hit hard, but the difficulty is to get a fair chance of hitting at anything sufficiently definite to mean an important and lasting success. I think it quite possible the postal and telegraphic communication may be cut before long. If so, I hope you will keep up a good heart, but it will all be finished one way or another before this reaches you. The troops have had terrible hard work. My best love to you and all my children . . .

Yes, it was the Transvaalers 'on the east and north-east of Ladysmith' that Sir George would try to hit first. British cavalry were bringing in reports that these Transvaalers, under General Erasmus and General Lucas Meyer, were occupying Pepworth Hill (to the north-east) and Long Hill (east) which were only three to four miles from Ladysmith.

Incidentally, Major Marling was on this reconnoitring job, and his diary betrays the nonstop tragedy of war:

Started at 3.30 a.m. on a reconnaissance to Lombard's Kop . . . Poor Molly Myers was killed. He was Adjutant of the Eton Volunteers, and a right good fellow. He gave me a wedding present of a hunting flask which I have now, with the inscription on it, 'Spike from Molly'.

Anyway, General White began to hope that if he could smash the Boers' right wing on Long Hill and Pepworth Hill, the remnants would be forced on to their centre and he could then drive them eastward, away from their allies, the Orange Free Staters. In addition to this plan he decided to send a separate force some seven miles north to hold a pass called Nicholson's Nek, just north of a hill called Kainguba. The object of this seemingly hazardous out-on-a-limb venture was to hold the Free Staters, protect the main British force's left flank and hold Nicholson's Nek open so that British cavalry could ride through and harass retreating Boers after the hoped-for British victory at Long Hill and Pepworth Hill. That was the brave but risky idea in Sir George's head.

This was to be his big military fling. He planned to use almost his entire army; simply leaving behind in Ladysmith a bare minimum garrison and presumably keeping his fingers crossed that the unpredictable Free State Boers would not pour into Ladysmith from the west.

He rested his Dundee column troops until 29 October and waited no longer. The Nicholson's Nek force comprised the 1st Royal Irish Fusiliers, the 1st Gloucesters and No. 10 Mountain Battery and was commanded by Lieutenant-Colonel F. R. C. Carleton. They marched out of Ladysmith at 10 p.m. that night.

To cover the right flank of the main British attack on Long and Pepworth Hills was a cavalry brigade consisting of the 5th Lancers, the 19th Hussars and a Natal regiment under Colonel Royston. The brigade was commanded by General French. Their job was to occupy some ridges northeast of Gun Hill, which lies to the south-east of Ladysmith. It was also hoped that this cavalry brigade would threaten the Boers' left. They rode out during the very early morning of 30 October. They were supposed to be in position before dawn.

The main central attack comprised two brigades. One, the 8th Brigade under Colonel G. G. Grimwood, consisted of five infantry battalions: the 1st and 2nd King's Royal Rifles, the 1st Leicestershires, the 1st King's Liverpools and the 2nd Royal Dublin Fusiliers. Attached to them were three batteries of the Royal Field Artillery and the Natal Field Battery. The infantry battalions of this 8th Brigade were not at full strength; nine companies were left in Ladysmith to hold the place.

The other body of troops was called the 7th Brigade and was made up of the 2nd Gordon Highlanders, the 1st Devonshires, the 1st Manchesters and eventually the 2nd Rifle Brigade. Attached were three batteries of Royal Field Artillery and cavalry consisting of the 5th Dragoon Guards, the 18th Hussars and the *crème de la crème* of volunteers, the Imperial Light Horse, – oh, and there were two companies of mounted infantry. This 7th Brigade was commanded by Colonel Ian Hamilton.

The plan was this: Grimwood's 8th Brigade was to take Long Hill, though the artillery of both brigades was to blast the way. That accomplished, Ian Hamilton's 7th Brigade would move forward to take Pepworth Hill, again with combined artillery support. That objective successfully won, Hamilton's cavalry was to sweep north-westward to and through Nicholson's Nek and attack the rear of sundry Boer positions. That was the plan and even now in the safety and warmth of this room, I get nervous at the thought of it.

In the earliest hours of 30 October 1899, Colonel Grimwood moved his 8th Brigade out of Ladysmith and a full hour before dawn he was where he should have been, south-east of Long Hill. Grimwood's personal location was almost the only thing that went according to plan on that black British day. Though he was where he should have been, as dawn came up like dread over the veldt, he discovered that two of his battalions, the Liverpools and the Dublin Fusiliers, had got mislaid. In the darkness they had followed the artillery off to the left. And then when Grimwood looked round for General French's cavalry which was supposed to cover his exposed right, no cavalry was to be seen! French and his horsemen were in the hills of Umbulwana and Lombard's Kop, considerably to the south-west of the proposed battle area.

Ian Hamilton and his 7th Brigade moved out of Ladysmith at about 4 a.m. on that morning of 30 October and quickly reached their initial position, Limit Hill, just west of the town. No sooner had they settled there, even before dawn, than a muleteer of No. 10 Mountain Battery, which should at that moment have been holding Nicholson's Nek seven miles to the north, arrived with the horrifying news that the mules (those same mules of No. 10 Mountain Battery that journalist Steevens had described at the battle of Rietfontein as 'stupid, uncontrolled creatures, you would have said') had stampeded in the darkness, in the middle of Boer territory. And then an officer attached to the Gloucesters, who should also have been up there at Nicholson's Nek, appeared and confirmed that the guns and ammunition of Carleton's column had almost certainly disappeared in the stampede.

Well, Steevens' first impression about those mules was now confirmed with a vengeance. But down here with the 7th and 8th Brigades a job had to be attempted.

As light came the British artillery began their duty by shelling Long Hill. But soon it was realized that those clever Boers had removed their guns and themselves from that place. The British were shelling a deserted mountain. And then to add to British embarrassment the Boers opened fire from Pepworth Hill beyond with an enormous 6-inch Creuzot gun, popularly known to the British as a 'Long Tom', and firing a 94-pound shell. This monster was supported by six smaller guns on Pepworth and they all outranged the British artillery. The British gunners with customary do-or-die courage moved their Royal Artillery pieces closer and splendidly but only temporarily silenced the guns of Pepworth Hill. But then Boer guns opened fire from various places on the field of action and the British artillery had to disperse to deal with them as best they could. Pepworth burst into painful life for the British once more.

The Boers pressed hard on Colonel Grimwood's 8th Brigade and outflanked it on the right. The brigade was forced to swing away from the vital objective of Pepworth Hill and face eastward. By this time General French's cavalry had managed to stretch itself northward and touch Grimwood's turned right flank.

On the Boer side a very significant occurrence had taken place. General Lucas Meyer, one of those old Boer patriarch leaders, had finally found this new, cruel warfare too much for him and he was actually assisted from his horse in a state of nervous collapse – and quite early that morning. The man who promptly inherited his responsibilities was the New Boer personified: young Field-Cornet Louis Botha. On that morning and early afternoon of 30 October 1899 Botha began to make a name for himself that was to be cheered around the world – except for those parts under the Union Jack!

Under Botha's command the Boers extended their line even further south and with disturbing mobility threatened even to outflank General French's right wing, down south by Lombard's Kop. And then the Boers pressed south from Pepworth and poor old Grimwood thought his left flank was turning. What was turning were the tables – with a vengeance. Grimwood's 8th Brigade was in a mess. Indeed the whole British enterprise was disintegrating. And Ian Hamilton's 7th Brigade had virtually disappeared, swallowed up by the demands of the 8th Brigade for reinforcements The conservative *Times History of the War in South Africa* was unexpectedly cutting about Colonel Grimwood:

The men fought well, but their efforts were directed to no definite end. Colonel Grimwood, to whom the fetish of seniority had assigned so all-important a command, proved quite unfit to grapple with the extremely difficult situation in which, largely by the mistakes of others, he was placed; completely un-nerved, incapable of issuing orders, too confused to remember the position of his men or to try and recover his missing battalions, he simply left his brigade to itself. With such a commander, what little chance remained of retrieving the situation on the right was thrown away.

Help for the British was now more than welcome from any quarter. Very early that morning a train squeezed into Ladysmith from the south. Aboard was the 2nd battalion of the Rifle Brigade; they had been hustled off the troopship *Jelunga* at Durban and bundled into this very conveyance. I will quote Mr H. Dawnay from his account in *The Rifle Brigade Chronicle for 1900*:

. . . we made our first acquaintance with Ladysmith at 3 a.m. on Monday, October 30th – a day the results of which were to give us such uncongenial employment for so long a period. We were greeted on detraining by Colonel Ward, ASC, who announced that the rest of Sir George White's army had already marched out, that we were to follow as soon as possible, and that a battle was imminent; so discarding all impedimenta except haversacks and water-bottles, we marched up to the Gloucesters' camp, where, thanks to the kindness of that regiment, we found a meal prepared for the whole battalion. As soon as everybody had partaken, and the battalion had assembled, off we started under the guidance of Captain Dixon, Sir George White's ADC, to join the rest of our brigade, under General Ian Hamilton, which was some four miles to the north-east of Ladysmith. The only hitch which occurred, and which we had good cause to remember later in the day, was our inability to refill our water-bottles, as nowhere could we discover a water supply.

As soon as we got clear of the hills round the town, we were greeted by shells from a Boer 'Long Tom' on Pepworth Hill, which made us deploy at the double, and, keeping extended, we made our way on, and eventually reached the rest of our brigade (the Devons, Manchesters and Gordon Highlanders) under Limit Hill about 6.30 a.m.

It reads like some awful school treat. Meanwhile the town of Ladysmith was not having a happy time. Since daybreak, the Boer gun 'Long Tom' was pitching 94-pound shells into the northern part, particularly around the railway station. Their unparalleled explosions together with the arrival of battered remnants of No. 10 Mountain Battery – mules dragging bits of guns and groups of shattered gunners – had thoroughly unnerved the inhabitants.

The man left in command of Ladysmith while the battle was fought was Colonel W. G. Knox RHA, and he anticipated an attack on the town itself. So few soldiers were available that he impressed every man to active duty that he could lay his hands on. He occupied the hill of King's Post, just outside the town, and dragged the two Boer field-pieces captured at Elandslaagte to make some semblance of defence for the northern perimeter of Ladysmith.

By mid-morning, Boers were seen from the town itself, up in the direction of Surprise Hill and shortly before 11 a.m. they were again seen around the Harrismith railway. That was enough for Colonel Knox. He promptly sent a message to Sir George White, out on the battlefield, that he feared the town was about to be attacked.

How critical could things get? A town full of panic-stricken civilians, with the army absent a few miles to the east and north and all engaged in a disastrous action. And now Boers were in the vicinity of a barely defended base. England in Africa was hanging by a not very sound thread.

But in all fairness to the civilians of Ladysmith, a soldier of the Borderers spoke about some curious and sadly cool ladies of:

Some of the more courageous had ventured on the hill beside us to see the battle, and were standing conspicuously dressed in white. On their being asked by a soldier to sit down and keep out of sight, as they made a splendid target for the enemy's guns, one lady calmly replied that she was not going to soil her dress by sitting on the dirty ground.

There were of course better women in Ladysmith, as the same soldier remembered:

At different parts of the town women were standing with cans of tea and coffee, which they served to the tired out men as they passed along.

At about 11.30 a.m. General White decided that withdrawal of all his troops was inevitable and indeed now a dreadful necessity, and he gave the command. The retreat was not orderly, though some have tried to argue that it was. For a description of what took place I would rather quote again *The Times History of the War in South Africa* than anti-British sources in America or Europe:

The moment the men stood up to retreat it became evident that the lull which had taken place in the action was purely temporary. A perfect hail of bullets greeted the first signs of retirement, and a minute later the Boer field and automatic guns were playing fiercely upon the retreating companies. As long as Grimwood's battalions had remained under cover their losses had been trivial. But directly behind them an almost unbroken stretch of level plain extended to Ladysmith.

Across the whole of this they were followed by a searching fire . . . In spite of the devoted efforts of Sir A. Hunter and some of the staff, the retirement soon lost all semblance of order. The two Rifle battalions were especially bad. It is possible that the retirement was begun too hastily, and that it would have been better to have waited a little in order to bring some of Hamilton's brigade closer up in support. As it was, the bulk of Grimwood's brigade just dribbled in a straggling crowd through the extended files of the Manchesters and Liverpools, who held their ground firmly. For a moment the situation looked serious.

The general atmosphere of the British soldiers on that 30 October was as if they had been infected by the political, imperialist, businessman's disease that had created the war. Often British wars have been diseased at their roots, but usually the British soldier has risen above Westminster and the City of London. But not on that day – though of course there were many noble exceptions.

The most notable exception was, as often before and since, the behaviour of the gunners. The 13th Battery, Royal Field Artillery, under Major Dawkins, stood unsupported in the middle of the plain and blazed away at the advancing Boers and thereby gave cover to the disorderly retreat of a large part of the infantry. Men and horses of the 13th Battery fell and it is said that their fire never slackened. For fifteen minutes they were entirely alone and then the 53rd Battery under Major Abdy came galloping up and in that murderous predicament unlimbered and gave support on the 13th's right.

General Hunter, walking about apparently unconcerned amongst the guns of the 13th, gave the order for the artillery to retire and they went, dying in good military order. All of the Royal Artillery engaged that day behaved with astonishing martial style; it is therefore a shade invidious to single out any particular battery.

The cavalry's retreat was not much to write home about. Once again I take the timid approach and quote directly from *The Times History*:

When the infantry were clear the cavalry began their retirement. For reasons which it is difficult to understand, the cavalry were allowed to save themselves by their speed alone. No attempt was made at a judicious withdrawal by regiments. Troop officers were not even given the time to form their troops. A seething mass of clubbed and broken cavalry charged down the narrow nek on the west of Lombard's Kop . . .

But it is a confident person who criticizes the conduct of men under fire. George Lynch, war-correspondent, reported the terrifying battle conditions and then, reader, judge for yourself how you might have left that field of battle:

The 5th Lancers were riding out on our right, when a single horse came galloping past them, clattering furiously over the stony veldt. No wonder the men stared; it was a sight to be remembered. The rider was firmly fixed in the deep cavalry saddle; the reins tossed loose with the horse's mane, and both hands were clenched against either side of his breast; and the head was cut off clean at the shoulders. Perhaps in the spasm of that death tear the rider had gripped his horse's sides with his long spurred heels; perhaps the horse also was wounded; anyhow, with head down, and wild and terrified eyes, his shoulders foam-bespewed, he tore past as if in horror of the ghastly burden he carried.

Commandant-General Joubert, then aged sixty-eight years, was present at this British rout. He was a gentle giant who hated war and its hidden outcome. He personally restrained his young burghers from riding after the fleeing enemy.

But at this disastrous culmination of the battle a fantastic piece of dramatic timing took place, which no improbable fiction could surpass. The British sailors from HMS *Powerful* arrived in Ladysmith, 280 of them, and, Hallelujah! – they were hauling four naval 12-pounder guns and two naval 4·7-inch guns! What a sight! The sailors were dressed for action in full sea-going rig. Then, under Captain the Honourable Hedworth Lambton RN, they quickly hitched their guns behind bullock teams and hustled out to Limit Hill and promptly squared up to giant 'Long Tom' and anything else Boer that was going. 'Long Tom' was quickly and viciously off the mark and, with its second 94-pounder aimed at the Royal Navy, struck the leading gun right under its wheels and overturned it, wounding every member of the gun's crew. The other naval guns took up a position on open ground, just north of Ladysmith, and at 12.30 p.m. replied to Pepworth Hill at a range of 6500 yards. After a few rounds, 'Long Tom' was silenced for the day and so were the rest of the Boer battery.

As the sailors and guns of HMS *Powerful* returned to Ladysmith, the sight did much to steady the cracking morale of the population. And what General Sir George White felt can only be imagined. The sailors quickly named their two 4·7-inch guns 'Bloody Mary' and 'Lady Anne' – the latter as a compliment to Captain Lambton's sister – though the soldiers, for some reason unknown to me, insisted on calling it 'Weary Willie'.

The Royal Navy gun race, which is such a popular event in the Royal Military Tournament, has its origins in the speed with which the Navy went into action at Ladysmith.

General White had a fair idea that the Nicholson's Nek column under Colonel Carleton was in some sort of trouble. Anyway the whole enter-

S WERE THE SAILORS WHO BROUGHT UP A GUN

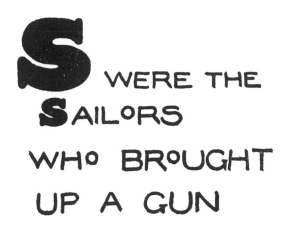

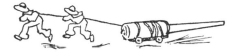

From An Active Army Alphabet

prise was ruined, so he signalled a heliograph order to the northern force: 'Retire on Ladysmith as opportunity offers.' Poor Carleton saw the message flash and he called for signallers to read it. One man began to read it and was shot; then another man and he was shot, and finally a third man went down with three bullets in him. Oh yes, he was in trouble!

Lieutenant-Colonel Carleton, with Major Adye of the Intelligence Department as guide, had led the 1st Royal Irish Fusiliers, the 1st Gloucesters and No. 10 Mountain Battery towards Nicholson's Nek. While it was still dark they reached Kainguba Heights, with their destination still two miles further north. At this point, the Colonel and Major Adye consulted about a potential hazard. They were worried about being discovered in the defile of Nicholson's Nek as dawn came up. These two officers therefore decided to occupy Kainguba and move on to Nicholson's Nek later. It was a disastrous decision.

The Irish Fusiliers diverted sharply to the left and began what became a difficult, steep climb over boulders. They were almost at the top when panic began, caused by none knows what. A number of the Irish Fusiliers came tumbling down and shouts were heard: 'Boer cavalry are on us!' The mules immediately behind also became frightened and broke loose, tearing down the mountain. The Gloucesters, just beginning the descent, heard the terrifying commotion in the night above them and fixed bayonets; a few shots were fired.

Well, until that havoc, it is unlikely that the Boers knew the British were there; now they did! However the officers managed to settle the men and the climb was continued to the top. But there they discovered the full implications of their predicament. Over 200 mules had disappeared into the night, carrying with them essential parts of the guns of No. 10 Mountain Battery and almost all of the reserve ammunition, only seventeen boxes being saved which allowed about twenty rounds per man. The water-kegs were gone and so were the heliographs for signalling. It was now just after 3 a.m.

Young Deneys Reitz, though an Orange Free Stater, was fighting with the Pretoria Commando and they were holding the Boers' right wing, just to the east of Nicholson's Nek. He wrote:

Shortly before daybreak, when it was growing light, two large mules came trotting up from below, their head-ropes trailing on the ground, and on bringing the animals to a halt we found that one of them carried on his back the barrel of a mountain gun and the other a leathern box containing shell ammunition.

A sinister discovery – for the British . . .

The Pretoria Commando's attention was directed towards Kainguba Heights and Deneys Reitz continued:

Meanwhile it was sunrise, and we could now make out this force on the level top of Nicholson's Nek [it was, in fact, south of the Nek] across the valley. The soldiers were working like ants, building sangars of stone, and we could see a knot of officers, standing around what looked like an outspread map, while men were pulling a tarpaulin over a tree for shade . . .

The range was too great for accurate shooting, but our volley had the effect of dispersing the officers, who hurriedly climbed up to join their troops on the hill-top above, where we could now no longer see any sign of life, as the men who had been working there had taken cover, and the plateau seemed deserted. Our shots had the further effect of arousing the commandos and, before long, horsemen came hurrying from the different camps to occupy the forward crest, and within twenty minutes there were hundreds of riflemen in position . . .

The London *Daily Mail* reported the memories of that day of Captain Rice, Adjutant of the 1st Royal Irish Fusiliers:

When it began to dawn we saw that our hill was completely surrounded by other hills, which towered above ours, and although we could not see a single Boer the enemy kept pounding us from every side.

As time went on the rifle fire became terrific, and our men began to drop on every side. The worst of it was that, of course, we had lost every gun, and had no ammunition but what was in our pouches.

We tried putting the best marksmen on to volley firing, but that did not seem to even shift the Boers. Then I was hit in the ankle, and compelled to lie down. My sergeant piled big stones round me to give some sort of shelter, but the bullets were plunging all round.

Mr E.W. Smith reported in the *Morning Leader* what the Boers thought of this British ploy:

The enemy . . . made the fatal blunder of indulging in volley firing. All [the Boers] had to do when they saw the preparations being made for a volley was to keep well behind the stones, then the moment the discharge was effected jump up and take careful aim at picked men.

This was certainly not the field of Waterloo! Captain Rice continued:

Our men took what cover there was, but there was not much of that. It was a terribly wearing and anxious business, and we were exposed to that fire and practically unable to reply from daybreak till 2.30 in the afternoon.

By that time the Boers had pushed up close, and we were occupying the other half of our hill.

Deneys Reitz gave his account:

Crawling forward, however, we came on small parties of Free State burghers lying behind rocks and other shelter in a rough line across the hill, and when we joined one of these groups they pointed out to us where the English troops lay posted, behind similar cover, 30 or 40 yards away.

Both sides were maintaining a vigorous short-range rifle contest, in which the soldiers were being badly worsted, for they were up against real old-fashioned Free State Boers for whom they were no match in sharpshooting of this kind. Time after time I saw soldiers looking over their defences to fire, and time after time I heard the thud of a bullet finding its mark, and could see the unfortunate man fall back out of sight, killed or wounded. We joined in the fight, and for the next hour we slowly but surely pressed the English to the far edge of the hill.

As we gained ground we began to come on their dead and wounded and realized what heavy losses we were inflicting, for behind almost every rock lay a dead or wounded man, and we knew that we should have possession of the hill before long.

Towards noon, as we were increasingly hustling our opponents, we heard a bugle ring clear above the rifle-fire, and at the same time a white flag went up.

Captain Rice reported from his side:

Then it was that we heard bugles sounding the 'Cease fire'. Our troops were so surrounded that some of the men thought they were our bugles. But we knew the difference in the note, and shouted to our men to go on firing.

The Boer bugles went on sounding the 'Cease fire' for a long time, and our men got so restive, as they had no intention of ceasing firing, that they gave the order to fix bayonets for a charge. The bayonets were fixed like a shot, but, of course, there wasn't anything to charge at. Anyhow, it kept the men quiet for a bit.

The poor fellows behaved splendidly, though they had had no food since Sunday night, and had been exposed to deadly firing from an unseen enemy for ten hours.

Things went on like that for a bit, and then the word came down to us that the white flag had been hoisted by some of the Gloucesters. When the news came along our men simply yelled with rage. That white flag, I may say, is a complete mystery to me. No one knows who hoisted it. But Father Mathews, our chaplain, who went on to Pretoria with the prisoners, says that it was raised by a subordinate of the Gloucesters, who found himself cut off with ten men, and quite believed that he and his companions were the only survivors. Whether that is the correct story or not I cannot say, and I don't know what the Father meant by 'a subordinate'. Probably he meant a sergeant. Now, as the white flag had been raised, and we believed by order, it was our duty to make the men put down their arms. We gave the order, but were not obeyed, and for some time the men flatly refused. In many cases we had to take their rifles from them. They were furiously angry, and though most of them had not a cartridge left, they had all made up their minds to fight to a finish.

The boys were the worst, and some of the subalterns refused to give up their swords. In fact, it was all most horribly painful.

Then the other officers and myself had to [and here Captain Rice hesitated for a moment as if disliking to utter the words] well, we had to break up our swords. That is not a nice thing at all. Finally, a lot of the men and the subalterns flung themselves on the ground and wept with rage. Even when they had no weapons they wanted to go on fighting. After that the Boers came along and we were made prisoners.

And what I want you to understand [concluded Captain Rice very earnestly] is that we did not surrender. We were surrendered against our will.

This account by Captain Rice, I find, is extraordinarily interesting – and tragic. In those words can be heard the total military conditioning of the British Empire. I doubt very much that the Boers ever sounded a deceptive 'Cease Fire' on a bugle. It was not in their character and anyway it was clear to them that the British were trapped and beaten. But Captain Rice could not accept that a British soldier had sounded it. And the white flag. Well, that was visible fact – but it must not be one of his regiment so it was a Gloucester. And he quickly interprets 'a subordinate' as 'Probably he meant a sergeant'. Well, maybe, but a commissioned officer could not suspect one of his own class. And finally ' . . . we did not surrender. We were surrendered against our will.'

That was the power of imperial jingoism. That was the power that often led British soldiers quietly forward to annihilation in a disgraceful cause. And he was conditioned not even to ask the fundamental moral questions. Moving, terrible and tragic.

What in actual fact had happened was that a small group of Gloucesters, including Captains Duncan and Fyffe and a Lieutenant Beasley, together with eight or nine men, were giving covering fire to the Gloucesters as they withdrew to the southern end of Kainguba Heights. This small group was in a ruined African kraal and finally was isolated completely. They began to assume that the entire British force had withdrawn from the field of action and were perhaps even now racing across the long plain to Ladysmith. Fyffe and Duncan were wounded; only Lieutenant Beasley and one or two men remained unscathed. They decided that they were truly beaten and could do no more. They raised a white handkerchief on a sword, which was not seen by the Boers, so they changed it for a white towel or sheet.

Colonel Carleton was faced with some panic-stricken Gloucesters who threw away their rifles as they ran and then he saw that white flag. Boers stood up and cheered. The Colonel decided to surrender and ordered a bugler to sound 'Cease Fire'. The bugler was so frightened that he couldn't blow properly, but after several attempts got out some semblance of the notes.

This unhappy effort was probably what Captain Rice heard and, like any good British soldier, assumed that its inefficiency must come from an untutored enemy.

Deneys Reitz saw the end:

Dead and wounded soldiers lay all around, and the cries and groans of agony, and the dreadful sights, haunted me for many a day, for though I had seen death by violence of late, there had been nothing to approach the horrors accumulated here.

Hundreds of khaki-clad figures rose from among the rocks and walked towards us, their rifles at the trail. We stood up to wait for them. The haul was a good one for there were 1100 prisoners, mostly Dublin Fusiliers. The commando responsible for this came from the district of Heilbron in the Northern Free State. They were led by Commandant Mentz, but the man who had chiefly urged on the fight was Field-Cornet Christian de Wet, afterwards the redoubtable guerilla leader. I saw him here for the first time as he made his way from point to point during the action, and I well remember his fierce eyes and keen determined face.

Shortly after the surrender I was talking to some of the captured officers when

I heard one of them exclaim, 'My God; look there!' and turning round we saw the entire British force that had come out against us on the plain that morning in full retreat to Ladysmith. Great clouds of dust billowed over the veldt as the troops withdrew, and the manner of their going had every appearance of a rout. There were 10 000 soldiers, but General Joubert had far more than that number of horsemen ready to his hand, and we fully looked to see him unleash them on the enemy, but to our surprise there was no pursuit. I heard Christian de Wet mutter, '*Los jou ruiters; los jou ruiters*' (Loose your horsemen – loose your horsemen) but the Commandant-General allowed this wonderful opportunity to go by, a failure that cost us dear in the days to come.

Melton Prior, the war-correspondent and artist, had been watching from a reasonable distance and he joined in the retreat:

On my way back to town I met Bennet Burleigh [war-correspondent of the London *Daily Telegraph*] in a most excited state rushing off to the telegraph officer. 'Prior, my boy,' he said, 'it is all over – we are beaten, and it means investment. We shall all be locked up in Ladysmith!'

Louis Botha and Christian de Wet were on the war scene. Consider what these two men achieved against overwhelming British odds during the coming two and a half years . . . If they had been in sole command at this battle of Ladysmith and immediately afterwards – well, the British must have been swept to the sea.

Old Commandant-General Joubert watched the British flee back to Ladysmith and when Boer officers pleaded with him to pursue, he turned on them and admonished: 'When God holds out a finger, don't take the whole hand!' The Boer Field-Cornet Isaac Malherbe remarked that: 'It might be sound theology, but it was no good in making war!'

In Ladysmith, there were only dark rumours and shreds of evidence – and then into the town came a Boer envoy, with a flag of truce, with the news that the entire force at Nicholson's Nek was taken prisoner and was, at that moment, on its way to a prisoner-of-war camp in Pretoria. But the dead and wounded Britishers were still on the scene of battle and could be collected without hindrance.

Mr Smith of the *Morning Leader* hurried on to Kainguba Heights with the Rev. E. G. F. Macpherson as soon as the battle was over. They met two Boers who were guarding the wounded and who volunteered to guide the two Britishers to the summit. The four men clambered up the precipitous side of the hill and near the brow observed a large white flag hanging in the still air; the Britishers guessed that it had been improvised from an officer's bed sheet. The elder Boer said:

'My friend says God is on our side, that we are fighting against injustice and must win.'

The younger Boer agreed:

'Yes, I believe God is with us.'

The older man, in the midst of the slaughtered British, said:

'I say for myself, that one Boer is as good as ten Englishmen in guerilla warfare in a country like this.'

Mr Smith observed over thirty British bodies in one small area. He looked at one dead Irish Fusilier who had several pages of *A Preparation for Confession* by his side. He wrote: 'It is pleasing to be able to state – and wounded men I met confirmed the official acknowledgement which has been made – that the Dutch doctors, and the enemy generally, treated our wounded and prisoners with every possible consideration.' An officer of the Gloucester Regiment confirmed: 'The Boers were very good about water, giving us all they had, and fetching more from the bottom of the hill, one and a half miles away.'

The Royal Army Medical Corps, of course, were up on top. A private of that merciful body of soldiers wrote:

I found one man propped up against a rock. When he saw me he called out in a weak voice, and I went up to him at once. I saw that both his arms were broken, and that he could not raise either of them. About two yards away there was a cigarette-case, which someone had dropped in the battle.

'I'm all right, old boy,' said the wounded man; 'there's lots worse than me all round. Get them on the stretchers first. I can last out a bit. I'll tell you what you can do. See that case of "fags"? Well, just take one out and stick it in my mouth. I've been watching it for ever so long, but I couldn't pick it up. I'd give anything for a smoke.'

I gave him a cigarette. It would have done your heart good to see how he puffed away at it. The poor fellow seemed quite contented and happy when he got it. I saw this inscription inside the cigarette-case: 'From Alice to Fred, in memory of happier days'.

The British official return of casualties was:

The total of missing of the Gloucesters and Irish Fusiliers was 843. Thirty-two of the Gloucesters, ten of the Fusiliers, and two men of the Mountain Battery were found dead on the field, while 150 wounded were brought into camp at Ladysmith. Between 70 and 100 of the men escaped and got back to camp.

The young Deneys Reitz wrote that 'Of our party under Isaac Malherbe not one had been hit, but the Free State men had eight or nine dead, and fifteen or twenty wounded.' The feelings of many a patriotic Englishman were expressed by the war-correspondent, G. W. Steevens, when he wrote: 'At the end, when the tardy truth could be withheld no more – what shame! What bitter shame for all the camp! All ashamed for England! Not of her – never that! – but for her. Once more she was a laughter to her enemies.'

General White took the news as best he could. Melton Prior spoke to him:

'Good morning, General; we seem to have had rather a bad time of it.'

'Yes,' replied the man on the very edge of destruction. 'I tried to out-flank the Boers, but as fast as I did so they outflanked me; in fact, they out-witted me.'

Melton Prior went away, asking himself: 'Who could help admiring a man who would speak so openly as that before his staff, before everyone?'

Sir George White composed his report for the War Office in faraway Westminster, London:

No. 128A of 30th October. I have to report a disaster to a column sent by me to take a position in the hills to guard the left flank of the troops in their operations today. The Royal Irish Fusiliers, the Gloucestershire Regiment and No.10 Mountain Battery, were surrounded in the hills, and after heavy losses had to capitulate. Losses not yet ascertained in detail. A man of the Royal Irish Fusiliers, employed as hospital orderly, came in under flag of truce with letter from the medical officer of the column, and asked for assistance to bury dead. I fear there is no doubt of the truth of report. I framed the plan in carrying out which this disaster occurred and am alone responsible for that plan. No blame whatever attaches to the troops, as the position was untenable.

They were honest words, and true. The hazardous military arrangements of the day were entirely his. In England, the news of the removal of two battalions of infantry to Pretoria hit home as nothing before. England could not hide or play down the loss of well over a thousand man at the hands of those farmers. But England liked Sir George's fair-play report. It smelt of the 'decency' of cricket. The decency which one might expect from a gentleman as against a player.

And then Sir George wrote to his wife before he sought sleep on that 30 October 1899:

It is doubly sad that the blow of my life has fallen upon me on this day. [It was their wedding anniversary.] I had promised myself the pleasure of wiring to you 'Viretum', the word you wrote on a sheet of paper for me on the way down to Southampton. You kept a copy of it, but it means, 'My very dear love to you on this day, and may I see you very soon.'

The newspaper boys are now calling in London the terrible disaster that I have only heard of two hours ago. I must tell you the history of it.

I had collected all the troops in the colony of Natal here, and I felt it my duty to the colony to try and hit the Boers so hard that they would not pass Ladysmith and invade the colony south of it. I may tell you in confidence that most of my staff were opposed to going out to fight. They said, 'Let us wait, until the enemy is nearer, and then let us strike.' I felt that this was to allow ourselves to be shut in and unable to strike out where we wished, so I insisted on fighting. I laid out a plan to attack a position which was held last night by the enemy with guns . . . As the attack on this position exposed my left flank to attack from the hills, I consulted a capital officer, Major Adye, who knew every inch of the ground, and he assured me he could, if a party marched at night, take a position which he and they could hold for two days at all events. I detailed the Gloucester Regt., the Royal Irish Fusiliers, and a mountain battery. They started at 11 o'clock last night, and when I got up at half-past three o'clock this morning I was told that there had been some firing during the night march, and that the mules with guns had stampeded. This was an unlucky beginning, but as the Boers hate night fighting, and Major Adye, who was the guide in the affair, said he could do the advance at night, but not by day, I had adopted that course as the one by which the position could be gained with least loss.

I went out at 4 o'clock in the morning and was fighting all day. The men were tired and done. I think it is certain that my plans were betrayed to the enemy, as the position I had intended to burst upon at daylight had been evacuated in the night. They must have heard our plans. We were then attacked by the Boers and forced into a fight that had not been planned. I think we hit the Boers harder than they hit us, but they can outflank us and move much more rapidly, as they all ride ponies. I fought on till I saw our men were failing and could not get on, and then I withdrew them quietly. When I got home I visited the hospital and some corps that had had heavy losses, and then came to my quarters to hear that the two regts. I had sent on the separate duty had been surrounded and had to capitulate. It had been a knock-down blow to me, but I felt I had to make an effort, and thought this plan afforded a fair chance of military success.

It was my plan, and I am responsible, and I have said so to the Secretary of State, and I must bear the consequences. I could have shut myself up or even dealt half-hearted blows with perfect safety; but I played a bold game, too bold a game, and I have lost. I believe every move I made was reported to the Boers. They are brave and very intelligent, and very hard to give a decided beating to.

I think after this venture the men will lose confidence in me, and that I ought to be superseded. It is hard luck, but I have no right to complain. I have had a very difficult time of it. I don't think I can go on soldiering. My mind is too full of this to write about anything else. It is far into the night, but I don't expect to sleep, though I have been up since 3 a.m. The story of the fate of the 2 regiments is too horrible to me to tell you of. The papers will tell it with every detail.

Later he was able to write to his wife:

I was heartbroken over the loss of the Gloucester Regiment, the Royal Irish Fusiliers, and the Mountain Battery . . .

It is easy to imagine General White's desperate depression. A nightmare disaster like this, towards the end of a long and famous career. But Britain stood by him fulsomely. On the following day he received a telegram from Lord Lansdowne:

Queen telegraphs to me as follows: 'Am much distressed to hear of this sad news. Trust it will not dishearten troops at Ladysmith; feel every confidence in Sir George White, although he naturally takes all blame on himself; am anxiously awaiting further particulars.'

And then three days later a second message arrived:

Queen telegraphs to me as follows: Begins, 'The despatch from Sir G. White just sent this morning has been a great relief, and quite clears Sir G. White of blame. – V.R.I.' Ends.

The old royal lady reached out to give the General comfort and support. And, of course, there is no shadow of doubt that his wife, Lady White, helped to keep him afloat with her love and trust. With all the question marks which hang over the relationships between men and women of that Victorian era, it is nostalgic to note that men at the helm of huge human events were strengthened through a female quality.

On top of Kainguba the British dead were buried and present was the Reverend Owen Spencer Watkins, the army's Wesleyan chaplain:

Forty-five men were found lying amongst the rocks, and having obtained from their clothing and description-cards their names, two long trenches were dug, and side by side those who had fought and died together were committed to their earthly rest – Mr Macpherson reading the service over one grave and myself over the other, whilst a crowd of armed burghers gathered round with heads uncovered and reverently bowed.

Well, there was now no question of the Ladysmith army challenging the Boers in face-to-face combat on an open field of war. It was back into the perimeter and defend until the army corps arrived and pray God they would come to the rescue in time!

The potential rescuer, Sir Redvers Buller, was ashore at Cape Town (not yet with his army corps, of course) and on 31 October he telegraphed Sir George:

> I doubt if Boers will ever attack you if entrenched. Hitherto you have gone out to attack them; can you not entrench and wait for events, if not at Ladysmith, then behind Tugela at Colenso? No reinforcements can reach you for at least 14 days. Why not try and play the game now played by the Boers? The only thing I can do is to send some of the fleet to Durban to protect our base. Let me know if you wish that done.

That telegram was not very comforting – except that it suggested what had now become inevitable, though damned un-British: entrenchment. But what was that bit about 'behind Tugela at Colenso'? Sir George had weeks ago pondered that one, but by this time had put the idea aside. He reasoned thus: it was some sixteen miles through difficult hills and south of the Tugela to Colenso. The general east–west line of the river from the foothills of the Drakensbergs in the west to the Buffalo river in the east was some eighty miles and when the weather got dry, men could cross it almost anywhere along the length. He argued that his force was not large enough to hold such an entrenched position, against an enemy that could be three times larger than his force and highly mobile. He feared a turning movement which would either destroy his army, or force on it the necessity to retreat – where? The coast at Durban 190 miles away?

General White also believed that Ladysmith was a symbol of Cape Colony and Natal Colony to the Boers as well as to the British. He had been informed that the fall of Ladysmith was to be the signal for a rebellion by Boers in these British colonies on behalf of the two Boer republics.

Again, he argued that Ladysmith was the rail junction for the lines from the Transvaal. Strategically, the withholding of that centre helped to separate the two Boer armies. And then there were the supplies and the civil population that would have to be abandoned.

On the basis of that thinking, Sir George replied to Sir Redvers as follows:

> 31.10.99. The Boers have established themselves in very strong positions in the hills west, north and east of Ladysmith. Each man has one or two ponies. They resent intrusion so much that it is impossible to ascertain their numbers. They live on the country, and their mobility gives them great advantages. They say themselves they will attack. Ladysmith is strongly entrenched but the lines are not continuous, and the perimeter so large that Boers could exercise their usual tactics. Our men want rest from fighting; but I have the greatest confidence in holding Ladysmith for as long as necessary. I could not now withdraw from it. I think it would be

politic to send some of the fleet to Durban to keep up public confidence there . . .
Hitherto I have considered the interests of the colony south of this required me to
hit out. Yesterday's fighting showed me there were risks and limits to this. I wired
Governor yesterday that I would send Dublin Fusiliers to guard bridge at Colenso
as best step I could take for protection of colony. I intend to contain as many
Boers as possible round Ladysmith, and I believe they will not go south without
making an attempt on Ladysmith.

Buller promptly replied:

31st October. I agree that you do best to remain at Ladysmith, though Colenso
and line of Tugela River look tempting, but I would suggest for consideration
whether, if you can reduce perimeter of defence, you might not send one Battalion
and one Regiment of Cavalry in direction of Albert or York, or even Greytown,
or somewhere covering Maritzburg from raid from North-East.

You have a large force of mounted troops now on the left [north] of the Tugela
River. Some of them might be better value on the right [south] of that river. It
will be at least three solid weeks before I can attempt to reinforce you, and at present
I fancy that the best help I can then give you will be to take Bloemfontein. Good
luck to you. You must have had some merry fights.

In this telegram, a characteristic of Buller begins to emerge. He suggests
certain actions might be taken but does not insist upon them. Though
agreeing with White about staying in Ladysmith he still harps on the attrac-
tion of retreating south of the Tugela river. At this time, in this particular
situation, his tentative advice sounds kindly and even wise, but later in the
campaign this quality was to cost the British soldiers very dear.

The news for White 'that the best help I can then give you will be to
take Bloemfontein' was not as alarming as it might sound to the layman.
Bloemfontein, the capital of the Orange Free State, and far, far over to the
west, would be the initial target for the army corps if Buller stuck to his
sound idea that strategically the Free State was the proper door to the Transvaal. If Bloemfontein were threatened it was certain that the Free State army
around Ladysmith would desert Natal and hurry to their capital's defence.

On 1 November, General White replied, making no further comment
about the 'merry fights':

I have information that a Commando estimated at 2000 men, Free State, with
guns, have arrived within a few miles Colenso. I had ordered French with two
Cavalry regiments and 400 Mounted Volunteers to try and help, but later information shows that all the roads are strongly held by enemy. I think the Cavalry could
not get through without heavy loss, so I have countermanded them. If road clears
will send one Cavalry regiment across Tugela. I cannot reduce perimeter without

President Paul Johannes Kruger – a signed photograph

General Schalk Burger

General Christian De Wet – a signed photograph

General Lucas Meyer

General Louis Botha

President Martinus Steyn – a signed photograph

General Sir George White

General Sir Redvers Buller – a signed photograph

General Buller with Bennet Burleigh

General Sir Charles Warren talking to a member of the Naval Brigade before entraining for the front

British prisoners captured at Colenso and en route for Pretoria, photographed with their Boer guards

yielding Artillery positions that would make Ladysmith untenable. Their guns are better than our Field guns. Don't ask me to detach another Battalion. The enemy are in great force.

The last three sentences betray a note of desperation. Though the British field guns were outranged by the Boer guns, Sir George does not mention the naval guns, which were not. On 1 and 2 November, these naval guns, manned and commanded by Jolly Jack Tars and their officers, fought long-range duels with the Boer guns on Pepworth Hill. Boer shells fell on Ladysmith.

Also on 1 November, troops were employed to consolidate the perimeter of defence on which Sir George White had decided. And on that day a small force of the 2nd Royal Dublin Fusiliers and the Natal Field Battery were riskily sent south to Colenso by rail – to fulfil the promise given to Sir Redvers Buller. Sir George must have seen them depart with very mixed feelings. He needed every man he could lay his hands on, to hold such an extensive defence, but on the other hand, he had reluctantly to consider the miserably thin British force south of the Tugela – less than 3000 soldiers. These soldiers might not only have to face a Boer army but also act as lines of communication. Anyway, they got to Colenso, where they set about protecting the bridge across the Tugela river. Danger was closing in.

On 2 November, General French rode south with a strong force of cavalry and a battery of guns, to see what he could do to keep the door open. They found a Boer camp, shelled it, and then returned to Ladysmith. The Boers were settling north, south, east and west. As French rode in he was given a telegram sent by Sir Redvers Buller, ordering him to get out of Ladysmith, and join the commander-in-chief at the Cape. At about midday (2 November) he took a special train and as it puffed southward, Boers rode at it in the vicinity of Pieter's station blazing away with their mausers. General French and Major Douglas Haig (later to command the British Army in France), who was with him, had to lie under seats for protection. Major Haig's portmanteau was hit but otherwise the train successfully ran the gauntlet, and French hurried to the Cape–Free State front, where he made a famous name for himself.

Having failed to stop the train, the Boers settled the matter for the immediate future by pulling up the rail-tracks. Ladysmith was now besieged.

6

THE SIEGE OF LADYSMITH
November 1899

*Our women and children shall not go out under a
white flag! They shall stay with the men under the
Union Jack.*

ARCHDEACON BARKER

BEFORE nightfall on 2 November 1899, the Boers had heaved their field
artillery on to Lombard's Kop, to the west-nor'-west of the town and were
throwing everything they could at the populace.

The Naval Brigade threw everything they could back at them, from a
kopje (hill) near the Newcastle road. Lieutenant Egerton RN lay close under
the barrel of his big 4·7-inch guns, directing fire. A shell came right through
the battery's earthwork, without bursting, but it hit the young man across
both his legs. He looked down and said: 'My cricketing days are over now.'
The doctors amputated one leg at the thigh and the other at the shin. By the
afternoon Lieutenant Egerton was cheerfully sitting up, drinking champagne
and smoking cigarettes. But during that night he died.

Shortly after this tragic event, Captain Lambton RN invited war-
correspondent Melton Prior to visit the naval guns:

> I declined as gracefully as I could, as I had heard that in the morning one of his
> gunners had had his head blown clean off by a Boer shell, and two other men were
> wounded. I said I thought I could see the bombardment much better from a certain
> kopje I knew, for the shells were coming over very thick.

Mr Watkins-Pitchford expressed to his wife the humiliation that the
Natal Volunteers suffered by getting trapped in Ladysmith:

> We heard that night that the wires were down, and the natives reported the line
> cut and held by large bodies of Boers just above Colenso. From that time we have
> heard nothing of the outside world, what England is doing, or how she is viewing

the criminal slackness which has left us in this position of peril. All is conjecture, but though we have been outnumbered, and for that matter out-generalled, all are confident of the ultimate outcome of the campaign.

Many civilians remained in Ladysmith who could have safely fled. But for various reasons, many stubbornly refused to budge. After persuasion, Major Marling persuaded his wife 'B.' to escape:

October 31st. Shells flying about all day off and on. Several fell for the first time in the town. Told 'B' she really must leave, though she does not want to go . . .

November 1st. 'B' went off to stay with the Governor at Pietermaritzburg. She went dreadfully against her will. Shells flying about all day. One fell in the garden of the hotel . . .

My wife, who was staying at Government House with Prince Christian Victor, took the last photograph which was taken of him before he died . . . She said Winston Churchill was staying there too, and one night at dinner laid down the law to the Governor as to his Colonial policy, and also to Sir Redvers Buller as to how he should conduct the campaign. Buller told him not to be a young ass. Redvers Buller didn't suffer fools gladly.

Some ladies did give way to what was expected of them in 1899 and had more than an attack of the vapours. Australia's Donald Macdonald related how 'on Wednesday night there was again a trying scene at the railway station. Many women were carried on stretchers utterly collapsed under the strain, often screaming hysterically.'

The two old war-correspondent veterans, Melton Prior and Bennet Burleigh, debated whether to stay or not to stay:

Burleigh had his cart and horses, and he soon made up his mind to go. He tried to induce me to follow him, but I said 'No'. I went to most of the other correspondents and I asked them what they were going to do. I said, 'The general opinion is that we are going to be invested. Are you going to stop, or are you going to get out?' and something like twenty said they were going to remain, and I determined to do likewise. I had seen previously almost every phase of warfare, but I had never been in an investment and I thought I would see what it was like. I think General French would very much have liked to remain, and I believe he was ordered out from home.

On 2 November, H. W. Nevinson, representing the London *Daily Chronicle* in Ladysmith, visited the Manchester Regiment, presumably on Caesar's Camp for that was where they were stationed.

I found the Manchesters building small and almost circular sangars (Indian or Persian word means wall of piled stones – from 'sang', a stone) of stones and sandbags at intervals along the ridge. The work was going listlessly, the men carrying up the smallest and easiest stones they could find, and spending most of the time in contemplating the scenery or discussing the situation, which they did not think hopeful. 'We're surrounded – that's what we are,' they kept saying. 'Thought we was goin' to have Christmas puddin' in Pretoria. Not much Christmas puddin' we'll ever smell again!'

Then Mr Nevinson went down into Ladysmith to send off his usual press report:

Early in the afternoon I took my telegram to the Censor as usual, and after the customary wanderings and waste of time I found him – only to hear that the wires were bunched and the line destroyed. So telegrams are ended; mails neither come nor go.

A queer Boer ambulance, with little glass windows – something between a gypsy van and a penny peep-show – came in under a huge white flag, bringing some of our wounded to exchange for wounded Boers. The amenities of civilised slaughter are carefully observed. But one of the ambulance drivers was Mattey, 'Long Tom's' skilled gunner, in disguise.

I wonder if that was true or one of those wonderful legends that are ever born in times of stress. I don't know.

A Major Kincaid was returned to Ladysmith by the Boers because he was sick with fever. He praised the Boer treatment of the British wounded prisoners, saying:

When our fellows were worn out, the Boers dismounted and let them ride. They brought them water and any food they had. Joubert came round the ambulance, commanding there should be no distinction between the wounded of either race.

As the siege of Ladysmith commenced on that 2nd of November 1899, there were 13 436 soldiers inside the perimeter, with Sir George White. The consisted of the following regular troops:

INFANTRY

1st Devonshires, 1st Gloucestershires (half battalion), 1st Manchesters, 2nd Gordons, 1st Royal Irish Fusiliers (half battalion), 1st Leicestershires, 1st King's Royal Rifles, 1st Liverpools, 2nd King's Royal Rifles, 2nd Rifle Brigade.

CAVALRY

5th Lancers, 18th Hussars (part only), 19th Hussars, 5th Dragoon Guards.

ARTILLERY

13th, 21st, 42nd, 53rd, 67th, and 69th Field Batteries (each six 15-pounders), rest of 10th Mountain Battery (two muzzle-loading 7-pounders, two 12-pounders, quick-firers), and two old 6·3-inch howitzers, firing 80-pound shells.

There were also the following irregulars and troops from Natal: Imperial Light Horse, Natal Police, Durban Naval Volunteers (one Nordenfeldt quick-firer), Border Mounted Rifles, Town Guard, Natal Artillery (with six 9-pounder muzzle loaders), Natal Mounted Rifles.

The Naval Brigade brought two 4·7-inch guns and four long naval 12-pounders.

On 3 November, General Brocklehurst, who had inherited cavalry responsibility from General French, took almost every mounted soldier in Ladysmith, plus a brigade division of artillery, to investigate what the Free State Boers were doing to the west of the town. It became a messy, incompetent ride, in which the entire Imperial Light Horse were nearly cut off and were only rescued with some difficulty by the 5th Dragoon Guards and the artillery. The probe lasted five hours and the British finally withdrew to the town with six killed and twenty-eight wounded. General French had hardly distinguished himself at the battle of Ladysmith; Brocklehurst looked like being no improvement.

Major Marling was on that jaunt but was not in critical mood:

5th Lancers, 5th Dragoon Guards, and Imperial Light Horse went down Long Valley at 9 a.m.; 18th and 19th Hussars and two Batteries went out at noon. Quite a nice little fight in the afternoon . . .

H. W. Nevinson of the London *Daily Chronicle* watched from afar and felt differently:

I could see many a poor fellow wandering hither and thither as though lost, as is common in all retreats. A man would walk sideways, then run back a little, look round, fall. Another came by. The first evidently called out and the other gave him a hand. Both stumbled on together, the puffs of dust splashing round them. Then down they fell and were quiet. A complacent correspondent told me afterwards, with the condescending smile of higher light, that only seven men were hit. I only know that before evening twenty-five of the Light Horse alone were brought in wounded, not counting the dead, and not counting the other mounted troops, all of whom suffered.

The bombardment of the town on this 3 November 1899 became pretty formidable. So, on the following morning, a notice was put up around the town, under the title *Suggested Permission For Non-Combatants To Leave the Borough*.

Sir George White has written to General Joubert to suggest that non-combatants – men, women, and children – be permitted to leave Ladysmith, and is awaiting his reply.

Meanwhile, Sir George suggests that, if the town is bombarded, he thinks the safest place is near or beyond the Grand Stand on the Race Course, and that anybody proceeding there may go under a flag to show they have no connection with the combatant forces of the garrison. (Signed) A. Hunter, 4th November, 1899, Major-General.

It was a Major Bateson who carried the letter to Commandant-General Joubert requesting safe conduct for civilians to travel south. The morning was relatively peaceful and many hopefuls began to pack at the prospect of escape from Ladysmith.

Back came Joubert's reply and another notice went up in Ladysmith entitled *Extract From The Translation Of A Letter Dated Nov. 4th, 1899, From Commandant-General Joubert To Sir George White, Lieut.-General Commanding The British Troops, Natal.*

Respecting your request that the townspeople may be allowed to leave for the South, this I cannot possibly agree to. The wounded, with their attendants and doctors, may, as requested by you, be taken to a chosen place; and I shall agree that the people of the town shall also be removed there.

The number of the civilians must be communicated to me, and the removal of the wounded and civilians must be effected within 24 hours of the receipt of this, and the locality must be distinctly marked.

I must further make it a condition that under the name of civilian there must not be sent out any who have taken up arms against the Republic.

True extract of letter received at Ladysmith on 4th November, 1899, at 12 noon. A. Hunter, Major-General, Chief of Staff, Natal.

Well, that put an end to Sir George's wildly optimistic hope. Joubert, embarking on a siege, which always entails the hope of starving the besieged into submission, could not release the militarily useless ones, thereby providing extra rations for the soldiers. Sir George should not have asked – though no harm in asking, I suppose – but out of his request came as generous and as humane an alternative as was possible.

General White advised the townspeople to accept General Joubert's offer and a site was selected some four miles south-east of Ladysmith, on the railway line, and the place was called Intombi Camp. It was almost in the shade of the Boer stronghold Umbulwana Hill, a little to the east.

Supplies for the camp were to come from Ladysmith, of course, and one railway train would be allowed to travel between the camp and the town, each day, under a flag of truce.

Many people gladly accepted the opportunity – but not all! An eccentric, unorganized public meeting was held on the front steps of the Ionic Public Hall (a hospital) and jingoistic emotions ran high. The suggestion that British women and children should be placed some four miles away from the strong protecting arms of straight-backed Englishmen . . . Never! It was suggested that wretched Boers would use the helpless innocents as a screen for some dastardly attack . . . The Mayor, Mr Farquhar, was present and so was the Anglican Archdeacon Barker.

The Archdeacon, a tall, upright, white-haired man, was a better imperialist than Christian when he thundered: 'Our women and children shall not go out under a white flag! They shall stay with the men under the Union Jack, and those who would do them harm may come to them at their peril!'

Would they accept Boer terms? 'Britons never, never will!' Shouts, cheers, parasols were waved and the National Anthem was raised: 'God save our gracious Queen . . .' The meeting gave the offer a very rude rejection.

However, the next day, Sunday 5 November, the train steamed out of Ladysmith, bound for Intombi Camp, with the sick and wounded on board, plus many civilians. The place was unkindly called 'Fort Funk'. The move was not well organized. Initially there was no water and no rations and a grave shortage of tents. H. W. Nevinson reported: 'In all that crowd of suffering men I did not hear a single complaint. Administration is not the strong point of the British officer. "We are only sportsmen," said one of them with a sigh, as he crawled up the platform, torn with dysentery and fever.'

Incidentally, it was soon tacitly agreed that no fighting should take place on Sundays. The Boers, being deeply preoccupied with the Old Testament as well as the New, dreaded any breaking of religious customs – and, of course, the British welcomed a bit of a breather.

Major Marling put it this way: 'Sunday, November 5th. A quiet day. Old Brer Boer does not shell on Sunday, as a rule.'

H. W. Nevinson overheard two soldiers of the Devonshire Regiment discussing the matter, while washing themselves in the river:

'Why don't they go on bombardin' of us today?'

'Cos it's Sunday, and they're singin' 'ymns.'

'Well, if they do start bombardin' of us, there ain't only one 'ymn I'll sing, an' that's "Rock of Ages, cleft for me, Let me 'ide myself in thee"!'

Indeed everyone seemed to have their feet up on that 5 November. Major R. Bowen of the King's Royal Rifles was writing to his wife at Sandgate in England. I am now holding the letter and am peering at the small neat writing:

My dearest Missy, We are at present having a very peaceful Sunday. They haven't yet fixed a shot at us, I wonder if you will soon get this at all as we are more or less shut in at present. I am commanding the Battn. as the Colonel has gone sick and Jimmy Riddell was dangerously wounded . . . I suppose you know far more about what's going on than we do . . . You would never recognise me with a grayish beard . . . The Boers are said to be sick of the war and I really don't wonder as the hardships on both sides are very great and so far as I can see most of them have nothing to gain and something to lose by fighting, whereas it is our business as soldiers and we have something to gain and only our lives to lose. I don't call them wonderful shots. But below us at present. I hope I shall see you again Dear some day. Love to the children. Yours ever
affecsly. R. Bowen.

Almost opposite Ladysmith Town Hall there was and is still the Royal Hotel. This place was for the elite of the siege and in it, surprisingly, was the notorious Leander Starr Jameson and Colonel Frank Rhodes, brother of Cecil. These men had been at the heart of the Jameson Raid in 1896 and therefore were deeply hated by the Boers. Whether through the activity of Boer spies or providential justice, Boer shells followed them wherever they went. On that 3 November, a shell pitched outside the packed dining room of the Royal Hotel, but actually exploded in a cottage, usually occupied by Mr Pearse of the London *Morning Post*. Mr Pearse was fortunately out at the time – but rumour insisted in Ladysmith that the Boers were ever aiming at the 'Rhodesians'.

Sir George White had now established his pattern for the defence of the town. His total defensive perimeter was about fourteen miles and at the beginning of the siege was held by just under 14000 men. The civilian population was now something under 7000. The General's headquarters were near the centre of the town, and incidentally, like so much in Ladysmith, remains exactly as it was, at least up to a few years ago. Close by was located his reserve force, mainly mounted men; the idea being to order them quickly to any part of the perimeter that might come under pressure.

The outer defences were divided into four sections: A, B, C and D. 'A' section was commanded by Colonel W. G. Knox CB and it ran from Junction

Hill, north of Ladysmith through Tunnel Hill and Cemetery Hill to Help-makaar Ridge. 'B' Section was under Major-General F. Howard CB, CMG, ADC, and ran from Gordon Hill due north of the town and included Cove Redoubt, Leicester Post, Observation Hill, and King's Post, all in a westerly direction, and then moved southward along the western defences, through Ration Post to Rifleman's Post. 'C' section was commanded by Colonel Ian Hamilton CB, DSO, and it stretched from Flagstone Spruit, through Range Post, and included Maiden Castle and the entire southern defences from Wagon Hill to Caesar's Camp in the south-east corner. Finally 'D' section was held by Colonel Royston and his Natal Mounted Volunteers. This length

„Splendid Isolation!"

stretched from the south-east corner to due east of Ladysmith and joined section 'A' at the Klip river. Incidentally this river ran through Ladysmith, supplying the place with not-very-good water.

The Boer positions held to a ring of hills, thirty miles in length and, as might be expected, encircling the British positions. The outstanding features were Umbulwana Hill, to the south-east, flat-topped, 500 feet above the level of the town and about 7500 yards distant. From it, through the clear, dry air that is common in this part of Africa, one can look down on the streets and buildings of Ladysmith and imagine that they are within rifle range – which they are not, but they are well within range of 'Long Tom' and his Boer artillery mates. Not only that; Umbulwana commands most parts of the British defence perimeter. Umbulwana was definitely a thorn in the side of Ladysmith during the siege.

Then nasty old Pepworth Hill, which had already given the British a bad time, lay nor'-nor'-east of the town, and again the Boers had easy range, but lacked the elevation to see clearly where they were hitting.

Other hills held by the Boers were Lombard's Kop to the east; Long Hill to the north-east; Surprise Hill and Thornhill's Kop to the north-west; Star Hill, Rifleman's Ridge and Lancer's Hill, around the south-west and south; Mounted Infantry Hill, Middle Hill, and End Hill. The Orange Free State headquarters (*hoofdlaager* in the Boer language) lay behind Telegraph Ridge to the north-west.

Provisions in all the shops of Ladysmith were commandeered by the military and every soul was on rations. People began to search for bomb-proof holes and shelters, and a favourite place was into the high banks of the Klip river. The cautious stayed there during the daytime bombing and then returned to their homes for the evening and night. Rather surprisingly the Boer artillery behaved a bit like clockwork. As H. W. Nevinson put it: 'Their hours for slaughter are six to six, and they seldom overstep them. They knock off for meals – unfashionably early, it is true, but it would be petty to complain.'

Splendid river-bank homes were constructed by the volunteer Imperial Light Horse, many of them experienced at tunnelling gold-mines under Johannesburg, for themselves and their ammunition, and also by the Arch-deacon of Ladysmith, who thereby betrayed that he had some doubts about Divine Providence.

The Boers heaved their 6-inch Creusot gun to the top of Umbulwana and it was on 8 November 1899 that they first let fly from their splendid elevation. It was immediately a great worry to the British. Donald Macdonald of the *Melbourne Argus* described the quiet deterioration of Ladysmith's citizens in the face of shell fire:

On the first day, when the shells were few in number people laughed – a mechanical crackling laugh, like the rustle of dry straw, but still a laugh. On the second day there was rather less laughter, and more of smothered swearing. On the third day there was an impressive silence, people answering curtly when spoken to, every one thinking a good deal. It was not a friendly act then to throw an empty bottle or a can amongst the rocks close to where a man stood. He was too proud to make any protests, but still his nerves betrayed him. On the fourth day men had a hunted look, and I never fully realized what a hunted look meant until the bombardment of Ladysmith. Most men were morose. It was not so much the Krupp shell that worried them as the waiting for it. The most courteous man in the world became short-tempered then. On the sixth day he was savage, and asked people whether the British soldier had deteriorated, that he didn't go out in the dark and take that cursed Krupp gun?

When a person was actually hit, the reaction to incipient death was apparently unpredictable. War-correspondent George Lynch witnessed a coming and going:

One afternoon a young fellow galloped past me in the main street of Ladysmith. He had just got opposite the Town Hall Hospital, when a shell from Bulwana burst right under his horse. When the cloud of dust and smoke cleared away, we found the horse lying on the road completely disembowelled, and the poor fellow flung onto the footpath, with a long piece of shell sticking in his side. As he was taken into the hospital he said: 'This means two more Dutchmen killed.' But the wound was obviously fatal; there was no use even in removing the piece of shell. The clergymen came to him and spoke to him for some time, and told him that there was no hope of recovery for him. He seemed to get tired of his ministrations and asked them to 'send down for my chum'. When this chum arrived he was unable to speak, but just pressed his hand and smiled, and went off into his death-sleep.

On 7 November, the convent, which flew the Red Cross flag because it was used as a hospital, was hit by several shells, and this for the umpteenth time. It was decided to evacuate patients and nurses.

On 9 November the Boers made a gesture of a general attack on Ladysmith. But because of their formidable individuality – at this early stage of the war burghers often decided for themselves what they would do and what they would not do – and also because it was an instinctive knowledge in them that their numerically small nations could not afford heavy casualties, the attack was ineffectual. However they did make their presence felt at Caesar's Camp, in the south. The total British losses were small: four killed, twenty-seven wounded. How many the Boers lost, I don't know – not many.

At midday a grand piece of English eccentricity took place. It was the unattractive Prince of Wales' birthday and Captain the Honourable Hedworth Lambton RN fired a salute of twenty-one guns at the Boers, in honour of the wretched fellow. And then the poor bloody sailors were ordered to give three cheers: they shouted first, this being their privilege as the senior service, and the call was repeated by the soldiers. As those voices echoed around the fourteen miles of hills, the Boers heliographed from hill to hill: 'What do you make of it all?', and as the reason dawned on them they must have shaken their heads sadly. And then in Ladysmith a congratulatory message was composed for His Royal Highness and sent by pigeon to

Durban. It is good value to report that the message actually reached those royal hands and in due course an acknowledgement was received back in Ladysmith.

Major Marling wrote in his diary:

Thursday, November 9th. We were fighting all day. The Boers attacked, principally at Caesar's Camp and Waggon Hill, and also a half-hearted attack at

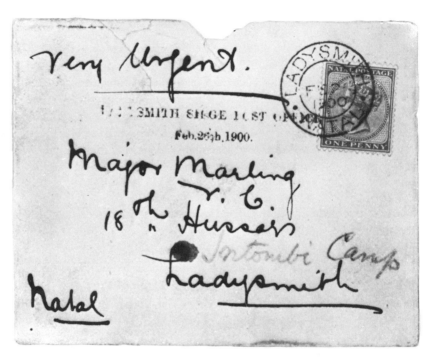

A cover addressed to Major Marling VC. In addition to the Ladysmith postmark it has the handstamp 'Ladysmith Siege Post Office'

Observation Hill. We beat them off, killing or wounding they say about 200, but I doubt myself whether their casualties were half as much.

The Prince of Wales's birthday, and the trumpeter blew 'God Bless the Prince of Wales', and the Brigadier of the Cavalry Brigade, a bit of a courtier, ordered a Royal Salute of twenty-one guns to be fired in honour of the event, and we all cheered.

The pomp and circumstance of a twenty-one-gun salute was already in cruel conflict with the actual state of the garrison. H. W. Nevinson of the London *Daily Chronicle* wrote:

It would be a good thing if the Army could be marched through Regent Street as the men look this morning. It would teach people more about war than a hundred pictures of plumed horsemen and the dashing charge. The smudgy khaki uniforms soaked through and through, stained black and green and dingy red with wet and earth and grass; the draggled great-coats, heavy with rain and thick with mud; the heavy sopping boots, the blackened, battered helmets; the blackened, battered faces below them, unwashed and unshaved since the siege began; the eyes heavy and bloodshot with sun and rain and want of sleep; the peculiar smell – there is not much brass band and glory about us now.

The Boers almost gave Captain Lambton, commanding the Naval Brigade, apoplexy. His courageous and skilful sailors fired several shells right into 'Long Tom's' emplacement. The Boers immediately sent up a white flag, and therefore it was quite clear, according to all the usages of war, that the monster gun had surrendered and would never again worry a Britisher. The gallant Captain ordered an immediate cease-fire and awaited further signs of capitulation. Suddenly, the white flag was hauled down, and 'Long Tom' resumed firing. The Boers had removed their casualties and effected the gun's repairs.

At some time during the middle of November, news reached Sir George White that some troops were being sent from the Cape to Natal. The idea of capturing Bloemfontein, and in that way drawing off besieging Free Staters, was fine enough, but this news of fresh British soldiers moving directly into southern Natal was more heartwarming.

Then Ladysmith learnt that efforts were to be made to improve communications from the outside British world. The General Officer commanding the line of communications telegraphed to Sir George: 'I am getting searchlight fixed on truck, and will flash signals with it from Estcourt by night. Watch sky for flashing signals. Try to effect means of reply.'

The idea did not work easily. The jagged range of high hills on the northern bank of the Tugela river were in the way. But after some days, messages were seen reflecting off the clouds. And the siege was not quite so lonely. What an eerie sight it must have been. A great light flickering on the night clouds, above the Tugela Heights.

Of course, what the Ladysmith garrison were always searching for was a heliograph message. This is created by the sun shining on a special manipulated mirror, which can send messages over many miles. But for a besieged soldier in Ladysmith to see one of those flashes from the south would mean that a British soldier had successfully crossed the Tugela and then pierced the mountains. Thousands and thousands were to try that cruel journey, but not yet awhile.

On 12 November, the Boers, with grand simplicity, appeared in the British ambulance camp and asked for some chlorodyne because they had run low and were suffering from dysentery, like the besieged. The British responded, it seems almost eagerly, not only giving them chlorodyne but a few bottles of brandy as well. We must set that gesture to counterbalance the excesses of Elandslaagte.

When Tommy Atkins heard the above story he invented one of his own. It was said General Joubert came into Ladysmith and asked General White for some forage for his horses because they were hungry. And Sir George replied, 'I would very gladly accede to your request, but have only enough forage myself to last three years.'

And on this very same day was born the first siege baby. The mother, a Mrs Moore, tried an underground shelter, but noting its dampness said she and the 'expected one would take their chances in the shell-pierced fresh air of their hilltop farm. All went well.

Also on this 12 November, Major R. Bowen of the King's Royal Rifles continued his letter to his wife in England:

Sunday 12 – I've not yet had any opportunity of sending this off. On the 10th they treated us to an extra strong Bombardment and an attack but not on my part of the line. I have made my part so strong with two or three forts . . . we were under a frightfully hot fire of Rifles and Shrapnel at Lombards Kop for several hours and didn't lose so many men considering in fact I expect that we got as many of them as they did of us. I should like very much a good tub and some clean clothes but both of those things are out of the question and have been for some time – The water we have to drink is more than a quarter mud and filth but as yet there has been no typhoid and only one or two cases of dysentry in fact we are wonderfully fit as the food and weather are both on the whole good and the water is the only danger. We are all getting tired of being besieged and only waiting the order to again attack them. Of course we have no news but by this time some troops should be out from England and soon we will move on. The colonel still keeps on the sick list thank goodness. At Lombards Kop we lost 2 officers and 10 men killed – 1 officer and 31 men wounded and 14 missing most of them I expect killed really and far more than ½ were shot close to me. My Coy and Capt Barnetts losing about ½ the total.

We want to pay them out. I hope I shall soon get this off – Yours ever R.B.

Excellent Colonel Ward had by this time organized the provisions in Ladysmith to last for eighty days. One could surmise that Colonel Ward had pondered more carefully than anyone else how difficult it would be for a relieving force to cross the Tugela river and break through the Tugela Heights. He bought up what beer and spirits remained, partly to dish out on special occasions and partly to prevent celebrations when there was nothing to celebrate.

The Ladysmith war-correspondents had to try, for professional reasons, to get messages to England. A pigeon-post to Durban was used, but more often they employed black African runners – who were not popular with the military authorities. The messages were not in cypher and if the courageous postmen were caught, it was of more concern that security was at risk than that the runners would probably be shot.

H. W. Nevinson described the departure of a 'postman' on 16 November:

> In the evening I sent off another runner with a telegram and quite a mail of letters from officers and men for their mothers, wives, and lovers overseas. He was a bony young Kaffir, with a melancholy face, black as sorrow. At six o'clock I saw him start. One pocket bulged with biscuits, one with a tin of beef. Between his black chest and his rag of shirt he had tucked that neat packet which was to console so many a woman, white skinned and delicately dressed. Fetching a wide compass, he stole away into the eastern twilight, where the great white moon was rising, shrouded in electric cloud.

Finally a press censor was appointed, Major Altham of the Engineers, and he organized a regular string of black runners who skilfully ran the gauntlet once a week. One of the envelopes which was carried from Lady-smith is reproduced on the next page. Headquarters staff fixed the price at fifteen pounds for each letter! Donald Macdonald described Major Altham as 'a man who combines the directness of the soldier with the literary sagacity of a sub-editor.' And then goes on to record a dialogue between a newspaper correspondent and the major:

Censor: Can't let you say this, you know.

Correspondent: Well, it's of interest to the public.

Censor: We're not considering the public, though; we're considering the enemy.

Correspondent [with a weary air]: Oh, very well, strike it out.

Censor: And here again you say, 'Great satisfaction expressed here arrival General Buller. Feeling that siege will not long continue.' That's a reflection on our General. You don't mean to say that we're skulking behind rocks, and that General Buller has only to come here and personally drive the Boers away.

One of the Ladysmith covers that came through the Boer investment and was post-marked on its arrival at Estcourt. The cover was folded for easier carrying by runners

Correspondent: No; but he has an army corps with him.

Censor: Then why don't you say so? Hum! Ha! What's this? Question of tactics. Where did you get your knowledge of military strategy?

Correspondent [triumphantly]: It's not so much a matter of strategy as of common sense.

Censor: Your conclusions in that vein, don't you know, are admirable, if the premises were correct, but unfortunately they're not. I suppose that doesn't matter, though.

Correspondent [seeing an opening]: I shall be very glad, major, if you will amend them where incorrect.

Censor: No doubt; but then, you see, I'm not acting as correspondent for your paper.

What a splendid exchange! I am an actor, and I cannot refrain from re-marking that dialogue of that subtle and humorous quality doesn't turn up in television plays from one year's end to the other.

The Boers remained regular in their firing habits – until 15 November.

Everyone could go to their beds with a feeling of considerable security; but on that ominous night, shortly after midnight, there was a tremendous roar and crash as the big Boer guns on Pepworth Hill and Umbulwana opened fire on the town. Horrified men and women scuttled about the dark streets in their night-attire. And then, to everyone's delighted astonishment, the British guns began to thunder their reply. Gunners, being thinking people, had taken the precaution each evening of training their guns on the Boer emplacements in case of precisely this eventuality.

Many debates took place the following morning as to what had prompted the Boers to break their sleep patterns in that quixotic manner, and it began to emerge that they were paying the British back for those Prince of Wales' birthday bangs.

About this time, a Boer wrote a letter to his sister about the effect of these shelling exchanges. The letter was captured and given to Sir George White, and he was so delighted with it that he quoted it in a letter he wrote to his wife:

Mr Englishman fights very hard indeed, and does not seem to mind the shells falling thick into Ladysmith. Our burghers do not like their shells, and cannot stand them. We have been before Ladysmith now for a month, and we don't seem much nearer taking it. I fear there will be great bloodshed before it falls . . .

Of course there is a danger to those who study this Second Boer War of imagining that all Boers were supermen; this is not so. A telegram was sent by a distinguished Boer outside Ladysmith back to a Field-Cornet in the Transvaal:

T.D. ZAR 16.11.1899. From Commandant Viljoen, Ladysmith
To Field-Cornet De Vries, Fordsburg, begins:

About twenty persons have arrived here from your ward. Some of them sick or disabled, others crippled, blind or cock-eyed. The majority possess medical certificates which have been ignored either by you or the Acting Commandant. What the hell do you think I have here, a hospital, a reformatory, or a war on my hands? These sick and disabled must suffer the greatest discomfort and privation amongst us, since not only are they quite unserviceable but they also need nursing and accommodation without which they must surely perish. Among others who have arrived here with chronic and grave diseases are J. Elliott who is blind, G. van der Walt who has a large rupture and J. F. van der Merwe with a gastric ulcer, whereas G. Roestof throws an epileptic fit every day. In addition there are many more. Why do you not commandeer plump, over-nourished persons like the officials, as well as Charlie du Plessis of Vrededorp? As for that fat braggart G. Bezuidenhout I cannot leave him there, he must come and defend his country. Besides, you have enough scouts in skirts to help you. And if Field-Cornet Lombaard will not come himself, why does he not send his clerk Pienaar and such-like types? Give Field-Cornet Lombaard a copy of this – ends.

On Friday 17 November, faithful to the British tradition when things are looking ugly, the Gordon Highlanders played the Imperial Light Horse at Association football, and thereby bluffed themselves and the enemy through sport. Regretfully and risking, once again, an anti-British reputation, I have to record a questionable incident of that game. The Boers, probably outraged at this piece of cheek, dropped a shell into the middle of the game and under cover of the explosion and smoke, the Gordons 'sneaked' a goal. The Imperial Light Horse objected. The Highlanders, being Scots, were immovably stubborn, and finally to settle the matter, a message was got to the Football Association in England 'as to whether such a contingency is covered by the rules of the game'. I don't know the outcome – but no one was hurt or killed by the shell.

In Ladysmith, during the siege, was a visitor from Torquay, England, whose name was Dr Starke. He was a widower and had travelled to South Africa on the eve of the war to 'witness great events' and he had chosen to remain in Ladysmith for the siege out of curiosity and in the hope of assisting in ambulance work. He was a tall man and was undoubtedly very eccentric, wearing a very long coat and usually carrying either a fishing rod or a butterfly net.

Despite his adventurous decision to remain in Ladysmith, he was of a nervous disposition and every morning, very early, he padded down to the safety of the river bank, carrying in one hand a basket containing his lunch and in the other an adopted pussy-cat. When the Boers had predictably packed in their shooting for the day, the doctor placidly returned, often receiving a little good-humoured and kindly banter: 'Well, doctor, got back from your daily picnic?'

As it grew dark on 18 November, Dr Starke reached the outside of the Royal Hotel and met Mr McHugh of the London *Daily Telegraph*, who engaged him in conversation. Out of the evening, as it were, came a Boer shell and struck the opposite side of the street. The two men turned, startled. Another shell hit the roof of the Royal – no doubt searching for Jameson and Frank Rhodes – wrecked two bedrooms (one of them Dr Starke's) without exploding, then came down the stairway and out of the front door, where it struck poor Dr Starke above the knees. Mr McHugh was unscathed but was covered in the harmless doctor's blood. Dr Starke fell forward on his face, moaning 'Look after my poor cat; look after my poor cat!' and died an hour later. The wreaths on his grave were made up of the little mountain marguerites. And if by any chance you pass the Royal Hotel, Ladysmith, look down closely and you will see a small brass plate set into the pavement, marking his death place.

The final irony of Dr Starke's death was that he was an outspoken Liberal and therefore had militantly opposed Chamberlain's policy and vigorously denounced the injustice of England's cause – even on the streets of Ladysmith where he died.

On 18 November, Ladysmith produced its first siege journal, *The Ladysmith Bombshell*, and perhaps if I extract a few items from this first issue, the very best spirit of the town will be conveyed:

Long Tom O'Pepworth's Hill

He doth not speak in parable,
Or Whisper soft and low,
So all the folk of Ladysmith
His every accent know;
For he can bend the stiffest back,
And mould the strongest will –
He's quite a little autocrat,
Long Tom o'Pepworth's Hill.

[Two more verses follow.]

There was a time at the Royal [hotel] when you got eggs inside and shells outside. Now you don't.

The climatic conditions continue unsettled; this morning is fair and dry. There are however, ominous clouds over the Umbulwana.

Mr Woodhouse, the ex-Mayor of P.M.B. [Pietermaritzburg], is making an extended visit to Ladysmith; he is anxious to get away.

Wanted: A few Dutchemen to enter the Town of Ladysmith. A Warm reception guaranteed.

For Sale: A few descriptions of the fights by eminent London correspondents. To be sold at a sacrifice.

At the police court this morning an application was made to the sitting Magistrate for an Order to arrest General Joubert, on the charge of disturbing the public peace, after the hour of 11 p.m. on the 14th inst. The necessary Order was at once granted. Sergt. M——r assured His Worship that, under a flag of truce, he would immediately effect service. It is anticipated the offender will be severely dealt with. (The maximum fine is £5.)

Officer with eye-glass meeting an aged mule in the street: 'Dear me, 'pon my word, this, surely, must be a Boah!'

Lost, a Pluck. Finder will be suitably rewarded upon returning same to Excavation No. 401, River Bank.

That you can talk about Ladysmith in any part of the civilized world now without being asked, Where is it?

(Printed and Published at Ladysmith, Natal, 18th Nov., 1899.)

By Sunday 19 November, after nearly three weeks of siege, life in Ladysmith was rough. Enteric fever was adding to the fighting casualty lists and the cheapest deal coffin was costing £10; so bodies were usually buried in brown African – or as they said in 1899 Kaffir – blankets. And on this day a Boer doctor visited Intombi Camp and told the inmates that an armoured train, operating with the British, far to the south, had been ambushed and many prisoners had been taken.

On that Sunday, Major R. Bowen continued his letter to his wife, a letter which was now becoming more of a weekly diary:

Still here had no end of a shelling last night but nobody damaged badly. The work and responsibility is very heavy and we are very tired of being always shut up and shot at. I take command of a place cailed Observation Hill at 3 a.m. one morning for 24 hrs then 24 hrs off, then on again. No sleep for those hours and your [*sic*] shot at if you move from behind the wall. I must try and sleep now.

The biggest problem in Ladysmith, as in all sieges, was psychological. Sir George White put it clearly to his staff: 'Gentlemen, we have two things to do – to kill time and to kill Boers – both equally difficult.' Captain Lambton RN expressed the fighting man's humiliation: 'we are being stuck up by a man and a boy.'

The Boers now shelled day and night. Donald Macdonald wrote: 'The 22nd and 23rd of November were tissue-wearing, nerve-shattering days in Ladysmith. On the night of the 22nd we had heaven's artillery and the Boers' at the same moment, and in the darkness the two combined made a paralysing din.'

Of course, rumoured Boer spies were made the scapegoats for every British military failure and no doubt there were many people in Ladysmith who did all they could to support the republican cause. One spy was clearly authentic and came to prominence on Friday 24 November.

His name was Oscar Meyer and he 'got wind' that he was suspected. Wearing the khaki uniform with the blue and white puggaree of the Guides he calmly went to the military horse-lines and rode off on a well-saddled mount. Reaching a British outpost, he was challenged by a sentry and he explained in perfect English that he was a Guide on a reconnoitring mission. 'Where's your pass?' asked the sentry. Oscar Meyer searched diligently for the pass, muttering the while, 'Confound that pass! I'm always losing it. It must be in one of my pockets though.' All this while his stolen horse seemed to be nervously edging away from the sentry, in the direction of the open veldt. Suddenly he stuck in his spurs, leaned low over the horse's withers and galloped full-tilt for the Boer lines. The sentry was so shocked by the whole audacity that he never fired once.

Also on 24 November, Ladysmith suffered a very serious loss. A military order had stipulated that any cattle that went grazing on the flats, close to the town, must be tended by armed and mounted men. But things were getting slack, and on that day about two hundred cattle meandered off, beyond the old camp, only accompanied by black Africans (unarmed, of course); whites in Africa were not accustomed to performing such menial jobs. The Africans went to sleep in the sun, and suddenly Boers were between them and their responsibility, quietly edging the cattle away from the British defences. Men of the Leicester Mounted Infantry saw the danger and galloped out, only to be met by heavy Boer covering fire. They managed to reach Star Hill, hoping to head the cattle back. Then the Boer guns, 'Faith', 'Hope' and 'Charity' as the British called them, opened fire from Telegraph Hill joined by other guns from Surprise Hill, Thornhill Kopje and Blueback Ridge, and the Leicesters beat a hasty retreat. The Boers then with circus-precision accuracy drove the cattle into their laagers by placing shells not too far behind them. About thirty to forty beasts were retrieved by the British but the Boers gained about £3000 worth of mainly transport cattle. It was criminal negligence, under the circumstances, but I can find no record of a court-martial.

The citizens of Ladysmith began to recognize the audible idiosyncrasies of the different guns, both Boer and British, and would remark, as the British did about German aircraft in the last war, 'That's one of ours.' The Boer guns were given characteristic names by their potential victims: 'Silent Sue', 'Jangling Jane', 'Gentleman Joe', 'Puffing Billy' – or 'Long Tom', 'Faith', 'Hope' and 'Charity'.

Sundays remained peaceful, but the Boers kept a puritan watchful eye on the town and if anything clearly transgressed the rules of the Lord's Day – watch out! On Sunday 26 November, some Mohammedan Indians brazenly walked out on to the river-flats and started to dig a trench. Very quickly a Boer shell landed in the construction, with five more in the vicinity. The Asians dived for the river bank.

The British would play cricket on the Sabbath and for that national religion were prepared to risk all. On these days of relative peace, the Boers rather ostentatiously paraded their lady-visitors. For some reason the British got very indignant about this pretty but distant view of white dresses and parasols.

Tommy Atkins was now hit where it hurt most: beer began to run low, and to add to his other miseries, ginger-beer was about the only substitute in the wet canteens. In a way, things could not get much worse.

But aggressive humour had not died. A rifleman went to sleep at the foot of a tree in the 'volunteer camp'. Suddenly he woke up to find that half of the barrel of his rifle and the top half of the tree had been blown off. He was heard to remark, 'These Boers are getting very careless with their shooting. If they don't mind they'll be hitting someone.'

Major Bowen continued his letter to his wife:

26 Nov. Still alive but we are all getting very tired of this. Perpetually shot at by big guns we cant reach. And sniped at all of every other day on Observation Hill. Major Cockburn R.B. [Rifle Brigade] and I take it alternate days. We have built ourselves shelters but nearly every time one comes out to get your food or go round the men or look through the telescope one is shot at. Yesterday I had 3 that I know were meant for me as they were so close. I've tried to shoot the man who does it myself and made him clear out once. I dont believe we will care for sleeping in a bed or in fact anywhere but on a stone and in ones clothes and boots again but I do want a change from a pound of Bullybeef and a pound of bread or biscuit a day and not be obliged to get up 2 hours before sunrise. At present we get up at 1.45 a.m. every day. However in spite of it all I'd sooner be here than in India hardships and all. There have been a lot of those duststorms lately and sheets of rain so we have been wet through for hours. I should like to get a few letters and see the papers very much. I hope people at home dont think us a laughing stock being shut-up like this. Nothing we should like better than to be led out at them, but I suppose the General knows what is best. If he doesn't he ought to. You might if you think of it keep any newspapers pictorial or otherwise that you think might interest me some day as I shall probably never see them here. Goodbye.

Yrs ever, R. BOWEN.

If anything happens to me you'll hear it as soon as possible. So no news means I'm alive.

Civilians were also beginning to change their attitudes about the shelling. The schoolmaster's wife had paid a soldier ten shillings for a fragment.

Two days later, on 23 November, while she was asleep in her bedroom, a 45-pound shell appeared through her fireplace and burst in the vicinity of the bed. The room was smashed to pieces, but the lady was only lightly wounded about the head. H. W. Nevinson wrote that 'Now she had a whole shell for nothing.' And went on about the new deluge of Boer shells: 'They came shrieking over our heads, and then a flare of fire and a cloud of dust and stones showed where they fell. At every explosion the women and children laughed and cheered with delight, as at the Crystal Palace fireworks.'

Mr R. J. McHugh, correspondent of the London *Daily Telegraph*, was enormously impressed by a fellow Scot whose house was in direct line between the Naval Battery and the Boer guns on Umbulwana. Almost daily shells exploded around his house and in his garden and apparently he always remarked, 'Ay, ay! Lord, man, that wuz a hummin'-bird damned well hatched!' – and proceeded with whatever he happened to be doing.

Though people were getting killed, casualties from Boer artillery fire were surprisingly low and familiarity was breeding a sort of fun-contempt.

The Boers on Umbulwana began to concentrate their fire on a new battery of British guns, close to the river and near the racecourse. It was calculated that about £300 worth of ammunition was hurled at it before the Boers seriously asked themselves why it never replied. The truth was that Colonel Knox had constructed it from wood and canvas, as a shell decoy.

On 25 November, those difficult Scots, the Gordon Highlanders, decided to brave Boer artillery outrage, and hold their sports meeting close to the Iron Bridge. Precautions, of sorts, were taken: sentries were placed at various points to warn about approaching shells. The drill went like this:

'Any more entries for the United Service mule race? Are you ready? Sentry, are you keeping your eye on that gun?'

'Yes sir.'

'Very well then, go!'

Of course, the ever present question was when the relief column would arrive. Spirits rose towards the end of November when the military headquarters issued the following bulletin: 'The enemy had been defeated at Mooi River by portion of the column advancing from the south for the relief of Ladysmith, and has retreated on the Tugela River. General Clery's force occupied Frere [about twenty-four miles away] on Monday, 26th inst.' It was relief enough, for the moment, to be reassured that there was an actual relief column.

In Ladysmith, a force was kept poised to go out and join a relieving column, should it meet with success and begin to break through. Many nights there were alarms and excursions, but they came to nothing except that after one such hoped-for action a sentry, going on duty in the darkness, actually caught a man working a lamp-signal, presumably to the Boers. The sentry shot the spy through the shoulder, and early next morning a British outpost observed a large force of Boers leave an ambush position where they would have caught the Imperial Light Horse, had they ridden out to try and join General Clery's supposed relief column.

The lamp-signaller was a Cape Coloured man (known euphemistically in South Africa as a Cape Boy) named Ventor, and the sinister discovery was made that he had been attached to No. 10 Mountain Battery as a mule-driver, on the night of the disaster at Nicholson's Nek. It was these very mules that had stampeded and led to the surrender of 1200 British soldiers. I wonder whether this unknown Mr Ventor should rank with Christian de Wet, Louis Botha and De La Rey as one of the grandest devastators of British soldiers during this Second Boer War?

Rumours were everywhere in Ladysmith and were about everything. Suddenly the whole town believed that an observation balloon had sighted the advance guard of the dreamt-of relief column only eight miles to the south of Umbulwana Hill. And then the excited people of Ladysmith learnt that the Boers were actually dismantling 'Long Tom' on Pepworth Hill. Conviction grew to certainty, and then from euphoria all hopes were dashed. The Boers were moving 'Long Tom' from Pepworth to a more effective position on Umbulwana – and were clearly adding to their siege artillery.

But on 7 November, as the Boers were putting up yet another 6-inch gun, this time on the hills beyond Range Post, Ladysmith hit back with pure creativity. On this date, the town published its second siege journal, called the *Ladysmith Lyre*, under the editorship of George Steevens of the London *Daily Mail*. And then the beleaguered burst into artistic life when Colonel Stoneman gave the first of his Shakespeare reading parties; it was argued that shell-fire intensified the literary sense. Truly Ladysmith was an outpost of the Empire.

The editor of The *Ladysmith Lyre* began his first issue with a statement of policy for his newspaper:

Prospectus: The *Ladysmith Lyre* is published to supply a long felt want. What you want in a besieged town, cut off from the world, is news which you can absolutely rely on as false. The rumours that pass from tongue to tongue may, for all you know, be occasionally true. Our news we guarantee to be false.

In the collection and preparation of falsehood, we shall spare no effort and no expense. It is enough for us that Ladysmith wants stories; it shall have them.

It is possible, however, even in the best regulated newspaper that some truths may unavoidably creep in. To save our readers the trouble of picking them out, these will be published in a special column by themselves. [The *True News – Up to the time of going to press* column was totally blank.] This division of news, into true and false, is an entirely new departure in the history of the public press. Whatever you read in the space devoted to truth, you may believe, or not, as you like.

Here is a selection of items from the first issue:

From our own Despondents: (By Wireless Telegraphy, London, November 5.) A shell from Long Tom burst in the War Office this afternoon. General Bracken-bury, Director General of Ordnance, accepted its arrival with resignation. Several reputations were seriously damaged. Unfortunately the Ordnance Committee was not sitting. A splinter broke into the Foreign Office and disturbed the siesta of the Prime Minister . . .

The artillery intended for the campaign in South Africa will be despatched as soon as the necessary ammunition has been received from the German factories . . .

The Second Army Corps has been discovered in the pigeon holes of the War Office . . .

Christmas puddings! Christmas puddings!!

Our Prize Competition: Do you want a Christmas pudding? You will! This is how you can get it.

This prize will be given for

The Most Miraculous Escape

from the shell fire of the enemy between the dates of November 2 and December 20. The competition will close on December 21st at 12 noon.

So if you want a Christmas pudding delay no longer. Go out and have a miraculous escape and send a description of it to the Editor of the *Ladysmith Lyre*.

Advertisements

(Personal) Pist: Return home at once. Everything forgiven. Paul.

If General Erasmus, or any duly authorised substitute, will call at Helpmakaar Hill (or Caesar's Camp, or Observation Hill, or Range Post, or Wagon Hill, or anywhere I could see him) at any time between the hours of 12.1 a.m. and 12 midnight, he will hear of something to his advantage. T. Atkins.

Publisher's Column

From Park Lane to Pretoria by Winston L. Spencer Churchill (in preparation).

Exchange and mart

Try Joubert's Hair Curlers. Hundreds of testimonials from the manager of the Royal Hotel, Mr Carter, prominent surgeons and others.

On 30 November from its new position, the Boer gun 'Long Tom' began to experiment with its range of fire. On that day it is believed that about one hundred shells were scattered over the small town. And they began to fall around the Town Hall which was still a military hospital. One shell burst in front of the building and was quickly followed by another that pierced the roof and exploded before reaching the ground. A soldier from the balloon section, who had only come into the hospital that day, was killed instantly and nine other patients were wounded.

This event made the British in Ladysmith very angry. A Natal Carabineer was heard to say: 'It's pure brutality, and may God Almighty help the first Boer who asks me for quarter.' This was all very fine, but who had caused the war and for what reasons? And do you place your military hospital in the very centre of a town that is under siege and subject to bombardment?

On this subject of root responsibility, H. W. Nevinson of the London *Daily Chronicle* reported a relevant conversation: ' "I tell you what," said a serious Tory soldier to me, "if English people saw this sort of thing, they'd hang that Chamberlain [The Tory Colonial Secretary]." "They won't hang him, but perhaps they'll make him a Lord," I answered . . .'

And 30 November was St Andrew's Day. Mr McHugh of the *Daily Telegraph* pondered the awfulness for Scotsmen in Ladysmith, without scotch whisky to drink and haggis to eat. But fortunately he met one of his nationality with formidable foresight:

One canny Scot of my acquaintance told me today as a dead secret, that he foresaw the terrible state of affairs that has arisen, and early in the siege he hid in a place, which no mortal man will wot of till to-morrow night, a supply of mountain dew sufficient to season haggis for half a dozen men . . . I trust we shall loyally celebrate the festival of Scotland's national saint.

Other Scots in Ladysmith reopened the battered Royal Hotel and celebrated as noisily as possible. But a dismal record was claimed for the occasion: that it was the only great Scottish gathering at which not one drop of the precious liquid was obtainable. With ginger-beer and Cape wine they did their best – but there was an awful bleak chasm.

Things were a bit better up in the lines of the Gordon Highlanders. Colonel Dick-Cunyngham was in the chair and they entertained their old

Colonel Sir George White. I believe whisky was handed about. Certainly the pipers marched around the table, playing Highland airs. Sir George exposed his generous nature by saying a few words on behalf of the Boers: 'In spite of appearances, I do not believe that the enemy have deliberately fired a single gun at our hospital in the Town-hall.' Captain Lambton of HMS *Powerful* availed himself of the freedom of the evening by replying, 'I don't agree with you, sir,' and it is written that there was 'a storm of approval' in support of the sailor's words. But few people in Ladysmith were as generous and kindly as Sir George White.

As the first month of siege ended, it was generally decided that things could be a lot worse. It was calculated that another month could pass before horses and rats would have to be eaten. Many food items were long finished; others had only recently ended, among them tinned meats, biscuits and jams. A new, dogged, second-wind determination was perhaps sensed; but on the other hand it was all beginning to hurt. H. W. Nevinson of the London *Daily Chronicle* had a conversation with a young officer: ' "I wish to Heaven the relief column would hurry up," sighed [the young man] to me. "Poor fellow," I thought, "he longs for the letters from his own true love." "You see, we can't get any more Quaker oats," he added in explanation.'

And on 30 November, the *Ladysmith Lyre* appeared again.

Leading Article The situation: The situation is unchanged.

Here are the first and last verses of an anonymous nine-verse poem:

The Poet under the River Bank

Wake for above Bulwan the coming day
Lights up the signal for the guns to play;
    How sweet to know 'tis but a living tomb
Awaits you, and there's time to creep away.

So when the peace shall find me safe and well,
'Twill be a further joy each night to tell
    How many a bullet nearly touched the spot –
And in my window place an empty shell.

Extracts from a Diary Of A Citizen.

November 19: Seems Buller went up Table Mountain to plan defences of Cape Town in case of Boer attack. Thick fog came down, and Buller not been seen since.

November 20: Misfortunes never come singly. HMS *Powerful* ran aground in attempting to come up Klip River; feared total loss.

November 26: Boer broke Sabbath, firing on our bathing parties. Believe they so infuriated by sight of people washing that quite forgot it was Sunday.

Localities

We are informed that the Colony of Natal is safe. Then 'God Save the Queen'.

Whisky is selling at thirty-five shillings a bottle. The Army Service Corps are waiting until the price is two pounds before disposing of the eleven thousand bottles in stock . . .

Major Blewitt and other artillery experts are anxious to inform their friends that fuses of live shells are removed with the utmost ease. All that is required is a sledge hammer and a coffin.

It was the last day of the month. About midnight that strange light from south of the Tugela stumbled a word over a starlit sky. Three times the word was repeated: 'Ladysmith'. The words were in cypher. Cumbersome words were 'called', but they were difficult to recognize – except the last two: 'Buller, Maritzburg', which was repeated twice. Ladysmith now knew that Buller was in Natal.

7

THE RELIEVING FORCE
November 1899

*No smoking, no talking, no firing – nothing but the
bayonet.*

ORDERS AT BRYNBELLA HILL

T H E *Dunottar Castle* had arrived at Cape Town on the night of 30 October
1899, but Sir Redvers Buller stayed aboard until the next morning. Winston
Churchill described the debarkation:

> Sir Redvers Buller landed in state. Sir F. Forestier-Walker and his staff came to
> meet him. The ship was decked out in bunting from end to end. A guard of honour
> of the Duke of Edinburgh's Volunteers lined the quay; a mounted escort attended
> the carriage; an enormous crowd gathered outside the docks. At nine o'clock
> precisely the General stepped onto the gangway. The crew and stokers of the
> *Dunottar Castle* gave three hearty cheers; the cinematograph buzzed loudly;
> forty cameras clicked; the guard presented arms, and the harbour batteries thundered
> the salute ... So Sir Redvers Buller came back again to South Africa, the land where
> his first military reputation was made, where he won his Victoria Cross [Zulu War,
> 1879], the land which – let us pray – he will leave having successfully discharged
> the heavy task confided to him by the Imperial Government.

Sir Redvers hurried to consult with the High Commissioner, Sir Alfred
Milner, with the Prime Minister of the Cape Colony, Mr Schreiner, the Naval
commander-in chief and the General Officer Commanding in Cape Colony,
Lieut-General Sir F. Forestier-Walker; and great crowds hysterically
cheered him on his way. The truth is that a large proportion of the inhabitants of Cape Town were panic-stricken. Buller to them was security personified. From the civil and military authority he heard, for the first time,
all that had happened in southern Africa since he left England. In Cape
Colony, Mafeking and Kimberley were besieged, and General Sir George

White's force in Natal was falling back and centring around Ladysmith.

There were three telegrams from Sir George White. The first, dated 28 October, stated: 'Have a very strong force in front of me with many guns. Natal Colony requires earliest reinforcements possible. Troops here very heavy work, especially Cavalry. I will do all my means admit of to conquer enemy. Very short of Staff and officers. Hunter indispensable.'

Though the worst – the siege of Ladysmith – had not yet begun, those words must have penetrated deep into General Buller. Sir George White had the only large body of British troops in South Africa, including just about the entire mounted force – and here he was, asking for reinforcements. But Buller, with only 4000 soldiers, hoped to hold the entire southern border separating the Cape Colony from the Orange Free State about 430 miles long. On top of that, the British colonial country around this small force was heavily populated by Dutch people, deeply sympathetic to the Boer cause. Not one of those British soldiers in the Cape could be spared for Natal.

Of the two sieges in that western theatre of the war, Mafeking, under the entertaining Baden-Powell, asked for nothing. Mafeking seemed to be looking after its own problems and having a laugh as well. But Kimberley, in the person of Cecil Rhodes, was making loud, threatening demands. The officer commanding Kimberley, Colonel Kekewich, behaved in a cool and soldierly manner, but it was the arrogant imperialist Rhodes who was making dangerous noises.

The next two telegrams were those that Sir George White had sent on 30 October and they ended with the news of the failure of the battle of Ladysmith and the awful loss of the Royal Irish Fusiliers, the Gloucestershire Regiment, and No. 10 Mountain Battery, on and around Kainguba Heights. But none of the telegrams suggested that events were so bad that a siege of Ladysmith was even a possibility.

Sir Redvers Buller, whatever his inner feelings were, read and heard the nerve-straining news with his customary impassiveness – the same stolid John Bull demeanour that he wore when great crowds cheered. So he exchanged the messages with Sir George White which culminated in the definite statement that a siege of Sir George's entire force in Ladysmith was inevitable: '. . . I intend to contain as many Boers as I can round Ladysmith, . . . I could not now withdraw from it . . .'

And so General Buller was compelled to readjust his original strategic theories of the great army corps advance through the Orange Free State. It was clear that the main Boer assault was being made on Natal and it was clear that White's army was trapped. What should Buller do? To protect the Colony of Natal south of the Tugela river, which included the capital Pietermaritzburg and the great port of Durban, were a mere 2000 soldiers, made up of the Royal Dublin Fusiliers at Colenso and the Border Regiment at Durban, plus one mountain battery. In command of this force was Colonel Wolfe-Murray and he was instructed to abandon Pietermaritzburg, if necessary – and only fight to hold the port of Durban.

Buller weighed up all the factors available to him and heard the political demands from both the Cape and Natal. High Commissioner Milner, having started the war, seems to have been confused by events and kept relatively quiet. On 10 November, after coping with a political delay as to whether the Orange Free State forces would or would not invade the Cape (they did), Buller telegraphed to England for an extra division of troops to be sent to South Africa, with all speed.

Buller now knew that about three to four thousand Boers had already crossed the Tugela river, south of Ladysmith in Natal, and were moving further south. The Royal Dublin Fusiliers had withdrawn from their exposed position at Colenso to Estcourt on 3 November and were now being joined by about 1000 Natal volunteers, bringing the combined British force up to 3000. At that time and for some days to come, Natal was wide open to the Boer forces, if they chose to take it. All Buller could do was to hope that miraculously nothing would happen, and to do his best.

On the day General Buller arrived in Cape Town he started raising two regiments of mounted infantry from South African volunteers: Brabant's Horse and the South African Light Horse. Now, later in the month, he had made what military decisions he could and was about to put them into operation. He organized a column under Lord Methuen for the relief of Kimberley, General French was sent to Colesburg to hold the centre of the Cape–Free State border, and General Gatacre was to do what he could further east along that border. By 20 November Buller was preparing to leave Cape Town for Natal and next day he composed a despatch of his decisions for the Secretary of State for War, Lord Lansdowne, in London:

Troops are slowly gathering in Natal. General Hildyard, with his whole Brigade, is at Estcourt. The last two battalions of General Barton's Brigade, and General Lyttelton with the 2nd battalion of his Brigade, left Cape Town for Durban the night of the 19th. Except, perhaps, the 1st Rifle Brigade, it seems likely to be some days before we get more Infantry.

The position in Natal is not a nice one. We are too short of mounted men. The Boers hold a strong position about 15 miles west of Estcourt, near the Tabanhlope Mountain, with about 3000 men, and have 800 at Weenen, . . . and they have about 1000 on the Blaaukrantz River north of Frere. I am not as strong in Natal as I should like to be . . .

I am in daily communication with General Clery [then commanding in Natal], who is doing well . . .

There are no more troops expected till the end of this week or early next.

Sir Redvers Buller was splitting his army corps as it landed in Africa, but what else could he do ? He had decided that he himself must lead the great confrontation in Natal. He left Cape Town on 22 November and landed at Durban three days later.

After the siege of Ladysmith had commenced, the new young Boer leader, Louis Botha, had managed to persuade the old conservative leader, Commandant-General Joubert, to invade Natal south of the Tugela river. Botha was given command of nearly 4000 mounted Boers, though Joubert decided to come along as well, presumably to keep an eye on Botha's youthful inventiveness. This force passed through Colenso, on the southern side of the river, and by 14 November, Boer patrols were in the vicinity of the British forward position of Estcourt.

On the day before the West Yorkshire Regiment had arrived in Estcourt and on 14 November two 12-pounder guns and one 7-pounder had arrived from HMS *Tartar* together with twenty-five sailors. Indeed, as each day arrived, so the British in Natal got that bit stronger; the weight of power was beginning to shift perceptibly away from the Boers.

At this time, Colonel Wolfe-Murray, who had been in command at Estcourt, was in Pietermaritzburg, supervising the arrival of General Hildyard's brigade and in his place, holding temporary command, was Colonel Long, Royal Artillery, a regular blood-and-guts man.

The only aggressive British gesture, during this keep-your-fingers-crossed period, was an almost daily armoured train expedition, which puffed up the railway northward towards Colenso. I am sure I don't have to explain to any reader why this was a highly hazardous jaunt . . . Pull up the railway line behind the train and where would it be ? Indeed the soldiers were well aware of its dangers and called the train 'Wilson's death trap'.

Winston Churchill was in Estcourt by 6 November. He had hoped to get to Ladysmith before it was invested, but failing this, he had pushed forward as far north as possible. On 8 November, ever inquisitive, he had travelled with this armoured train to within half a mile of Colenso, and had viewed, without Boer opposition, the looted village, deserted except for a few black Africans. On 9 November, back in Estcourt, he had listened to the thudding of distant guns up Ladysmith way; this was the abortive Boer attack.

Also in Estcourt was Captain A. Haldane DSO, an officer of the Gordon Highlanders who had been wounded at the battle of Elandslaagte, and so was not in Ladysmith. On the evening of 14 November, Captain Haldane was warned that he would command the armoured train the following day and he has written about his reaction to that news: 'Up to this time . . . I had not had to take out the armoured train, which was one only in name and had been extemporised by the railway workshops, but from what I had heard officers say who had had that experience I cannot confess that I received the warning to do so with pleasure.'

By that date reports had come in to the British that Boer patrols had been seen even within a few miles of Estcourt, which intensified the bleak atmosphere about the proposed train ride for the following day. Captain Haldane, knowing this, set off for Colonel Long's brigade office in a depressed state, thinking about the loud puffing noise the engine made on steep gradients – of which there were many – and what an advertising sound this would be for any Boers that might be cantering in the vicinity.

However Colonel Long was as keen as mustard about the morrow's trip. Captain Haldane has inscribed: '. . . he told me, as if he were lavishing a favour, that besides my company of the Dublin Fusiliers he was giving me another of the Durban Light Infantry, a volunteer unit, and a 7-pounder gun, with its detachment from HMS *Tartar*.'

Colonel Long went on to explain to Captain Haldane that his duty would be to 'reconnoitre with caution' towards Colenso. Captain Haldane allowed himself to think that one man on horseback could do that job probably more efficiently – and would avoid the risk of losing perhaps 300 men.

As Captain Haldane came out of Colonel Long's office, he noticed Winston Churchill, as he wrote, 'hanging about' with some other newspaper correspondents. Captain Haldane went up to the young journalist:

I told him what I had been ordered to do and, aware that he had been out in the train and knew something of the country through which it was wont to travel, suggested that he might care to accompany me next day. Although he was not at all keen he consented to do so, and arranged to be at the station in time for the start . . .

Next morning, before leaving my tent, having a presentiment of coming evil, I told my servant to pack up my things and take care of them in my absence.

Captain Haldane and his soldiers and sailors gathered around the armoured train in the early morning darkness and Winston Churchill turned up, as he had promised. At 5.30 a.m. the train steamed off. The 7-pounder gun, manned by the men from HMS *Tartar*, was in the leading truck and behind that was the first armoured wagon, full of Dublin Fusiliers; then came the locomotive, followed by two more armoured wagons, one of which was full of more Dublin Fusiliers together with soldiers of the Durban Light Infantry, and lastly came a low truck, packed with tools and other equipment for repairing the railway track. The men in this last conveyance were platelayers and a telegraphist with his equipment. Haldane and Churchill decided to travel in the leading gun truck.

Cautiously they puffed their way to Frere station and there met a small patrol of Natal Police who told them that there were no Boers within the next few miles. This news they telegraphed back to Colonel Long, at Estcourt.

Captain Haldane decided that they would risk pushing on to Chieveley. All was clear on this lap, but as the train reached Chieveley station, Winston Churchill saw '. . . about a hundred Boer horsemen cantering southwards about a mile from the railway. Beyond Chieveley, a long hill was lined with a row of black spots, showing that our further advance would be disputed.'

The telegraphist wired back to Colonel Long in Estcourt this information, and the Colonel replied: 'Remain at Frere in observation guarding your safe retreat. Remember that Chieveley station was last night occupied by the enemy. Do not put faith in information obtained from native sources.'

They couldn't put much faith in information obtained from the Colonel either; he had failed to tell them until now that Chieveley had been occupied by the Boers the night before.

Captain Haldane began to question himself as to why on earth he had penetrated so far northward, under these uncomfortable circumstances. He came to the conclusion that 'I do not wish to lay blame on anyone but myself, but had I been alone and not had my impetuous young friend Churchill with me, who in many things was prompted by Danton's motto, "de l'audace, et encore de l'audace et toujours de l'audace", I might have thought twice before throwing myself into the lion's jaws by going almost to the Tugela. But I was carried away by his ardour . . .'

Anyway, Haldane now gave the order to the engine driver to retreat and no one was arguing with him!

The first part of the retreat was uneventful and, as Captain Haldane wrote, 'I think that I and my companions felt rather elated as the pace grew faster and faster . . .' Then about a mile and three-quarters from Frere, rounding a corner of the track, the occupants of the train noted that a hill about 600 yards ahead of them and commanding the line, was occupied by waiting Boers.

The four sailors loaded their 'antiquated toy', as Winston Churchill described it, and the soldiers loaded their rifles. But Churchill claims that at this stage no one on the train was 'much concerned', because the armour plating on the wagons was bullet-proof and Churchill confessed to some glee: ' "Besides," we said to ourselves, "they little think we have a gun on board. That will be a nice surprise." '

Churchill stood on a box in one of the armoured trucks and through his binoculars got an excellent view of the Boer position. Suddenly 'three wheeled things appeared on the crest, and within a second a bright flash of light . . . opened and shut ten or twelve times . . . Then came the explosions . . . The Boers had opened fire on us at 600 yards with two large field guns, a Maxim firing small shells in a stream, and from riflemen lying on the ridge. I got down from my box . . .'

From An Active Army Alphabet

The train driver reacted as the Boers hoped he would. He slapped on full steam and the armoured train leapt forward, tearing round the curve of the hill, and then hurtling down the gradient on the other side – 'and dashed into a huge stone which awaited it on the line at a convenient spot'.

The leading break-down truck was lifted high into the air, with its occupants, and landed upside down on the embankment. The next armour-plated wagon, packed with Durban Light Infantry, ploughed on for about twenty yards and ended up on its side, throwing the soldiers about like confetti. The next got stuck on the railway track 'half on and half off'. The rest of the train, including the locomotive, miraculously remained on the rails.

And then Churchill wrote one of my favourite sentences in all literature: 'We were not long left in the comparative peace and safety of a railway accident.' The Boers swung their heavy guns round and started pummelling the train-wreck. The sailors managed to fire three rounds from their 7-pounder before the Boers scored a hit and the gun actually fell out of the wagon. It was a very hot spot!

Captain Haldane wrote:

> For a few seconds I was so dazed by the suddenness of the crash that the power of collecting my thoughts to decide what had best be done deserted me, but Churchill, quick witted and cool, was speedily on his feet. He volunteered to see what the situation was, and soon he returned with the suggestion that if I could keep in check the fire from the Boer guns and rifles . . . he thought he might manage to get the line cleared. As my association with him had only been military, I naturally regarded him from that point of view. I knew him well enough to realise that he was not the man to stand quietly by and look on in a critical situation . . . I therefore gladly accepted Churchill's offer . . .

The Boers pounded the shambles with every missile they had. Though the bullets rarely penetrated the insides of the armoured wagons, which were slitted for returning fire, the shells had no such difficulty. Churchill noted that four shells penetrated one wagon, but did not explode until they had passed out through the farther side.

Churchill's problem of clearing the line, under this devastating fire, was formidable. But no one present has even hinted that he hesitated for a second. The first problem was to detach the wagon partly off the rails from the one completely off. The driver of the locomotive had taken precarious shelter behind armour plating and Churchill argued with him to return to his cab. The man was outraged. 'He was a civilian. What did they think he was paid for? To be killed by bombshells? Not he. He would not stay another minute.'

Young Churchill debated with him. 'Yet when I told this man that if he continued to stay at his post he would be mentioned for distinguished gallantry in action, he pulled himself together, wiped the blood off his face, climbed back into the cab of his engine, and thereafter during the one-sided combat did his duty bravely and faithfully – so strong is the desire for honour and repute in the human breast.' I have been told that years later, Winston Churchill used his influence and secured for this engine-driver an award for gallantry.

Of course, Churchill underrates his own contribution. Not only did the young man inspire the driver, but he inspired soldiers to come out into the open with him, to assist in the work.

They managed to uncouple the partly derailed wagon, and then the locomotive pulled it back clear of the wreckage; finally it had to be thrown clear by human strength. Churchill called for volunteers to do this pushing, while under aim from Boer artillery and rifle fire. Nine men were prepared to sacrifice their lives to assist the young man in his daring scheme. With the aid of a little shoving from the engine they succeeded. All seemed, unbelievably, successful. But not quite. As the engine moved forward on its first few feet towards safety, the tender and a corner of the footplate caught a corner of the newly overturned wagon. The engine drew back a few feet and jabbed forward. And then again and again. The more it was done, the more the wagon became wedged. Then an attempt was made to loosen the obstruction by coupling the wagon to the engine and easing it backwards – but the wedging was not overcome. Winston Churchill wrote:

I have had, in the last four years, the advantage, if it be an advantage, of many strange and varied experiences, from which the student of realities might draw profit and instruction. But nothing was so thrilling as this: to wait and struggle among these clanging, rending iron boxes, with the repeated explosions of the shells and the artillery, the noise of the projectiles striking the cars, the hiss as they passed in the air . . . all this for seventy minutes by the clock with only four inches of twisted iron work to make the difference between danger, captivity, and shame on the one hand – safety, freedom, and triumph on the other.

The locomotive continued to hit the wrecked wagon. The Boers poured in more fire-power. Churchill was afraid that the engine would itself become derailed. And then a shell struck the front of the locomotive, setting the wooden parts alight. That was too much for the driver. He pulled the train, turned full steam on and charged. There was a deafening collision and a great shuddering and then to the accompaniment of tearing metal, the train broke through. Chieveley lay clear ahead!

But not for everyone. Looking behind, it was seen that the wagons had not followed the locomotive. Perhaps a shell had severed the couplings. Efforts were made to pull the wagons through, but in the terrible circumstances it was impossible.

Captain Haldane described what it was like inside the armoured wagons, while Churchill's efforts were under way:

It crossed my mind that our situation was comparable to what it would be if under fire of rifles at one hundred yards' range, while packed inside a large biscuit tin . . .

Suddenly I heard Churchill's voice and I climbed out of the wagon and joined him near the engine, which looked to me as if it were in a bad way, for flames were issuing from the fire-box and volumes of steam pouring out from other parts of it.

Haldane and Churchill decided to get the wounded on to the engine, 'standing in the cab, lying on the tender, or clinging to the cow-catcher'. The locomotive would also have to travel slowly, so giving the unwounded soldiers a chance to take cover on the far side of it, away from the Boer gunfire.

As the battered object puffed and smoked and groaned away, Maxim shells hit it time and time again, rewounding some of the suffering soldiers.

Poor Captain Haldane, with his old leg-wound from the battle of Elandslaagte, couldn't keep pace with the locomotive, so he heaved himself aboard. No sooner had he managed that, than someone trampled on his clinging hand and he fell off and was left behind while 'bullets and shells were striking the ground all around. I was feeling desperate at the hopeless situation into which my haste had brought me, and I prayed fervently that one of the bullets would come my way and put an end to the business.'

Captain Haldane hobbled along the track in a southward direction and then to his horror he saw a group of British soldiers on a bridge ahead, 'and white handkerchiefs being waved'. He hurried forward, as best he could, then suddenly:

. . . rifles were pointed at me and a voice shouted, 'Put down your arms!' Having nothing in my hand but a walking-stick I replied, 'I have no arms.' The rifles were at once lowered and the next thing that happened was that I was seized by a stalwart Boer who tried to wrench from me my Zeiss glasses. As I was resisting, someone called out, 'Better let him have them or he'll shoot you!' So discretion took the better part of valour and they fell to him as his share of the plunder.

Winston Churchill had travelled away on the burning locomotive but when it reached some houses where he and Captain Haldane had thought a possible stand could be made by the surviving soldiers, he jumped off. He looked round for the escaping British soldiers so that he could rally them, but there was not one to be seen. At this point he was unaware that they had surrendered. Suddenly two men appeared at the far end of a cutting, through which the locomotive had come:

'Platelayers,' I said to myself, and then, with a surge of realisation, 'Boers.' My mind retains a momentary impression of these tall figures, full of animated movement, clad in dark flapping clothes, with slouch, storm-driven hats poising on their rifles hardly a hundred yards away. I turned and ran between the rails of the track, and the only thought I achieved was this, 'Boer marksmanship.' Two bullets passed, both within a foot, one on either side ... Another glance at the figures; one was now kneeling to aim. Again I darted forward. Movement seemed the only chance. Again two soft hisses sucked in the air, but nothing struck me.

Winston ran for it, but finally he was cornered:

Should I continue to fly? The idea of another shot at such a short range decided me ... So I held up my hand, and like Mr Jorrocks's foxes, cried 'Copivy'. Then I was herded with the other prisoners in a miserable group, and about the same time I noticed that my hand was bleeding, and it began to pour with rain.

As Winston Churchill and Captain Haldane were marched away in the general direction of a place of imprisonment in Pretoria, their moods were very different, as the Captain has recorded:

At this time we were all feeling, not unnaturally, very disconsolate, but Churchill must have been cheered by the thought, which he communicated to me, that what had taken place, though it had caused the temporary loss of his post as war correspondent, would help considerably in opening the door for him to enter the House of Commons.

Commandant-General Joubert himself took an interest in young Winston. He despatched a telegram to his government:

T.D. ZAR 21.11.1899. From Commandant-General, H.Q. Ladysmith

To Government, Pretoria, begins:

19.11.99. I understand that the son of Lord Churchill claims to be nothing more than a press correspondent and as such entitled to release. From a newspaper dated the . . . [Memo Telegraph Dept.: No date filled in here] his status appears something totally different. Thus I deem it advisable that he be guarded and regarded as one potentially dangerous to our war effort. In short, he must be imprisoned for the duration of hostilities. It was through his active participation that a part of the armoured train escaped – ends.

A famous young Boer hero named Danie Theron put the hat on it for Winston's hopes of an easy release:

T.D. ZAR 28.11.1899 From Captain Theron, i/c Dispatch-riders, Colenso

To Secretary of State, Pretoria, begins:

I beg to inform you that on the 17th inst. full reports have appeared in the *Natal Witness* and *Natal Mercury* of the active and prominent part played by the press correspondent Winston Churchill in the fight with the armoured train at Frere station. When the officers were in difficulties Churchill called for volunteers and was their leader. According to the *Volkstern* and *Standard and Diggers News* he now declares he took no part in the fight. This is a pack of lies; nor would he stand still when warned by Field-Cornet Oosthuizen to surrender or do so till covered by the latter's rifle. In my opinion he is one of the most dangerous prisoners in our hands. The Natal papers make a great hero of him – ends.

When the Bishop of Natal heard about the armoured train incident, he wrote in his diary that 'We are far too innocent for these wily Boers.'

But the ambushing of the armoured train had consolidated a new hero for England. The Honourable Canon of Carlisle, H. D. Rawnsley MA celebrated him in a ballad:

To WINSTON CHURCHILL – Estcourt, November 15 1899

Not yet the Blenheim seed
Has failed us at our need,
   Still does the name of Churchill ring like gold,
Whether at Omdurman
A warrior in the van,
   Or where the Estcourt ridges are uprolled.
He, having just ungirt his sword, took pen
To fight as brave for us home-staying men.

There, when the armoured train
Was wrecked, and fast as rain
   Boer bullets fell on our devoted band,
Did not this swordless one
Remember great deeds done,
   And, hero, call on heroes all to stand?
Did he not clear the wreckage, rails relay,
And speed the wounded on their homeward way?

Yea, and with lion-heart
Did he not backward start,

Clutch rifle, turn again to face the foe,
To fight – if need be, fall –
For country, Queen, and all
   That made him great those many years ago?
Ah! Churchill, let the thanks of Britain be
The balm and calm of your captivity.

After the Boers had marched their prisoners away, they, as always when given a chance, reverently buried the dead. The 'armoured train' grave is by the side of the railway and I have visited that strange atmosphere. But it was in the burying of these British dead at that place that one of the ugliest legends of the whole war was born. A legend that grew until it was believed by many British soldiers that Boers made a practice of burying their adversaries alive. The most balanced British account of that event, that I have read, was chronicled by Corporal Haydn of the 1st Durham Light Infantry, in a letter to his parents who were living in Northampton:

The poor fellows killed are buried close by. We have cemented their bodies over and fixed empty cartridge cases in the cement with their names in memory. [The cartridges cases are there to this day.] There is one lonely grave by itself. A poor fellow of the Dublins had his leg shot off, and it is supposed he crawled away, and the Boers buried him alive, for afterwards he was found with his other leg out of the ground. And when we dug up his body he was found to be clutching the ground with both hands. Our doctor said he could not have lived, and the Boers doubtless thought him dead, so we don't blame them for it.

This story then degenerates as the weeks go by. On 28 December, Private John Maker of the 2nd Lancashire Regiment wrote a later version:

The Boers did a dirty act at the last fight the Dublins were in. After the fight they went round the battlefield and stripped all the dead and wounded of their boots and socks and any money or anything they had on them. One fellow who was not so badly wounded refused to give them up, so they dug a grave about two feet deep and put him in alive, and covered him in. He got out again, and they kicked him in again, and covered him over with bags of dirt and big stones, and left him there.

Having settled the armoured train business, Louis Botha was anxious to press down into Natal; Commandant-General Joubert was uneasily at his coat-tails. Botha, with enormous confidence, because the British were already numerically superior, split his 4000 burghers into three parts. One column, under himself and Joubert, bypassed Estcourt to the west and another column bypassed it to the east. The third group stayed to the north of Estcourt and prodded in a threatening way.

However, the Boers were not quite quick enough. On 16 November, General Hildyard and his staff got into Estcourt, together with the 2nd Queen's and the 2nd East Surrey Regiments. And next day the 7th Field Battery and Bethune's Mounted Infantry squeezed in. Also on that day the West Yorkshire Regiment and some mounted troops moved south of Estcourt to a place called Willow Grange, for the purpose of hopefully keeping in touch with the next British base at Mooi river, a little further down the railway line.

But Botha pincered round all this, and his two converging forces joined and dominated Mooi river from the railway line north of that place. Estcourt was now virtually isolated. In Mooi river, the British force was building up to a formidable degree. On 16 November the 2nd Royal Irish Fusiliers had arrived and on the 18th General Barton was there with the 1st Royal Welch Fusiliers and Thorneycroft's Mounted Infantry. The 19th saw the arrival of the 14th Battery RFA and on the 20th the 2nd Devonshire Regiment had arrived. Botha with his 4000 horsemen was a cool customer!

During these few days there was mass cattle-raiding by the Boers, and rather nervous skirmishing by both sides. What settled a positive action was the discovery by the British that the Boers had placed a gun on Brynbella Hill, about six miles south-south-west of Estcourt, in the vicinity of Willow Grange. General Hildyard didn't fancy being shelled, so decided to have a go.

It was to be a night attack and the enterprise was under the command of Colonel F. W. Kitchener, brother of Kitchener of Khartoum. He took with him his own West Yorks, seven companies of the East Surreys and four companies of the Queen's and of the Durban Light Infantry. Artillery comprised the 7th Field Battery and the ubiquitous Royal Navy 7-pounder. They moved out of Estcourt on the afternoon of 22 November and before daybreak of the 23rd, five companies of the Border Regiment and the mounted troops left to join them as supports. It teemed with tropical rain. The force got to about 5000 yards north of the Boer position on Brynbella Hill, and at that point General Hildyard joined Colonel Kitchener and took over the command of the operation.

Kitchener with his West Yorks and the East Surreys were to carry out the actual night attack, and once on top, Hildyard would co-operate tactically and then they intended to drive the Boers into Barton's force down Mooi river way. That was the general theory.

Just before sunset, some British soldiers showed themselves on the skyline and the Boer gun fired. The British naval gun replied like a reflex and it looked as if the night attack would no longer be a surprise. Indeed, one of the purposes of the operation was to capture the Boer gun. In view of the artillery exchange, and sensing that something was afoot, the Boers very wisely removed their gun at 2 a.m.

The rain-storm renewed its strength and every soldier was drenched to the skin. Indeed one Boer and several horses were killed by lightning that night.

Just after 11 p.m. Colonel Kitchener took his two battalions towards the base of Brynbella and there a most unfortunate accident took place. In an understandably miserable but nervous state, the East Surreys mistook some West Yorks for Boers, and not only fired into them but used the bayonet. Several were wounded. Whether the Boers heard this fracas above the thunder and the pelting rain is not clear. Anyway up Brynbella went the British, led by Major Hobbs of the West Yorks. A Sergeant Woodhouse from Methley wrote that a 'cold chill' passed over him when he first heard the command: 'Fix bayonets!' And then he recalled that Colonel Kitchener clapped him on the shoulder and said: 'Now lads, give them a bit of Yorkshire!' Instructions were spoken along the ranks: 'No smoking, no talking, no firing – nothing but the bayonet.'

They got to the crest and were challenged by a surprised sentry. The order to use only the bayonet was promptly broken. The British fired a volley and advertised their presence further by cheering. This warning gave the Boers sufficient time to hurry back some 1500 yards to a dominating ridge, where they took up their new position. There were only 150 Orange Free Staters and fifty Johannesburg Police. All the British captured were some still-warm blankets and the odd mug of coffee.

The arrival of the British at the crest of Brynbella Hill was described by a corporal in the East Surrey Regiment: 'We had to rest about a dozen times, going from rock to rock, and we got about twenty yards from the top when we were challenged by a sentry in pure English, "Halt! who comes there?" when one of the West Yorks shouted out, "Half of old England, you ——", and put a bullet into him . . . '

As dawn came Colonel Kitchener placed a forward firing line of his West Yorks behind boulders, withdrawing the rest behind a wall. But by this time, the Boers, fully warned, were reinforced by Louis Botha himself and the Krugersdorp Commando with two field guns and a quick-firing 'pom-pom'.

Louis Botha and his burghers began to attack. For the first two hours they crept forward and began to envelop the British from both sides of the hill; the Boer guns converged their fire on the British. There was no effective reply from the British artillery. At 9 a.m. Kitchener decided that his position was hopeless and ordered the withdrawal. As they hurried away, the Boers manhandled the very gun that the British had planned to capture back into its original place and shelled the retreating soldiers.

The total forces in this battle, of whom only a small minority were actively engaged, were 2000 Boers and 5000 British. The British casualties were sixteen killed and over sixty wounded, mainly West Yorks. Major Hobbs and seven of his soldiers were taken prisoner because they stayed on to tend the wounded.

Louis Botha sent his report back to Pretoria:

The Infantry [British] was about two thousand strong. On reaching the top they gave loud 'Hurrahs!' and yelled 'Majuba is now avenged', while we maintained a heavy and steady fire on them. We had two men killed at this stage.

... Under cover of [our] guns we [the Krugersdorp Commando] reformed with the Free Staters and the Police and stormed the position held by the English troops and drove them off with apparent heavy loss. They retreated in disorder towards Estcourt. The engagement was very hot. Ambulance reports to me were that the British losses were 120 killed and wounded. Our losses were one killed and four wounded – Krugersdorp men. My horse was shot from under me.

But at last the tide had turned, formidably, against the Boers. Both the British force to the north at Estcourt and the force to the south at Mooi river were very much larger than Louis Botha's army of burghers, victoriously wedged between. Boer scouts reported to Joubert and Botha that more troop trains and naval guns had arrived at Mooi river on 24 November. On top of all that, the Tugela river was beginning to run full. What if the British found the initiative to get behind them and blow up Colenso bridge and the drifts were too deep for passage?

Botha simply wanted to forget the vast numbers of enemy soldiers congregating around him; he wanted to take his 4000 straight at Pietermaritzburg and then on to Durban. Perhaps the hour for a sweeping Boer victory was gone, but not in Louis Botha's mind. However the Boer army was, at this time, a totally democratic affair and no one could dictate. A *Krygsraad* (a Council-of-War) was called on 24 November and Botha was overruled. Commandant-General Joubert was not in a happy state of mind. He hated the deaths, and just at this time the old man had been thrown from his horse and had sustained internal injuries. It was decided that the Boers would withdraw to the northern side of the Tugela river and there would await with their other comrades the worst that Buller and this great impending army could do against them.

As late as 25 November the Boers were even firing artillery at Thorneycroft's Mounted Infantry around Mooi river. But the main body of Boers was moving northward. Their herds of looted cattle and waggons stretched from Mooi river to Weenen! By 27 November the whole expedition had crossed the Tugela river, mainly at Colenso. A great cavalcade had lumbered northward unmolested, and one should really ask 'Why?'

An angry British citizen living in Scottsfontein, Natal, wrote on 7 December 1899 to the London *Times*:

For four days 650 Boers held a track of country with a frontage roughly 25 miles either way, and held it at their leisure, raiding cattle, driving about with traps and horses, mule-waggons, etc., picking up what they wanted; killing time buck shooting and guinea-fowl shooting – all this with 13 000 British troops within eight and ten miles of their main camp on either side of them.

Ideally, General Buller would have liked to have stayed in Cape Town and to have directed the campaign he had planned, advancing through the Orange Free State from that central position – and, of course, there would have been no qualms from Britain about his doing that, if expedience demanded. He could have remained in Cape Town, awaiting the arrival of his battalions from the Empire and hoping that the Boers would not show too much aggressive initiative, while leaving the awful problems of Natal to Generals Clery, Lyttelton, and Hildyard. But this senior trio asked Buller to take personal command and he was, perhaps uneasily, persuaded; they always found it extremely difficult to *see* what he really felt, behind that rather blank, enigmatic, stoical face.

Also, of the three generals, only Lyttelton had had any recent field service experience; he had commanded a brigade at the battle of Omdurman (Sudan War, 1898). The other two had not seen active fighting since the Egyptian Campaign of 1882, when they were both junior staff officers. Of course, as we have already noted, Buller had very strong reservations about holding an independent command, which, let us remind ourselves, he had never done before. But he was holding one now, and was on the very eve of exercising that sobering authority. And, of course, we should also not forget that as commander-in-chief, he was totally responsible for the separate campaign way over to the west on the Cape–Orange Free State front. But about that front, because of the emergency in Natal, he had to delegate responsibility. Faced with the now obvious perils of fighting these Boers on the African terrain that they understood so well and according to their own ideas of warfare, he could not have been boundlessly confident about the immediate outcome. And I wonder if it entered his strange mind that if he failed, he could be superseded by another soldier? But who? That was an uneasy question; senior army officers were a small, not always friendly, club . . .

One other little worry: Sir George White in Ladysmith was senior to the other three generals apart from Buller, and should Ladysmith be successfully relieved by them, Sir George would normally take over the general command. Buller felt, particularly after the battle of Ladysmith on 30 October, that Sir George was not up to that overall responsibility. And Buller had been given the sort of diplomatic sanction (not exactly an order) that he could replace Sir George White by General Hunter, who, of course, was with him in Ladysmith. But this act Buller could not have borne to do.

Buller has been criticized for leaving his military staff in the Cape. This is unfair; someone had to run the Cape show. And, of course, his original choice of staff, including his much needed chief-of-staff, General Hunter, were trapped in Ladysmith. He has also been severely criticized by high authorities, such as L. S. Amery in *The Times History of the War in South Africa*, because he 'neither took counsel nor informed others of his intention' to move to Natal. This cannot be fair to Buller. He must have discussed the matter with Alfred Milner, because the High Commissioner begged him to stay in the Cape. And he must have discussed it with the generals Clery, Lyttelton and Hildyard, because they begged him to go – to Natal. With whom else should he have discussed it?

On 26 November, Buller was in Pietermaritzburg, and wrote to the Secretary of State for War, Lord Lansdowne, back in London:

> The situation in Natal has improved in the last twenty-four hours. On the night 22nd–23rd General Hildyard from Estcourt attacked the force of the enemy, who were camped on his communications, with a force of about three battalions and a battery [the battle of Willow Grange]. I have no particulars of the fight other than the information I am sending by telegram to-day. There are rumours that it was not an entire tactical success. I don't know how that may be, but it certainly seems to have been an entire strategical success. The Boers evacuated their position . . . There are about 13 200 men, including three batteries RFA and four naval 12-pr. guns at Mooi river and to the north of it.

General Buller then went on to enumerate the additional troops that were landing at that time and to discuss the military fortunes at the Cape, which were cheering up a bit. He then continued:

In this Colony [Natal] I anticipate the enemy will make a final assault on Ladysmith and think they are concentrating for that purpose. If they do not succeed, and I do not see why they should, I think their disheartenment, of which we already hear some tidings, will become more acute . . . I have extraordinarily little news of Ladysmith, but it was all well on the 22nd.

General Clery had been in command of the British military in Natal until the arrival of General Buller, and had laid the groundwork for the organization of the Natal Field Force – but it was only the barest groundwork. Buller stayed in Pietermaritzburg for the next ten critical days, organizing and organizing. He apparently showed no inclination to hurry up north to Mooi river and Estcourt to see for himself. He has been criticized for that. But one of his many characteristics was to conserve his energy by deciding on his priority and, in his introspective, stubborn way, ploughing on with it.

As soon as the Boers retreated northward towards the Tugela river, Buller ordered General Clery to move up to Frere and make that place the forward British base.

In Pietermaritzburg, Buller supervised the equipping of the new troops as they arrived there from the ships at Durban. And he paid particular attention to their bodily welfare by giving considerable prominence to canteen arrangements and above all to hospital organization. No one had been more solicitous about the physical care of poor Tommy Atkins since Florence Nightingale. And that really accounts for the fearsome loyalty of the ordinary soldier towards Redvers Buller. They were about to die in droves, often through the military stupidity of their commanders, but they generally loved 'Old Buller'. Even to this very day. I have talked to old veterans of the Natal Field Force – men who had lived through the bloody shambles of Spion Kop – but don't say a word to them against 'Poor Old Buller', or, if you do, expect ancient eyes to flash a reproving glare at you. Sir Redvers loved his tummy, but he was not a selfish man: he was also concerned about the private soldier's tummy, and his men were to suffer the very minimum of pain possible.

He organized an Intelligence Department – and about time! There was a monstrous lack of dependable maps; they did exist, but were all captured by the Boers, up at Dundee.

Buller's report on this subject:

By the energy of Captain Kenny Herbert, RA, and with the willing help of the Surveyor's department of the Natal Government, a map was created and was a very creditable production. The formation of the Intelligence Department was undertaken for us by the Hon. T. K. Murray, Member of the Legislative Assembly, who placed his thorough knowledge of the country and unbounded energy absolutely at our service. He obtained for us a Corps of Guides, whose services were invaluable, but all this work had to be done from the beginning. The threads of the Intelligence Department that had been prepared before the war were all in Ladysmith and inaccessible . . . I had the advantage of knowing Natal very well, and of possessing a good general knowledge of the country round about Ladysmith, and of the Dutch character. I felt nearly certain that as long as Ladysmith held out the Boers, having failed in their first attempt to invade South Natal, would not repeat it, and that I should not run any very serious risk if, while careful of my communications, I, in the ensuing operations, departed from the best principles and took liberties in the way of uncovering them. I knew the Colenso position (by which I mean not the village of that name on the south side of the Tugela, but the low hills immediately adjacent to it on the north side) and I felt that the assault on that position would be a very dangerous undertaking . . .

I am a little worried by 'I should not run any very serious risk if, while fairly careful of my communications, I, in the ensuing operations, departed from the best principles and took liberties . . .' Surely the best military principles are the surest and safest for success. Why does he think of departing from them? What he meant was that an attack on the Boers' centre at Colenso was the most obvious thing for him to do, but that he was already thinking of attacking much further west and crossing the Tugela river at a place called Potgieter's Drift (see map, page 15). But it was a funny way to put it, in a report to the Secretary of State for War, Lord Lansdowne. Louis Botha was preparing formidable gun pits, sangars and trenches among those 'low hills' around Colenso, that is for sure! So Buller's instinct not to cross there was a very good instinct.

All was not ideal in British efforts to learn and understand the peculiar characteristics of that part of Natal where battles would have to be fought. A Mr de Lasalle wrote from Natal to his father, Colonel de Lasalle who lived in Surbiton, England: 'The Imperial officers are creating a very bad impression by their supercilious airs of knowing all about the country much better than men who have lived here thirty or forty years, and their manner of turning up their noses at all things and persons Colonial.'

Earlier in this month of November 1899 a very interesting and gallant soldier, Lieutenant-General the Earl of Dundonald, had arrived in South Africa. Much to his disappointment he had not been selected to go to the war but like many other patricians, he was so anxious to serve that he travelled out at his own expense, and, offering his services to General Buller at Cape

Town, he was quickly appointed to the command of mounted troops in Natal. I would like to digress at this point and allow the Earl to describe his departure from his aged mother, in Scotland:

I thereupon decided to go to South Africa without a definite appointment, as I felt sure Sir Redvers Buller would employ me when I arrived there.

I was then staying with my mother, who was much opposed to the war, and did not like my having offered my services to Sir George White. She said President Kruger was a God-fearing man and the war was an unrighteous one, and she gave me these beautiful lines:

> Some will hate thee, some will love thee,
> Some will flatter, some will slight;
> Cease from man and look above thee,
> Trust in God and do the right.

I told my mother that the Army was my profession and that it was right that I should go where duty called me. But that day I had not courage to say that my passage was already taken by the *Carisbrooke Castle*, which was to sail for South Africa on 28 October.

Though she was now over 80 years of age we walked as usual to the little Congregational Chapel which she attended; then towards evening there she sat with the Bible on her knees, as was her custom to do every Sunday, and many other days as well. Suddenly she said, 'I do not like your going out to fight the Boers; it is an unrighteous war and Kruger is a religious good man and reads the Bible, so I am glad Sir George White cannot have you.'

This scene has been for ever printed on my mind, and so have all those quiet Sundays with my mother, so different they were from regimental Sundays with great dinners; it is those quiet Sundays I often think of now and shall to the end of my days.

Anyway, on 28 November, Lieutenant-General the Earl of Dundonald took some of his mounted soldiers, together with a battery of Field Artillery, within 2000 yards of the village of Colenso. It was a reconnaissance to discover exactly where the Boers would make their stand. Lord Dundonald soon gleaned this information when the Boers suddenly opened fire with their artillery, from the Colenso Hills, and thirty-four 'well directed shells' came at the British; 'marvellously' no one was injured. British artillery replied from 4000 yards, and in due course Dundonald took his force back to Frere.

On 29 November, Buller sent a message towards Ladysmith by flashing that searchlight on the clouds:

Am organizing relief force, and only waiting for artillery. Have driven enemy north of Tugela, except small force at Weenen. They have destroyed bridge at Colenso . . . All is quiet in Europe. No chance of intervention. If you hear me attacking, join in if you can. I do not know which way I shall come. How much longer can you hold out?

The signal was very difficult to read in Ladysmith. All they did get was 'I do not know yet which way I shall come. How much longer can you hold out? From Pietermaritzburg. Buller.' A little later they were able to decipher 'If you hear me attacking, join in if you can.' An important, though sadly desperate, bit of the message.

Sir George White replied:

Situation here unchanged, but enemy still mount additional guns, against some of our [?essential] positions. I have provisions for seventy days, and believe I can defend Ladysmith while they last. S.A. ammunition, $5\frac{1}{2}$ millions; 15-pr. guns, 250 rounds per gun; 4·7 in. naval gun, 170 rounds per gun; 12-pr. naval gun, 270 rounds per gun; 6·3 in. howitzer, 430 rounds per gun. Hay or grazing is a difficulty. I have thirty-five days' supply of this at reduced rations. Enemy learns every plan of operations I form, and I cannot discover source. I have locked up or banished every suspect, but still have undoubted evidence of betrayal . . . Hospital returns: Wounded, 225; dysentary [*sic*], 71; enteric fever, 15; other fevers, 12; other diseases, 10 . . . Will look out for you and do what I can.

It was not an optimistic message for Buller to get and the most worrying sentence was 'Enemy learns every plan of operations I form, and I cannot discover source'. Who was the unknown traitor? It made prearranged co-operation between the relievers and the besieged impossible.

8

THE SIEGE OF LADYSMITH
December 1899

*When I come home I shall want to sleep in my clothes
out on a path in the garden in a blanket, if it isn't
raining I should like someone to pour a watering pot
over me every now and then. And the gardener come
out and shoot every hour or so in the night . . .*

Letter from MAJOR R. BOWEN to his wife

THE general spirit in Ladysmith at the beginning of December was dogged.
Hearts were lifted when, unexpectedly, heliographic communication
was received from the British to the south. It was certainly not from a column
breaking through the Tugela Heights – no one had tried yet – but it came
from a place called Weenen, far to the south-east. But from now on as long
as the sun was shining, the beleaguered garrison of Ladysmith could know
what was going on in the outside world.

Good news came in as well as bad news. Sir George White wrote to his
wife:

In one of the heliographic messages I have received since we got into communication with Sir Redvers Buller's force by signal, I was given an extract from
Reuter that 'Lady White at Windsor'. If this means that the dear old Queen has
asked you in acknowledgement of my services it was *too* good of her. It gave me
the first sensation of pleasure I have had since the Bell's Sprut [*sic*] disaster . . .

On 2 December, the second *Ladysmith Bombshell* was published, and
here is a selection of items:

Strange accident: A very singular accident, anatomically considered, occurred on
Friday morning near the Post-Office. Mr Craddock, while attempting to sit upon
the shaft of a Scotch-cart, fell in such a manner as to strike the larynx, or upper part
of the wind-pipe, upon a projecting nail with such force as to break through the

larynx, though the skin was not wounded; and although he did not at first seem much hurt, he looked extremely uncomfortable and the air came rushing out with fearful rapidity. There being no external opening, it passed into the cellular texture and was driven on under the skin, obliterating every natural feature of his countenance, closing his eyes, elevating the scalp, and then passing down, nearly surrounded the chest and upper abdominal integuments. Dr Rouilliard was passing at the time, and the necessary relief being afforded, Mr Craddock proceeded on his way with Mr Lotter to breakfast.

£10 Reward to the first Boer who enters Ladysmith in any capacity other than bearer of a white flag or as prisoner of war.

Amid all the din of shot and shell may frequently be heard the dulcet tones of the Deputy-Mayor's cornet.

To be raffled: The last bottle of old Gaelic. 25 members at 1s. each. Optional on winner's part to stand drinks. Mr Murray, the Club.

One of our young ladies, a refugee from Dundee, is so refined in her language, that she never uses the word 'black-guard', but substitutes 'African Sentinel'.

A large collection of white flags to be disposed of in the Boer lines; these flags have been repeatedly used, but are good as new.

Pretoria, November 19th, 1899. – From Joubert to Kruger. Having heard that England has annexed the moon, last night opened a vigorous fire on it. Eventually moon retired behind a cloud. Casualties on our side, 53 men moonstruck; enemy's loss unknown.

Notice: As we find it impossible to send a separate reply to the numerous enquiries as to whereabouts of friends and relations we publish for general information that –

> They've gone far away to a peaceful clime,
>   To get cured of their liver or bile;
> But where the foe lurks as the screaming shell bursts –
>   Not there, not there, my child.

(Printed and Published at Ladysmith, Natal, 2 Dec., 1899.)

On 4 December Major R. Bowen continued his weekly letter to his wife in England. He had now given up his original hope of getting it through the Boer lines:

Ladysmith Dec. 4

Dearest Missy

I've written one letter and shut it up ready to post on first chance so now I start on another which will be old no doubt by the time you get it. We are still struggling on, but have run short of drink and vegetables and the Klip River which we have to drink is more sand and mud than water. I don't believe you would let your dog drink it at home. No milk of course. We are in communication with the relieving column by signal so I trust 'this tyranny will soon be over passed'. I rather wish I was with them, as although this siege is an experience still it has been very dull and we have never been in a successful action and next time I want to see the Dutchmens backs and a little closer too than we ever see their faces. They have up to now always been in large numbers and a long way off and we have not got into them properly – and I am sick of 100 pound shells dropping in from 5 miles or more. The flies here are very annoying. Everybody has so far kept very well and fit – except the Colonel. When I come home I shall want to sleep in my clothes out on a path in the garden in a blanket, if it isn't raining I should like someone to pour a watering pot over me every now and then. And the gardener come out and shoot every hour or so in the night. A stone or the door scraper or something will do for a pillow. I must up at 2.45 a.m. and stand about till 5, and then lie down again till breakfast. We feed alright but everything is mixed with flies and we only have one plate and knife and fork for everything but we are very happy. During the siege we have lost 1 man died of typhoid and about 10 men wounded. The total losses are under 100 killed and wounded. It is marvellous how shells explode right among men and perhaps touch nobody at all. I can't say I like them all the same. They are most alarming to nervous people but people are so used to them now that the moment they fall they run out with spades to dig them up when they don't explode. Even the women do so in the town. I suppose it will surprise you to hear that there are lots of nice looking English women in all these towns, and a good many have stopped here. One has no idea till you come here to the Colonies how important they are, and how very like England it is after all. . .

On 5 and 7 December, the besieged soldiers began a series of aggressive prods against the Boers. Detachments of infantry went out to surprise Boers in outlying farmhouses, which they usually occupied as forward outposts. On both occasions the farms were empty. Had the Boers been warned? The question of security was getting a bit nightmarish.

About this time, war-correspondent George Steevens visited a section of the Naval Brigade, and carefully recorded stylish sea-going chat, on top of a craggy African kopje:

'There goes that stinker on Gun Hill,' said the captain. 'No, don't get up; have some draught beer.'

I did have some draught beer.

'Wait and see if he fires again. If he does we'll go up into the conning-tower, and have both guns in action toge—'

Boom! The Captain picked up his stick.

'Come on,' he said.

... As we passed through the camp the bluejackets rose to a man and lined up trimly on either side. Trust the sailor to keep his self-respect, even in five weeks' beleaguered Ladysmith ...

'That gunner,' said the captain, waving his stick at Surprise Hill, 'is a German. Nobody but a German atheist would have fired on us at breakfast, lunch, and dinner the same Sunday. It got too hot when he put one ten yards from the cook. Anybody else we could have spared; then we had to go.'

One can smell the sea salt in the air – but as to those references to the Boer gunners on Gun Hill and Surprise Hill, others in Ladysmith were thinking hard about them too.

Issue number three of the *Ladysmith Lyre* appeared on 5 December and for the first time had an item under that unusual heading *True News*:

Lord Methuen [over to the west on the Cape–Orange Free State front] has defeated the enemy in three engagements [even this was not exactly the truth; in fact the Boers had on early occasion made a tactical withdrawal in the face of a larger force after having given that force a varied but cruel pasting] at Belmount, Graspan and Modder River.

Immediately followed a poem:

> There was an old man of Pretoria
> Whose conduct got gorier and gorier
> Till a splinter of shell
> Sent him screaming to ——
> And he gave up his place to Victoria.

Our Children's Corner

Tommy's Natural History: (The Boer) This kwaint little creture lives almost intirely on billtong and copies. His boddy is covered with shells, wich he throus at you wen he's angry, thow it doesn't nevver hit you. Nurse says you can find him round Ladysmith any day you like, thow you don't nevver see him as he always hides behind rox and fings. He doesn't never throw fings on Sunday, but sits still and redes his prair book, which ma says all good littel boys ort to do. He haits pointed fings like bainetts and lances. Pa says he is a woman haiter, but he doesn't hait peticotes as much as kilts. I don't kwite see wot he means, do you? He is such a funny littel creture no one older than a seccond leftenant ever understands wot he'll do next.

New Songs (sung by the leading vocalists):

'Way down upon the Mooi River.' By General Joubert.
'A ittle bit off the top.' By Medical Officer in charge of Town Hall.

THE LADYSMITH LYRE.

" Let him Lie."—Old Song.

Vol. I. No. 3.   5th DECEMBER, 1899.   PRICE—6D.

TRUE NEWS.

Lord Methuen has defeated the enemy in three engagements, at Belmont, Graspan and Modder River. At Graspan our losses appear to have been heavy, four Naval Officers being mentioned as killed. Lord Methuen's official account of the Modder River fight is as follows:—

" November 28th.—Reconnoitred at 5 a.m. Enemy on the Modder; found them strongly entrenched and concealed. No means of outflanking. Action commenced with artillery, mounted infantry and cavalry at 5.30 a.m. Guards on the right. Ninth Brigade on the left, attacked the possession in widely extended formation at 6.30, and, supported by artillery, found itself in front of the whole of the Boer force, 8,000, two large guns, four Krupp guns, etc. The Naval Brigade rendered great assistance from the railway. After desperate hard fight which lasted ten hours, the men, without water or food, in a burning sun, made the enemy quit their position, General Pole-Carew being successful in getting a small party across the river, gallantly assisted by 300 Sappers. I speak in terms of high praise of the conduct of all engaged. One of the hardest and most trying fights in the annals of the British Army. If I can mention one arm particularly, it is the two batteries of artillery."

The Capetown and East London line is interrupted by the breaking of a bridge, near Steynsberg. General Gatacre is advancing north from Queenstown. The Boer outposts appear to be between Molteno and Stormberg Junction.

There was an old man of Pretoria
Whose conduct got gorier and gorier
    Till a splinter of shell
    Sent him screaming to ——
And he gave up his place to Victoria.

THE RELIEF OF LADYSMITH.
Reprinted from *The Times* of December 5th, 2099.

A WONDERFUL DISCOVERY.

The eminent German archæologist, Dr. Poompschiffer, has recently contributed to science the most interesting discovery of the century. It will be remembered that the learned professor started in the spring on a tour of exploration among the buried cities of Natal. When last heard of, in October, he had excavated the remains of Maritzburg and Estcourt, and was cutting his way through the dense primeval forests on the banks of the Tugela. By cable yesterday came intelligence of even more sensational finds. Briefly, Dr. Poompschiffer has re-discovered the forgotten town of Ladysmith. Crossing the Tugela, the intrepid explorer pushed northward. The dense bush restricted his progress to three miles a day. On the third day Poompschiffer noticed strange booming sounds frequently repeated; none of his party could guess what they were, and curiosity ran high. On the sixth day the mystery was explained. The party came suddenly upon a group of what were at first taken for a species of extinct reptile, but which the profound learning of Poompschiffer enabled him to recognise as

THE LAST SURVIVALS OF THE PREHISTORIC BOERS. Their appearance was almost terrifying. They were all extremely old. Their white beards had grown till they trailed beneath their feet, and it was the custom of the field cornets to knee-halter each man at night with his own beard to prevent him from running away. Their clothes had fallen to pieces with age, but a thick and impenetrable coating of dust and

melinite kept them warm. Their occupation was as quaint as their appearance. They were firing obsolete machines, conjectured to be the cannon of the ancients, in the direction of a heap of cactus-grown ruins. That heap of ruins was the fabled fortress of Ladysmith.

Students of history will remember the Boer war of 1899, from which public attention was distracted by the great War Office strike. The learned will also remember at a later period, after the closing of that office, the controversy in our columns on the question whether Ladysmith existed or not, which the general voice of experts finally decided in the negative. It is now proved that so-called *savants* of that rude age were mistaken. Not only did Ladysmith exist, not only was it besieged, but up to the day before yesterday

THE SIEGE OF LADYSMITH WAS STILL GOING ON. The site of the town at first appeared uninhabited. But when Poompschiffer commenced excavating he came, to his amazement, upon signs of old workings at a depth of only a few feet below the surface. For an instant, he tells us, he thought some other antiquarian had been before him. Next moment some creature blundered along the tunnel into his very arms. It was secured and brought into the light. It was the last inhabitant of Ladysmith.

It was apparently one of the children born since the beginning of the siege, and was about a hundred years old. From living in underground holes it was bent double, and quite blind. It appeared unable to speak, only repeating constantly, in a crooning voice, the syllables, " Weeskee, weeskee," which Poompschiffer was unable to translate. The professor was anxious to secure this unique specimen for the Kaiser William Museum of Antiquities, at Berlin. But the moment it was removed from Ladysmith it began to pine away. Having never known any state of life but bombardment, it was terrified by the absence of artillery fire. Time after time it attempted to escape to its native shells. Poompschiffer endeavoured to maintain life by artificial bombardment, letting off crackers in its ear and pelting it with large stones. But all was in vain, the extraordinary creature was not deceived, and in a few hours, with a last despairing wail of " Weeskee," it expired through sheer terror at the safety of its surroundings.

WHERE TO SPEND A HAPPY DAY.

(SEE ILLUSTRATED SUPPLEMENT.)

To the ladies of Pretoria.—Messrs. Kook and Son beg to announce a personally conducted tour, Saturday to Monday, to witness the siege of Ladysmith. Full view of enemy guaranteed. Tea and shrimps (direct from Durban) on the train. Four-in-hand ox-wagon from Modder Spruit to Bulwan. Fare 15s. return; one guinea if Long Tom is in action. Lovers half price.

Mother (acting on above advertisement): " Come along, children, here we are at last. Oh, what a journey we've had! Now, be good, baby! Look at the pretty soldier with his gun. Isn't he fierce? Piet, don't get too close to him, you never know what a gun mayn't do. I wonder where your dear father is! Oh, he's up that hill, is he, sir! Thank you very much, I'm sure. You see, you couldn't expect me to know. It's the first time I've ever been to war. Sannie, mind you don't dirty your Sunday dress; you might just hold my white parasol over me and baby. Now take the basket,

The first page of the third issue of The Ladysmith Lyre

They're after me, they're after me,
To capture me is everyone's desire,
They're after me, they're after me,
I'm the individual they require.

By Col. Rhodes.

Skill Competition: A bottle of Anchovies – useless to owner on account of prevailing whisky famine – will be awarded to sender of first opened solution of this competition. The problem is to name date of Relief of Ladysmith, by relief being understood re-opening of railway connexion with South. Generals, conductors, and inhabitants of Ladysmith that say 'Ja' instead of 'Yes' will be disqualified as possessing exceptional sources of information. Send answers, with small bottle of beer enclosed to Puzzle Editor, Mulberry Grove, I.L.H. Lines, Ladysmith.

On the night of 7 December a big adventure was planned. To the east of Ladysmith, four miles distant, just in front of Lombard's Kop, was 'Gun Hill'. The Boer guns there were selected as a target for a night sortie. Leading the force was Sir George White's chief-of-staff, Major General Hunter, and he took with him 500 men of the Natal Volunteers under Colonel Royston, and 100 men of the Imperial Light Horse, under Lieutenant-Colonel Edwards, together with eighteen men of the Corps of Guides, under Major Henderson of the Intelligence Branch. Also with this formidable body of British South Africans were a few military engineers and artillerists, survivors of the ill-fated No. 10 Mountain Battery, armed with explosives and sledge-hammers, for the purpose of the expedition was to destroy any 'stinking' Boer guns they could find.

Colonel Knox, who had originally put this idea of attacking Gun Hill to General Hunter, was also to take a small force northward to Limit Hill and disturb the Boers there and, in doing so, cover the left flank of the Gun Hill party.

Everyone was worried about security and maximum secrecy was slapped on the enterprise. Would the Boers be expecting them? That was the painful question. At 10.15 p.m., Hunter led his mounted men eastward from Devonshire Post. They marched wearing light boots in complete silence to the northern base of Gun Hill and Lombard's Kop and halted. Major Henderson knew that there was usually a Boer picket on a northern spur of Gun Hill. At this point, General Hunter detached 100 men of the Border Mounted Rifles (Volunteers) and ordered them to remain where they were to give cover, and then detached a much bigger group under Colonel Royston to watch Lombard's Nek, in case of a counter-attack from that direction. Hunter himself led the assault group, comprising the Imperial Light Horse and 100

Volunteers (representing the different corps) and they were at the western foot of Gun Hill at 2 a.m., where they deployed into line. The Light Horse, led by Colonel A. Edwards and Major Karri Davies, formed the left wing, and the Natal Volunteers formed the right wing, under Major Addison.

Up went General Hunter and his brave men. The side of Gun Hill which they had selected was 250 feet of cruel boulders and seemed in the night to be perpendicular. As they neared the top, and much to their shock, came a challenge, from their left rear, '*Wier kom daar?*' It was repeated time and time again – until it dawned on the Boer sentry who, in all certainty, *was* going there! He then shouted back into the darkness, '*Schiet, Stephanus, hier kom de verdomde rooineks, schiet, schiet!*' which I translate very uneasily as: 'Shoot, Stephanus, here come the damned English, shoot, shoot!' And the Boers did shoot into the blackness. The British South Africans clambered all the harder, up into the night sky, and they got within about twenty paces of the crest of Gun Hill. Immediately the Boers fired down into the blackness. Boer officers were heard to shout orders to hold fire. And at that moment Colonel Edwards' voice bellowed the awful order, 'Fix bayonets!' How this command was received by the British, I don't know, because they weren't carrying bayonets, but it had a profound effect on the Boers; they turned and beat an extraordinary hasty retreat. Whether that shout of 'Fix [non-existent] bayonets!' was according to the decent, cricketing usages of war, I can't decide – but it saved quite a few British blokes' lives.

Colonel Edwards and his men groped and stumbled across the plateau and came to the awful gun. Solemnly the words were spoken: 'I annex "Long Tom" in the name of the Imperial Light Horse.' They also found, to their delight, a 4·7 howitzer and immediately Captain Fowke and Lieutenant Turner, with their few sappers, inserted gun-cotton charges into the breech and muzzle of the guns – while the assault party wisely disappeared below the crest of Gun Hill – and blew both into a nasty mess.

General Hunter said a few words in the African night and called on his men for three cheers for Her Majesty the Queen, which was rousingly complied with. Those were extraordinary days! Surely the answer should have been a fusillade of mauser bullets? But nothing came . . . first the threat of imaginary 'cold steel' and now a noisy tribute to the Queen Across the Water was more than those Boers could take. It was a British triumph. Of course, they now had to get back to Ladysmith . . . Well, they got back, reasonably unscathed, and carrying with them the breech-block of the 6-inch gun and a complete Maxim-Nordenfeldt gun, together with anything else they could loot.

A few years ago, Major Karri Davies' daughter told me that long after the war was over, the famous Major returned the breech-block to Field-Marshal Jan Smuts. And then, into the Chelsea room where we were having tea, came her son and he asked me what was special about his grandfather.

The casualties were very light: seven wounded, including Major Henderson, who led the way.

Colonel Knox's party, up north, were not quite as successful, though they did sever the telegraph line between Lombard's Kop and the Boer head laager at Modder Spruit. Opportunities were a bit fumbled, up there, and they finally withdrew, losing three killed and fifteen wounded. The Rev. Owen S. Watkins, Acting Wesleyan Chaplain, had hurried towards the sound of gunfire and met, on his way, a young medical officer, riding to obtain help for the wounded:

So having with me a Red Cross flag we turned our horses' heads and rode out to their assistance. For the first few seconds the bullets flew fast around us, but as soon as our flag fluttered out on the breeze and the burghers could see what it was the firing ceased, we released our friends from their uncomfortable and dangerous predicament, and sent back the wounded man in a dhooli.

We were then met by two armed burghers carrying a white flag who told us of other wounded men lying within our lines, and offered to guide us to them ... The burghers had shown every kindness to the wounded, supplying them with food and drink; and nothing could exceed the courtesy and goodwill manifested towards ourselves by these men who were in the very act of firing upon our comrades.

It was a strange experience: between us and the town was a ridge, from which the Boers were firing busily upon our men, and as we passed them at their work they would stop firing, clamber down the kopje side, shake hands with us heartily, and chaffingly refer to their speedy entrance into Ladysmith. 'When you go back to town,' said one young fellow, 'engage a room at the Royal for me, will you? We shall be in tomorrow evening.' 'Hear you've got Dr Jameson in there,' jeered another; 'tell him we are longing to meet him, and,' patting his bandolier lovingly, 'have a little present here we are going to give him.' 'Well, goodbye and good luck to you; mustn't waste any more time; going to try and shoot a few more of your fellows before they get in.'

On the following day, Sir George White ordered a special parade for all the men who had taken part in the raid on Gun Hill. The soldiers drew up in line to receive their General, and, as they did so, the Boer gun 'Puffing Billy' threw a shell very close to one of the flanks. The soldiers broke into close column with a short front, so that they were better hidden by houses and trees. General White, together with General Sir Archibald Hunter and

General Brocklehurst, rode on to the parade ground, and the commanding officer addressed the heroes:

General Hunter, who planned and carried out the very successful movement of this morning, has reported to me the very efficient help that he received from the men of the Imperial Light Horse as well as the other corps who were employed . . . It will be a great pleasure to me to report to General Sir Redvers Buller, whose name brings confidence wherever it is mentioned . . . your behaviour is an honour not only to your own country and colony, but to the whole empire. Colonel Edwardes, I don't wish to keep you any longer, owing to the circumstances that 'Long Tom' of Bulwaan [Umbulwana] may interfere in this conference, but once more I thank you one and all.

The Boers, of course, were livid about this British success, and immediately began to scuttle around for someone to blame. One man, Major Erasmus of the State Artillery, took the very rare course, in human affairs, of blaming himself. Telegrams were being passed around very freely:

T.D. ZAR 8.12.1899 8.40 p.m. From Chief Trichardt Commandant State Artillery, H.Q. Ladysmith.

To Commandant-General Volkrust, begins:

. .. Major Erasmus then told him that the Big Gun and the Howitzer has fallen into the hands of the enemy . . . Major Erasmus has himself asked the State Attorney to be placed under arrest and I thought it advisable to arrest Lieutenant Malan as well. As soon as the reports of Major Erasmus and Commandant Weilback are received, a *Kriegsraad* will be held to investigate the affair and to punish the guilty. While awaiting, sir, your further instructions, I fully concur that if this affair is to be ascribed to the negligence of any officer or officers – be they permanent or citizen force – the guilty person or persons be made a salutary example. The casualties of today's fight cannot as yet be assessed with certainty. As far as I know, we have one dead and two wounded, while the enemy losses are much greater – ends.

The regular soldiers in Ladysmith shared the delight that was felt about the Volunteers' success, but it was clear to them that they must now have a go themselves. So Colonel Metcalfe received permission to take soldiers of the Rifle Brigade to attack a 4·7-inch howitzer which was located on Surprise Hill, to the north-north-west of Ladysmith.

On 10 December, at 10 p.m., Colonel Metcalfe led five companies of the Rifle Brigade, with Major Wing RA and the two guides Mr Thornhill and Mr Ashby, together with a blasting detachment of Royal Engineers under Lieutenant Digby Jones, from the camp behind King's Post. Initially, the Colonel only dared take his party about a mile outside the British perimeter, to a donga (a dried-up water-course) because the moon was not due to set until about midnight. There they lay in no-man's-land to await comparative darkness. It was said to be a strange and eerie wait. The moon lit up the open veldt which stretched away to the west. The waiting soldiers saw the intermittent flicker of a searchlight, trying to signal messages to Ladysmith from the great relief force forming about twenty miles to the south. Then a blinding light would glare in their direction from much closer, from the Boer position on Telegraph Hill. This searchlight would move its great beam along the edge of the town and pause knowingly at every possible exit and would then shoot upwards to meet the thin British signal and thereby destroy the hope of watchers in the town deciphering any message. And then down it would come, searching for such a group as the Rifle Brigade and their comrades were. But they bent low in their natural entrenchment. And as through any other night, there was the irregular sound of rifle fire.

About midnight the moon disappeared and the time for commitment had come. The five companies moved forward across the rough veldt. When they came to the Harrismith (Orange Free State) railway line, they left half a company there to help protect their left and then, under Bell's Kopje, they left another half company to cover their right. The remaining four companies expected their first encounter around rising ground, about one mile in front of Surprise Hill. The Boer General Ben Viljoen, who had commanded this area, had always placed a strong picket there, but a few days before he had been ordered to the upper Tugela area, and his successor was not so efficient and withdrew this forward precaution. All was going very well for the British.

By 2 a.m. the Rifle Brigade and comrades had reached the foot of Surprise Hill. Here Colonel Metcalfe ordered two of the companies to form outwards to give support to the two remaining companies that were to do the actual assaulting. Up Surprise Hill went these men. Perhaps their army boots and accoutrements made a little more noise than the Volunteers had made on Gun Hill. Nevertheless they were reaching the brow of the hill when 'Who goes there?' was challenged in Dutch ('*Wie daar?*') And these Boers wasted no time; they blazed away at the direction of the approaching British. On pressed the Riflemen, on to the flat top of Surprise Hill. The gun had gone! What was that great tarpaulin? The infantry soldiers spread out into a semicircle beyond the object. Yes, it was the gun. Young Lieutenant Digby Jones placed his explosive charge and the infantry ducked where they could. They waited. Nothing happened. The cool Lieutenant returned to the lethal object and fastened another fuse – and up went the Boer gun with a suitable bang. This time there was a more hurried cheer, but cheer there was, and the British force were hurrying back the way they had come.

As the British soldiers came tumbling to the foot of Surprise Hill – horror upon horror – a line of some twenty mausers opened fire almost, it seemed, at their feet. A party of Pretoria burghers, belonging to the well-educated minority and including mainly lawyers and businessmen, had bravely hurried forward at the first noise of gunfire, to cut off the British retreat.

Colonel Metcalfe immediately ordered his soldiers to charge the brave Boers and fortunately they obeyed him; this time the British really did have bayonets fixed. The Pretorians blazed away with their mausers until the Riflemen were amongst them, killing and wounding with bullet and bayonet as they passed through. They, the British, reaching the flat veldt, made their way back to Ladysmith as best they could, under the protection of Observation Hill. The survivors were back in Ladysmith just before dawn. Their casualties were fourteen killed or mortally wounded, and fifty wounded.

Amongst that group of Boers who placed themselves between the Riflemen and Ladysmith was seventeen-year-old Deneys Reitz, and he wrote to his father, now the Secretary of State for the Transvaal:

In the meanwhile, the English were approaching. We could hear what they said. They were in high spirits, and they were quite unaware of our being in front of them. We waited till we could see them. They marched in close order, about 300 in number. They were then about ten yards away from us. We then fired amongst them. They stopped, and all called out, 'Rifle Brigade'. They must have supposed that we belonged to their people. Then one of them said, 'Let us charge.' One officer, Captain Paley (I am writing this letter with his silver pencil-case), advanced, though he had two bullet wounds already. Joubert [not, of course, the Commandant-General] gave him another shot, and he fell on top of us. Four English got hold of Jan Luttig, and struck him on the head with their rifles, and stabbed him in the stomach with a bayonet. He seized two of them by the throat, and shouted, 'Help, boys!' His two nearest comrades shot two of the nearest soldiers, and the other two bolted. But then the English came up in such numbers that we all lay down as quiet as mice along the bank . . .

Tell Ati he must not insist on coming to the front, for it is no picnic.

I shall now conclude with love to all – Your affectionate son, Deneys Reitz.

Once again that ever-faithful Christian, the Rev. Owen Watkins, hurried to the scene of suffering:

Amongst the killed, I found one who was a comrade of many past experiences. Only the day before we had planned to dine together on the following evening, but instead I attended his funeral. Such is war! . . .

At the foot of the hill we laid the brave Riflemen, marking the place where they lay with stones heaped over the grave in the form of a cross. Then sorrowfully we returned to our camp, and wearily withal, for the day was far spent, and no food had passed our lips since dawn.

In the evening I was again called to the sad ceremony of burial; four men had succumbed to their wounds during the day. In the darkness we buried them in the cemetery just outside the town; no light was permitted lest we should draw the enemy's fire upon us, so, with only the stars to light us, the words of the service, which daily were becoming more and more mournfully familiar, were recited over the graves. Strange, thus to bury our comrades by stealth, but alas! in the days that were coming it ceased to be strange by reason of its frequency.

These two raiding actions out of Ladysmith swung the psychological warfare in favour of the British. Everyone inside the perimeter was cheered by the achievements. And the Boers outside were very angry and then very depressed. In fact the Boers were completely thrown by these two escapades, and in wild desperation after the second raid, began to point a nervous finger at any of their burghers who had been in the vicinity of the guns and had the misfortune to have a British name. The result of the two raids was far in excess of the actual military gain, as can be deduced from this telegram:

T.D. ZAR 21.12.1899. From Assistant-General Erasmus

To President, Pretoria, begins:

I am sending up five persons from here today, in custody of P. Beyers and Van Doorn, upon whom grave suspicion rests in connection with the lost cannon and with other events, as will become apparent in the declarations I have handed over to the State Attorney. Their names are Tossell, Cooper, McArthur, Walker and Miller – ends.

Not a Van der Merwe in the whole bunch!

Also on 10 December, a curious official notice went up in Ladysmith, touching on the dwindling food supply:

Market: Notice is hereby given that the Morning Market is for a time discontinued; the re-opening of the Railway will see its resuscitation. (By order), G. W. Lines, Market Master.

The war-correspondent of the *Morning Herald*, the *Echo* and the *Illustrated London News*, George Lynch, had a strange adventure. Getting very bored, and thirsty for 'copy', like the good journalist he was, he quietly decided on a risky expedition. Apparently a Lancer had wandered in a certain direction towards the Boer lines, had met a Boer at an outpost, and had had a bit of a chat, returning safely to Ladysmith. Mr Lynch was not dwelling on the fact that other British soldiers had wandered too far and had got a mauser bullet in them. Anyway he rode off on his horse named 'Kruger' – captured at Elandslaagte – towards the Boers with optimism. He arrived at the reputed location of the outpost 'where the veldt, from being bare, commenced to be thickly covered with mimosa trees' but there was nothing there, except a 'springbuck'. And then Mr Lynch realized that he could perhaps be 'the first white man to bring the news from Ladysmith out of the beleaguered town'. He decided to ride south towards Buller's force.

He did very well. He got between Umbulwana and Lombard's Kop without being challenged, but there he saw a Boer laager. He dismounted and succeeded in passing the Boer siege lines. All was now relatively easy and a great newspaper scoop confronted him. He decided to lie low until darkness, but unexpectedly from behind a voice shouted at him in Dutch. A Boer was standing ten yards away and was pointing a rifle.

The Boers treated him very well: indeed like a privileged guest. They had discussions about the rights and wrongs of the war, and he listened to their hymn singing in the darkness:

They sang, without any drawl or nasal intonation, straight out from their deep chests. The chant rose and fell with a swinging solemnity. There was little of pleading or supplication in its tones; they were calling on the God of Battles; the God of the Old Testament rather than the Preacher of the Sermon on the Mount was He to whom they sang; and sometimes there was a strain of almost stern demand about it that gave it more the ring of a war-song than a prayer. Entering the door of that tent seemed like going into another century. It could not be but luminously evident to the onlooker that these men were calling on an unseen Power whose actual existence was as real to their minds as that of their Mauser rifles stacked around the tent-pole. One could not help contrasting this obvious sincerity with the perfunctory church parade on our side . . .

Mr Lynch asked his captors to do him a favour, and the following telegram resulted:

From Commandant-General, H.Q. Ladysmith

To Secretary of State, Pretoria, begins:

Mr George Lynch, a prisoner of war here, requests that the following telegram be allowed through.

Begins: From George Lynch, Boer Camp, Ladysmith, R.T.P. *Morning Herald*, London. Went Sunday evening Boer lines to exchange our newspaper *The Ladysmith Lyre* for *Diggers News*. Most hospitably entertained and kindly treated . . . Comfortable night, good breakfast. *Ladysmith Lyre* caused much amusement. Hear reports Boer casualties in English papers grossly exaggerated. Men excellent spirits, chaffing me when I proposed football match for team each side for Saturday afternoon – one suggested that they prefer playing with cannon balls. The more one meets genuine Boer, more one learns to admire him as chivalrous enemy – ends. Please despatch if you have no objection – ends.'

Mr Lynch was hoping to appease his captors with that very tall story about exchanging newspapers and to explain why he was in the middle of their investment line. And appeasement almost topples into sycophancy with his other words; but the Boers were usually suspicious about the motives of all Britishers, and this exploit was no exception. The Boers sent a telegram of their very own to Pretoria:

From Commandant, H.Q. Ladysmith

To Secretary of State, Pretoria, begins:

Yesterday a certain Mr Lynch entered Commandant Weilbach's lines and was captured by his pickets. He claims to be a reporter, and asserts that his sole purpose was to exchange newspapers. He is under the firm impression that as such he should be released by us. Will send you further particulars about him and, since I consider him a highly dangerous person, will send him to Pretoria . . .

Major R. Bowen's saga to his wife was continued on 11 December:

I'm just recovering from another severe go of Indian fever which has left me rather weak. It is too sickening. I've had it now 5 times in the last 3 months since I left India twice on board ship and 3 times here. Thank goodness it doesn't last long, but is awful while it lasts and any hot day which causes ones temperature to rise naturally is very apt to bring it out again. I've just saved it too several times by taking extra quinine. On Friday night the Imperial Light Horse and others took 1 gun and destroyed 2 other big ones which were seriously annoying us with very little loss and early this morning the R.B. [Rifle Brigade] destroyed another without loss, but unfortunately fell into a trap coming home and suffered rather severely but I believe they accounted for as many of the enemy . . . We have lost 100 men here killed and wounded in the last 4 days. The Boers seem a good deal annoyed about the loss of their guns. I do trust and hope England will take over the place after this it will be too wicked if all our lives are to be risked and so many lost for nothing. I hope Buller will soon force the Tugela and join us. We are not told the cause of the delay. Typhoid and Horse sickness are both beginning and we ought to get out of this valley as soon as possible. The troops have been very healthy so far, but it wont last for ever. Riddell is off the sick list he has made a marvellous recovery. We are just as I write catching a very hot shelling from a very big gun that has just been put up a good deal too close to us and we have no gun in position to reply. They began while we were at luncheon and after the third shell we luckily moved the table round to the other side of the magazine, and made one company move as the fourth struck the ground about 15 yards of where we had been sitting and would most likely have knocked some of us out if we hadn't moved.

I sometimes think I have been unsympathetic and not humoured you as much as I might have and that has had something to do with our not getting on very well together. If this is so I must ask you to forgive me and try and think kindly of me. My life has not been a very happy one doubtless mainly through my own faults. Every sin of every kind brings its own punishment. I wish I could write like Adam Lindsay Gordon. I think I'd better shut this up now. I'll put it in with the other letter. Give my love to the Boys. I fear the eldest especially will be too like me. [The Major then wrote a sentence which he thoroughly crossed out.]

Goodbye Dear,

Yrs. ever – Robert Bowen.

Everyone in Ladysmith was aware that the time had at last arrived when General Buller was expected to meet these puritan Boers and begin his great movement to cross the Tugela river, and pierce the Tugela Heights, towards the freeing of their town. On 7 December Sir George White had received the first positive statement from General Buller on the subject, that 'I have definitely decided to advance by Potgieter's Drift. Expect to start on 12th December, and take five days.'

Potgieter's Drift is a shallow crossing of the Tugela river about eleven miles west of Colenso. It lies between the heights of Spion Kop and Vaal Krantz which are on the northern side of the river. If Buller came through that way, he would approach Ladysmith from the south-west across open veldt and presumably come up Long Valley into the town.

General White was now very anxious to carry out his duty to the best of his ability. It is true that he had been perhaps over-cautious in arranging aggressive moves against the besieging Boers. Nevertheless the Boers had recalled some burghers from the Tugela Heights to help strengthen the encirclement of Ladysmith and thereby inadvertently eased Buller's potential problem; it has been argued that as many as 2000 Boers returned. But now White's job was to co-operate with Buller's proposed assault from the south, and Sir George threw all he could into this scheme with great enthusiasm.

General White reorganized his mobile columns and to free Colonel Royston's mounted troops for this purpose, he once again embodied the Town Guard (12 December). He riskily brought some of the guns from their artillery combat positions into the town, and moved two naval guns, a 4·7 inch and a 12-pounder, from their positions on the northern defences, to Caesar's Camp and Wagon Hill in the south, so that they could cover Buller's army as it came up Long Valley. He made arrangements for feeding the relieving force with what food he had left and made preparations to receive a large number of wounded.

While Sir George White was making these ambitious arrangements to co-operate with his rescuers, he received another message from Sir Redvers Buller on 11 December which betrayed an area of uncertainty. The General suggested that White should not begin any movement of his force until the relievers were actually at Lancer's Hill, some seven miles west-south-west of Ladysmith, 'unless', added Buller, 'you feel certain of where I am.' What was worrying about that message, inside Ladysmith, was that it implied that Buller himself wasn't sure where he would be . . .

And then, on 13 December, literally out of the blue, came a big surprise message from Buller that he had 'been forced to change my plans; am coming through via Colenso and Onderbrook Spruit [behind Colenso]'. This was all a bit unnerving to Sir George White and his staff. Why was Buller *forced* to change his plans? This was to be, apparently, a direct frontal assault by the shortest possible route.

Sir George White replied, 'Your No. 78 of today received and understood. Shall be very glad if you will let me know your probable dates.' Buller answered, '. . . 13th December. Three brigades concentrate in Chieveley today. Fourth brigade go there tomorrow. Actual date of attack depends on difficulties met with; probably 17th December.'

Perhaps Buller made these messages deliberately vague so that the Boers would know very little; certainly poor Sir George White knew very little. But that didn't stop his new beaver-like energetic arrangements. On 14 December he published a special order, disclosing his plans of co-operation. He would personally lead out of Ladysmith almost all of the best troops he had. To guard the town itself he would leave behind the thinnest garrison, a mere four battalions, one battery of guns, one cavalry regiment and a few Natal Volunteers, all under the command of Colonel Knox.

Now, in mid-December, the sun was very hot; African dust was everywhere and, from the polluted Klip river, disease was becoming epidemic. An Irish soldier wrote a letter on 13 December from Ladysmith, and a runner got it through the Boer lines:

My Dear Pierce, . . . a soldier's is a nice life until war breaks out – then it is quite the reverse, for it is in a time like this that one looks back to the old times, to the gay companions, the pretty girls, and, best of all, your parents, brothers and sisters, and your dear old Irish home. May God help us! I often think of our rambles together over the dear green hills of Ireland when we were young and innocent. How foolish I must have been when I enlisted. I have often been sorry since – still, for all that, I am readily willing to die for England, but would to God it was for Ireland! Dear Pierce, as this may be my last letter, I will ask you to pray for me that I may come off safe . . . Good-bye once again. Remember me to all the boys. – I remain your friend till death.

Even indomitable Major Marling was getting pushed under. He had written:

Flies, if possible, worse than ever. You have to sweep the flies off your spoon before you can put anything into your mouth, and unless you cover up your cup with a book or saucer or something, you have about ten drowned flies in as many seconds. However, in spite of everything, we continue to keep pretty jolly.

But by 9 December, he was writing:

Hardy, our medico, insisted on my going to the hospital, and sent me up in a doolie. Heat and flies awful. My temperature 103. They say I have congestion of the lungs and fever. Feel pretty cheap, whatever it is. Tent like an oven.

And after being moved into Klip Cottage, as the guest of Lord Ava and Colonel Frank Rhodes, he wrote on 18 December:

No proper food, only flies and shells. The flies were worse than the shells, whilst the whole of Ladysmith smells. Heat awful. Doctor decided to send me to Intombi.

The people in Ladysmith waited as patiently as possible for 17 December to arrive, but on the 15th, early in the morning, they heard a distant commotion far to the south, in the direction of Colenso; it sounded like a great battle. Heliograms began to arrive for Sir George White and so he learnt that Buller had started to fight without even informing him. Sir George must have wondered why he had not been told, and why so little value had been placed on his great efforts to help. But he presumed that the battle would continue and that probably on the morrow he would receive his orders to march out and fight. What Buller did send him on the following day was something very different; indeed the precise opposite:

Buller to White. No. 88 Cipher, 14th December: I tried Colenso yesterday but failed; the enemy is too strong for my force, except with siege operations, and those will take one full month to prepare. Can you last so long? If not, how many days can you give me in which to take up defensive positions? After which I suggest your firing away as much ammunition as you can, and making best terms you can. I can remain here if you have alternative suggestion, but, unaided, I cannot break in. I

find my infantry cannot fight more than ten miles from camp, and then only if water
can be got, and it is scarce here. – Buller.

General White and his staff read and re-read the heliogram message,
and since it was beyond military comprehension, they snatched on the hope
that somehow the Boers had got hold of the British cipher and that they had
concocted the shocking words. But the message was repeated and repeated
by heliograph and they finally accepted the fact that something dreadful
had happened; not only with the battle, but apparently with Sir Redvers
Buller personally.

Then another message arrived from the south:

Buller to White. No. 92 Cipher, 16th December: Also add to the end of message:
'Whatever happens, recollect to burn your cipher, and decipher and code books,
and any deciphered message. – Buller.

To White and his staff in Ladysmith these words from Buller read like
complete demoralization – or had his army been wiped out? Was that possible?
Buller was suggesting that they should fire away their ammunition, burn
their intelligence records and surrender. Not even to come out fighting as a
last resort.

Sir George White was ageing, was ill, and had proved that he was an
uneasy tactician and latterly a very conservative strategist (except for his
plan of co-operation with Buller) but now, looking at Buller's statement, he
came into his own once again. Perhaps he had found the spirit of Charasia,
the battle of his prime which he had used as a symbol when writing to his
wife. He replied to his commander-in-chief:

White to Buller: Your No. 88 of today received and understood. My suggestion
is that you take up strongest available position that will enable you to keep touch
of the enemy and harass him constantly with artillery fire and in other ways as
much as possible. I can make food last for much longer than a month, and will not
think of making terms till I am forced to. You may have hit enemy harder than
you think. All our native spies report that your artillery fire made considerable
impression on enemy. Have your losses been very heavy? If you lose touch of
enemy, it will immensely increase his opportunities of crushing me, and have worst
effect elsewhere. While you are in touch with him, and in communication with me,
he has both of our forces to reckon with. Make every effort to get reinforcements
as early as possible, including India, and enlist every man in both Colonies who will
serve and can ride. Things may look brighter. The loss of 12 000 men here would be
a heavy blow to England. We must not think of it. I fear I could not cut my way to
you. Enteric fever is increasing alarmingly here. There are now 180 cases, all

within last month. Answer fully; I am keeping everything secret for the present till I know your plans.

What a turn-up for the book this was! Bearing in mind what Sir George White had become since the war began, and what even his friends were beginning to think about him; indeed, what he was beginning to think about himself . . . What did he write to his wife after the awful mess-up of 30 October? 'I think after this venture the men will lose confidence in me, and that I ought to be superseded.'

And now, here he was, taking over – as best he could from a besieged town – the military and moral leadership of the British Army in Natal. Please consider very carefully Sir George White's reply. Advice to his commander-in-chief about further military action; reassurance that Lady-smith was still full of steam and far from giving up; encouragement to Buller for what he had achieved against the Boers; a tentative and diplomatic in-quiry about the extent of the disaster. Optimism. And then a solemn stiffener about their responsibility to England. And finally an explanation why he must stay besieged but, nevertheless, fight.

The Boers on Umbulwana signalled a message to the Gordon High-landers at Fly Kraal Post: 'Where is Buller now? He has presented us with ten guns in place of three you took.' Could it possibly be true? Had Buller lost ten heavy guns?

The people in Ladysmith, civil and military, became depressed by the news of a British defeat Colenso way, but then were cheered by Sir George White's spirited rejuvenation. News began to seep through to them that their British comrades over on the Cape front were having a bad time; there were rumours that the British had been defeated at Stormberg and a place called Magersfontein. But Ladysmith was finding a new pride, born out of adversity. If England was crumbling elsewhere in Africa (though Baden-Powell and Mafeking were always a famous exception) Ladysmith was not going to crumble.

What was going wrong for the all-powerful British with their vast Empire? The American war-correspondent, Mr Easton of the *New York Journal*, wrote:

The Boers are fighting for everything a man holds dear. They are fighting against a machine soldier. I have seen General Joubert's wife load his guns for him; I have seen grandfather, son and grandson fight side by side. The Boer soldier is fighting for a prize worth winning; Tommy Atkins is fighting for a shilling a day. Hence the difference.

On 17 December, General White made the new situation official by informing the garrison that:

The General Officer commanding the Natal Field Force regrets to have to announce that General Buller failed to make good his first attack on Colenso. Reinforcements will not, therefore, arrive so early as was expected. Sir George White is confident that the defence of Ladysmith will be continued by the garrison in the same spirited manner as it has hitherto been conducted until the General Officer Commander-in-Chief in South Africa does relieve it.

And then, almost as though in response to that belt-tightening admission, came a scrap of good news from, of all people, General Buller:

December 17th: Fifth Division just arriving at the Cape. Have telegraphed for it to come on at once. It will make me strong enough to try Potgieter's [Drift]. How long can you hang on?

Sir George White replied:·

December 18th: Your 97 cipher of yesterday received and understood. Delighted to get it. I have provisions for men for 6 weeks, and I have confidence in holding this place for that time, but bombardment becomes more trying. I had 22 casualties this morning from one shell. Enteric and dysentery increasing very rapidly. I can get on well for 3 weeks, keeping even horses moderately fit. If you wish to wait for siege-guns, it is worth waiting a little to dominate and overwhelm the enemy's guns . . .

Major Robert Bowen faithfully put his pencil to paper:

Dec. 17: Although Buller is so near that we can hear his guns I see no immediate prospect of being relieved. We are all very tired of being shut in by a lot of farmers. I cant say all I think, but some of us think a good deal. At any rate we have underrated the Dutchman especially have the people at home. The poor uncivilized Boer! has not got much the worst of it so far. I am on the Observation Hill game again. Up at 1.30 every morning – 'so-long'.

Three days before, on 15 December, the fourth and final issue of the *Ladysmith Lyre* was off the humble press and was circulating the British-held kopjes. The editor, Mr George Steevens, kicked off a with song:

Two Jolly Little Sailor Guns

(Sung with immense success by Capt. Lambton.)

'It is very dangerous to attack the town. They have two naval guns from which we receive a very heavy fire, which we cannot stand.' (Extract from a letter taken on Gun Hill from Gunner Groenwald to his sister.)

We are two jolly little sailor guns,
And they've hauled us up
A long way from the sea.
We've given up the ocean,
With its undulating motion,
For the rocks that are steady as can be.

Och, Puffing Billy,
Why your shootin's only silly,
You may puff, puff, puff,
But you cannot shoot like we.
Though we're only 4.7,
We can send your men to heaven,
Or their craven hearts with terror inspire.

Intercepted Letters

To Miss Muggison, 15, Paradise Lane, Bethnal Green, London. (November 15, 1899.)

My dear ol' gal,

This ere Ladysmith is horful. We sits, and sits, and sits, and don't do nothink. Rations is short, taters is off, and butter is off. We only gets dubbin, and the shells from them bloomin' guns is a fair snorter. To ear 'em 'um do make you sit up, it do. Anyhow I ain't in Pretoria yet, like some I knows on. 'Ope this finds you as it leaves me.

Your affectionate
Bill.

On 20 December, during lunchtime, the big gun on Umbulwana Hill achieved a memorable bull's-eye. It fired a shell which whizzed across Ladysmith and hit the tower on the Town Hall, without exploding but carrying away one corner of the edifice. This damaged piece of civic pride became the most famous symbol in Ladysmith; today it is smugly mended.

On this same day a deputation including the mayor, Mr Farquhar, and town councillors called on Colonel Ward and made a disgraceful request. They humbly prayed that the parties of soldiers who bathed below the town in the Klip river on Sundays, would be henceforward stopped, because it shocked the feelings of the womenfolk. Colonel Ward got very angry with the unctuous petitioners and refused to listen to the formal words. He asked quite simply, 'Why do the women go to look?'

The enteric fever problem was now getting out of hand. At this time there were about 900 sick people in Ladysmith. General White himself went down with fever during mid-December and he was compelled to stay in his bed. For some time the Boer gunners had been throwing shells in the direction of his headquarters, a small house at the base of Convent Hill – which emphasized that the Boers knew well-nigh everything there was to know about the arrangements inside the town. And on 21 December, while the poor old boy was weakly sweating and shivering in bed, a large shell hit the house and actually burst in the next room to where he lay. The wall and furniture were blown to smithereens, but miraculously no one was killed, and Sir George was unscathed, at least physically . . . Lieutenant-Colonel St John Gore wrote that 'Unfortunately, it [the shell] landed among the "English stores" and the liquor, and it pains one even to think of the sad destruction of good drink and stores at such a time!'

The General was just lucky. Now more and more people were getting knocked over by the increasing bombardment. A newspaper correspondent saw a driver in the Royal Artillery hit by shell fragments:

His arms and breast were severely injured – far more severely than he thought. As he lay on his back he exclaimed, 'I can't drive any more, I can't fight, and I can't die. I can do nothing now.' This he repeated over and over again to each knot of sympathizing comrades who gathered near. And as he spoke relief came. 'Form up, No. 4 Company!' he cried, and the face turned grey and then rigid. The driver had been able to do something – he had died for his Queen and his country.

Another issue of the *Ladysmith Bombshell* appeared on 23 December and a few items are here selected:

Nevermore (With more apologies to E. A. Poe)

Once upon a midnight dreary, while I pondered weak and weary,
Over all the quaint and curious yarns we've had about the war,
Suddenly there came a rumour (we can always take a few more),
Started by some chap who knew more than the others knew before –
We shall have the Reinforcements in another – month or more:
Only this, and nothing more.
[five verses omitted]

For we're waiting rather weary. Is there such a chap as Clery?
Are there really reinforcements? Is there any Army Corps?
Shall we see our wives and mothers, or our sisters and our brothers,
Shall we ever see those others who went southwards long before?
Shall we ever taste fresh butter? Tell us, tell us, we implore:
Shall be answered nevermore.

The Song of the Besieged

When Buller wheels round Lombard's Kop,
When Piet Joubert has done a 'hop',
We'll sing, if only over 'dop',
'For this relief, much thanks!'

[Seven verses omitted]

Dear Ladysmith! Sweet, pretty thing,
Fond memories you'll ever bring;
But please excuse us, while we sing –
'For this relief, much thanks!'   (J.S.D.)

The Convent is now empty. Nun left.

The Home-Coming

The flags unfurl! Beat loud the drums!
  Shout out the victor's song –
At last the day of triumph comes,
  For which we've waited long.
Yet while o'erhead bright garlands wave,
  And fragrant roses rain,
Forget we not those heroes brave
  Who'll ne'er come home again.

If the relief column takes a day and a half to march a yard and a half, how much longer will the price of eggs be 10s 7d. per dozen?

Is the *Powerful* only waiting for a heavy dew to be able to get steam up for the relief of Ladysmith?

(Printed and Published at Ladysmith, Natal, 23 Dec., 1899 – G.W.L.)

It was generally hoped in Ladysmith that on Christmas Day 1899 the Boers would not fire a shot. Peace on earth and goodwill to all men! Optimism was soon dashed. The morning was heralded by salvos of Boer shells. The first two fell into the Natal Carabineers and Imperial Light Horse camps, but they did not explode. Collectors of these souvenirs (known in Ladysmith as conchologists) rushed to the holes in the ground and dug out the uneasy prizes. Both shells were unusual: the fuses had been removed and wooden plugs inserted in their places. When these plugs were gingerly pulled out, the shells were found to be stuffed with Christmas plum puddings and engraved on the outsides of the shells were the words 'With the Compliments of the Season'.

This story is no happy invention. I myself have stood in Ladysmith, holding one of these precious shells in my hands . . .

What did the British themselves do to celebrate Christmas Day? A public auction was held to dispose of the small stock of luxuries that still remained in private hands, and remembering the low cost of food in 1899, enormous prices were bid. There certainly was not much to sell; the entire supply fitted on to 'one long table'. The auction was held in a secluded alley, so that the Boer gunners could not see the activity, and the time selected was dusk. Eggs were sold at nine shillings a dozen – and freshness was not guaranteed. Thin ducks cost half a guinea each, and scrawny fowls were nine shillings and sixpence. Tinned butter was eight shillings and sixpence a pound. Three tiny cucumbers 'no longer than one's hand' fetched five shillings and when two Gordon Highlanders witnessed twenty-eight new potatoes being sold for thirty shillings, one said to the other, 'Come awa, mon! We dinna want nae sour grapes.'

But Colonel Ward and many others, as we shall see, displayed a fine sense of responsibility towards the non-capitalists of Ladysmith. The splendid Colonel had put aside a large supply of raisins for this very day. Boer gifts or no Boer gifts, the British would make their own Christmas puddings! Suet was a major problem, and, indeed, even after these many years I would rather not discuss how or where a substitute was found. Britishers were tougher then. Unhappily there was no rum for flavouring; what there was had to be husbanded for medicinal purposes. But the Christmas pudding was achieved and was eaten by every soldier, after he had partaken of a full ration of roast beef. And then there were inter-regimental sports, grandly entitled a 'Royal Military Tournament'.

The officers of one or two of the posher regiments refused to eat like plebs, whatever the shortages were. The 5th (Princess Charlotte of Wales) Dragoon Guards, produced a menu:

Ladysmith, Christmas Day, 1899. Menu:

Potages

Julienne (tinned – kept specially for Christmas)

Entrées

Nil

Rôti

Rosbif à la Anglais (Trek ox)

Légumes

Pomme de terre bouillees (one for each man)
Petits Pois (one small tin)

Relevés

Jambon au General Hunter (God bless the General for it!)

Entremets

Plum-pudding au Bulwan (nobody asked for a second helping)

Desserts

Apricots, peaches (several of the deserted houses in Ladysmith
have orchards attached).

Vins

Eau de Klip River (ad lib), cognac de Ladysmith (one bottle), Port
d'Afrique (one bottle), Rhum (commissariat quarter bottle).

N.B. The 'Rosbif' was slightly spoilt as the bakery was shelled when the meat
was in the oven, and the cooks left somewhat abruptly.

A special effort was made on behalf of the sick and wounded at Intombi
hospital. The morning train was loaded with fruit and flowers and with what
delicacies the beleaguered town could find.

The greatest and most moving achievement was accomplished for the
children of Ladysmith. The people who made themselves responsible for
this good task were the very men who had created the war, under their old
leader, Cecil Rhodes. Colonel Dartnell was relatively innocent in this respect,
but he was assisted by Colonel Frank Rhodes, Major Karri Davies, Lord
Ava, and others.

Karri Davies bought up every unbroken toy he could find in Ladysmith.
The others acquired four Christmas trees and, assisted by ladies of the town,
festooned them with decorations and presents. And round the bases of the
four trees were the imperial words, 'Great Britain', 'Australia', 'Canada' and

'South Africa'. Jingoes they were, but good jingoes on 25 December 1899. Above the four trees were festooned the folds of the Union Jack.

Father Christmas made an appearance, dressed in a costume of snowy swansdown – a brave Santa Claus in that sweltering African heat. They say that wherever he walked, feathers floated away from him. The imperial élite present worked like servants and suffered the little children willingly. General Sir George White VC arrived with General Sir Archibald Hunter and their staff officers. Sir George looked slowly around at the 200 children and was heard to remark, perhaps to himself, 'I had no idea that so many children remained in Ladysmith.'

There was only one sad fly in this ointment. The military and municipal announcement, giving notice of the children's party, read as follows:

Christmas Tree: All European children in Ladysmith are invited by Colonel Dartnell, C.M.G., and Major K. Davies to attend a Christmas party and Christmas tree in Messrs Walton and Tatham's Hall this evening at 7.30 till 9.30.
Ladysmith, 25th Dec., 1899.

It is only proper that the British people should acknowledge that, until quite recently, they practised cruel and open racial discrimination.

That evening of Christmas Day there was a dance and the young people who were not on duty celebrated until midnight.

On 26 December Major Robert Bowen wrote home:

Dear Missy, That repulse of Bullers since I last wrote was rather a disappointment and some of the fainter hearted (principally among the Staff) pulled very long faces over it. A Boer one day said to one of us – 'We think the British soldiers very brave men – braver than many of ours – but we place great reliance on *your* Generals!'

Perhaps this slight check to Buller may do good as it will show some of them the difference between a battle with modern weapons and an Aldershot field day or a day with the Soudanese of frontier tribes. Of course one can't write all you think but I may say there are some of these nigger whackers who have made themselves 'undieing reputations'. However they will write the accounts themselves and will doubtless pose as heroes and collar all the best rewards, instead of the poor fellows who are constantly shot at, while they the writers live in holes under ground – (all this of course is more or less confidential).

I have often thought about it for some years, but I had no conception of the effects of modern fire at distances of over a mile for rifles and over 3 miles for field guns till now. And my admiration for the courage of our men, but in especial of the gunners, is very high. Our field batteries are really splendid. I didn't imagine men would behave as they do, but there *guns* are inferior to the Boer guns. Yesterday

Lady White's New Year card, 1900

was fairly quiet and I had a day off so rode up to Wagon Hill to see Gore Browne and 3 coys of the 1st Bn. Had an excellent lunch with them then rode round the town with Campbell and the remainder of the 1st and 2nd Battns. except 10 coys on duty (outposts) and the Colonel who suffers from nerves and never dares leave a little hole in ground dined together. Each man had ⅓ of a pint of champagne, a spoonful of rum and ditto of whiskey – all of which had been saved up. We have been teetotalers for a fortnight so that was a big night. Thank goodness we have lots of Transvaal tobacco, but those common little Yankee cigarettes they sell at home for 10 a penny box are now at 5/- a box 6d each. I don't smoke them luckily. We've no vegetables so have to eat lots of sugar. I hope there is still plenty. The water is awful it is often quite thick with sand and filth and never lighter coloured than cafe au lait.

I expect you've had enough of grousing – I am perfectly happy and honestly prefer the hardships and dangers of this life, coupled with good health to the miseries of India, coupled with constant suffering. I sent you a telegram. I forget what it means yesterday [Christmas Day] . . . I end up each section of this letter so that it will be ready to send. Goodbye. Yrs ever – R. Bowen

There is a short message added in ink: '31.12.99 All right', and on that last day of the nineteenth century, Major Robert Bowen of the King's Royal Rifles had written his last words to his wife in England.

On 28 December 1899, another official notice went up on the walls of Ladysmith that suggested that though the inhabitants were having a rough time, they also knew that they were participating in a Famous Siege:

A Souvenir: As soon as circumstances will permit it is intended to have all residents of Ladysmith during the prolonged siege photographed in a group. A register is now open, and bona-fide residents are requested to communicate their names to the Town Clerk. – J. Farquhar, Mayor.

Who could not have been a bona-fide resident of Ladysmith, inside the siege? Spies and prisoners of war, I suppose. Major Marling, still ill at Intombi Camp, dealt with such a one on that very day:

December 28th . . . Sat on a court-martial on a civilian for holding correspondence with the Boers. Gave him three years' penal servitude just to steady him. Treacherous brute. We feed him with Government rations, although the fighting men are terribly short, and this is his gratitude.

Every human being inside Ladysmith was now hungry, but other living creatures were worse off. Mr H. W. Nevinson of the London *Daily Chronicle* wrote:

Almost the saddest part of the siege now is the condition of the animals. The oxen are skeletons of hunger, the few cows hardly give a pint of milk apiece, the horses are failing. Nothing is more pitiful than to feel a willing horse like mine try to gallop as he used, and have to give it up simply for want of food. During the siege I have taught him to talk better than most human beings, and his little apologies are really pathetic when he breaks into something like his old speed and stops with a sigh. It is the same with all.

As the month of December ended, the temperature rose in the day to 108° and fell during the night to 65°. It was recorded that on 31 December 1899 there were 1650 sick people inside Ladysmith.

9

THE RELIEVING FORCE
December 1899

Die, for God's sake, men, but don't leave your guns.
REDVERS BULLER

WHAT *had* been happening to Sir Redvers Buller and his Natal Field Force since the beginning of December? Let's start on the first of the month. On that day a telegram arrived for Sir Redvers in Pietermaritzburg from Lord Lansdowne, Secretary of State for War in London, stating that the 6th Division was being got ready and asking whether it was likely to be needed; and Buller replied:

1st December . . . I still think situation extremely grave. It seems to me that Methuen's force [over on the western Cape–Free State front] has all it can do to get to Kimberley, and I have a hard job to relieve Ladysmith. Situation in centre of Cape Colony [General Gatacre] becomes worse, and even with 5th Division we shall not be too strong to deal with it. Meanwhile, Mafeking will certainly fall . . . we shall certainly want another Division, or its equivalent in men . . . People here declare that ammunition of all sorts is being smuggled into Delagoa Bay [ammunition for the Boers through Portuguese East Africa]. In my opinion it is essential to blockade Delagoa Bay absolutely . . .

The reply came from London:

1st December . . . We cannot blockade Delagoa Bay in full sense of the word without going to war with Portugal, but cruisers are searching all doubtful vessels . . .

From Buller to Lansdowne:

8th December . . . I am aware of the difficulties attending the blockade of Delagoa Bay, but it is the only course I can think of for putting real pressure on the Transvaal . . . I do not think you realize the difficulties under which we carry on war here. The enormous distances, the extreme mobility of the enemy's troops compared with ours . . . that we shall succeed I do not doubt, but it will be at great cost of time and money. To give you an idea, I find I cannot force the Boer defences between here and Ladysmith and must turn them. To do this, I have to march 50 miles . . . They [the Boers] are also being told that a strong peace agitation is growing in England, and this, of course, hardens their wants . . .

These telegrams from Buller to Lansdowne are very important if one is to comprehend the size of the canvas and what was about to be painted on it. Buller's responsibility for the whole far-flung war (not merely Natal). His unease about his Generals, Methuen and Gatacre, over in the Cape. His miscalculation about Baden-Powell and Mafeking. His mind ranging far and wide to Portuguese Africa in a hope of stopping Boer arms supplies, by means of imperial threats to a neutral country. Finally, and very significantly, his categorical statement that he cannot break directly through the Tugela defences (at Colenso) but will have to perform a wide flanking movement with his great army. Back in November he had already thought about moving west and assaulting the Boer positions from across Potgieter's Drift.

After Lord Dundonald had carried out his reconnaissance towards Colenso on 28 November, and had been fired on, three more similar expeditions took place on 3, 6 and 8 December, and on the last two occasions General Buller went along personally. He peered through his telescope at the natural defences above and beyond Colenso and hoped that the Boers would again fire and disclose their gun positions, but nothing happened. The craggy hills presented a quiet African rural charm but Buller and his staff were not placated; they sensed a sinister deception.

So there was General Sir Redvers Buller VC thinking hard about the inevitability of that move west, parallel with the Tugela river, and there he was staring at his new maps and focusing on Potgieter's Drift and the Heights beyond, on the northern bank, and thinking, no doubt, of Ladysmith beyond them. The date was 10 December 1899. And it was on that day that he received news that General Gatacre and his British force had met with a disaster over in the Cape at a place called Stormberg. Out of the 3000 British soldiers involved, 25 were killed, 110 wounded, and 561 taken prisoner. There was also the peculiarly military disgrace of the loss of two artillery guns. General Gatacre and his surviving soldiers were falling back on Queenstown, in the Cape.

General Buller seemed to keep his head. He sent a kindly telegram to the defeated Gatacre, wishing him better luck next time and warning him to retire and take no risk of getting surrounded. Buller had already suffered enough from the siege predicament. But the Boers, as in Natal, were not following up their success. Gatacre was allowed to march away.

So presumably Buller hid his nightmare and began to think about crossing Potgieter's Drift once again.

On the following day, 11 December, another telegram was handed to Buller. General Lord Methuen had led his British soldiers, with the Highland Brigade to the fore, against the Boer positions at the foot of the low-lying Magersfontein Hills, south-west of Kimberley in the Cape, and out of his 15 000 soldiers, 948 were either killed, wounded or missing. Methuen was pulling his battered force back to their base at Modder river.

The machinery of Buller's plans to march westward continued to turn. On that fateful day, 11 December, orders were issued for his army to move west to Springfield and then on to Potgieter's Drift. On the 12th, soldiers began to move, but then, suddenly that evening, Buller called a halt and completely changed his mind. He would make a frontal attack on the Colenso position. It was a dreadful decision; he had reiterated to his staff, the War Office in London, and to Sir George White in Ladysmith, the impossibility of that frontal attack and now, suddenly, he was going to do just that. What was the message he had sent to Lord Lansdowne in London, four days before? 'I find I cannot force the Boer defences between here and Ladysmith and must turn them . . .' That had certainly been a categorical statement.

The horrific news from the Cape had affected Buller's nerve. He rationalized his new decision in a message to the War Office in London:

This operation [to the west across Potgieter's Drift] involved the complete abandonment of my communications, and, in the event of success, the risk that I might share the fate of Sir George White, and be cut off from Natal. I had considered that with the enemy dispirited by the failure of their plans in the west, the risk was justifiable, but I cannot think that I ought now to take such a risk. From my point of view it will be better to lose Ladysmith altogether than to throw open Natal to the enemy.

Was Buller unbalanced at this time? I have the greatest sympathy for him but the answer to that question must surely be in the affirmative. He was suggesting in that telegram that it was less of a risk to attack an impossible position than risk his lines of communication, and all because of defeats elsewhere. And what had attacking Colenso to do with losing Ladysmith?

On 13 December, he signalled those messages to Sir George White in Ladysmith: '. . . am coming through via Colenso . . . Actual date of attack depends on difficulties met with; probably 17th Dec.'

What would Buller's soldiers have to do, to succeed at Colenso? South of the Tugela river (the British side) the land was virtually an exposed, open plain; they would have to cross that. The river itself was said to be fordable at perhaps two places and that depended on the flow, which varied wildly according to the African rainfall; they would have to get across that. And beyond that river were the Colenso Heights, no doubt formidably held under the supervision of Louis Botha. That, of course, is the simplest description; there were many other geographical problems for the British – the main ones being that just to the west of Colenso, the river hooks up north and then south as it approaches the village (not an important village but incidentally on the south side of the river), then runs a short distance east and then strikes northward for about three miles, before flowing eastward again. Parallel with this northward thrust of the Tugela, but on the 'British' side of the river, runs a long, narrow hill named Hlangwane – held by the Boers.

There were a number of tactical options open to Buller now that he was set on attacking the Colenso position. Over to the west, on the Boers' central right flank, was Wagon Drift, a shallow in the Tugela river, and if this could be crossed and the heights above taken, it would make the Boer Colenso centre untenable. Secondly, and the most obvious: if Hlangwane Hill could be captured by the British, the Boers above Colenso would be dominated. And if the Boers on Hlangwane put up any formidable resistance to the attacking British, Buller's force could concentrate on them and annihilate them before tackling any other position. This should not have been very difficult to achieve, because the Boers on Hlangwane would have the Tugela river between them and their main force, and they didn't like that thought. Indeed, so unnerved were the Boers on Hlangwane at the thought of being on the 'British' side of the river, that they deserted their stronghold on 13 December. Botha argued, threatened and pleaded with them to return. All to no avail. Botha telegraphed Commandant-General Joubert, who was in Pretoria. Back came the reply that Hlangwane must be reoccupied at all costs. It was the key to the Colenso position. It was as important to the Boers as it was to the British – that is the point to remember. Still the burghers tried to dodge the uncomfortable issue. Lots were drawn and fate selected the Wakkerstroom burghers, together with volunteers from other commandos. They crossed the Tugela river and reoccupied Hlangwane at 3 a.m. on 15 December.

Buller decided that he would not cross at Wagon Drift, to the west, nor would he take Hlangwane. Well, crossing at Wagon Drift would seem a good idea, as any hope of outflanking a strongly held centre is a good idea, but no more. The taking of Hlangwane, on the other hand, was a dire necessity. Buller confessed that capturing Hlangwane was 'tempting' but gave as his main reason for refusing the temptation 'that its possession did not in any way assist the crossing' – which depends on how one might try to cross; if the British were on Hlangwane they could certainly make things difficult for the Boers in their central position, who would be opposing the main British attack towards the Iron Railway Bridge. No, Buller seemed to be suffering from some blind desperation. He was going to go at Colenso like an unthinking bull at a gate.

The overture to battle was a general bombardment of supposed Boer positions north of the Tugela river. General Buller's official report stated that 'All visible defences had been heavily shelled by eight Naval guns on the 13th and 14th [December], but though some of the defences were damaged and accurate ranges obtained, we failed to induce the enemy to disclose his own position, or to reply in any way to our fire.' Incidentally, the naval guns had arrived at their battle position, quickly named 'Gun Hill' on the morning of the 13th. They were manned by sailors from Her Majesty's Ships *Forte*, *Philomel* and, primarily, *Terrible*, all under the command of Captain E. P. Jones RN.

On 14 December, General Buller called his senior officers together and announced that they would attack Colenso on the following morning. These senior officers were Major-General Hildyard, commanding the 2nd Brigade, which consisted of the 2nd East Surreys, the 2nd West Yorks, the 2nd Devons and the 2nd West Surreys; Major-General Hart, commanding the 5th Brigade, which consisted of the 1st Connaught Rangers, the 1st and 2nd Royal Dublin Fusiliers, the 1st Royal Inniskilling Fusiliers and the 1st Border Regiment; Major-General Lyttelton, commanding the 4th Brigade, which consisted of the 1st Rifle Brigade, the 1st Durham Light Infantry, the 3rd King's Royal Rifles and the 2nd Scottish Rifles; Major-General Burton, commanding the 6th Brigade, which consisted of the 2nd Royal Fusiliers, the 2nd Royal Scots Fusiliers, the 2nd Royal Irish Fusiliers and the 1st Royal Welch Fusiliers; and finally Major-General the Earl of Dundonald, commanding the Cavalry Brigade, which comprised the 13th Hussars, the 1st Royal Dragoons, the South African Light Horse, Thorneycroft's Mounted Infantry, Bethune's Mounted Infantry, the Natal Carabineers (one squadron) and the Imperial Light Horse (one squadron).

General Buller disclosed his plan of action. The 5th Brigade (General Hart) was to attempt a crossing of the Tugela river at Bridle Drift, about two and a half miles west of Colenso, just west of the northern hook of the

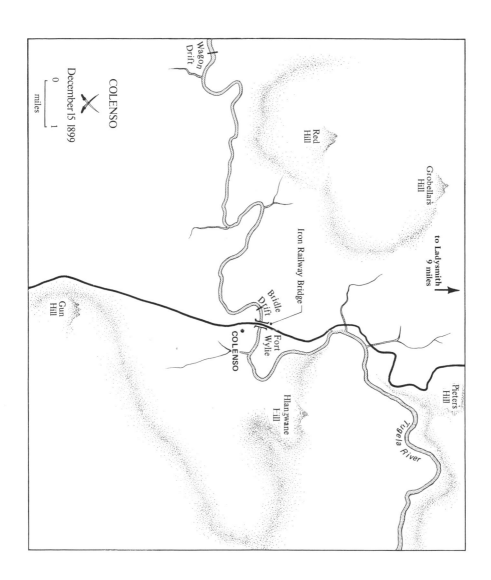

COLENSO

December 15 1899

0   1
miles

Wagon
Drift

Red
Hill

Grobellars
Hill

to Ladysmith
9 miles

Iron Railway Bridge

Bridle
Drift

Fort
Wylie

Gun
Hill

COLENSO

Hlangwane
Hill

Pieters
Hill

Tugela River

river. The 2nd Brigade (General Hildyard) was to attempt to cross the Iron Railway Bridge itself and a possible drift a short way down river. Lord Dundonald and his cavalry were to make a gesture against Hlangwane Hill (cavalry seem to me to be the most unhappy choice for this job, even if dismounted for the actual assault). The 4th Brigade (General Lyttelton) was to stand in reserve to assist either the 5th or 2nd Brigades, when required. The 6th Brigade (General Barton) was to support the right flank of the 2nd Brigade and Lord Dundonald's mounted men. And though this order of battle suggests a thin concept of tactics, the hard essence of the scheme was to go straight at the Boers' centre, with a blatant frontal attack by General Hildyard's 2nd Brigade. It is reported in *The Times History of the War in South Africa* that General Buller's officers accepted this military plan without discussion. It seems that though they must have been taken aback by Buller's change of ideas they had, at this time, some sort of mystical faith in his infallibility. A strange incidental to all this neurotic revamping of strategy and tactics was that the orders were put out under General Clery's name, the man still nominally in command of the South Natal Field Force. But Buller was our man . . . From this point onwards Buller was responsible for many strange and mysterious actions, and they came thick and fast. As I hope you will remember, Buller's last calculation to Sir George White in Ladysmith was, 'Actual date of attack depends on difficulties met with; probably 17th Dec.' This information was sent for a practical purpose, so that Sir George White could synchronize a second attack in the rear of the Boers' Tugela positions. And now, with Buller planning to attack two days earlier, on 15 December, he failed even to inform Sir George White. As we already know, the first hat Sir George White and the inhabitants of Ladysmith knew of the battle of Colenso was the distant sound of heavy gunfire, far to the south.

Before daylight on the morning of 15 December, the heavy naval guns – 4·7s and 12-pounders – were ready for action. By 5.30 a.m., at 5000 yards range, they had opened fire on the Colenso Hills and in particular the rock bastion called Fort Wylie. These guns pounded the area with lyddite shells (the latest horror of modern warfare) and it was felt by watchers that few men could have survived the holocaust of flying earth and stones and fire and green fumes. No Boer guns replied; the British began to wonder whether Fort Wylie and the Colenso Hills around were occupied by the Boers at all.

And then, just after 'McCormick', as Victorian soldiers called the sun, rose above the horizon, there began a British move which is keenly felt in Royal Artillery circles to this day. Colonel Long, who had recently ordered out Winston Churchill's disastrous armoured train, and was now, at the battle of Colenso, in command of the artillery, moved forward with the 14th and 66th Batteries of Royal Field Artillery, plus six naval 12-pounders. His orders were to cover General Hildyard's attack on the Boer centre, but his orders were also that he should only move under cover of General Barton's 6th Brigade, which was there in support. Now Colonel Long was an emotional and impetuous chap, as we have already sensed, and therefore protecting General Hildyard was fine, but the fact that he should have to be protected himself by General Barton's infantry was not so fine. He seems to have been totally opposed to caution in any manoeuvre that he was responsible for, whether it was an armoured train or, now, heavy guns. He quite clearly expressed his belief on what his British guns should do in this battle of Colenso. Colonel Long said, with imperial ardour: 'The only way to smash those beggars is to rush in at 'em.' And this is precisely what he did.

Colonel Long and his guns were three miles from the Tugela river on the east side of the railway when he gave the order to advance. In front were a detachment of mounted battery scouts. About a quarter of a mile behind were Colonel Long, his staff officer Captain Herbert, Colonel Hunt, and Lieutenant Ogilvy, Royal Navy. They trotted past their infantry escort belonging to Barton's brigade, and behind them came the guns. General Barton sent a message requesting Colonel Long to wait; the Colonel ignored it, and continued to ride his guns further and further ahead. There were more requests from Barton, and on rode Long with his guns. Soldiers in the rear watched Long's eccentricity with fascination. The mounted battery scouts had actually reached the scrub bushes which grew along the vicinity of the river and Colonel Long and his guns were only 700 yards from the Tugela itself when he gave the order to go into action. Not a sound had come from the Boers. The British began to unlimber when one single round was fired from the Colenso Hills. Was it a Boer signal? Immediately, from the far side of the river, the Boer mausers blazed away from their hidden trenches at Colonel Long and his gunners – Barton's infantry were over a mile to the rear. The British guns were speedily arranged in their parade order and began to fire, and the horses were raced back to a donga (a dried-up stream) about 400 yards to the rear. The naval guns were being pulled by oxen and therefore were a little behind the field batteries. The navy came into action where they happened to be when the Boers opened fire.

A Gunner Platt described the Boer onslaught: 'Colonel Long was so confident he could sweep the Boers off the face of the earth that he took the guns right into the Boer camp. Then what a surprise they got. About 2000 rifles went bang, and about 10 guns, and before they could say "Jack Robinson" the troops were nearly cut to pieces.'

It has been calculated that something between 1000 and 2000 Boer rifles were firing on the British guns and gunners. It was an appalling situation. Within a few minutes Captain Schreiber and Captain Goldie were killed, and Colonel Hunt and three other officers were wounded. But the survivors were heroic; they simply fed their guns in a storm of flying lead. The British concentrated on Fort Wylie, from which direction the mass of Boer fire came. Fort Wylie was at 1250 yards range and the British guns actually succeeded in beating down the volume of Boer rifle fire, but not Boer shell fire, which increased in intensity. At 6.30 a.m. tragic Colonel Long was cut through the body by a shrapnel bullet and, as brave men carried him back to a little ditch behind the guns, he kept repeating: 'My brave gunners, my brave gunners!' In the ditch, Colonel Long was amongst his wounded and dying men, and there he refused point-blank to accept medical attention until every single soldier had been attended to.

Artillerymen continued to feed the guns. A gunner from Birmingham described the awful scene:

Everything was done as cool as if it was on a drill-field, instead of a battlefield. My off horse had his two hind legs blown clean off in the first half hour. I got another, a steel-grey, and had not had him handed to me ten minutes when a shell entered his side and literally blew him to atoms. My riding horse was next struck slightly. After about an hour and a half we expended all our ammunition. We found that the ammunition supply had been cut off. We were then left in a trap, but our men stuck to the guns. It was nothing but horses and men falling on all sides. The cries were something awful to listen to. Every now and again a man would give a cry such as: 'Oh, my poor wife!' and would fall from his horse.

By 7 a.m. the British guns were running out of men to serve them, and ammunition was almost gone. Orders were given to the survivors to retire back to the big donga and there await the ammunition columns to come forward; it was discovered that these columns were still three miles behind. Back to the donga came the British gunners, in quiet order, carrying their wounded with them. Captain Herbert then rode back towards the distant ridge where General Buller and his staff were located. His job was to report the terrible event and to try to get ammunition for the abandoned guns.

Yet still British soldiers remained with the artillery. Bennet Burleigh of the *Daily Telegraph* reported:

Four men persisted in serving two guns and remaining beside their cannon.

One of either pair carried the shell; the others laid and fired their beloved 15-pounders. But two men were left. They continued the unequal battle. They exhausted the ordinary ammunition, and finally drew upon and fired the emergency rounds of case, their last shot. Then they stood to 'attention' beside the gun, and an instant later fell, pierced through and through by Boer bullets. These, I say, by the light of all my experience in war, these gunners of ours are men who deserve monuments over their graves and even Victoria Crosses in their coffins.

But General Buller was not concentrating on Colonel Long's disastrous predicament, nor even at that time aware of it. Nor was he considering General Hildyard's central movement towards the Iron Bridge. No, General Buller's telescope was focusing on General Hart's Irish Brigade, the 5th, over on the left flank. There was horrible trouble there.

The Irishmen had taken breakfast at 3 a.m., but before that, their tents had been struck and packed. They 'fell in' at 3.30 a.m. and General Hart drilled them until 4 a.m. Then, in parade ground style they marched towards the Tugela river, with General Hart riding in front and carrying the traditional sword. Riding with him were his staff officers, and guiding them was 'a trusty Kaffir', who was under a civilian, a Mr Norgate, who was an 'official colonial guide'. You may recall that General Hart's orders were to cross his brigade at Bridle Drift, a little to the west of the Tugela's hook northwards. First marched the 1st and 2nd Royal Dublin Fusiliers in 'fours from the right of companies at deploying intervals', and behind came the Inniskilling Fusiliers, the Connaught Rangers and the Border Regiment – all in 'mass of quarter columns', which is a hazardous manner to advance on any enemy armed with decent guns. On the Irish Brigade's rear left were two batteries of Royal Field Artillery under Colonel Parsons, and guarding the brigade's left flank were the Royal Dragoons under Colonel Burn-Murdoch.

Then the African guide made an unexpected pronouncement. He insisted that Bridle Drift (the shallows where Hart's brigade was to cross the Tugela) was not west of the sharp loop of the river, but right in the centre, where it curved sharply into Boer territory. General Hart does not seem to have questioned this new information. He *should* have questioned whether it was possible for his soldiers to expose themselves on this tongue of land. If Boers were about, they could fire not only into his centre but into both his flanks as well.

Colonel Burn-Murdoch, far out on the left flank with his Dragoons, could see the Boers waiting for the Irishmen. They could see them waiting in their well-constructed trenches. Colonel Burn-Murdoch hurried the news to General Hart. But Hart did not waver in his advance – into an inevitable death trap.

A Private Dwyer wrote to his father in Darlington, England:

The formation was quarter columns, which were very close. We marched along until some of our scouts came in with the news that the Boers were entrenched in front. I don't think the General believed them, for, instead of opening us out, as is the rule laid down in every military book that ever was printed, he closed us up together until we were a solid mass, thus being a target for artillery at nine or ten miles. But the mistake was not found out, as usual, until the Boers dropped a shell into the right of the Dublins, which left the best half of a company of the poor fellows lying there . . .

General Hart belonged to a very old school of active service behaviour. He was usually against the military precaution of spreading his men. He believed in keeping his Irishmen 'well in hand' and steamrollering forward regardless of losses. Shortly after 6.30 a.m. the leading companies were about 200 yards from the river when Boer rifles and artillery exploded into them. The Boers fired from the front and from both flanks. The Irishmen were sent spinning right, left and centre.

General Hart himself described this moment of impact:

A tremendous rifle fire was poured into us from our front, and a considerable rifle fire from our left front. There was no smoke and not a sign of the enemy himself, or even a horse, but the streaks of dust as the Boer bullets showered in, grazing the ground, plainly showed where they were . . . The infantry lay down flat. Fire was new to them . . .

Sergeant Wood of the Inniskillings wrote:

The very earth seemed to rise in front of us, and we were torn by shot and shell. I shall never forget the confusion. The Colonel sprang from his horse and cried: 'Deploy', but between the Connaught Rangers pressing back and old mules kicking, we had some difficulty in getting in order. As we lay down I heard some tall chap cry, 'Oh God!' and when I looked round his face was clean smashed off by a shell.

A soldier of the Inniskillings named Jack Hendry accused the Borderers and Connaught Rangers of lying down and refusing to advance:

The Borderers and Connaughts were thrown into terrible confusion by a terrible fire from the Boers who were hidden so well in their trenches that they could not be seen. These two regiments wavered, and got the order to lie down from their officers. After about quarter of an hour the General [Hart] rode up and gave an

O WERE THE OFFICERS LEADING THE WAY

P WERE THE PRIVATES ENJOYING THE FRAY

From An Active Army Alphabet

order to the Border Regiment to go on, but I am ashamed to say that not a single man of them moved, although the General threatened to shoot them.

General Hart described his persuasive powers differently, in a letter to a friend:

Nevertheless they [shells] alarmed our inexperienced soldiers greatly. Still they held their ground. There was no retreat, but they lay flat, and to a great extent were deaf to every effort of mine to go on.

I could see officers here and there urging on the advance; and all this was so far successful that a slow advance was made. Here and there men with better nerves pushed on. There was no panic, and once when I said to a lot of men who were deaf to my commands to advance – 'If I give you a lead, if your General gives you a lead – will you come on?' they answered quite cheerily with their brogues 'We will sir', and up they jumped and forward they went . . . The Kaffir [the 'trusty Kaffir' guide, who had persuaded Hart to advance up into the loop of the Tugela] disappeared directly the first shots were fired and was not seen afterwards, but Mr Norgate [the official colonial guide] a civilian gentleman, not called upon by his engagement to risk life, kept near me under that heavy fire, in case he could be of any use to me; very gallant, patriotic conduct that I hope will be recognized well; and, poor fellow, an hour or two after he ruptured himself helping to carry a wounded man.

Without knowing how to cross the river, Irishmen were now crowding the southern bank and were getting slaughtered for their efforts. The river at this point was about ten feet deep and flowing strongly. A boy-bugler named Dunne, who had been ordered to the rear when the metal began to fly and had disobeyed the order, put his bugle to his mouth and sounded the 'Advance'. A bullet struck Dunne in the right arm and men of the Dublins fixed their bayonets and went into the river.

Bugler Dunne was wounded, and Canon Rawnsley was at the story as sharp as a bayonet:

The Bugler's Wish

What shall we give to you, bugler boy,
For the bugle they lost in the Tugela's wave,
The day you fell on Colenso plain?
And the bugler-laddie he answered brave,
Give? – give me leave, in the Queen's employ,
To go to the Front with my bugle again!

Poor little Bugler Dunne! If it hadn't been for his military conditioning, I think he should have had his bottom smacked for sounding that 'Advance'. The Queen gave him a new instrument on which was inscribed:

Presented to
Bugler JOHN FRANCIS DUNNE,
1st Battalion Royal Dublin Fusiliers,
by
QUEEN VICTORIA,
To replace the Bugle Lost by Him on the
Field of Battle at Colenso on the 15th
December, 1899, when he was Wounded.

My friend, Peter Strong, flew Mr Dunne over Ladysmith and along the Tugela river in 1950, on the fiftieth anniversary of those famous days!

Sergeant George Murray of the Royal Dublins wrote:

Fire and water could not stop the Dublins. We had to hold our rifles over our heads, ploughing through muddy water, which was half-red with blood, and the water was getting very deep. A general halt was called five yards from the opposite side of the river. 'What on earth can be the matter?' we asked. 'Lead on, men – lead on, men,' was the command given by Captain Gordon, as he plunged to the front, but was checked by the barbed and netted wire concealed underneath the water. There our men formed a target for the enemy.

Another soldier related:

What a scene! Fellows groaning and the fellows that were dead were black! There was a continual shout of 'Doctor', 'Stretcher!', etc. And all the men were cool. My chum said to another fellow, 'Give me a light for my cigarette before I get shot.' The next minute I heard a groan: he was shot. One of our fellows – a drummer boy about fourteen years, who had been doing his best for the wounded – was shot dead.

General Buller viewed the disaster from Gun Hill where the heavy naval guns were firing at the Boer positions at about 4500 yards range. He despatched his Military Secretary, Colonel Stopford, to General Hart, with orders to retire his brigade, and then followed in person. Immediately afterwards he rode across to General Lyttelton, whose 4th Brigade was waiting in reserve, and said to Lyttelton: 'Hart has got into a devil of a mess down there; get him out of it as best you can.'

General Hart wrote:

I therefore gave the order to *retire slowly*, and almost immediately a tremendous fire from our artillery (Naval and Military) passed over my head, and shells rained into the positions the Boers apparently occupied, though no sign of them was ever visible.

Under cover of this fire we retired slowly. There was, here and there, an attempt to double back, but I drew my sword and stretched out my arms and ordered a halt at once, and then retirement again when the rear-most men retiring were up.

About ten soldiers of the Connaught Rangers and twenty of the Inniskilling Fusiliers, all under a Colonel Thackeray, were left stranded out on the far right flank. Indeed they had heard of no order to retire. They were forced to cease firing when ambulance wagons began to appear. And then, suddenly, they were surrounded by Boers. One of the Irishmen recounted what happened:

The Colonel and his few men were at last surrounded by the Boers, and their leader asked Colonel Thackeray to give up his arms, but he replied that they could take him prisoner, as he couldn't help himself, but he refused to part with his arms.

The upstart was that the Boer told him that he was a brave man, and let him go, telling him that if he came to Pretoria, he would have a bottle of brandy waiting for him.

When the old colonel returned to camp the old Irish Brigade hurried out and cheered him again and again.

Though Hart's brigade was smashed, General Buller still hoped to force the passage of the Tugela and battle on to Ladysmith. He still had three relatively unscathed brigades and forty-four guns – at least, so he thought. He decided to throw all his remaining military strength at the centre. General Hildyard's 2nd Brigade, consisting of the 2nd East Surreys, the 2nd West Yorks, the 2nd Devons and the 2nd West Surreys, would move up, west of the railway, straight through Colenso. Already the Queen's and Devons were moving in attack formation. But now Captain Herbert galloped up with the awful news of Colonel Long's guns. Twelve were out of action, standing abandoned except for the dead and dying gunners. It was 8 a.m. Buller decided to break off the action. He ordered one of the leading battalions across the railway to support the guns and allowed two other battalions to continue towards Colenso village, but not to become 'too hotly engaged'. Then he himself, accompanied by General Clery, rode towards the donga just behind the abandoned guns, where the survivors lay amongst 'pools of steaming blood'. It was an extraordinary ride for a general of independent command to make. He was under heavy fire. Trooper Billing, of the Natal Mounted Field Force, and one of General Buller's bodyguard, described the situation:

... we had to ride with him right through the enemy's fire, and the shells were bursting all around us with one perpetual roar. One of our men had a shell burst over him, and another went right through his saddle and never hurt him. I had a spent bullet hit my horse as I was riding along, and they were hitting the ground just like hail ... I was expecting to feel one hit every moment ... All the time we were going along at a walk with General Buller in front; he did not seem to care a bit for all the bullets or shells, and I saw them bursting all round him; he never even turned his head, but walked on as if nothing had happened.

I think General Buller is about the bravest man I have ever seen, and he is also a very nice man to speak to. The screaming of the wounded and the yelling of the dying was awful to hear.

Buller was finally struck by a shrapnel bullet and his personal doctor, Captain Hughes, anxiously rode to his side. A Private Richardson, of the Royal Army Medical Corps, witnessed the event and related that: 'He [Buller] calmly replied that it had only just taken his wind a bit.' And then Private Richardson went on to comment: 'If he is not worth following, I don't know who is. He is as brave as a lion. If all the officers were like him this war would soon be at an end.' The doctor, Captain Hughes, was then killed at Buller's side.

In the donga, a Colonel Hunt, who had been shot through both legs, suggested to Colonel Long, who was wounded in arm, liver and kidneys, that it would be best to abandon the guns. Long recovered sufficiently to reply: 'Abandon be damned! We never abandon guns.' The layman should understand that in the Royal Artillery, the guns are, as it were, their 'colours' also. To lose a gun was to lose a 'colour'. It was reported in the London *Westminster Gazette*, quoting an officer, that when General Buller arrived at the donga he cried: 'Die, for God's sake, men, but don't leave your guns!' He was not simply making a plea to save hardware.

Then General Buller called for volunteers to try to retrieve those symbolic weapons. But first a Natal transport driver, Driver Fred Hinton, with a comrade whose name I cannot discover, galloped into the appalling fire and retrieved a load of ammunition. As they got back their shattered horse dropped dead. General Buller told his ADC, Captain Schofield RHA, to take charge of the rescue bid. And Gunner C. H. Young claims that the General added his voice to the appeal for volunteers: ' "Now, my lads, this is your last chance to save the guns; will any of you volunteer to fetch them?" We sat half stunned for a minute, and then Corporal Nurse got up, and as soon as we saw him we volunteered at once to fetch them. There were six gunners and one corporal.'

These soldiers were all of the 66th Battery RFA. And with them, two officers had stepped forward, Captain Congreve, Rifle Brigade and from the headquarters staff, and Lieutenant the Hon. Fred S. Roberts, 60th Rifles, ADC to General Clery, and only son of Field-Marshal Lord Roberts of Kandahar. The latter, in volunteering for so lethal a mission, must have added awful drama on awful drama. In a way he was under the personal supervision of Buller. Lord Roberts, his father, was the most famous and most loved soldier in the British Army. But there was no way of preventing the gesture.

Captain Schofield got to the guns with two teams, but fifty yards from the little ditch behind the guns, Lieutenant Roberts was shot from his horse, mortally wounded. A corporal of the 66th Battery, whom I believe to be Corporal Nurse, has left this account:

I got the horses over to the limber, and Lord Roberts's son held my horse while I helped to hook in.

As soon as I got them mounted I started off at a gallop for the guns, half a mile away. The enemy were following us with a perfect storm of shot and shell, one of which burst overhead just before we mounted and took the off-centre's eye clean out. Lord Roberts's son was shot as we were going up.

Captain Congreve himself remembered the details:

All one could see were little tufts of dust all over the ground, a whistling noise, 'phut', where they hit, and an increasing rattle of musketry somewhere in front. My first bullet went through my left sleeve, and just made the joint of my elbow bleed. Next, a clod of earth caught me a smack on the other arm; then my horse got one; then my right leg one and my horse another. That settled us, for he plunged and I fell about 100 yards short of the guns we were going to.

The corporal continued his account:

When we got to the guns I went to the left hand one, and tried to pull it up to the limber, but it was stuck in the stones. I ran across to the others, some twenty yards away, and helped the staff officer to limber up. I then ran back to the other one, and managed to get it on the hook. The bullets were pattering around us like hail. One went through my haversack, piercing a hand-glass and piece of bread I had in it, hit my revolver pouch and splintered one of the fingers of my right hand in two places. I got the two guns back safely, despite the heavy fire we experienced going and coming. General Buller watched it all, and sent down for our names the same day. Next day he sent his aide-de-camp to thank me for our gallant conduct, etc., and for the cool way in which we behaved. I saved the honour of my battery.

All this time, young Lieutenant Fred Roberts was lying out in the open,

229- (COPYRIGHT) - MR WINSTON CHURCHILL AFTER HIS
ESCAPE FROM THE BOERS REVISITS THE SCENE OF HIS HEROISM
THE ARMOURED TRAIN DISASTER - BOER WAR-1899-1900

J.E.M.
Photo

Winston Churchill revisits the wreck of the armoured train

Field artillery cross the Tugela River

General Clery watches the effect of the naval guns in action during the Battle of Colenso

The Battle of Spion Kop. British soldiers carry the Red Cross flag

The dead on Spion Kop

A shell explodes in a Boer gun emplacement

A section of British troops advances in line during the Battle of the Tugela Heights

Major R. Bowen
and part of the last letter he wrote to his
wife in England (see page 159)

A civilian shelter at Ladysmith

The British Naval Brigade in Ladysmith

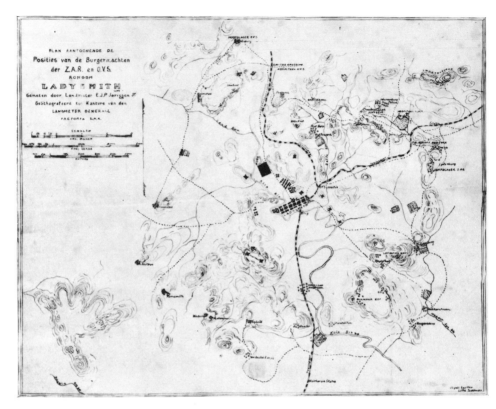

A map of Ladysmith, used by the besieging Boers

The Base Hospital Camp behind the Town Hall, Ladysmith

British troops resting after the official entry into Ladysmith. Note the shell damage to the tower of the Town Hall

The first and last shells – from *The Leaguer of Ladysmith*, a contemporary book by Captain Clive Dixon, who served with the besieged garrison

still alive, but under a heavy fire and suffering a cruelly hot sun. As soon as
Captain Congreve saw his situation, although wounded himself, he began
to crawl towards the lonely body. Major Babtie of the Royal Army Medical
Corps, who for the previous two hours had been tending the wounded in the
donga, also crawled out to assist, and together these two officers brought
Lieutenant Roberts into comparative shelter.

A little later, Captain Reed of the 7th Battery RFA out on the left flank,
led three wagon teams in an attempt to save the remaining guns. This also
was an astoundingly heroic effort, covered in blood. Before these soldiers
reached the guns they had lost thirteen horses out of twenty-two, and seven
men out of thirteen. Captain Reed was shot in the leg and this effort was
abandoned. Bombardier Stephenson was one of the survivors:

> The wheel driver who came up with me and was shot in the leg, got shot
> again through the left cheek and died immediately. You can imagine how excited
> and frightened we were. We took his jacket off and covered him up; and then we
> lay along with the dead, with bullets flying all around us, and now and again shells
> hitting the limbers, just grazing our bodies. We gave up all hopes, but not one of us
> showed our fear . . .
> The 14th and my own battery [the 7th] lost 110 men killed, wounded and miss-
> ing. My section officer was killed; a major, a captain and a lieutenant were wounded.
> Another lieutenant was taken prisoner, as was also the sergeant-major. The officers
> were pecked off like skittles.
> We hadn't one of our officers left; they were all wounded, and one was shot
> dead; but next morning the General came up to our camp, and he told us he never
> witnessed such a grand display of gallantry in his life as when we tried to save the
> guns. Out of 175 horses we returned with 64; 26 of them wounded and 38 sound.
> Out of 165 men only 91 returned, but half of them were in charge of the baggage.

Major Babtie, Captains Congreve and Reed, Lieutenant Roberts and
Corporal Nurse all received the Victoria Cross. At first, General Buller
refused to recommend Captain Schofield for this award, on the ground that
he had 'told' him to make an attempt to save the guns. But finally the powers-
that-be moved and Captain Schofield also got the Victoria Cross. Eighteen
non-commissioned officers and artillery drivers received the Distinguished
Conduct Medal.

At 11 a.m. General Buller collapsed in his own curious way. He decided
simply to abandon the guns and by 11.30 a.m. a general retirement of his
army was under way.

Lord Dundonald's mounted brigade had not been able to achieve very
much with their limited resources against Hlangwane Hill. He had attacked

from the south and from the south-east, but here, led by Lieutenant-Colonel Thorneycroft, of Thorneycroft's Mounted Infantry, the British found themselves in danger of being outflanked on their right and being taken in the rear — which wouldn't do at all. Lord Dundonald appealed to General Barton, commanding the 6th Brigade, but the General had already been forbidden to move eastward by Buller. So Dundonald held on as best he could. His force began to withdraw, under difficulties, at about 11.30 a.m.

A last tragic spasm of the battle happened in a break in the ground, a little way in front of the abandoned guns. There Colonel Bullock, commanding the Devons, was isolated with two sections of his men. No order to retire had reached him — understandably, that far out. Some Boers of the Vryheid and Krugersdorp Commandos and some Johannesburg Police, all under Field-Cornet Emmett (a man not without noble Irish blood), brother-in-law of General Louis Botha, approached to collect the ten 'great, splendid cannons'. Colonel Bullock's men fired. Field-Cornet Emmett collected a British ambulance orderly, who was looking for wounded, and went under cover of a Red Cross flag to ask the Devons to surrender. Colonel Bullock ordered the Boers back, stating that he wished to fight. But some Devon soldiers, parched for a drink, began to raise white emblems. It is said that Colonel Bullock reached for his revolver. What is certain is that a Boer clouted him over the head with the butt of his rifle, stunning Colonel Bullock.

It might be interesting to examine several versions of the above episode; certainly it would prove how difficult it is to realize what exactly has happened in history.

A French officer, M. Galopaud, who had resigned his commission in the 9th Chasseurs to fight with the Boers, reported his version in France's *Matin*:

... in a dip of ground, 150 men and nine officers have remained, and after its surrender. Among the officers are two colonels, one of whom commanded this artillery. As he is throwing up his arms he discharges five revolver shots almost point-blank on the unlucky man who is advancing with trust in the honour of an officer ... The Boers did not kill him. One of them struck him on the head with the stock of his rifle, wounding him rather severely in the eye.

Captain Congreve was there, wounded:

It was half-past four that the Boers rode up and asked us to surrender, or they would shoot us all. Colonel Bullock was the senior unwounded officer, and had perhaps twenty rifles all told. He refused, and they at once began a fusillade from fifty yards distant, and our people returned it. It was unpleasant, and only a question of minutes before they enfiladed our trenches and bagged the lot. Bullock's men knocked over two, and they then put up a white flag, parlayed, said we might remove our wounded, and the remainder either be taken prisoner or fight it out. However, whilst we were talking, a hundred or so crept round us. We found loaded rifles at every armed man's head, and we were forced to give in.

Or Private Glanfield, of the 2nd Devons:

When the Boers came to take the Colonel, he refused to give up his revolver, and one of the Boers gave him a crack across the head with his rifle, and one of my section put a bayonet through him, and then they shot him afterwards.

Well, who tells the truth? Certainly Captain Congreve, being badly wounded, was allowed to return to his own people; a colour-sergeant of the Devons carried him on his back – so it is said.

As for Colonel Bullock, a letter from Pretoria related that:

The Colonel who commanded two batteries at Colenso and lost ten cannons arrived here on December 19th, ill and in very low spirits. The last hour in the ambulance train he had pinned a paper on his breast, on which was written 'I am the officer who lost ten cannons at Colenso.' With the greatest difficulty they took this paper away from him.

If that story is true, how tragic! Colonel Bulloc, was certainly not the loser of ten cannon at Colenso. Perhaps the whack on the head deranged him.

The *Manchester Guardian*'s war correspondent saw General Buller at this time of acknowledged defeat:

Sir Redvers Buller and his Staff came by me on their return. The General climbed down limply and wearily from his horse like an old, old man. I thought he was wounded with vexation; I did not know then that he was wounded.

The British suffered a grand total of 1127 casualties. Seven officers and 138 men were killed, 43 officers and 719 men wounded, 21 officers and 199 men missing and prisoners. The Boer casualties were about forty altogether.

What did the Boers think about it all? As the sun sank behind the Drakensberg Mountains, they began to sing their favourite psalms, and young General Botha composed his battle despatch for old President Kruger, back in Pretoria: 'Colenso, Dec. 15 (8 p.m.): The God of our forefathers granted us a brilliant victory today.'

Of course, as General Buller slumped wearily from his horse, and General Botha composed his simple puritan words, the physical agony of many men was only beginning. Frederick Treves, Surgeon Extraordinary to Her Majesty the Queen, etc., and Consulting Surgeon with Her Majesty's Troops in South Africa, was waiting for the wounded, just behind Gun Hill. It was the first time that he had gone to war, and in his memorable book *The Tale of a Field Hospital* he movingly described what he experienced:

When I arrived the ambulances were already coming in – the dreary ambulances, each one with a load of suffering, misery, and death! Each wagon was drawn by ten mules and driven by a Kaffir, and over the dusty hood of each the red cross flag waved in the shimmering heat . . .

What a spectacle it was! These were the very khaki-clad soldiers who had, not so long ago, left Waterloo [station] spick and span, amid a hurricane of cheers, and now they were coming back to camp silent and listless, and scarcely recognisable as men. They were burnt a brown red by the sun, their faces covered with dust and sweat, and were in many cases blistered by the heat; their hands were begrimed; some were without tunics, and the blue army shirts they wore were stiff with blood. Some had helmets and some were bare-headed. All seemed dazed, weary and depressed.

Some still gripped their rifles or dragged their bandoliers along as they limped to the tents. Many were wandering about aimlessly. All were parched with thirst, for the heat was extreme. Here a man with a bandaged, bootless foot would be hopping along with the aid of his gun, while another, with his eyes covered up, would be clinging to the tunic of a comrade who could see his way to the tents. One or two of those who were lying on the ground were vomiting, while nearby a poor fellow, who had been shot through the lung, was coughing up blood.

The surgeons and their orderlies worked to save life and alleviate the suffering as fast as they could. It was a nightmare.

Yet, although the whole ground seemed covered with stricken men, the dismal ambulances were still crawling in, and far over the veldt the red cross flag of other wagons could be seen moving slowly up to the naval ridge.

Would this procession of wagons never end!

Surgeon Treves, in this sudden exposure to war and the poor soldier in it, was forced to consider the awful panorama of stupidity, when greed and arrogance sends men into physical conflict:

I could not fail to be reminded, over and over again, of the remark made by many who were leaving England when I left, to the effect that they hoped they would reach the Cape 'in time for the fun'. Well, we *were* in time, but if this was 'fun' it was humour of a kind too ghastly for contemplation.

Among the stricken crowd who had reached the shelter of the hospital, there was many a groan, but never a word of complaint, never a sign of whining, nor a token of fear. Some were a little disposed to curse, and few to be jocular, but they all faced what had to be like men . . . As one man said, pointing to the overworked surgeons in the operation-tent, 'They will do the best they can for the blooming lot of us, and that's good enough for me!'

Frederick Treves saw the best side of human nature, behind Gun Hill:

Innumerable instances came under my notice of the unselfishness of the soldier, and of his solicitude for his friends in distress . . . An orderly was bringing some water to a wounded man lying on the ground near me. He was shot through the abdomen, and he could hardly speak owing to the dryness of his mouth, but he said: 'Take it to my pal first, he is worse hit than me.' This generous lad died next morning, but his pal got through and is doing well.

Another poor fellow, who was much troubled with vomiting, and who was indeed dying, said, as he was being hoisted into the train, 'Put me in the lower berth, because I keep throwing up.' How many people troubled merely with sea-sickness would be as thoughtful as he was? He died not long after we reached Chieveley.

On the following day, 16 December, a Mr E. J. Bearcroft was working with the British Ambulance Corps:

. . . at sunrise we were busy loading the trains with wounded until 12, when two sections were told off to bury the dead. I had to take my section over to Colenso, where I witnessed one of the most ghastly sights it is possible to conceive. The bodies were scattered about in small heaps and, hovering over them, were thousands of vultures, looking for all the world like so many fiends. The stench was simply unbearable.

When news reached Britain on 15 December that Buller had been defeated at Colenso, the Secretary of State for War, Lord Lansdowne, hastened a telegram to him, saying, 'Very sorry to hear of your ill-fortune. Give us, as soon as you can, an idea of your intentions, and say whether there is anything we can do to help you.'

On receipt of the above, Sir Redvers replied with the first of several doom-laden and ominous telegrams:

No. 87 Cipher. 15th December. My failure today raises a serious question. I do not think I am now strong enough to relieve White. Stop. Colenso is a fortress, which I think if not taken in a rush could only be taken by a siege . . . My view is that I ought to let Ladysmith go, and occupy good positions for the defence of South Natal and let time help us. Stop. But that is a step on which I ought to consult you. Stop. I consider we were in face of 20 000 men today. They had the advantage both in arms and in position. They admit they suffered heavily, but my men have not seen a dead Boer, and that dispirits them. My losses have not been very heavy. I could have made them much heavier, but the result would have been the same. The moment I failed to get in with a rush, I was beat. I now feel that I cannot say

I can relieve Ladysmith with my available force, and the best thing I can suggest is that I should occupy defensive positions and fight it out in a country better suited to our tactics.

The effect of this telegram on the British Government was, naturally, devastating. The bit that sent them reeling in the vicinity of Whitehall, London, was 'I ought to let Ladysmith go . . .' Later, and particularly in front of the Royal Commission on the War in South Africa, Buller tried to talk his way out of the content of those words. He said: 'It is a well-understood expression. I think every soldier really understands it . . . "let go" does not at all mean "let fall".' Unfortunately for Buller's poor effort at semantics, he had also sent that clear piece of advice to Sir George White in Ladysmith: 'I suggest your firing away as much ammunition as you can, and making best terms you can . . .'

General Sir Redvers Buller wrote his account of the battle of Colenso, and it is in this that we see his continually growing weakness as an independent commander of a large field force. After reviewing in some detail the happenings of the day, as he understood them, he sums up:

So far as the fight of the 15th of December goes, my intentions for the day were frustrated by the action of my subordinates. Of that fact I do not in the least complain. A General one day may find himself in difficulty because a subordinate has not done right, and another day he may reap immense and unexpected advantage because a subordinate does right, though contrary to his orders, at a critical moment. But these are the chances of war. To gain balance of those chances on one side the co-operation of all Commanders towards the success of the principal idea is necessary, and it is because Colonel Long forgot to realize the necessity for this co-operation that he is, in my opinion, to blame.

Poor Colonel Long! As if things weren't bad enough for him, seriously wounded, deeply disturbed by the fate of his gunners, the awful military shame of the loss of his guns – and all due to his old Balaclava-like mentality. But now, nightmare upon nightmare, Buller was squarely writing that Long was responsible, and Long alone, for the defeat at Colenso. That could not be true. A continuing effective bombardment of Boer positions by Long's batteries could not have made the world of difference to the fate of Hart's Irish Brigade, over on the left flank, or to anybody else. Not at that late stage of the awful game. Lost guns never help; but these lost guns did not lose the battle of Colenso.

Indeed, on the contrary, it is important to consider what young General Botha felt about Colonel Long's impetuous action. General Botha gave strict orders to his farmer-soldiers not to fire a single shot until the central

British attack had crossed the wagon bridge at Colenso. Then the Boers were to open fire, and Botha believed that the British would have been annihilated, with the flooded Tugela at their backs and with Hlangwane Hill on their right flank. The sight of Long's guns in such close proximity was too much for one burgher, and he let fly, which started off all the others. General Botha always held the view that Colonel Long unwittingly saved Buller's army from destruction.

But many proud British soldiers found some relief from their shame in making Colonel Long the scapegoat. Lieutenant George Salt of the 1st Battalion Royal Welch Fusiliers wrote home:

Chieveley Camp, 15th December. I feel very depressed, so must write to you to try and cheer myself up. This morning we were defeated by the Boers, the whole disaster arising out of a gross blunder committed by the Colonel commanding the Artillery . . .

Colonel Long did not die of those wounds, and he wrote a letter which is very simple – almost like a schoolboy explaining a misdemeanour:

[Sir Redvers] pointed out to me on a rough map in general terms that he wished me to come into action east of the railway, in order to support the attack of the 2nd Brigade, indicating as an objective entrenched positions on three kopjes *behind* Fort Wylie . . . The impression left on my mind was that Sir R. Buller wished me to come into action at a medium range, and I wished to select a position at from 2000 to 2500 yards, but the light was deceptive, and I got a bit closer than I intended.

Well, he sure did. But Lieutenant Fred Ogilvy RN later reported that he had warned Colonel Long and Colonel Hunt that they were getting too close to the enemy's rifles. Anyway, the argument must rest there – except to quote another ballad from the Canon of Carlisle, H. D. Rawnsley. That professional Christian wrote a piece which is nearer in spirit to Milner than Jesus:

A Gunner's Story

The Battle of Colenso, December 15, 1899

> I am the eldest of mother's sons,
> She is a widow, she drew my pay,
> I fell in trying to save the guns,
> But my heart was glad when the ball went through,
> How else could I dare to be talking with you,
> Seeing we gave away the guns?

Timber of limber and coil of steel,
Light to gallop with, strong to steel,
None are made swifter death to deal.
But ah! I was glad when that ball went thro',
If I had been spared to be seen of you,
How could I face my native land?

No scouts ahead! it may well seem strange,
Of foes in the river we had no thought,
Our Colonel wanted a closer range,
I was glad when the rifle ball went thro',
How else should I dare to be talking with you,
Seeing we knew not what we ought?

My breech-block scarcely had closed on shell,
When forth of the ambush volleyings came,
And every horse of the battery fell,
Ah! sir, I am glad that the ball went thro',
For now I can dare to be talking with you,
It is easier here to bear the blame,
And out of the silence, I tell you true,
We died at our guns and we both died game.

It began to look as if Buller had found a scapegoat in Colonel Long and that would suffice, but the ramifications of his curious paranoid temperament began to worm in other directions. General Hart, in spite of his 553 casualties was apparently feeling fairly innocent, even on the following day (16 December 1899) when General Buller rode into his camp and the two men had a bit of a chat. General Hart remembers that 'Not a disagreeable word passed between us'. However, General Hart took the opportunity to blame his men to the extent of telling Buller that his main trouble had been to stop his soldiers lying down and 'how difficult it was to get them on'. He complained about the men taking instinctive cover from a murderous onslaught of lead, but was apparently oblivious to his own blunder. Hart was a corker; he went on to write: 'but I took a cheerful view of it [the soldiers lying down], ascribed it to first experiences of fire, and said they would do much better next time.' What was left of them . . .

But General Hart was being lulled into that famous false sense of security by General Buller. Five days after the battle (20 December) the two met again at headquarters, which were then at Frere. The meeting started well with Buller handing a glass of brandy and soda and saying, 'How are you, my dear Hart?' But with that, the honeymoon was over. General Hart described it thus:

> To my surprise he began to censure me about the losses I had suffered on the 15th. As he spoke he worked himself up into angry tones. It was impossible to reason with him. He paced up and down the room and spoke in such an extraordinary way that I wondered if he was quite in possession of his senses . . .
>
> Why this outburst did not come until days after the fight, during which time I had seen him daily, I do not know . . .
>
> On the 22nd, two days after the above interview . . . he sent for me to his room and alone told me his intention to send me in command of my brigade and other arms, to a certain important forward position, with certain objects, . . . [As] he did not mention the subject of our last interview, and was going to employ me in this way, I might well suppose that the matter had dropped.
>
> Judge of my surprise, next day, on my going to see him on the subject of my next move, to find him sitting in a gloomy state, alone as before, and to hear from him that he had written a letter asking for me to be deprived of my command, but was not going to send it; he spoke sadly and quietly at first; but he got a little excited as he went on to blame me again for the heavy losses in my attack; and especially when he said everyone was talking about it and the papers were full of it.

General Hart went on to describe the conclusion of this unnerving encounter. Particularly unnerving, I feel, for the poor soldiers under their command, who would soon have to face again the formidable enemy.

> What I had heard [wrote General Hart] – right and left – but I did not tell Sir Redvers Buller so – was . . . wonderment why, having decided to force the passage of the Tugela, two brigades only made any attack and two took practically no part in the action!
>
> He deplored the loss of life: so do I. I could only say 'I am very, very sorry,' and he softened then and said 'I know you are, my dear Hart', and he concluded by saying these words, viz: 'I am not going to say anything more about it.'

This graphic account was written by General Fitzroy Hart after the battle of Colenso and before any other fighting action by the South Natal Field Force. It was written in a long diary-style letter, and the concluding paragraph is well worth revealing:

> Please God, I shall survive it and prove my ability, but if not, I should not like to leave my side of this story untold, and therefore I confide it to you . . . in this letter, and to . . . who will read it before I post it . . . feeling assured you will go on and prosper, until we have united this lovely country, this matchless climate, this wealth of nature into one great South Africa under the British flag, happy and free.
> – I remain, yours, etc. A. FitzRoy Hart.

You recall that laconic despatch from General Botha to President Kruger on the evening of 15 December? Well it was not really as simple as that for the Boers. God helps them who help themselves, and then He might be ready to grant 'a brilliant victory'. And the Boers, led by Louis Botha, had helped themselves.

General Botha made a visit to Johannesburg and was waylaid by a keen reporter of the *Standard and Diggers' News*. I have that old paper from the Golden Rand in front of me now. Botha was thirty-six years old and was a farmer by profession. He spoke concisely and in detail:

My first idea was that the positions I believed about to be assailed should be strengthened in such a manner as to be unknown to the enemy. According to my notion, there would be three points assailed, and at these three points I and the burghers commenced to thoroughly prepare ourselves. I kept the intention foremost that nothing should be seen by the other side of these defensive arrangements. My conjecture as to the enemy's lines of ordnance proved to be absolutely correct, and I had no need to modify it as the fight proceeded. In fact, so complete was the surprise, that at the first point of conflict the Imperial Light Horse [many Britishers from Johannesburg] and the British regulars came with their rifles slung over their shoulders, in careless order, to within sixty yards of my men and guns – the hill of Langweni [Hlangwane] – before we opened fire. Then, as you may imagine, the slaughter was terrific, and the discomfiture complete. That was the British right wing [under Colonel Lord Dundonald].

Then General Botha spoke about General Hart's Irishmen, as he saw them:

The second point of attack was at the Bridle Drift, made by the British left wing, and distant about six miles higher up the river from Langweni. There, one of the British Generals [Hart] marched with a large force, and opposing them were the Zoutpansberg and Swaziland commandos. My men allowed them to come within 200 yards and then opened fire. The British did their best to get through, and I must say that I never saw anything more magnificent than their charges at this point which was the main objective, being the easiest point of attack. But all to no purpose. They were driven back time and again, and though one or two stragglers got through the river, they were taken prisoners, and the main body repulsed. No less than five times they charged, and I never want to see finer bravery than I saw there.

It is interesting to compare Botha's words about the Irish Brigade with the words (or perhaps lack of praising words) of both Buller and their critical leader, Hart.

General Botha spoke about Long's guns:

Meanwhile the gunners of the Armstrong batteries had been shot away, and I sent Lieutenant Pohlmann, of Johannesburg, with his men to reinforce the Krugersdorpians to stop any attempt to retake the guns. In this they were successful, as is known.

Did I see General Buller wounded or killed? It is impossible for either me or any one else to say. There was one officer stricken down, for the recovery of whose body desperate and eventually successful efforts were made, but my impression is that he was Lieutenant Roberts, son of Lord Roberts . . .

I wish to add with regard to the battle of Colenso, that I never wish to see any one better prepared for the heavy duty before them than were the burghers; they were resolute and determined and fully imbued with the seriousness of the task before them. They were animated with any amount of courage, and under the heaviest of fire they implicitly carried out my instructions. Their dominating idea was that the fortune of the day, with the assistance of the Almighty, would be given to them . . . They saw the immense columns moving out against them, and it is marvellous, when men think they have twenty to one against them, as they did [General Botha was far out in his estimation of the ratio; it was more like three to one] that they should never flinch an inch from early dawn to late afternoon.

As for the enemy as I have said, their bravery was astounding. Sometimes they advanced at a walk, in regular order, and when they were mowed down those that were left simply dropped in the grass and waited until the next lot came up. They were men of pluck and no mistake!

Afterwards, I received a letter from the British commanding officer, asking for a twenty-four hours' armistice in which to bury the dead. Of course I readily granted the request. But I must say that they did not perform the task in a proper manner. In many instances, the dead were buried so hastily and so imperfectly that a few days afterwards the battlefield presented a woefully pitiable sight – there were arms and legs, and even bodies, sticking out of the ground.

Early on 16 December, young Lieutenant Fred Roberts, wounded in three places, was removed from the 4th Brigade field hospital to Chieveley. Sir Frederick Treves had seen him and had already stated that 'from a surgical point of view the case was hopeless'. That evening the young man died. His Victoria Cross was posthumous. Buller must have suffered this news acutely. Obviously the only son of the great Field-Marshal Lord Roberts of Kandahar was under Buller's personal care to some extent. But volunteers had been needed for a lethal enterprise, and now he was dead. The Right Reverend A. H. Baynes, Bishop of Natal, participated at the burial:

. . . poor young Roberts, the brave leader of one of the forlorn hopes to recover the guns on Friday, had died at 12 o'clock last night. The whole camp seemed to grieve for him, and for his father. I went to consult the principal medical officer about the funeral, and we arranged that it should be at 4 o'clock in the afternoon, when other poor fellows who had succumbed to their wounds would be buried too ... Came the sad ceremony at the grave-side. A large number of officers, including General Clery, General Hildyard, and Lord Dundonald, came to pay their last respects to Lord Roberts's son. The bearers were his Colonel [Colonel Buchanan Riddell], Colonel Stuart Wortley, Prince Christian, Major Bewick Copley, and two others. Mr Gedge and I together read the service. The graves lie about 200 yards this side of Chieveley station, and within about 60 yards of the line on the east.

Incidentally, there is a legend about Lieutenant Roberts' posthumous Victoria Cross which is probably true. It has been reported that Queen Victoria gave the medal to the young man's mother, Lady Roberts, in 'a sealed packet' and said: 'Do not open it till you get home, no other hands but mine have touched this.' The roles of both Queen and mother had greater significance in 1900 than they have today.

The link between Buller and Roberts was about to grow dramatically. Lord Roberts had spent forty-one years in the Indian Army and now, at this time, was commander-in-chief in Ireland. But ever since the disgraceful Jameson Raid of 1896, with its increasing push and shove from England's imperialists, he had expressed his interest in any potential military conflict in South Africa. He had written to Lord Lansdowne that if the disagreements got out of hand, he hoped that he would not 'be considered too senior, or too old, to be employed'. He even stated that he would be prepared to serve as a General and would drop his Field-Marshal status.

As war looked more likely in South Africa, Lord Roberts pressed the harder. It is my opinion that he saw clearly that he was probably the best man for the job and having a simple dedication to the service of his country, he felt compelled to push for himself. His estimation of his own qualities was about right. He was a humble, quiet and pleasant man, and a courageous and skilful soldier.

The war came and Lord Roberts was not called. He watched with unease from 6000 miles' distance, and as Buller began his build-up, on 8 December 1899, Roberts once again addressed himself to Lansdowne, the Secretary of State for War. It was almost as if he foresaw what was about to happen and all of the tragedy personified in the death of his son. He pointed out the devastating fact that 'not a single commander in South Africa has ever had an independent command in the field'. He was worried by the spirit of Buller's telegrams – before Colenso – and felt, painfully, that he could save an impending disaster. He was also conscious of the wretched and selfish in-fighting that went on in the War Office, 'for, impossible as it may seem,

I am sorry to say I cannot help feeling they would prefer running very great risks rather than see me in command of a British army in the field'. He finished with: 'I shall hope, with God's help, to end the war in a satisfactory manner.'

This appeal was written on 10 December. On 15 December arrived Buller's telegram about Colenso. On Saturday the 16th, a meeting of the Defence Committee (what a strange euphemism) was held in Prime Minister Lord Salisbury's room at the Foreign Office. The instigator, above all, of the suffering along the Tugela, Jo Chamberlain, was not present – he was away in Ireland, of all significant places, receiving an honorary LL.D. degree at Trinity College, Dublin, to that establishment's shame. But he gave a telegraphic nod and wink for Roberts. It was proposed that Roberts of Kandahar should go to South Africa as the new commander-in-chief and Kitchener of Khartoum should be his chief-of-staff. At the end of this meeting a telegram was despatched to Buller in Natal:

16th December. No. 53 Cipher. Her Majesty's Government considers abandonment and consequent loss of White's force as a national disaster of the greatest magnitude. We should urge you to devise another attempt to relieve it, not necessarily by way of Colenso, making use, if you think well, of additional troops now arriving in South Africa.

On Sunday morning, 17 December, Lord Roberts arrived in London from Ireland and formally accepted the command at a meeting of ministers in Downing Street. He had already been informed by Buller that his only son was wounded and had been recommended for the Victoria Cross. That very evening – of the day he received his command – news arrived of Lieutenant Fred Roberts' death. The Secretary of State for War, the Marquis of Lansdowne, took it upon himself to break this most awful news. Lansdowne has described the scene: 'For a moment I thought he would break down, but he pulled himself together. I shall never forget the courage he showed, or the way in which he refused to let this disaster turn him aside from his duty.'

Lord Roberts attended Queen Victoria at Windsor Castle for a farewell. The Queen wrote in her journal: 'He knelt down and kissed my hand. I said how much I felt for him. He could only answer, "I cannot speak of *that*, but I can of anything else . . ." ' However, some time later he was able to express his feelings. He wrote a letter, replying to the Primate of New Zealand:

It was a terrible blow . . . He was all we could wish a son to be – a dear good fellow in every way. I know he is infinitely happier in heaven than he ever could have been on earth; but I have been quite unable to keep from wishing often and often . . . that he could have been with me.

Field-Marshal Lord Roberts VC was sixty-seven years old.

The British Government was worried that General Buller would prove embarrassing and resign on news of Roberts' superseding him. Field-Marshal Viscount Wolseley, the commander-in-chief of the British Army, was sure he would. Wolseley had not been given the courtesy of a consultation with the Cabinet – he was a Liberal – and was informed of the decision by Lansdowne on Sunday afternoon, 17 December. Wolseley wrote:

He sent for me to say that the Cabinet *yesterday* decided to send out Lord Roberts as C-in-C. to South Africa, with Kitchener as his chief-of-staff. . . . I was nearly struck dumb and said I thought it was a very unwise decision and that, in my mind, and according to my opinion, Buller was much the abler soldier of the two, and that of course he would resign. I said 'Were I in his place, I should resign at once, and I think you will have his resignation back as the answer to your tele-gram.' . . . In the meantime news just in to say that young Roberts has died of his wound. I feel for Roberts and his vulgar wife from my heart.

But old Buller didn't resign. The news of his supersession was communicated in a telegram despatched on 18 December:

Distinct operations of the utmost importance are now in progress in Natal and in Cape Colony. The Campaign in Natal is being prosecuted under quite un-expected difficulties, and in the opinion of Her Majesty's Government it will require your presence and individual attention. In these circumstances Her Majesty's Government have decided to appoint Field-Marshal Lord Roberts as commander-in-chief, with Lord Kitchener as chief of the staff.

Lord Lansdowne, out of pity or unease or a bit of both, sent a separate, private telegram to Buller:

No. 58 Cipher. Private and Personal. Decision communicated to you in my telegram No. 57 may, I fear, be distasteful to you, but we have arrived at it from a strong sense that the step is inevitable. I have seen Lord Roberts, and I am quite sure you need have no misgivings as to your relations with him.

Buller replied by letter on 20 December:

If I may be allowed to say so, I entirely agree with the reasons that guided the action of Her Majesty's Government. I have for some time been convinced that it is impossible for any one man to direct active military operations in two places distant 1500 miles from each other. I was aware when I left the Cape for Natal that I was, so to speak, leaving the front door open, but the conditions here were so critical, and the General Officers coming here were all so anxious that I should be present myself, that I felt I had no other course open to me. Lord Lansdowne is kind enough to suggest that the decision may be distasteful to me, but I trust that any decision intended for the interests of the Empire will always be acceptable to me.

But the above does not encompass all Buller's attitude to the changes in the hierarchy of command. He remarked that Lansdowne's personal telegram 'read like one to a girl who was being put in charge of a strict governess'. And four months later his feelings were distilled in a letter to Lansdowne: 'I received two telegrams on the 18th December 1899, one from the Government I thought brusque, the other from the Secretary of State for War [Lansdowne himself] I thought brutal. I confess I deeply resented the cruel and, as I thought, quite uncalled-for sneer contained in the latter.'

But the old lad remained. The soldiers of the South Natal Field Force remained in his unpredictable hands.

Before the appointment of Lord Roberts as commander-in-chief, South Africa, another unexpected choice had been made: that of General Sir Charles Warren to command the 5th Division, the next addition of British soldiers to face the Boers.

Sir Charles was a true son of that ancient and distinguished breed of Englishmen, the military eccentrics who have done so much to keep the Empire famous – even to this day. He had been an abnormally bright soldier-student at Sandhurst and Woolwich, had gone for the Royal Engineers and liked to specialize in trigonometry and such. He had surveyed for the army in 1876, along the borders of the Orange Free State and Griqualand West – diamond country, and old Britannia was always interested in diamond country. He had fought Africans in the Transkei and threatened Boers who had strayed across Britain's intended path northward in Bechuanaland. He had stood for Parliament as an 'Independent Liberal' – with a remarkably and unexpectedly liberal ticket – and then, after service with the British Army in Egypt, became Chief Commissioner of the Metropolitan Police – where he exercised less than liberal instincts, particularly against the new, dreaded Socialists. Then, after a spell of duty as the First General Officer Commanding at Straits Settlements (Malaya) he returned to 'the old country' and to his astonishment and delight, on 7 November 1899, was appointed commander of the 5th Division, destined for South Africa.

Now Warren was difficult as most eccentrics are, and Buller knew about him very well. Two old military buffers were about to collide in South Africa, and at a difficult time, too.

On the ship, steaming towards South Africa, General Warren insisted that his staff officers played war games. Since they were expecting to join Lord Methuen around Modder river, they played on maps of that area. One officer would command the Boer Army and another the British Army; Warren liked to be referee.

Sir Charles Warren landed at Cape Town on 13 December; that is, two days before the battle of Colenso. On that day he received several hot messages. The first was the news that he had been given the euphemistic 'Dormant Commission'. The Dormant Commission was a pre-appointment; in the event of Buller's dying or being incapacitated, Warren would inherit the position. Then there was a straight letter from Lord Wolseley, commander-in-chief of the whole British Army, laying it along the line: 'I look to Sir Redvers Buller and you to put an end to this folly. Our men and Regimental Officers have done splendidly. Our Generals so far have been our weak point.' And that was before Colenso; diplomatic chat was evaporating fast.

The final surprise came in a telegram from the War Office in London, informing Warren that he was to supersede Methuen on the Modder front. The defeated generals, Methuen (Modder river) and Gatacre (Stormberg) were to command the lines of communication; apart from their failure to win these two battles protocol had come into play: Warren was senior and with this Dormant Commission was elevated even more.

Now Buller was very touchy about implied judgements from the War Office back home. If Methuen and Gatacre were being demoted, might the powers-that-be in London try the same thing with himself? On the day after his own defeat at Colenso, he set about correcting this reflex by calling London:

I cannot agree with the commander-in-chief and allow Methuen, who has done very well, to be superseded by Warren. Commander-in-chief, comfortable at home, has no idea of the difficulties here. It would, I think, be a fatal policy to supersede every General who failed to succeed in every fight, but I may say that, as I myself have since failed, I offer no objection in my own case, if thought desirable.

As we have learnt before, Buller was a clever manipulator of psychology. The War Office climbed down by allowing Buller to have Warren and his 5th Division over in Natal. Warren was already 500 miles northward into the Cape, on his way to Methuen at the Modder, when a young Major handed him a telegram sent by Lieutenant General Sir F.W. E. F. Forestier-Walker, in military command of the Cape, which starkly read: 'You will instruct General Warren to return at once.'

Warren was getting very edgy as his train puffed him back south to Cape Town. On 25 December he and his staff officers boarded the *Mohawk*, bound for Durban, and were on their first leg to join Buller. A new map – this time of Natal – was produced, and new war games began. These games must have worked, because from them it was concluded that Hlangwane Hill, the place that Lord Dundonald had failed to capture, was along the correct military route for Ladysmith. But Warren and his officers finally rejected it 'because General Buller had given it up, and it was therefore assumed that there must be some unknown difficulty that way'. That is what General Warren wrote in his diary – but sadly there was no 'unknown difficulty'. The 'unknown difficulty' was in Buller's head.

Then the two old boys met. Warren felt that Buller was 'rather reserved'. Probably this was a polite way of putting it. Nevertheless he pressed on in a helpful way, raising the tactical importance of taking Hlangwane Hill. Buller growled, like a very large schoolboy: 'What do you know about it?' I suppose Warren must have mentally flapped about a bit before he replied: 'General knowledge, and war games.' Good luck, Tommy Atkins!

On 23 December 1899, Lord Roberts sent a telegram to General Buller; it was the beginning of a hoped-for useful relationship between the two senior men, and it was, in actual fact, the first invitation to show each other their respective cards:

As far as I can see at present, the best way I can co-operate with you on my arrival in South Africa will be by carrying out the original plan of campaign, and advance in force through Orange Free State. The following expression of my view may facilitate our co-operation. From what I learn here, I hear that you are only waiting for sufficient reinforcements to enable you to hold an entrenched camp at or near Chieveley, while with the rest of your force you would turn enemy's strong position on Tugela River. If you succeeded, situation will have sensibly improved, and it would then, I imagine, be advisable to evacuate Ladysmith and hold the line of Tugela River until the time comes for a general advance. Please consider what number of troops you will be able to spare when this operation is completed . . .

While Lord Roberts was on the high sea, bound for the war, General Buller replied:

Frere Camp, December 28th, 1899. . . . The whole Tugela River is a strong position; there is no question of turning it; the only open question is whether one part of it is easier to get through than another. I tried Colenso because, though unaided, I could not have forced the defile north of Colenso; it was the only place in the whole line in which Sir George White's force could aid me in my advance from the Tugela. I am now waiting for reinforcements, and am going to try and force a passage at Potgieter's Drift. If I can find water to use in the subsequent advance I think I ought to just pull through; but the difficulties are very great. If I succeed it should be about the 12th January, and if then I join hands with Sir G. White I think together we shall be able to force the enemy to retire and so free Sir G. White's force . . .

Ladysmith is a terrible nut to crack . . .

I attacked Colenso, because I found that if I went by another route I should have to take 9 miles of ox wagons. This for little more than a Division, ten naval guns, five batteries and 1500 mounted men . . .

This letter, like so many things that Buller said and did, must be questioned. His words and actions seem to be peppered with holes. First, 'there is no question of turning it' (the Tugela river position). West of Potgieter's Drift, west of Taba Nyama Height, the elevated ground runs out, and there

'I've lost the key.' From a contemporary Dutch paper

is clear low land right round through Acton Homes and then east, behind looming Tugela Heights to Ladysmith. And then he states that he tried Colenso because 'it was the only place in the whole line in which Sir George White's force could aid me . . .' Not true. Sir George was prepared to attack the Boers at any time in conjunction with a Buller attack from any direction. And indeed, when Buller did attack at Colenso, he did not even inform Sir George White. How could Sir George co-operate when all he knew was that something was afoot because he could hear distant guns? And so his pathetic words go on and on. And the pessimistic tone is there. About this time he began to make morbid calculations. They went like this: the Boers had 145 000 men in the field, 85 000 came from the Transvaal and of these about 46000 were in Natal or around its borders. When Lord Lansdowne got wind of this paranoid preoccupation, he tried to bring Sir Redvers down to earth by reminding him, that as far as Her Majesty's Government knew, the entire population of the Transvaal before the war – man, woman, and child – was about 90000. Buller could not be convinced; Buller believed they were there. At this time there were about 20000 Boers in and around Natal, about half around Ladysmith and under 10000 along the Tugela.

But even this number of Boers was beginning to diminish seriously. The easy-going, over-democratized Boers were filtering back to the Old Transvaal and the Old Free State to see their families and inspect their farms. Fortunately for them, Buller was not in a fast-striking mood. He had set up his headquarters at Frere, and as Christmas came and went, all Buller did to the Boers was to bombard slowly and even monotonously the Colenso positions. And all the Boers did was to reply with cheeky signals across the Tugela river: 'How's Mr Buller? When is he coming for his next hiding?'

And then the first day of the twentieth century arrived and, with its coming, General Warren and his 5th Division began to step ashore at Durban. With this new lot of lads, Buller now had some 30000 under his command.

10

THE SIEGE OF LADYSMITH
January 1900

Our lingering faith is growing small;
'Where's Buller?' is the weary call;
'Where's French? Where's Clery?' They are all
Marking time.

LADYSMITH BOMBSHELL

BACK in Ladysmith, the garrison and population were pondering more urgently than anyone else what Buller would try next. On 1 January 1900, Sir George White received a heliograph message from General Buller, announcing his hopes for a second attempt to relieve the town. Buller stated that he hoped to leave Frere on or about 6 January and march his army westward. He added that by that date he hoped Warren's 5th Division would be with him. The message ended: 'I will inform you later of my exact date of departure from here, and will endeavour to keep you informed of my movements, but my telegraph line may be cut.' What Buller meant by his 'telegraph line' being cut, I cannot fathom. That had been cut long ago!

Anyway, General White and Ladysmith generally bucked up at this information. Sir George hastily and humbly replied: 'If you will trust me with further details of your plan, I hope to be able to assist you in the later stages of your advance on Ladysmith; but to do this effectually, I should require to know on which line or lines you intend to force passage of Tugela.'

On 2 January, Buller replied with a bit of hard information. He would cross the Tugela river at Potgieter's Drift, which was about twenty-three miles north-west from Frere. He would march via Springfield. The message suggested specific co-operation:

I expect a stiff fight when crossing the river, possibly a fight at the place I camp, between river and Lancer's Kop, and another fight there. If you can recommend me any better point of attack than Lancer's Kop, please do so. As troops are not arriving up to time, I doubt if I can start until the 8th January. I calculate it will take me seven days to reach Lancer's Kop.

White immediately replied:

As you intend crossing Tugela River at Potgieter's, Lancer's Hill [Kop] becomes an essential point on your line of advance. If you can keep me informed of your progress, I can help you by attacking Lancer's Hill from north when you attack it from south-west. Communication by signalling from hill above Potgieter's [Tugela Heights] should be easy. Do not hurry on date of starting on our account if recently arrived troops [Warren's 5th Division] need rest, as I am quite confident of holding my own here.

Well, General White's confidence was about to be brutally tested. The soldiers in Ladysmith doubted any prospect of a direct military assault on them. The Boers could not afford massed casualties. It was contrary to every hunting instinct they had. The siege of Ladysmith had become a simple matter of how long the garrison could ward off starvation and, therefore, how long they could find the strength to defend themselves. The Boers had last attempted to attack on 9 November 1899 – but now, in early January 1900, time was visibly swinging against them. From the Tugela Heights and through their spies they knew that Buller's army was growing, and must attack again soon. Probably they actually knew details of Buller's plans to move westward along the Tugela. If only they could hasten the fall of Ladysmith, then could their besieging burghers join Botha along the Tugela, and – if it were not too late – strike south into Natal?

Deneys Reitz, then a teenager, wrote:

For weeks there had been talk of an attack by the Free State forces against a loose-standing kop called Wagon Hill [the western end of the southern defences of Ladysmith], considered to be the key of the Ladysmith defences. We had so often heard of the proposed attempt that by now we had ceased to believe in it, but this time it looked as if something was on foot at last, for Commandants and Field-Cornets came riding in from the neighbouring camps to attend the meeting. Here I learned that it had been decided to storm the hill within the next day or two. It was said that Piet Joubert was growing impatient at the delay of the Ladysmith garrison in surrendering and hoped to help them to make up their minds by the capture of this commanding position. I had a good look at Wagon Hill, but I came away somewhat dubious of success, although the Freestaters were eager to have a shot at it.

The Boer council of war, or *krygsraad*, for the proposed attack on Ladysmith was held on 2 January. For all that Deneys Reitz thought it is more probable that General Joubert opposed the idea of an assault. He was a very old-fashioned gentleman. His wife travelled with him, and an American journalist, Webster Davis, communicated the unorthodox atmosphere of his marital arrangements. Webster Davis was introduced to Mrs Joubert at the general's headquarters, or *hoofdlaager*:

'Why,' said I, 'Mrs Joubert, do you accompany the general on his campaigns?'

'Oh yes,' said she, 'Piet [Joubert] couldn't get along without me. If I were not with him he would not be properly cared for, and as I have been with him in every battle since Majuba Hill, I shall continue following around until one or the other of us is killed.'

'Yes,' said the general, 'I try to keep mother [his wife] at home, but it is useless to try, she will be a camp follower. Why, the other day, during the battle of Elandslaagte, I was horrified to see her sitting calmly on a huge boulder on a mountain side within range of the British guns with one of my field glasses in her hand viewing the fight. She will surely get killed some day.'

The younger Boer officers nagged General Joubert at this meeting, and when it became clear that Presidents Kruger and Steyn reluctantly supported them, the attack was settled. To preserve maximum security, the timing of the attack was left to Joubert. As darkness came on the evening of 5 January 1900, he called his commandants together and announced that they would attack Ladysmith, moving at 3 a.m. the following morning. The all-out effort would be aimed at the southern defences of Ladysmith, stretching from Wagon Point on the west to the eastern extremity called Caesar's Camp. Two thousand Boers (mainly Orange Free Staters) would fight there, while another three thousand burghers would demonstrate around the town, mainly at Observation Hill, to the north of Ladysmith. The line Wagon Point to Caesar's Camp runs west to east. The general elevation above Ladysmith is 600 feet. Wagon Point is a hill of small area, then comes a dip and so up to Wagon Hill; another dip and then the long oval plateau of Caesar's Camp. The entire length of this line of hills is about four miles. But Ladysmith, the centre of Ladysmith, is no more than 3000 yards north. Control these hills and you have the town at your mercy.

Sir George White and his staff were very conscious of all these facts. And they had taken a precaution of arranging an inner position round Ladysmith should Wagon Hill and Caesar's Camp fall. They believed that they could hold out for some time in the 'inner Citadel' as General Hunter called it, but they knew that they must suffer very heavy casualties.

In command of this whole southern area was Colonel Ian Hamilton. His organization for defence was carefully worked out, to suit the limited number of men at his disposal. The depth of the plateau – by this I mean the distance north–south of the tops of the hills – varied from 300 yards on Wagon Hill to 1000 yards on Caesar's Camp, and the tendency was for the ground to slope gently southward. Therefore, Colonel Hamilton made his line of defence on the northern edge, that is, nearest the town. This was a series of elaborate stone sangars made from the boulders that cover, particularly, the sides of these hills. On the southern edge there were occasional small sangars which acted as outposts. I have visited this area and to this day, all these positions are there to be seen – and some of them still retain names and military insignia cut into the hard rock, all those seventy-odd years ago. And from these various military posts Colonel Hamilton had arranged a telephone network, finally connected to Sir George White's headquarters in Ladysmith.

At about midnight of 5–6 January, an Imperial Light Horse picket on the southern side of Wagon Hill heard Boers singing hymns over in their lines beyond Bester's Valley. Now this was a very common sound for the British outposts to hear – but not at midnight. Someone amongst the Imperial Light Horse, particularly since they were British South Africans, should have twigged the strange significance of this unexpected puritan gathering. But no one put two and two together. And it was perhaps the only security blunder that the Boers made.

The Boers began to ascend the southern face of the southern defences at around 3 a.m. on 6 January 1900. Without normal military discipline, some of the burghers crept away from the incipient conflict in the darkness. But others climbed steadily upwards through the night – and those Boers who were farthest ahead were over to the west, at Wagon Point.

Now here a curious coincidence was taking place. When Sir George White sensed that Buller was going to attack the Boers for the first time, at Colenso, he moved several naval guns from Wagon Point to a more convenient place, to co-operate with the hoped-for relief column. Colenso having failed, and after the weary weeks of hopeless waiting, General White chose, of all nights, 5–6 January to replace those guns. Lieutenant Digby Jones of the Royal Engineers with thirty-three sappers arrived in the dark to carry out this work. Two 12-pounder guns were put in place and then a 4·7-inch gun was brought to the northern foot of Wagon Point, escorted by thirteen sailors and 170 Gordon Highlanders. It remained there while the Royal Engineers prepared its emplacement. My friend, Mr George Hall of Newcastle, England, was one of those thirty-three sappers. I have recorded our conversation as he remembered that dark early morning of 6 January.

He described how 'everybody was doing something – the [gun] cradle was being mounted . . . this has got to be lifted. Now the master-gunner [Royal Navy] was doing all this – he was a gentleman bully! What a man! When we got the gun up, we couldn't swivel it – you should have heard this master-gunner! You could have cut his language. We had to take the gun down again, dismantle it . . . when there was flip, flop, flip, flop – what the – ? A report of rifles! We kicked the lamps out and dashed for our rifles. Into the sangar we went. Some poor devils panicked – they couldn't find their rifles and began to run. Young Digby Jones jumped on to a rock and drew his revolver and said [to the stampeding men], "The first man that passes me I'll shoot him dead – " and then poor old Digby got it, right through the throat.'

I then asked Mr Hall if he was close to Lieutenant Digby Jones when he was killed.

'I was within fifty yards of him.'

There was a long pause from Mr Hall as his memory went back to that night. Finally, I said: 'So Digby Jones won the Victoria Cross fifty yards away from you.'

'Yes,' replied Mr Hall, still, in his mind, a long, long way from me.

I persisted: 'It was hand-to-hand fighting?'

'The Boers were within a hundred and fifty yards. Why, one old devil,' said Mr Hall with great affection and admiration, 'de Villiers, came over the top [of the sangar] and told us to surrender. A bloke put up his rifle and missed him. Yes, can you imagine him [de Villiers] in the gun-pit, about sixteen feet across, telling everyone to surrender?'

I asked Mr Hall what happened after Lieutenant Digby Jones was dead.

'Well, now you're asking me something – because we were engaged in shooting at those fellows – that were shooting at us!'

I asked who took command.

'Nobody that I know. We lost our two lieutenants – lieutenant and sub-lieutenant; we lost the sergeant; we lost a corporal, and a lance corporal. There was only the master-gunner. He was in force. He was bossing the sangar . . . All this started roughly at about half past two in the morning. It went till about four o'clock in the afternoon – then we heard a cheer, and it had started to rain . . . Men were lying there – shot through – it was better when their heads were covered up . . .'

Well, dear reader, you and I will never get nearer to the awful truth of that Second Boer War than Mr Hall's memory, all those years afterwards. I am sure you will agree that that is the authentic voice of Queen Victoria's soldiers.

I cannot embellish Mr Hall's story; I can only place his memory of Wagon Point in its historical context. Initially, three regiments were represented on the southern defences. Covering Wagon Point and including the first dip were less than eighty men of the Imperial Light Horse; then came three companies of the 2nd King's Royal Rifles, as far as Caesar's Camp, and then that whole area eastward was held by the 1st Manchester Regiment, together with the 42nd Battery of the Royal Field Artillery and the Royal Navy detachment with one 12-pounder gun, and a detachment of the Natal Naval Volunteers with a Hotchkiss gun.

Some time between 2 a.m. and 2.30 a.m. an officer of the Imperial Light Horse returned from the direction of Bester's Valley, where the forward positions of the Boers were located, and reported that all was quiet. At 2.40 a.m. a forward picket of the Imperial Light Horse heard a movement in the ravine below. A challenge was spoken into the night and received no reply; a shot was fired. Alternatively, it has been reported that a reply was given, 'A friend,' in excellent English. Either way, there came an immediate explosion of Boer rifle fire and the Imperial Light Horse picket scrambled up the southern face of Wagon Hill. But they were then met by Boer fire from above! Boers had bypassed them and had already reached the southern crest of Wagon Hill. Several men of the Imperial Light Horse were shot as they tore towards comparative safety. It was at this moment that Mr George Hall, Lieutenant Digby Jones and the other Royal Engineers and sailors came under fire.

Colonel Ian Hamilton, who was sleeping in a gully, at the north-eastern corner of Caesar's Camp, was awakened by the gunfire. He immediately ordered three reserve companies of Gordon Highlanders, who were stationed at Fly Kraal, just to the north of Caesar's Camp, to get on to the hill. He himself hurried westward along to Manchester Fort, the central defensive position on Caesar's Camp. He arrived there at 3.45 a.m. By this time the Boers were attacking along the whole southern crest, but the Manchesters had moved forward at the first sound of trouble and were holding their southern forward sangars in double the normal strength. Therefore Colonel Hamilton felt reassured enough to hurry further westward to Wagon Hill and Wagon Point, where clearly there was very serious trouble. When he reached the headquarters of the King's Royal Rifles (the 60th), the bullets were flying thick and very fast, and he promptly got on the telephone to Sir George White, who had now moved from his partially wrecked house to 'Christopher's House' on Convent Hill – which, incidentally, is still occupied by the Christopher family whose happy guest I have been. But the old General had already been alerted; he had been out of bed since 3 a.m. Now, fortunately recovered from his fever, he had speedily despatched reinforcements towards the southern conflict. The whole of the Imperial Light Horse, held in reserve, was to go to Wagon Hill, and the 2nd Gordon Highlanders were to go to Caesar's Camp. Half an hour later, four companies from each of the 1st and 2nd King's Royal Rifles were also on their way. And then the remaining soldiers of the Gordon Highlanders marched to support. As they left their camp at the south-west corner of Ladysmith, by some terrible mischance a Boer bullet struck their commander, Lieutenant-Colonel Dick-Cunyngham VC and he was mortally wounded. This sinister bullet must have travelled about 3000 yards before hitting him. The Gordons moved on without their leader who, incidentally, was a famous Scottish hero, and, from all accounts, a true gentleman.

The first reinforcements arrived at Wagon Hill at 5 a.m. These were the fast moving and ardent fighting volunteers, the Imperial Light Horse, and the Gordon Highlanders who had been brought up by Ian Hamilton. These reinforcements threw themselves at the Boers and helped check a critical situation.

As daylight came there were about 250 Free State Boers actually on the summit of the south-western corner of Wagon Hill. They occupied about half an acre of boulders and had other burghers covering their left and right flanks from the southern crests. Immediately facing these Boers were the survivors of the Imperial Light Horse, who had fired the first shot, now joined by twelve Gordon Highlanders and nine soldiers of the King's Royal Rifles. It was very close and grim fighting.

The situation was glaring with danger. The Boers had actually succeeded in moving round the back of Wagon Point to where the naval 4·7-inch gun was still waiting to be pulled to the top. Fortunately the soldiers guarding the gun fought them off. The decisive area was centred on that half-acre inroad on the top of Wagon Hill. The outcome no one could foretell. The Boer leader, General de Villiers, had been badly let down by some of his burghers. The Winburg Commando had failed to support him. But he knew the strength and killing power of his position. He would not advance unless the whole battle turned against the British, and turn it might.

Colonel Ian Hamilton could not risk even a desperate defensive position. He ordered attempts to be made to charge at the advanced Boers. First went Captain Codrington of the Imperial Light Horse, who got to his feet and moved into the curtain of lead. It is said that such was the noise of war that no one heard his shout to advance. Only one man was behind him when he fell. Then the King's Royal Rifles had a go and Major Mackworth fell dead as he led them and they were driven back. Lieutenant Raikes died leading the next charge. Then Lieutenant Tod led twelve men into that awful open space. Three yards they covered and the lieutenant was dead and seven of the twelve were hit. And then – and it is difficult to comprehend – our letter-writer, Major Bowen of the King's Royal Rifles, and eight men got up and moved forward virtually to commit suicide. No more words for his wife and son. Enough was enough. Boer and Briton lay facing each other, within talking distance, if talk could have been heard. They blasted at each other across a narrow strip of grass.

Sir George White described the conditions at this juncture:

. . . the whole position was enveloped in a confusion of musketry; the defenders, who were in many parts intermingled with or actually in advance of the enemy, finding themselves attacked from so many directions at once, that no man knew whether to meet with the bayonet the Boers close upon him or to reply to the rifles of those more distant.

After Colonel Hamilton had moved from Caesar's Camp to the more lethal area of Wagon Hill and Wagon Point, the military situation for the British at the eastern extremity of Caesar's Camp began to deteriorate. The Transvaal Boers there, finding the frontal assault on the southern face difficult – the Manchesters had doubled their forward positions – had crawled their way round the eastern end of Caesar's Camp, and there suddenly appeared on the crest, pouring fire not only into the flank of the Manchesters' northern main position, but also into the rear of their forward positions. These Boers were mainly Transvaalers, and seeing the formidable stone 'forts' along the northern edge of Caesar's Camp, they balked attacking there and thereby missed an opportunity to swing the battle in their favour. These forts manned by the Manchester Regiment were not strongly held because soldiers had been ordered from them to strengthen the southern crest. If they had pressed at these forts and taken them, they would have been in the rear of the forward Manchesters, and would have been commanding any path from Ladysmith, thereby preventing reinforcements. This probably was the key to a Boer victory. But, once again, the Boers who had got to the top were poorly supported. There were about fifty of them and that was hardly enough. Nevertheless, they decided to do the next best thing and swung round to the rear of the Manchesters on the south-east corner of Caesar's Camp. Here it became another cruel, close battle. Slowly and terribly the Boers annihilated groups of British soldiers. A company of the

Gordon Highlanders was ordered to the north-east corner of Caesar's Camp to support. A few Natal Mounted Rifles and Natal Carabineers also came in support. Then a few soldiers of the 1st (King's) Liverpool Regiment arrived. Gradually the courageous Boers were held, and a bitter, murderous stalemate set in. And then, with the Boers clinging to the eastern end of Caesar's Camp, and particularly on the eastern face of the hill, shrapnel came bursting amongst them. It was unexpected and lethal. There below them, but to the north-east, was the 53rd Battery, Royal Field Artillery, under Major Abdy. Their fire was devastating, straight into the totally exposed Boers, at 2200 yards' range. The Australian war-correspondent in Ladysmith, Donald Macdonald, wrote: 'The biggest rocks were useless against the downward burst and the hail of splinters, which searched every corner, and after the fight no corner of that bloody field was so horrible a spectacle. There were men lying there who apparently had not a whole bone in their bodies. They were literally torn to shreds . . .'

Then the Gordon Highlanders fixed bayonets and drove at the Boers who were still on top of the hill. These Boers from Heidelberg, in the Transvaal, turned and fired point-blank at the charging Scots. But, nothing daunted, on came the Highlanders, and the few burghers left turned and scrambled down the south-eastern corner of Caesar's Camp.

The 53rd Battery, however, was not allowed to have an easy time. Since daylight, Commandant-General Joubert – and his wife, of course – had been directing the great 6-inch gun on Umbulwana on to the British positions at Caesar's Camp. Now that gun and every Boer heavy piece within range turned on the 53rd Battery. The 53rd Battery never returned the fire; they simply plugged away at the Boer riflemen on the hillside. The extraordinary fighting spirit of these British gunners is exemplified in Sergeant Boseley, who had his left arm and leg shot off. The last his men saw of him – at least for the time being – was the sergeant being carried from the field, waving his remaining arm at them and instructing them to 'buck up'. Some say that he was actually waving his severed arm at them, but I presume that that detail is apocryphal. Anyway, Major Abdy and Sergeant Boseley and the Gordons and others had really settled the emergency over on the east of Caesar's Camp.

Over to the west, at Wagon Point and Wagon Hill, the fighting was still fierce and undecided, and then out on to the plain beyond to the north-west came the 21st Battery, Royal Field Artillery, which plastered Mounted Infantry Hill where the Boer supporting burghers were firing, and thereby held Boer action in that area. That was at 6.30 a.m.

General White had now moved from Christopher's House to his headquarters, where he was in direct telephonic communication with all his sectors. Fighting was going on elsewhere around the perimeter, but it was already clear where the Boers were making their supreme effort. Soon after 6 a.m., Sir George had ordered the last of his reserve infantry to the southern defences; only his cavalry remained for the next emergency. At about 8 a.m., the requests for reinforcements became so urgent that he threw caution away and ordered his cavalry into the fray. Three squadrons of the 5th Lancers and two of the 19th Hussars hurried to Caesar's Camp, and the 18th Hussars raced to Wagon Hill. By 9.30 a.m. Sir George had nothing left; all was committed. A heliogram was flashed to Buller, lurking beyond the Tugela Heights: 'Attack continues, and enemy been reinforced from south. All my reserves are in action. I think enemy must have weakened his force in front of you.'

Again, a humble, indirect plea from White to Buller. For all its inoffensiveness, it was a desperate appeal. Was this not the time to hit Botha along the Tugela? Surely the Boers there must be, to some extent, distracted by the conflict in their rear. Buller did demonstrate in front of Colenso and bombarded the Boer trench areas, but he believed that the burghers were at full strength. No, Sir George and Ladysmith would not get much help from that direction.

Back at Wagon Point and Wagon Hill circumstances were giving more comfort to the British than to the Boers. On Wagon Point things were definitely looking up. Two companies of the King's Royal Rifles had got there and then at 10 a.m. those 18th Hussars were on the Point, without, needless to write, their horses. About 11 a.m. news reached the British on the western area of these southern defences that things were going very well over on the east.

General de Villiers now knew that his fortune was declining. The strength of Wagon Point on his left flank was a growing threat to his men. He promptly decided to take extreme action. He ordered about twenty Harrismith (Orange Free State) men, under Field-Cornets Japie de Villiers and Zacharias de Jager, down from the fighting crest, to collect other burghers at the base of the hill, and then take them round to the extreme western end of Wagon Point and assault the British from there. On top of Wagon Point the British were feeling a bit overconfident; some had been allowed to descend the northern face to grab some food, and it has been said that others were taking a nap.

The Boers, led by Japie de Villiers and de Jager, climbed the seemingly impossible precipice and were well-nigh on the summit when their slouch hats and beards were first spotted by the British. The Boers gave them a point-blank burst, and the truth is that most of the British decided that discretion was the better part of valour and ran in a northward direction! 'Here they come!' the British shouted as they hastily withdrew.

Now, as it happened, Colonel Hamilton had previously decided that a British effort to turn the Boers' left flank would be a timely idea, and for that purpose he was approaching Wagon Point with Major Miller-Wallnutt of the Gordon Highlanders, as the Boers came over the top and the British stampede began. Six known men stood their ground and ordered a halt. They were Colonel Hamilton, Major Wallnutt, Captain Fitzgerald, Sergeant Lindsay and Trooper Albrecht (Imperial Light Horse) and Gunner Sims, Royal Navy. They stopped the flight. About twelve Boers were on top. Then, from the Imperial Light Horse 'fort', which was about 200 yards to the rear, came a blast of fire at the Boers. All, save three, took cover; these three were de Villiers, de Jager and Gert Wessels. These men, apparently, were incapable of going backwards. They raced for the gun-pits. But also Colonel Hamilton and company were set on the gun-pits. What a lethal race! First was Hamilton, who leaned on the sandbag parapet and fired at the nearest Boer with his revolver. Trooper Albrecht fired. And then Lieutenant Digby Jones with a Corporal Hockaday, Royal Engineers, appeared, each firing at a Boer. It was like that over-publicized gunfight in America's O.K. Corral. Suddenly, almost everybody was shot. De Villiers, de Jager and Gert Wessels lay dead. Miller-Wallnutt got a bullet through the head and Trooper Albrecht fell a moment later. Mr George Hall's Lieutenant Digby Jones ordered some of his nerve-shattered men back to their positions and was then, as Mr Hall described, shot through the throat, and died. Lieutenant Dennis, Royal Engineers, ran to his side to help and was also shot. Colonel Ian Hamilton, who had braved other such hair-raising events on other occasions, miraculously stood unscathed. It is said, and it was the opinion of Colonel Hamilton (later, of course, to become General Sir Ian Hamilton) that de Villiers shot Miller-Wallnutt and Digby Jones shot de Villiers. Anyway, that courageous carnage seemed to settle Wagon Point and the charmed and charming Hamilton returned to the battle at Wagon Hill.

The situation on Wagon Hill had not changed. Hamilton had seen enough blood and was not in a mood to spill one more drop unnecessarily. He was reluctant to order another charge. But, of course, he was not the commander-in-chief, and he was about to be overruled. General White was getting increasingly anxious as the terrible day wore on and the Boers remained a threat to Ladysmith. Sir George ordered three companies of the Devon

Regiment, under Colonel Park, to prepare themselves to cross that open piece of ground on the west of Wagon Hill, where so many men had already died that day. It was 4 p.m. Sir George White sent his last message of the day to Buller: 'Attack renewed; very hard pressed.'

And then the sun, which had mercilessly burnt the dead, the dying and the fighting, disappeared behind giant black clouds, and no more information was forthcoming. Buller and, later that day, Britain, waited and waited in shocked awe, as they wondered what had followed – but there was now no way of telling.

The thunderstorm broke. It was no ordinary thunderstorm even by African standards. Ian Hamilton described it as 'Terrific rain – *never* – before or since – have I seen anything like it.'

This storm had a curious effect on both Boers and Britons. Both sides could not see far ahead and the noise of thunder and the flash of lightning added to the horror of the day. Both sides seemed to fear an attack from out of the storm and, therefore, blazed away with their rifles in the general direction of each other. It was difficult to describe the terror that reigned over Wagon Hill. Indeed, on Wagon Point, most of the soldiers broke and ran, for a second time – only the Royal Engineers, with Mr Hall amongst them, remaining at their posts. However, once again, they were rallied and returned.

By 5 p.m. those three companies of the Devons were in position, just below the skyline from the south and therefore invisible to the Boers. Ian Hamilton joined these men of the West of England and explained to Colonel Park exactly what was being asked of them. They would have to advance over the brow of the hill, into the open where men had failed to advance for more than three yards and live. And then Colonel Hamilton turned to the Devons and asked a terrible direct question: 'Devons, can you clear the top of the hill?' Colonel Park quietly answered for them: 'We will try.'

War-correspondent Donald Macdonald was on the spot as these words were spoken. He wrote:

The Devons were making ready for it, and how unready a man might feel at such a moment! The line of brown riflemen stretched away to the left of us, and it seemed that every trivial action of every man there had become an epic. One noticed most of all the constant moistening of the dry lips, and the frequent raising of the water-bottles for a last hurried mouthful. One man tightened a belt, another brought his cartridges handier to his right hand, though he was not to use them. It was something to ease the strain of waiting. Every little thing fixed itself on the mind as a photograph. There was no need of mental effort to remember. One could not see and forget, and would not, for his patriotism and his pride of kinship, forget if he could. Then the low clinking, quivering sound of the steel which died away from us in a trickle down the ranks as the bayonets were fixed – and a dry, harsh, artificial laugh, in strong contrast to the quiet of the scene – everything heard easily somehow above the rush and clatter of the storm, and lost only for an instant in the sudden bursts of thunder. A bit of quiet tragedy wedged into the turmoil of the great play, and all unspeakably solemn and awe-inspiring. One must see to understand it. One may have seen yet can never describe it. The situation was not for ordinary language; it was Homeric, overmastering.

The three companies were then formed up in column with bayonets fixed and magazines charged. Colonel Park said, 'Now then, Devons, get ready,' and gave the order to advance at fifty-pace intervals in quick time, and when the top of the ridge was reached to charge the position occupied by the Boers.

The storm was at its monstrous height. Blinding hail joined the tumult and Colonel Park considered the moment propitious and ordered the 'Charge'. Lieutenant Field commanded the leading company, and as this man emerged on to the open slope, he shouted, 'Company, double charge!' The Devons were on their way; they gave a loud cheer.

Ten yards behind came Lieutenant Masterson's company, immediately followed by Captain Lafone and his men. The Boers hesitated when they saw the West of England coming at them; it was difficult to concede that men could do such a thing – indeed, it still is – then the Boers fired, with all their skill and tenacity. At this moment, an English voice was heard 'clear and ringing' above the tumult, 'Steady, Devons, steady.' Of the five officers on that famous charge, first Captain Lafone went down dead, then Lieutenant Field was dead. Lieutenant Masterson was shot in both legs, but staggered on until hit again, and then he struck the ground. Soldiers of the Imperial Light Horse, in the most forward British sangar, dragged him under cover. Finally Lieutenant Walker, Somerset Light Infantry, was shot dead, fifteen yards short of the Boer position. At that critical point the Boers broke and raced forty yards back and took cover below the crest of Wagon Hill. From there they fired back – but the battle was virtually over. The Boers would simply defend themselves until darkness, when they would retreat.

The strength of the Devons before the charge was five officers and 184 non-commissioned officers and men. Three officers and, astoundingly, only fourteen men were killed, and one officer and thirty-four men were wounded. It was found that half the survivors were shot through their clothing. Most of the dead were shot through the head. This was because the Boers were down-hill of them, and explains why so many Devonshire men survived to wear their 'Defence of Ladysmith' bar to their medal; the Boers were tending to fire over their heads.

My friend, Mr George Hall, on Wagon Point, could only hear what was going on but told me: 'About four o'clock we heard a bit of a cheer, and it started to rain – nearly every battalion extended all over the hills, and that finished it as far as we were concerned – we were glad, absolutely glad.'

That was the finish of it. The Boers withdrew at nightfall. By today's awful standards the casualties were not great – but as far as besieged Ladysmith and the Boers were concerned, they were monstrous. The British suffered 424 casualties, including 17 officers and 158 non-commissioned officers and men killed or mortally wounded. The Boers officially announced that 64 burghers were dead and 119 wounded, but it is generally accepted that they lost between 220 and 250 men. The survival of fighting Ladysmith had been in the balance. Poor Major Marling VC was at Intombi Camp, in hospital, and he shakily wrote in his diary: 'Desperate fight on Wagon Hill. Poor Ava killed [Lord Ava]. For 24 hours it was touch and go if we were kicked off or not.'

The interesting argument to consider is what would have been the war situation if the Boers had taken Ladysmith. Both at Wagon Point and Wagon Hill and over on the north-eastern corner of Caesar's Camp the situation was at times critical for the British. What if the Boers had pushed home their gains in strength and with disciplined determination? It was extraordinary what they achieved with simply the independent will of a minority. Ladysmith could have fallen. Then those thousands of burghers would have been released, shining with victory, to join the new disciplined spirit of young General Botha. Could they then have broken stiff, unsure Buller? Yes, they could have. And then, would the European powers have come to the aid of the Orange Free State and the Transvaal? Germany would have liked to see Britain overthrown. And well-nigh every foreign country hated Britain, and, I fear, envied her. Could one argue that old George Hall, living in simple austerity in Newcastle-upon-Tyne, England, saved the British Empire because he didn't run, when nearly all about him were running? I wish we respected our debts towards the George Halls of our country more than we do. With all the criticisms heaped on the Boers of today over their racial predicament, it is a fact that they know where every one of their surviving veterans live and they honour and look after them. We do not.

Sir George White wrote to his wife about the battle of 6 January 1900:

Johnny Hamilton was in command where the principal attack was made and did invaluable service. Everybody under him is full of his praises, and I have reported on him in the highest terms. The Boers have, I believe, been very heavily hit, and they cannot stand loss as we do. They entered upon this war under the impression that they were going to kill all of us without being killed themselves . . .

Some of the Boers showed most determined bravery . . . When we handed over the dead to the Boers next morning [Sunday], as each succeeding hero was brought down – they were heroes – the Boers wrung their hands and owned we had killed their best . . .

Sir R. Buller is still coming. I hope he will be here before the 9th of next month [February]. The only effect of the approach of his force we have yet felt is that we have been receiving many shells from the Field Battery guns captured at Colenso on the 15th December . . .

The Reverend Owen Watkins helped the Boers remove their dead from the southern hills. 'It was a tragic sight to see the white-headed patriarchs with flowing beards lying dead side by side with mere boys. The one seemed too old to be engaged in such grim work, the other far too young.'

The British decided to bury their dead on a small plateau halfway down the northern side of Caesar's Camp. I have spent some time in this special graveyard, and it is difficult to convey in words the spiritual aura of the place. It shares a quality common to all British military burial places in South Africa. There is the unexpectedness, the incongruity of men of the British shires in those far-off, alien bits of the earth. And then there is the isolation; the awful loneliness. The air can be crystal clear and even larks sing – but this simply adds to the obliquity of the scene. And because there has been no distraction over the intervening years, I have sensed that the trauma of death has only just happened.

When the dead soldiers were carried to this area, they were laid in separate rows, regiment by regiment. The chin-straps of the helmets were cut away, so that the men could be more easily identified. Black Africans dug the long graves, and – it has been recorded – vultures wheeled overhead. Soldier friends came up the side of the hill and sometimes removed a button or a badge as a memento.

Again Mr Donald Macdonald was present, and he described one of the visitors:

A private of the Manchesters came. 'I hear my brother is missing from the King's Royals,' he said; 'I hope he's not in this lot.' He walked along the row of brown-clad riflemen, who wore the black cross-belts, then sank upon one knee, with his hands over his face. He had found his brother, the most boyish-looking of all that grim group. I put my hand upon his shoulder, and offered him the consolation of sympathy, which at its best is weak and insufficient. 'He was the youngest of us;' the poor chap said. 'I always hoped he would go back to the old people; I myself never shall.'

I have looked at Major Robert Bowen's grave, and felt that I knew him through the letters which I have quoted.

Father Ford and the Reverends Thompson, Tuckey and Watkins united for the burial service. Sir George White stood very still and bare-headed as he watched his soldiers into the African earth. And Donald Macdonald asked himself the question on behalf of the shattered corpses: 'In life and death, in right or wrong, first, last and always – my country?'

Mr J. S. Dunn composed a poem for the *Ladysmith Bombshell*:

> Ye thousands raise your deafening cheer
>   As onward proud they go!
> But there are wives and mothers dear,
>   And sires with locks of snow,
> Who scan with tears the serried rows,
>   They look – but ah! in vain,
> To catch the longed-for smile of those
>   Who'll ne'er come home again.
>
> The vacant chair stands as it stood;
>   Fresh let their mem'ry live;
> Sweet life that gave for others good,
>   'Tis all a man can give!
> They, too, were victors in the fray –
>   Then let us not restrain
> A tear for those far, far away,
>   Who'll ne'er come home again!

On 8 January Sir Redvers Buller heliographed congratulations to Sir George White on the gallant defence of Ladysmith and gave special praise to the Devons, but omitted the volunteers, the Imperial Light Horse, altogether. Sir George White repeated the omission, and a certain bad feeling was generated.

Colonel Hamilton righted the wrong in an official letter:

I write this line to let you and your brave fellows know that in my despatch it will be made clear that the Imperial Light Horse were second to none. No one realises more clearly than I do that they were the backbone of the defence during that long day's fighting. Please make this quite clear to the men. To have been associated with them I shall always feel to be the highest privilege and honour.

Ian Hamilton was right; no unit had fought harder or more tenaciously that day.

A message was bravely smuggled south through the Boer investment:

Ladysmith, Jan. 8 (By Runner to Pietermaritzburg Jan. 17).
Yesterday (Sunday) Jan. 7th, a solemn thanksgiving service to Almighty God for His blessing upon our arms, was held in the Anglican Church. The building was crowded, chiefly by soldiers. The congregation also included General Sir George White, General Sir Archibald Hunter, Colonel Ian Hamilton, and other Staff Officers.
At the conclusion of the sermon by Archdeacon Barker, General White and his staff, at the invitation of the Archdeacon, proceeded to the altar rails, and there stood whilst a *Te Deum* was sung. It was a most impressive spectacle, and it came to a thrilling conclusion by the singing by the congregation of 'God Save the Queen'.

The battle of 6 January 1900 pretty well settled what Sir George White and the Ladysmith garrison could and could not do. On 7 January, Sir George telegraphed details of the preceding day, and then added: 'Troops here much played out, and a very large proportion of my officers have, up to date, been killed or wounded, or are sick. [230 officers out of 592 were unfit for duty.] I would rather not call upon them to move out from Ladysmith to co-operate with you; but I am confident enemy have been very severely hit.'

Sir George's predicament was painful. How could his depleted, physically weak soldiers march out in any aggressive spirit? And yet he hated the idea of total passivity. On 8 January he was told that Buller was making some sort of a move, and he immediately reformed the Ladysmith 'flying column', which had been disbanded after the Colenso failure. The flesh was now weak, but the spirit remained strong. Indeed, Sir George White began to ponder on the most desperate solution. He began to think that if he once knew that Buller was finished, before total starvation took over Ladysmith, he would lead his tottering men out, southward, in a do-or-die effort to break through to Buller's army. He waited on the dreadful alternatives day by day.

But from all the accounts I have read, the ordinary British soldier in Ladysmith restraightened his back at this particular time. After 6 January it was no time to give up. Mr Watkins-Pitchford, volunteer Natal Carabineer, wrote to his wife:

We understand and respect Tommy more every day, for we know him as he is, not as the children and nursemaids know him in the park! Worn by constant guards and pickets, exhausted by dysentry [*sic*] and bad feeding, drenched by every shower which falls, and burnt by our fierce summer sun, he is the same cheery patient fellow as ever, though his tattered and patched clothes hang loosely round him, and his features have lost their roundness. He *looks* a deplorable scarecrow, one that would convulse a music-hall audience at home. But he holds the 'windy outpost' of Britain's honour here, and maintains it with his life.

The *Ladysmith Bombshell* exploded for the last time, and it reflected the situation in a poem entitled 'Marking Time'. A few verses:

> The New Year comes, so let us fill
> The flowing bowl with right good-will,
> Though Buller's at Colenso still
>   Marking time.

> We dreamed of battles fought and won,
> We dreamed our scattered foes would run
> Before us – but we haven't done
>   Marking time.

> Our lingering faith is growing small:
> 'Where's Buller?' is the weary call;
> 'Where's French? Where's Clery?' They are all
>   Marking time.

> The New Year comes, and we are here,
> With every prospect still to fear
> The dawning of another year –
>   Marking time!

One more verse, that communicates the message, goes:

> Buller, Buller, hear our loud entreaty,
> Under dire bombardment we are laid;
> Let thy legions come to us in pity,
> Let them come, and lend us all thy aid.
> Endurance has been tried, and stood the test right well,
> Relieve and aid us; oh, hear the besiegers yell.

And finally:

> Let Buller come or Buller stop
> We'll stick this show out till we drop,
> And never leave this blessed shop,
>   Though bad it be.

The population of Ladysmith was now hanging on precariously from day to day. On 13 January there were 2150 men in hospital; three days later, on 16 January, there were 2400. That was the unalterable acceleration of disaster. And of the soldiers still on their feet, there were 'many very weakly men on duty'.

Enteric fever was now decimating civilians and soldiers alike. The London *Daily Mail* war correspondent, George Steevens, was dying of this disease, and a colleague and friend named Maude of the *Graphic* was advised by a doctor to break the news to Mr Steevens, in case he wished to send a last message. Mr Maude said, 'Do you know, old chap, the doctor says you are very ill – very ill indeed?' Steevens, it is reported, looked very hard at his friend, and replied, 'Very ill? Why, I thought I was getting better . . . I suppose you mean by that that I am going to die? Mr Maude answered, 'Well, I am afraid, old chap, that is what the doctor means, and he wished me to tell you in case you had any particular message, or had any particular thing that I could do for you.' George Steevens knew what his last instructions were, and then expressed his last wishes, and having seen to that, said, 'Well, Maude, we have been very good chums, and if I am going to die let's have our final drink together. Get that last bottle of champagne that I have reserved for the relief of Ladysmith.' Mr Maude filled two tumblers, and Mr Steevens raised himself 'as well as he could' and touched Mr Maude's glass, saying, 'Well, goodbye, old chap.' Three hours later George Steevens was dead. With him, of course, died the *Ladysmith Lyre*, a journal which had helped the people in Ladysmith so much – through humour. R.I.P. It was 15 January 1900. I cannot claim that that was a typical enteric death in Ladysmith. But, nevertheless, let it represent all the others.

H. W. Nevinson of the London *Daily Chronicle* wrote a piece about the burial of George Steevens, who was a much respected man:

Tonight we buried him. The coffin was not ready till half-past eleven [15 January]. All the London correspondents came, and a few officers, Colonel Stoneman and Major Henderson, of the Intelligence Department, representing the staff. Many more would have come, but nearly the whole garrison was warned for duty. About twenty-five of us, all mounted, followed the little glass hearse with its black and white embellishments. The few soldiers and sentries whom we passed halted and gave the last salute. There was a full moon, covered with clouds, that let the light through at their misty edges. A soft rain fell as we lowered the coffin by their ropes into the grave. The Boer searchlight on Bulwan was sweeping the half circle of the English defences from end to end, and now and then it opened its full white eye upon us, as though the enemy wondered what we were doing there. We were laying to rest a man of assured, though unaccomplished, genius, whose heart had still been full of hopes and generosity. One who had not lost the affections and charm of youth, nor been dulled either by success or disappointment.

On 12 January 1900, Buller's heliograph began to flash at Ladysmith from a new direction. It came from the west-south-west, from a hill beyond the Tugela Heights. The Tugela Heights in that direction are Taba Nyama or Black Mountain to the west, and then eastward of it, a significant pile called Spion Kop, in English 'Prospect Hill'. Beyond and below these high hills flowed the Tugela river, and thereabouts was the possible crossing-place of that river called Potgieter's Drift. It seemed certain to the watching people of Ladysmith that Buller had pulled his army westward, and hopes focused there. But on 14 January Buller telegraphed: 'I find the enemy's position covering Potgieter's Drift so strong that I shall have to turn it, and I expect it will be four or five days from now before I shall be able to advance towards Ladysmith. I shall keep you constantly informed of my progress.'

On the following day General White replied: 'Your No. 156 of yesterday just received. I can wait. Wish you best of luck.'

Then two days went by without a word from Buller. This reticence was not due to thoughtlessness, but to military security. The Boers were almost certainly breaking the British code. But on 17 January H. W. Nevinson of the *Daily Chronicle* was gazing south-westward towards the Boer camps, north of the Tugela Heights, when he saw:

. . . near 'Wesse's Plantation', a great cloud of smoke and dust arise and slowly drift away. Beyond doubt, it was the bursting of a British shell. Aimed at the camp it overshot the mark, and landed on the empty plain. As a messenger of hope to us all it was not lost. The distance was only fourteen miles from where I stood – a morning's walk – less than an hour and a half's ride . . .

Shortly before the sun disappeared, Buller signalled:

I crossed one bridge at Potgieter's today, and am bombarding their position. Warren, with three brigades and six batteries, has crossed by Trichard's Drift [five miles west of Potgieter's Drift], and will move to the North to try and out-flank Boer position. I somehow think we are going to be successful this time . . .

Every man in this force is doing his level best to relieve you. It is quite pleasant to see how keen the men are. I hope to be knocking at Lancer's Hill in six days from now.

What a wonderful message this was for the hungry people of Ladysmith. Lancer's Hill was midway between Spion Kop and the besieged town. And there was a touch of humorous style in 'knocking at' – the message almost demanded confidence! Yes, Sir George spelt it out, in his reply of 19 January: 'Congratulate you and ourselves on your successful progress, and have greatest confidence in seeing you soon.'

Black African runners, or Kaffir runners as they were commonly called at the time, came into Ladysmith with news that General Lyttelton's division had crossed the Tugela river at Potgieter's Drift, that Sir Charles Warren's had crossed at Trichardt's Drift, and most exciting of all, that Lord Dundonald was in the vicinity of Acton Homes, out in the plain, west of the Tugela Heights, with a force of Irregular Horse, some of whom wore 'sakkabulu feathers in their hats and carry assegais'. Lancers? Relief seemed to be imminent.

Ladysmith waited as patiently as the uncomfortable circumstances would permit. Sir George White, having gazed like everyone else at the distant Spion Kop and pondered its forbidding silhouette, wrote to his wife on 19 January: 'Buller knows his business however, and we have only to sit down and wait until his men appear on the top of the said hill. We can see . . . his great Lyddite shells bursting on the enemy's side.'

But after two days of not seeing Buller's soldiers on Spion Kop, or hearing any more of Dundonald's 'assegais', White heliographed to Buller: 'If you can let me know when you intend decisive attack on Boer position, I will demonstrate from here and draw as many as possible away from you. Experience leads me to think I can draw away a considerable number.'

Back came Buller's reply: 'We are slowly fighting our way up the hill. I will let you know when help from you will be of most assistance.'

It was the first positive news for Ladysmith that British soldiers were actually lodged on the far side of the Tugela Heights. It was heartening, but thinking people in Ladysmith must have wondered what happened to Lord Dundonald's mounted force around Acton Homes. Why just slowly slog a way up a mountain, into the mausers, when you could, apparently, so easily outflank them on comparatively flat land? But there were many imponderables in Ladysmith. On 22 January, H. W. Nevinson lay on Observation Hill, a favourite vantage point, and watched British shells breaking over the ridges of Taba Nyama and Spion Kop. He could see for himself, though fourteen miles away, 'the mass of Boers . . . lying under the shelter of Taba Nyama'. A hard conflict must be imminent.

Inside Ladysmith, apart from enteric fever and typhoid fever and the usual deaths from explosions, there were other hazards. Again on 22 January Captain Jennings Bramley of the 19th Hussars was on picket duty when he sensed something slide over his legs. He turned and faced a five-foot-long *rinklolz* – or spitting snake – which immediately spat him in the eyes. This blinds, and is said to be agonizing. However, after a few days, Captain Bramley regained his sight.

On the evening of 22 January, it was noted that Boers were moving away from Ladysmith towards Taba Nyama and Spion Kop, obviously to support whatever action was going on there. Sir George White ordered his gunners to open a strong artillery fire on them 'to call them back'.

On 23 January, Buller signalled to White that his artillery duel was going well, and that on the following day his soldiers would attempt to seize Spion Kop. In Ladysmith, eyes and thoughts dwelt on the sombre height. Sir George heliographed back on 24 January: 'Many thanks for the efforts you are making. We await news of result with utmost anxiety.'

However, General White did not order any of his soldiers out in a diversionary manoeuvre. Physical weakness was now the better part of valour.

On the preceding day, the garrison of Ladysmith had been given a full ration and the Field Force orders stated that 'the relief of Ladysmith may now be held to be within measurable distance'. This was presumably to buoy up spirits and physical well-being so that the men could be helped to tackle a fight, if it came to them. But all they could do on the 24th was to watch the top of Spion Kop being plastered by bursting shells. Were they Boer shells or British shells? No one in Ladysmith could know.

Then, in the late afternoon, spirits soared in Ladysmith. The evidence of a British victory was a panorama to the south and south-west of them. The Australian journalist, Donald Macdonald, wrote:

. . . the Boer army in full retreat. Nothing could be more convincing. There were hundreds of wagons, heavily convoyed, thousands of cattle being driven – it was the great trek without a doubt moving back over the veldt towards Van Reenan's Pass.

That the enemy had been shelled out of the heights overlooking Potgieter's Drift seemed too great a certainty for argument.

Yet Ladysmith had to continue with her own unique way of life. On that significant 24 January 1900 a notice went up in the town:

Sale of Whiskey: To be sold by public auction at Scott and Hyde's Office on Thursday, 25th January, 1900, at 5 o'clock in the evening, one case Scotch whiskey (upset price £100), for the benefit of the widow of an officer who was killed in action.

Scott and Hyde, Auctioneers, January 24th, 1900.

No news came on the 25th, but it was heart-sinkingly noted that one Boer laager was seen to return to the northern foot of the Tugela Heights in the evening. What could it mean? Then the ever watchful H. W. Nevinson began to fear the worst. About 4 p.m. he saw a large party of men tramping through the dust. And Boers rode horses; they didn't march.

They were in khaki uniforms, marched in fours, and kept step. Undoubtedly they were British prisoners on their way to Pretoria. Their numbers were estimated at fifty, ninety, and 150 by different look-out stations. In front and rear trudged an unorganised gang of Boers, evidently acting as escort. It was a miserable and depressing thing to see.

On the 26th, there was no sun, so no news – and certainly no British relieving soldiers. Sir George wrote to his wife on that day:

Today has been very thick and rainy. There has therefore been no communication with Buller by sunflash [heliograph]. Last night his signallers sent part of a message by lamp, and then ran out of oil before the message was half delivered. So far as it goes it is not encouraging, and looks as if Buller had failed in his attack on Intaba Nyama on the 24th.

Lieutenant-Colonel St John Gore of the 5th Dragoon Guards, known as 'The Green Horse', made an interesting observation:

An almost unique situation! Everyone in the world has known what has happened long ago, except ourselves, the interested parties, under whose very eyes the battle has taken place! They know in London, America and Australia. Every Boer around us knows. But *we* don't know!

Sir George White wrote to his wife on 27 January:

There was a thick mist all night. I was up several times in hopes it might be clear enough to signal by lamp, but no hope of it. This morning, 11.0 a.m., the sky is blue and the horizon towards the West [Buller's direction] clear. I wonder what I shall hear. Will the helio belie its bright face and convey sinister intelligence to me and my force? The time is one of intense anxiety and our position here critical.

About midday, Buller's heliograph began to flash towards Ladysmith. Of course it did not come from the Tugela Heights, but from the hills south of the river. The words seemed to spell doom. They had been composed on the 25th but because of cloud in the day and mist at night, could not be sent until now. A cruel pause.

No. 170, January 25th. Warren took Spion Kop the 24th, and held it all day, but suffered very heavily. General Woodgate dangerously wounded, 200 killed and 300 badly wounded, and his garrison abandoned it in the night. I am withdrawing to Potgieter's, and mean to have one fair, square try to get with you, but my force is not strong enough, I fear. I shall send particulars tomorrow.

Sir George White signalled back the hardest facts about his situation. If the Boers read them, what was the difference? The coin, as it were, was already spinning in the air, and everyone knew it.

No. 55 P, January 27th. Your No. 170 of 25th only received today. We must expect to lose heavily in this campaign, and be prepared to face it. If you try again and fail Ladysmith is doomed. Is not 7th division available to reinforce you? I could feed the men another month, but not all the horses, and without guns my force could do nothing outside. My medical supplies are nearly out, and the mortality is 8 to 10 daily already. I put it to you and the Government whether I ought not to abandon Ladysmith and try to join you. I could, I think, throw 7000 men and 36 guns into the fight. If you would commence preparing an attack and draw off the enemy, say, in the afternoon of a day to be settled between us, I would attack that night and do my best to join you. The attack from here ought to have great effect, but I fear my men are weak, and some instances morally played out. The fall of Ladysmith would have a terrible effect, especially in India. I am deeply impressed with the gravity of the situation, and trust you will repeat this to the highest authorities. Deserters report Boers lost heavily on 24th, and were quite disheartened by your artillery fire. If we stick to them we may effect a junction, but my proposal is a desperate one, and involves abandoning my sick and wounded, naval guns and railway rolling stock. I could not keep the field more than **two or three days**. I would hold on to the last here if political considerations demand it, or if there is a prospect of sufficient reinforcements to relieve us.

I cannot pass that reference to the effect the fall of Ladysmith would have in India. It suggests that India was held by a sort of national hypnosis. The Raj must be invincible or all could collapse. Sir George detailed this argument in a letter to his wife:

The fall of Ladysmith would be a *terrible* blow to England's prestige. It would have even a worse effect in India . . . The fact that I, a late Jangi Lord Sahib, have had to haul down my flag . . . would shake India's belief in British power. Coupled to that it would be known that Lord Roberts Sahib, who is held throughout the length and breadth of India to represent England's military power, was in command and could not save us.

Buller replied to White's statement that he planned to have another go across Potgieter's Drift and that the Ladysmith garrison could co-operate towards Lancer's Hill. The message continued:

Your No. 55 P received . . . I agree with you that breaking out is only a final desperate resort. I shall try to force this position, and then we shall see. Some old Boers, who were very civil to our Doctors on Spion Kop told them that there were 16 000 of them in front of us, and not more than 4000 left at Ladysmith. I have no means of knowing how true this is, but deserters say that most of the men are here. Lord Roberts says he cannot reinforce me, but that if you will wait till the end of February, he will by then be in Bloemfontein and will have relieved Kimberley, which will, he says, reduce the pressure on Ladysmith. I doubt Roberts' forecast coming off, and think I had better play my hand alone, and as soon as I can. What do you think?

Everything that Buller was is to be seen in the words he wrote and spoke. Donald Macdonald lost his Australian patience and wrote:

Would blunders never end upon the Tugela? Would British officers never learn that they were fighting, not simple rustics, but men of matchless resource and cunning – men with a natural gift for tactics, ever ready, as at Amajuba or Tugela Heights, to take advantage of a strategical mistake?

On the same day, Sir George White received through Buller's head-quarters a message from Lord Roberts:

I beg you will yourself accept and offer all those serving under your command my warmest congratulations on heroic, splendid defence you have made. It is a matter of the deepest regret to me that the relief of Ladysmith should be delayed, but I trust you will be able to hold out later than the date named in your recent message to Buller. I fear your sick and wounded must suffer, but you will realise how important it is that Ladysmith should not fall into the enemy's hands. I am doing all that is possible to hurry on my movements, and shall be greatly disappointed if, by the end of February, I have not been able to carry out such operations as will compel the enemy to materially reduce his strength in Natal.

Sir George replied to Lord Roberts:

Many thanks from self and force for message and congratulations. By sacrificing rest of my horses I can hold out for six weeks, keeping my guns efficiently horsed and 1000 men mounted on moderately efficient horses. I should like to publish your intention to advance via Orange Free State as early as you can permit me to do so. It will encourage my garrison, and will be certain to reach and discourage Orange Free State men.

The final pattern of Ladysmith was now settled and immediately the scheme was put into action. Each regiment was ordered to dispose of all its horses, except the seventy-five that were strongest. The disposal of the weakest was in two ways. The first was simply to drive the horses out on to the sunburnt veldt to fend for themselves. This caused a pathetic situation for the highly-conditioned military animals. The second was to eat the horses. But for a horse-loving nation – at least as far as social privilege was concerned – it must not be a crude butchery job. A Lieutenant MacNalty of the Army Service Corps had begun to tinker 'in the engine shed' with a machine of his own invention for boiling down horses into soup. Mr H. W. Nevinson relates that: 'After many experiments in process and flavouring, and many disappointments, he has secured an admirable essence of horse.'

But Mr Nevinson was also conscious of the predicament of the horses that were not slaughtered for food. He wrote:

One of the most pitiful things I have seen in all the war was the astonishment and terror of the cavalry horses at being turned loose on the hills and not allowed to come back to their accustomed lives at night. All afternoon one met parties of them strolling aimlessly about the roads or up the rocky footpaths – poor anatomies of death, with skeleton ribs and drooping eyes. At about seven o'clock two or three hundred of them gathered on the road through the hollow between Convent Hill and Cove Redoubt, and tried to rush past the Naval Brigade to the cavalry camp, where they supposed their food and grooming and cheerful society were waiting for them as usual. They had to be driven back by mounted Basutos with long whips, till at last they turned wearily away to spend the night upon the bare hillside.

Of course, this fate so many horses met was almost as traumatic for the soldiers of the cavalry regiments. Lieutenant-Colonel St John Gore, of the 5th Dragoon Guards, called it 'a terrible blow to the regiment: we have tended and cared for our fine horses all the siege with such labour and zeal, and now all our work is to be thrown away!'

Well, this was the end of January 1900 in Ladysmith. A terrible month. But, as in all terror, there were intervals of light-heartedness. Carabineer H. Watkins-Pitchford closed the month with a bit of news which he wrote to his wife, who was returning to England from South Africa: 'The nearest shave I think I have seen is that of a dhoolie-bearer who has just come in with both his thighs scorched on the inside. He was stooping down cutting grass when a large shell passed between his legs and burst safely yards in front of him.'

11

THE RELIEVING FORCE
January 1900

Where will British privates not rush at the word of command? and, in the name of pity, why are such commands given?

LIEUTENANT-COLONEL GRANT

AT the turn of the century, down with General Buller's Natal Field Force, Lieutenant C. R. N. Burne RN was celebrating with his sailors who were 'on watch'. 'Good old 1899!' he wrote. 'Well, it is past and gone, but it brought me many blessings, and perhaps more to come. We gave the Boers some 4·7 liver pills [shells], which we hope did them good . . . Winston Churchill came up to look at our firing.'

Yes, irrepressible Winston had escaped from Pretoria and had hurried round by sea from Portuguese East Africa and was back, a little bit forward (northward), of where he had been captured. Gun Hill, facing Colenso, to be exact.

Winston had his own thoughts about the beginning of the twentieth century: '. . . war with peculiar sadness and horror, in which the line of cleavage springs between all sorts of well-meaning people that used to know one another in friendship; but war which, whatever its fortunes, certainly sweeps the past into obscurity. We have done with "a century of wrong". God send us now "a century of right".'

Her Most Gracious Majesty Queen Victoria sent Buller and the whole Natal Field Force a telegram: 'Wish you all a bright and happy New Year – God bless you. V.R.I.'

Lieutenant-Colonel Grant, writing under the nom de plume of 'Linesman', described the very early morning of 6 January 1900:

The pickets were just standing to arms an hour before dawn . . . when they heard a single cannon shot come thudding through the dark, still air from the north. Then a pause, then another dull boom, then a dozen together, far away, muffled, and ominous. Something must be happening at Ladysmith, but it was not until some hours that the big camp learnt what a terrible something it was.

Winston Churchill heard it. 'I lay and listened. What was happening eighteen miles away over the hills? Another bayonet attack by the garrison? Or perhaps a general sortie: or perhaps, but this seemed scarcely conceivable, the Boers had hardened their hearts and were delivering the long expected, long threatened assault.'

Thousands of soldiers of Buller's Natal Field Force gazed northward. At 9 a.m. Ladysmith's heliograph began to wink the news: 'Enemy attacked Caesar's Camp at 2.45 a.m. this morning in considerable force. Enemy everywhere repulsed, but fighting still continuing.' It has been said that the whole of Gun Hill breathed relief. Then, at 11 a.m., came 'Attack continues, and enemy has been reinforced from south. All my reserves are in action. I think enemy must have weakened his force in front of you.' That must have cut deep into the vast audience. Buller, who was down at Frere, telegraphed to General Clery, who was in charge. 'I think White is hard-pressed. Move out all troops you can and make demonstration in front of Colenso. Look after your flanks as you do it.'

Half the day had gone, and no one had yet moved. Thousands and thousands of the relief force did nothing but watch, with binoculars and telescopes.

Lieutenant-Colonel Grant wrote: 'In Heaven's name are we to do nothing? For the only time in the whole campaign I saw an army angry and despondent that day. Where was the General? *Was* he a general? If Ladysmith has fallen this day he must be so no longer!'

At about 1.30 p.m., when the firing at Ladysmith had almost ceased and, as far as Buller and company knew, all there was lost, the bugles of the relief force sounded the 'alarm'. Colonel Grant expressed the feelings of many:

. . . alarm, forsooth! And the force fell in for a 'demonstration' towards Colenso. [Incidentally, the definition of a military 'demonstration' is to pretend to do something that there is no intention of actually doing.] There was not a muddle-headed private in the ranks who did not see the egregiousness of it. If Ladysmith had fallen, of what use could a demonstration be, except to demonstrate what was already obvious, our criminal folly and dilatoriness? If not, was it likely that pressure which would not be felt until evening could cause the enemy to relax his upon his prey? But we demonstrated, nevertheless, feebly and slowly towards the river, with every tactical mistake of Colenso repeated, and some new ones discovered for the occasion. Had the enemy engaged the confused lines it is probable that another long casualty list would have blocked the cables to England. But he was contemptuously silent, and watched our artillery scientifically missing a herd of wild horses with ill-fused shrapnel . . . Of the deeds of the Devons, Imperial Light Horse and other fighting-men on the bullet-swept hills above Ladysmith I have no space here to speak. So much glory should find its chronicler amongst those who won it, not from one who in the most desperate hour of all was standing within sight and sound of it, idle amongst 20 000 unwilling idlers.

At 3.15 p.m. came the oppressive message from White in Ladysmith, 'Attack renewed, very hard pressed', and clouds obscured the sun. Not until the next day did Buller receive this devastating, unfinished news at Frere, where he still was. What was he doing at Frere at a time like that?

Winston Churchill, of course – though he was a liberal man in 1900 – didn't quite see the command's failure to strike in the same light as Colonel Grant. But he did acknowledge the wisdom if not the contempt of the Boers, in not giving away their artillery situation by replying. Churchill wrote: 'It needs a patient man to beat a Dutchman at waiting. So about seven o'clock we gave up trying.'

There was nothing but silence from Ladysmith on 7 January. And no heliograph; no sun. On the 8th came the news that Ladysmith had repulsed the attack.

On 6 January 1900, General Sir Charles Warren had visited Sir Redvers Buller at Frere, and announced that his 5th Division was now complete and ready to march. This division added a significant 50 per cent to the Natal Field Force's artillery as well as to their infantry.

Buller had made up his mind to march westward and, somehow, outflank the Boer right wing. On 8 January he issued an Army Order directing the following moves to take place under the orders of Lieutenant-General Sir C. F. Clery KCB, commencing on the night of 9–10 January:

2nd Division and Attached Troops

(a) Major-General Hildyard's Column

Mounted Brigade: 400 of all ranks (including one squadron 13th Hussars).
2nd Infantry Brigade: 2nd East Surreys, 2nd West Yorks, 2nd Devons, 2nd West Surreys.
Divisional Troops: a battery of Royal Field Artillery.
Corps Troops: 2 naval 12-pounder guns.

To move from Chieveley by the south of Doorn Kop to the camp already selected in the vicinity of Pretorius Farm.

(b) Major-General Hart's Column.

Mounted Brigade: 400 of all ranks.

5th Infantry Brigade: 1st Connaught Rangers, 1st and 2nd Royal Dublin Fusiliers, 1st Royal Inniskilling Fusiliers, 1st Border Regiment.

73rd Battery Royal Field Artillery.

17th Field Company Royal Engineers.

Corps Troops: 6 naval 12-pounder guns.

To move from Frere by the Frere–Springfield road to the camp selected south of Pretorius Farm.

(c) Headquarters and Divisional Troops (2nd Division)

Mounted Brigade: Headquarters and main body Supply Column (from Frere), Medical Unit.

Divisional Troops: a battery of Royal Field Artillery, Ammunition Column, Supply Column (from Frere), Field Hospital (from Frere).

Corps Troops: 2 squadrons 13th Hussars, 2 guns 66th Battery Royal Field Artillery 2 naval 4·7-inch guns, Supply Column (from Frere).

To move from Chieveley (except where otherwise mentioned) by the Frere–Springfield road to the camp south of Pretorius Farm, except that one squadron 13th Hussars for the 5th Division and 2 guns 66th Battery Royal Field Artillery will be left at Frere.

5th Division and Attached Troops

The following troops will move on the evening of 10th January from Frere to Springfield, under the orders of the Lieutenant-General Sir C. Warren G.C.M.G., K.C.B.:

(a) 5th Division

4th Infantry Brigade (Major-General Lyttelton): 1st Rifle Brigade, 1st Durham Light Infantry, 3rd King's Royal Rifles, 2nd Scottish Rifles.

11th Infantry Brigade (Major-General Woodgate): 2nd Royal Lancasters, 2nd Lancashire Fusiliers, 1st South Lancashires, 1st York and Lancaster.

Divisional Troops.

(b) Corps Troops

10th Brigade (Major-General Coke): 2nd Dorsets, 2nd Middlesex, 2nd Somerset Light Infantry, Imperial Light Infantry.

Artillery: 61st Battery Royal Field Artillery (Howitzer), 78th Battery Royal Field Artillery, Ammunition Column.

Engineers: Pontoon Troop, Balloon Section, Section Telegraph Division.

Supply Park.

Cavalry Brigade (Major-General Earl of Dundonald): 13th Hussars, 1st Royal Dragoons, South African Light Horse, Thorneycroft's Mounted Infantry, Bethune's Mounted Infantry, Composite Mounted Infantry, Natal Carabineers (one squadron), Colt Battery of four guns.

Naval Brigade: Two 4·7 quick-firing naval guns, eight long-range, quick-firing naval 12-pounders.

This fighting force totalled 15 000 infantry, 2500 cavalry and mounted infantry, and 64 guns – though six of these, being mountain guns, were not actually used; they were of short range and from a security point of view were dangerous because they used block powder.

The 6th Brigade, which was left at Chieveley to cover southern Natal, was commanded by Major-General Barton, and comprised the 2nd Royal Fusiliers, 2nd Royal Scots Fusiliers, 2nd Royal Irish Fusiliers, 1st Royal Welsh Fusiliers, six long-range, quick-firing naval 12-pounders, the remnants of the two field batteries lost at Colenso, and two 'dummy' 4·7 naval guns!

From Frere Camp, on 9 January 1900, the following detailed memorandum was issued:

1. The General proposes to effect the passage of the River Tugela, in the neighbourhood of Potgieter's Drift, with a view to the relief of Ladysmith.

2. Forces (already detailed) will be left at Chieveley and Frere to hold these points, while the remainder of the army is operating on the enemy's right flank.

3. Springfield will be seized and occupied, and the march of the main body and supplies to that point will be covered by a force encamped about Pretorius Farm.

4. With reference to Field Orders, dated 8th instant, paragraph 2 (a), the primary duty of Major-General Hildyard's column is to protect the march of the troops from Frere to Springfield during the formation of a supply depot at Springfield, but he will also operate so as to induce the enemy to believe that our intention is to cross the River Tugela at Porrit's Drift [seven miles south-east of Potgieter's Drift].

5. As stated in paragraph 2 (b) and (c) of the Field Order above quoted, the remainder of Lieut.-General Clery's force will encamp south of Pretorius Farm. Major-General Hart will, under General Clery's orders, assist in every way the supply columns as they pass his camp, and he will also be prepared to support Major-General Hildyard, if necessary.

6. On the afternoon of the 10th instant General Clery will send a sufficient force from the Mounted Brigade with Artillery to reconnoitre and, if possible, occupy Springfield.

7. The force under General Warren's command (Field Order, dated 8th instant, paragraph 3) will reach Springfield on the morning of the 11th instant, in support of the mounted troops referred to in paragraph 6 of this order.

8. The General Commanding-in-Chief will proceed to Springfield on the 11th instant.

That was Buller's military declaration of intent. And on 8 January the hard incidental facts of war were appearing at Frere. The field hospitals arrived in an ambulance train, and in the evening 700 civilian stretcher-bearers were assembled there, in an ominous context. They were volunteers from very varied social and racial backgrounds: businessmen from Johannesburg and Asians from Durban. These stretcher-bearers were about to demonstrate unobtrusive heroism – and Tommy Atkins humorized their duties by calling them the 'Body-snatchers'.

W. K-L. Dickson and his Biograph always stuck very close to the friendly Naval Brigade and their 4·7 ship's guns. Therefore, Mr Dickson was a delighted witness to the cunning of the sailors when they constructed dummy 4·7s to replace the real ones that were to move westward. 'The building of the dummies took place right under our eyes, whereas sentries were placed in every direction to keep all the other civilians at bay. The intention is to keep firing as usual, morning and evening, with the two twelve-pounders placed near the dummies.'

But just as the Naval Brigade was leaving Gun Hill, on 10 January – with the Biograph unit in tow – they received a heliograph message from the Boers above Colenso: 'Do you take us to be such fools as not to know a dummy from a real gun?' It was one of the few occasions that the Boers disclosed their presence, without the fair certainty that they would kill their enemy.

Of course the Boers never monopolized heliographic jibing. The Bishop of Natal noted the British signalling: 'Would you rather have Cecil Rhodes or Winston Churchill as President?' And then His Grace added, in his diary: '. . . war is just a big exciting game with all these light-hearted young officers.'

Buller's army began to move early on 10 January. It was vast; mile after mile of it. Everything a campaigning soldier could wish for – and some encumbrances that he would have reason to wish had not slowed him up. The Boers were not deceived by the dummy guns, and now they were being given every opportunity to view exactly where Buller was going. There were traction-engines puffing mile after mile along with the column. Since tropical rain began to beat down and turn the African dust to deep mud and empty water-courses (spruits) into raging rivers, these traction-engines proved useful. But young Winston Churchill, quite rightly, was not happy about it:

The vast amount of baggage this army takes with it on the march hampers its movements and utterly precludes all possibility of surprising the enemy. I have never before seen even officers accommodated with tents on service, though both the Indian frontier and the Soudan lie under a hotter sun than South Africa. But here today, within striking distance of a mobile enemy whom we wish to circumvent, every private soldier has canvas shelter, and other arrangements are on equally elaborate scale. The consequence is that roads are crowded, drifts are blocked, marching troops are delayed, and all rapidity of movement is out of the question. Meanwhile, the enemy completes the fortification of his positions, and the cost of capturing them rises. It is a poor economy to let a brave soldier live well for three days at the price of killing him on the fourth.

Lord Dundonald's orders for 10 January were:

You will leave General Clery's camp [Pretorius Farm] at about 2.30 p.m. to reconnoitre, and if possible occupy Springfield. If you can occupy Springfield you will hold it until the arrival of General Warren's column tomorrow morning. You will keep in communication with General Clery and report your movements and dispositions.

After covering only two or three miles of his journey from Chieveley, Lord Dundonald could stand the snail's pace no longer and secured permission from General Clery to ride forward with his Mounted Brigade and secure Springfield Bridge. They arrived at Pretorius Farm, halfway to Springfield, at 12.30 p.m. and after an hour's rest for off-saddling, watering and feeding, pushed on to Springfield, where they found the bridge intact. Dundonald decided to use his discretion – brave soldier that he was – and, leaving 'a force' to guard the bridge, pushed on to Spearman's Farm and Mount Alice above it, which overlooked the Tugela and, over on the far northern side of the river, the Tugela Heights, with Taba Nyama to the left and a little nearer the bastion called Spion Kop – though the Boers spell it Spioenkop.

Dundonald and his men reached Spearman's Farm and then occupied Mount Alice unopposed. They pulled their guns to the top and entrenched themselves.

Spearman's Farm had been looted by marauding Boers, who had probably only just hastened back across the Tugela river, as the water rose, due to the heavy rainfall.

Here I would like to relate a personal experience at this same Spearman's Farm – some ten years ago. While reconnoitring this area of Natal for a film I was about to make for the British Broadcasting Corporation, I reached this unidentified farmhouse. It is in an extremely isolated part of the country; visitors are rare. I was with a BBC colleague, Mr Lawrence Gordon Clark, and we wanted to know how to get on to Mount Alice. I volunteered to ask the farmer. Leaving our car at a discreet distance I walked through the well-cared-for farmlands, where black Africans were working, and approched the neat farmhouse. I knocked on the door and it was opened by a handsome middle-aged man, with close-cropped silver grey hair. Without more ado, no questions asked, I was invited in for hospitality. I fetched Mr Clark. The gentleman introduced us to his kindly wife and we learnt that they were Mr and Mrs Pretorius. Mr Pretorius was the inheritor of Pretorius Farm, but now had also bought Spearman's Farm, where they lived.

Mr Pretorius told me a story about the days immediately preceding Dundonald's arrival. His father, who lived at Pretorius Farm, and Mr Spearman were the closest of friends. They had been boys together. They were inseparable. But one of them, Mr Pretorius, was a Boer, and the other, Mr Spearman, was an Englishman. Came the war, and Mr Spearman told his friend that he must leave the farm and go south to join the British volunteer soldiers at, presumably, Pietermaritzburg. Mr Pretorius said that he must cross the Tugela river and join his people, the Boers, and fight with them. The friends parted and Mr Spearman hurried southward with his family. Immediately, Mr Pretorius collected together all of Mr Spearman's valuables – cattle, furniture, and the rest – and promptly sold them, presumably to the invading Boers. Two and a half years later the war was over, and both men had survived and returned to their ruined farms. The two friends met and after greeting each other like the lost brothers that they were in spirit, Mr Pretorius took Mr Spearman to a hole in the ground and produced coins from it. He gave the gold to Mr Spearman, explaining what he had done all that time before and saying, 'I didn't want either the Boers or the British to rob you.'

Anyway, on 10 January 1900, Lord Dundonald was in possession of Mount Alice and Spearman's Farm, and now he was anxious to get a report of his activities back to General Clery. He wrote, '. . . this difficulty was solved by Lieutenant Winston Churchill . . . he came up to me and volunteered to take a message to Sir Francis Clery at his camp 18 miles away. I thought his offer was a gallant one, as neither he nor I knew what parties of Boers might be lurking in the neighbourhood.'

The next morning, Lord Dundonald studied the river Tugela, far below him, and his attention focused on Potgieter's Drift and, in particular, the large ferry barge moored on the far (Boer) side of the river. He could also see a few hundred yards further back, among dongas and clumps of scrub, the forward Boer pickets guarding this very crossing. He turned to the officer commanding the South African Light Horse, Lieutenant-Colonel the Honourable Julian Byng, and asked him to call for volunteers to get the barge over to the southern (British) side of the river. The response was 'large', and one officer, Lieutenant Carlisle, and six men were selected. These seven men slipped into the river and were halfway across before the Boers noticed them. The Boers opened fire and the river began to be peppered with mauser bullets. The British covering party fired back and held the Boers in their dongas. After a few minutes the barge was pulled to the southern bank, and within a few days it was to prove very valuable to Buller's army. All of the South African Light Horse men got safely back, though one did get cramp and had to be rescued. The whole enterprise was in the best Bulldog Drummond tradition.

Lord Dundonald pursued his individualistic enterprise by heliographing a message to Sir George White in Ladysmith, informing him that they were at Mount Alice and asking him if he could bring him any stores and, if so, what would he like? Sir George replied: 'Very many thanks. Brooke, 7th Hussars, is arranging for me. Give him all the help you can, but your confident message is better than many stores.' Yes, Sir George and his garrison very badly needed a confident spirit south of Ladysmith.

The concentration of the main body of the army at Springfield was a slow, toiling process. Deep mud was the worst hazard. On 11 January, near Pretorius Farm, one of the many great traffic jams occurred. Engineers were constructing a road and the Naval Brigade was manhandling one of their great 4·7 guns across a spruit. Most of the sailors were smoking clay pipes as they heaved, and General Buller stood in the mud personally giving orders to keep his field force moving. Before that day was gone those sailors had got their 4·7's in position on top of Mount Alice, and their 12-pounders 'across a loop of the very tortuous river'.

By 12 January Buller himself was up Mount Alice, and for the first time gazed across at the breathtaking panorama in front of him. He gazed for a long time through his telescope, as was his wont, in complete silence. Well, this could be his Waterloo! Ten miles over to the west was Acton Homes, through which passes a road from the Orange Free State to Ladysmith. It is not an area of dangerous heights, but more of undulating hills. Then came the high land of Taba Nyama and about five miles away, to the north-north-west was the mass of Spion Kop, and just to the east of it the Twin Peaks. Six miles away, to the north-east, were the heights of Vaal Krantz. This was the new puzzle: how to get through – or around. Through his telescope he could clearly see the Boers digging trenches and building schanzes and gun emplacements. Yes, they had a fair idea that he was there.

Bishop Baynes had come along with the army and had climbed to the top of Mount Alice:

. . . when Murray brought his telescope and explained the position, the interest grew more vivid and exciting. For there we could see (even through the telescope looking no bigger than ants) the Boers riding from the east to the west to occupy these new hills which we are threatening. I counted about 120 passing. Then, looking along the lower hills and kopjes which skirt the meandering river on the north, one could make out long lines of intrenchments, and could see the Boers at work in them with pick and shovel.

Yes, that was exactly what Buller saw, but of course, he wasn't so forthcoming about the sight. Then the Bishop got chatting to the soldiers who were operating the heliograph and who were actually in communication with Ladysmith. The Right Reverend Baynes was allowed to send his own messages into the beleaguered town:

I was able to tell one man that his wife and family had landed safe in England. To another I mentioned the fact that we were badly off in a building operation for want of £1000 which he had, along with others, made himself responsible for. Curiously enough I got no answer to this. Perhaps he thought that to be shelled daily, and fed on bully-beef for three months, was public spirit enough without being asked for £1000 . . .

On that day, Sir Redvers issued an address to his soldiers:

The Field Force is now advancing to the relief of Ladysmith where, surrounded by superior forces, our comrades have gallantly defended themselves for the last ten weeks. The General commanding knows that everyone in the force will feel as he does; we must be successful. We shall be stoutly opposed by a clever unscrupulous enemy; let no man allow himself to be deceived by them. If a white flag is displayed it means nothing, unless the force who display it halt, throw down their arms, and throw up their hands. If they get a chance the enemy will try and mislead us by false words of command and false bugle calls; everyone must guard against being deceived by such conduct. Above all, if any are even surprised by a sudden volley at close quarters, let there be no hesitation; do not turn from it but rush at it. That is the road to victory and safety. A retreat is fatal. The one thing the enemy cannot stand is our being at close quarters with them. We are fighting for the health and safety of comrades; we are fighting in defence of the flag against an enemy who has forced war on us from the worst and lowest motives, by treachery, conspiracy and deceit. Let us bear ourselves as the cause deserves.

14 January was a Sunday, and I have in my possession Major-General Talbot Coke's diary for the war period. The General's entry for this day

adds curious and terrible fuel to Buller's sentiments. I quote as he carefully inscribed it:

Church parade at 9.0 a.m.; as no Chaplain present I read the service; had three hymns, and asked the men to say a hearty 'Amen' to the special prayer in the Book for Time of War. After singing the 'Queen' I called on the Brigade Major to read Sir R. Buller's special order to the troops about unscrupulous conduct of the Boers and added a few words about closing with the bayonet, and warning the men about the terrible losses entailed by retreat, ending up with the words 'May God Bless us all!' It was an impressive service.

The Right Reverend Baynes held a service (with Buller present) in another part of the field of operations. He wrote in his diary, 'I preached from the second lesson, "Follow me, and let the dead bury their dead." '

On 15 January 1900, Buller issued 'secret orders' to General Sir Charles Warren. Here they are, in full:

1. The enemy's position in front of Potgieter's Drift seems to me to be too strong to be taken by direct attack.

2. I intend to try and turn it by sending a force across the Tugela from near Trichard's Drift, and up to the west of Spion Kop.

3. You will have command of that force, which will consist of the 11th Brigade of your Division, your Brigade Division, Royal Field Artillery and General Clery's Division complete, and all the mounted troops except 400.

4. You will, of course, act as circumstances require, but my idea is that you should continue throughout, refusing your right and throwing your left forward till you gain the open plain north of Spion Kop. Once there you will command the rear of the position facing Potgieter's Drift, and I think render it untenable.

5. At Potgieter's there will be the 4th Brigade, part of the 10th Brigade, one battery Royal Field Artillery, one howitzer battery, two 4·7 inch naval guns. With them I shall threaten both the positions in front of us, and also attempt a crossing at Skiet's Drift, so as to hold the enemy off you as much as possible.

6. It is very difficult to ascertain the numbers of the enemy with any sort of exactness. I do not think there can be more than 400 on your left, and I estimate the total force that will be opposed to us at about 7000. I think they have only one or at the most two big guns.

7. You will take two and a half days' supply in your regimental transport, and a supply column holding one day more. This will give you four days' supply, which should be enough. Every extra wagon is a great impediment.

8. I gathered that you did not want an ammunition column. I think myself that I should be inclined to take one column for the two Brigade Divisions. You may find a position on which it is expedient to expend a great deal of ammunition.

9. You will issue such orders to the Pontoon Troop as you think expedient. If

possible, I should like it to come here after you have crossed. I do not think you will find it possible to let oxen draw the wagons over the pontoons. It will be better to draw them over by horses or mules, swimming the oxen; the risk of breaking the pontoons, if oxen crossed them, is too great.

10. The man whom I am sending you as a guide is a Devonshire man: he was employed as a boy on one of my own farms; he is English to the backbone, and can be thoroughly trusted. He thinks that if you cross Springfield flat at night he can take you the rest of the way to the Tugela by a road that cannot be overlooked by the enemy, but you will doubtless have the road reconnoitred.

11. I shall endeavour to keep up heliographic communication with you from a post on the hill directly in your rear.

12. I wish you to start as soon as you can. Supply is all in, and General Clery's Division will, I hope, concentrate at Springfield today. Directly you start I shall commence to cross the river.

13. Please send me the 10th Brigade, except that portion which you detail for the garrison at Springfield, as soon as possible; also the eight 12-pounder naval guns, and any details, such as ammunition column, etc., that you do not wish to take.

Not an ideal document to go into battle with. In the second paragraph, what does he mean by 'up the west of Spion Kop'? Up the west side of it? Up the ravine between Spion Kop and Taba Nyama? If he meant either of those, each must mean annihilation; but he doesn't make it clear. There is a rough road over the eastern end of Taba Nyama, through Fair View Farm, right over the high hill, north-eastward to Rosalie Farm, out on to the plain behind, with a clear run to Ladysmith eastward. However, there is a school of thought that believes that Buller meant, or hoped, that Warren would take the road through Fair View Farm, north-westward to Acton Homes and thereby outflanking, certainly, the main Boer right position. But no one does know. Perhaps Buller did not want to commit himself. Let Warren make the decision and take the awful chance. And one should remember that Warren was very eccentric. There was no telling what he might do.

Once again, what about the poor soldiers?

And then, in the sixth paragraph, the estimations of the number of Boers that Warren would face. Very much smaller than Buller's estimation of what he faced at the Colenso disaster. Four hundred on Warren's left and a total force of seven thousand. Was this a persuasion for Warren to refuse his right and to throw his left forward, as suggested in paragraph 4? It all seems unnerving psychological teeterings when so many men's lives were in hazard. And then all that pernickety detail, when the main decision is wildly vague. The guide who comes from Devon; the chauvinistic bit which is so positive, is not reassuring.

On 15 January, Sir Redvers made a last entreaty: 'We are going to the relief of our comrades in Ladysmith; there will be no turning back.' The British soldiers caught the words with great enthusiasm, and wherever Buller went, at that time, he was greeted with shouts of 'No turning back this time'.

On the night of the 15th to 16th, the army began to move. Lieutenant E. Blake Knox of the Royal Army Medical Corps, wrote:

To one watching the column it was a very picturesque scene: the Royal Artillery, their huge horses, the rattling of their chains, the rumble, rumble of the gun-wheels; the lances of the cavalry; the nodding cocks' feathers in the plumed hats of the South African Light Horse waving in the warm night breeze. Our ambulances jogged along merrily, bumping up and down, the Red Cross flags flapping and fluttering, and the Kaffir boys playing sjamboks and swearing at their companions as one team of mules fouled another.

What a strange deceptive atmosphere in that African night. How ghost-like! I have got very near to a belief in ghosts in that part of South Africa.

To add to the strangeness was the order that soon arrived, to be as silent in the advance as possible. The black Africans must now be quiet and no one must show a light. The Boers were that much nearer. Before dawn, the main column came to a halt and breakfast was to be taken. A bugler boy, thirteen years old but already conditioned by Aldershot, put his bugle to his mouth to sound 'Cook-house'. Fortunately for security, someone managed to snatch it away before he made a sound. And he was not allowed to have his bugle back, for the time being.

On 16 January, as the great army left the area of Spearman's Farm to engage the enemy, Frederick Treves arrived with No. 4 field hospital, and the doctors and nurses and orderlies started to make their arrangements for the return of some of the soldiers. And the Bishop of Natal thought of his duty. He wrote in his diary:

I ventured to suggest to the General [Lyttelton] that it would be very nice if each battalion before going into action could have a short prayer, and he quite approved . . . So when the camps were all struck, and the tents, and baggage packed on wagons, and the men had fallen in, I explained to them that some of the men had remarked that the Boers asked God's blessing before going into action, and we did not . . . I said a collect, an extempore prayer for all the special needs, the Lord's Prayer, and the Blessing. Then the word of command was given, and they marched off.

In the early hours of 17 January, Lord Dundonald had got his 1542 moun-ted soldiers to the vicinity of Trichardt's Drift, ahead of Warren's infantry.

Sir Charles arrived, and ordered, 'Move the cavalry out of the way – fifteen thousand men marching along this road tonight.' That order was reasonable enough, but General Warren never showed any liking for cavalry, as we shall see; he was always high-handed with them. Lord Dundonald sent a small patrol of Imperial Light Horse volunteers across the Tugela – they swam and were fired on – then moved his force 'about half a mile lower down', and crossed the fast-flowing river, by swimming their horses; surprisingly only one soldier, of the 13th Hussars, was drowned. But they were on the north bank, and they bivouacked there that night 'in the neighbourhood of Wright's Farm'.

Back at Trichardt's Drift, Warren was getting his infantry and artillery across on two pontoon bridges constructed by the Royal Engineers. Before the end of the afternoon, they were all across. The 5th and the 11th Brigades were immediately pushed to the foothills south of Taba Nyama and Spion Kop. At the same time, to the east, at Potgieter's Drift, General Lyttelton sent two of his battalions across, plus a howitzer battery. These troops seized the Maconochie Kopjes – named after the famous soup firm – and, therefore, by the evening of the 17th, the British were substantially holding important positions on the Boer side of the Tugela – and the human losses incurred had been small in number.

About 7 a.m. on 18 January, Dundonald moved his mounted soldiers – the 1st Royal Dragoons (412 men), two squadrons of the 13th Hussars (260), the 'Composite Regiment' (270), the South African Light Horse (300), and Thorneycroft's Mounted Infantry (300) – westward, across the Boer front. His intention was to carry out Buller's wish (there were no specific orders) to refuse the right, and push forward continually with the left. This is what he was doing, with all alacrity; unfortunately, Dundonald was the only fast-moving commander on the British side at that time. His mind was refreshingly clear, amid the vague jumble that was already slowly building up. He wrote: 'I knew that there was only one thing for me to do, and that was to make for the Acton Homes road a few miles to the west of Trichardt's Drift, where the hills are not so high, and where the road runs from the Orange Free State through Acton Homes to Ladysmith.'

His mounted troops held as closely to the foothills of the Tugela Heights as possible, but they observed Boers riding parallel to them on the tableland above. They were under observation.

Halfway to Acton Homes, the mounted brigade came to a stream called Venter's Spruit, and here Dundonald took the precaution of detaching Thorneycroft's Mounted Infantry before pushing north-westward. Every-

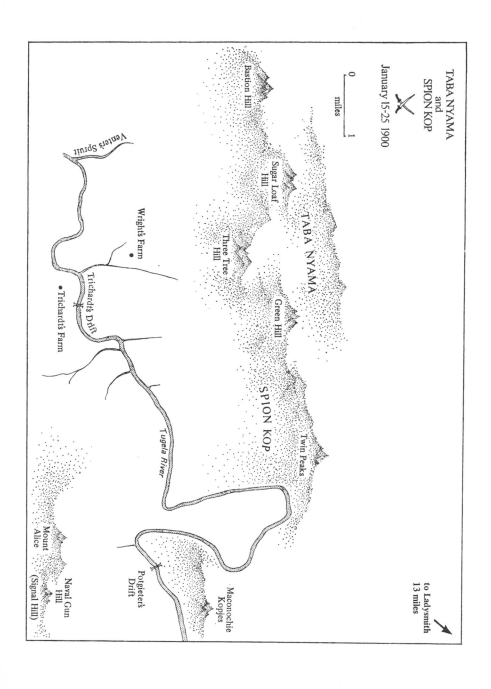

TABA NYAMA
and
SPION KOP

January 15-25 1900

0   1
miles

to Ladysmith
13 miles

Bastion Hill

Sugar Loaf
Hill

Three Tree
Hill

Green Hill

TABA NYAMA

Twin Peaks

SPION KOP

Venter's Spruit

Wright's Farm

Trichardt's Drift

Trichardt's Farm

Tugela River

Potgieter's
Drift

Maconochie
Kopies

Mount
Alice

Naval Gun
Hill
(Signal Hill)

thing was going remarkably well. Dundonald felt that he was very close to outflanking the Boer right wing and perhaps capturing a position commanding the Acton Homes–Ladysmith road, and he also believed that Warren's artillery and infantry would be following close behind. At this point he received a distressing and astonishing message from General Warren:

> O.C. Mounted Troops or next senior:
> The G.O.C. as far as he can see finds that there are no Cavalry whatever round the camp, and nothing to prevent the oxen being swept away. You are to send 500 mounted men at once to be placed round the camp . . . 18/1/00.

The message was imbecilic. Warren had the river Tugela at his back, plenty of Africans to prevent his oxen from straying, and if he needed mounted soldiers for this purpose he did have his divisional cavalry. Dundonald could not argue and sent back his 412 Royal Dragoons. He continued to advance with his seriously weakened force.

Soon after the Royal Dragoons had departed, Dundonald's mounted scouts saw about 300 Boers, riding in their direction from the Taba Nyama Heights. The British force waited in ambush behind a kopje and opened fire at about 300 yards' range. The action was short, sharp and decisive. Needless to say, Winston Churchill was on the spot. He found a position sheltering in a donga, which was already occupied by two Natal Carabineers.

> . . . one a bearded man of the well-to-do farmer class, the other a young fair-haired gentleman – both privates, both as cool as ice. 'Very astonishing outburst of fire,' said the younger man in a delicate voice. 'I would recommend your remaining here with your horse for the present.' . . . The young gentleman put his helmet over the crest on the end of his rifle, and was much diverted to hear the bullets whistle round it. At intervals he substituted his head for the helmet and reported the state of the game. 'Bai Jove, the Rifles are in a hot place.'

Despite the young carabineer having a bit of fun, he participated in a British victory. Some fifty of the Boers were either killed or captured. The British lost six men, but two of them were killed by dum-dum bullets, the illegal, soft-nosed variety. Winston Churchill looked at those two men, and wrote:

> Further on lay our own two poor riflemen with their heads smashed like egg-shells: and I suppose they had mothers or wives far away at the end of the deep-sea cables. Ah, horrible war, amazing medley of the glorious and the squalid, the pitiful and the sublime, if modern men of light and leading saw your face closer, simple folk would see it hardly ever.

The Boers were angry about this defeat, and did not show themselves as good losers. They blamed, in particular, a volunteer Austrian scout. One Boer prisoner was reported to have said: 'It all comes of trusting these cursed foreigners! If we had only had a veldt Boer out we should never have been caught.'

Dundonald had achieved a lot more than the destruction of fifty Boers. His men were now holding a strong position on some kopjes at the right flank of Botha's army, and were commanding the Acton Homes–Ladysmith road. Dundonald communicated his success to General Warren and requested heavy guns to combat any the Boers might bring up, and Dundonald also asked for the return of his Royal Dragoons. Warren sent no guns and only one and a half squadrons of the Royal Dragoons. They arrived at 11 p.m. on 18 January. Dundonald's force then waited anxiously for the expected infantry. Haste was important. The British were now holding a direct road to Ladysmith, which led behind the Boers on the Tugela Heights. If only guns would come to hold down the Boer artillery, what was seriously to hold up the infantry rolling up the Boer from west to east, on their very march to Ladysmith? Nothing happened through the night of the 18th to 19th.

And what was General Warren doing himself, on the 18th? Not very much, according to General Talbot Coke's original diary: 'January 18th. Thursday . . . Afterwards rode up to Naval guns and sorry to see Sir C. Warren's force *halted* not half way up the mountains. I really cannot understand the cause of all this delay.'

Worse was to come. On the morning of 19 January, Dundonald received an urgent message to attend on Warren personally. Dundonald hurried back the way he had advanced the day before and found General Warren, sitting on the bank of Venter's Spruit, personally urging on the drivers of military wagons who were struggling across. Warren stopped shouting and, turning to the shocked Dundonald, said, 'I want your cavalry close to me.' He then returned his gaze to the spruit and started shouting again. Dundonald remonstrated, and Warren simply repeated, 'I want you close to me.' No explanation was given. For Dundonald it was heartbreaking. But he simply wrote: 'When I left Sir Charles Warren I was completely puzzled. One thing was, however, clear; Sir Redvers Buller's plans for a great turning movement were not being rapidly carried out, and every hour's delay meant increased opposition.'

Major Denny, transport officer of the mounted brigade, rounds off this tragic tale of military lunacy. Major Denny was supervising some transport across Venter's Spruit when Warren appeared and pounced on him.

'Whose wagons are those?'

'Mounted brigade, sir,' replied Denny.

'Can't pass,' said the potty General. 'If I let them go, Lord Dundonald will try and go on to Ladysmith.'

J. B. Atkins, of the *Manchester Guardian*, recalled the words of the American military attaché, after the disastrous frontal assault on Colenso: 'Say Colonel, is there no way round?' Well, Dundonald had demonstrated the way round, but Warren would not take it. He was uncomfortable about 'outflanking' and 'rolling up' tactics. No, he wanted a simpler, more direct conflict.

General Warren had decided not to take the Acton Homes route, but to follow the Fair View–Rosalie road, which led north-east between Taba Nyama on its west and Spion Kop on its east. He decided to assault Taba Nyama. General Clery's 2nd Division (Hildyard's 2nd Brigade and Hart's 5th Brigade) were to do the job. On 20 January the British soldiers moved up the southern face of Taba Nyama. They fought their way to the apparent crest, but then found the usual South African problem: it was a false crest. Ahead of them was 1000 yards of totally exposed glacis, and at the top of this was a final ridge where the Boers were waiting in force. General Hart wrote in a letter: 'I fought on the 20th, and took a strong hill position successfully from the Boers at a cost of 365 officers and men.'

He also had under his command that day the 11th Brigade, comprising the York and Lancasters and the Lancashire Fusiliers. General Hart spoke to this brigade and said that he would not deprive them of the privilege of front place and that he would arrange for them to attack abreast, followed by his other three battalions in three successive lines. This 'privilege' brought soldiers to an early death. What strange rituals lie in the ramifications of such a military philosophy.

Lieutenant Colonel Grant described the struggle in more detail:

About 3.0 p.m. on Saturday, January 20th, the Lancashire and Irish brigades, under General Hart, rushed the two right gorges, with a dash that was positively startling in its unexpectedness. The artillery preparation was a mere form. There was a hasty bang, bang, bang from the artillery position on Three Tree Hill, a terrified crackle of musketry from the occupants of the re-entrant, and up from the shadows burst the Irish and North-Countrymen with a typhoon of yells, and a momentum that nothing but death could stop. But death was there: a tremendous fire broke out from the ridge behind, as the cheering soldiers flowed over the level above the re-entrants. The foremost men fell in heaps, the rearmost were stopped, as all should have been stopped, at the crest-line. 'Thus far, and no farther,' sang the Mausers.

The 2nd Division stayed where they were throughout the night of the 20th.

On the morning of 20 January 1900, over to the west, Dundonald had received an urgent message from Warren, in triplicate, to pull back towards the main body of troops. The orders were not specific, so Dundonald did what he could to salvage some good from his lost success. He sent his 'Composite Regiment' on a demonstration, up the road towards Ladysmith, hoping to draw off some of the Boers facing Warren on the southern part of Taba Nyama. Then moving with the remainder of his soldiers south-east towards Warren, he stopped under Bastion Hill and decided to try and take it. Dundonald could see that this hill would dominate the 2nd Division's attack, if it were strongly held by the Boers. The dismounted South African Light Horse led the assault and attacked with astonishing speed. The crest was reached and held. Leading this attack was a middle-aged volunteer, though formerly a Royal Horse Guardsman, Major Childe. As far as I can discover Major Childe had never been in action before, and yet here he was, leading a do-or-die venture. Winston Churchill, working like a beaver, carried a message to him on the summit. 'I . . . found him sitting on this dangerous ground, partly sheltered by a large rock – a serene old gentleman, exhausted with his climb, justly proud of its brilliant success.'

The Major had suffered a presentiment that he would be killed. The previous night he had felt it so strongly that he had discussed it with some brother officers. He went so far as to give them his epitaph and requested that it should be put above his soldier's grave. He had selected a quotation from the Bible (2 Kings 4. 26), 'Is it well with the child? It is well.'

However, the hazardous ascent had been accomplished. Lord Dundonald arrived on top and sat talking to the Major who quite happily repeated his premonition. Lord Dundonald left him to examine the rest of the captured position and after a few minutes' absence, returned to find Major Childe dead from a wound in the head. Lord Dundonald wrote:

He was carried down to the bottom of the hill by volunteer stretcher bearers of the Queen's, and we buried him close to a field of Indian corn; we buried him affectionately and reverently in his clothes just as he was; he had a fearful wound in his head – it seemed almost that the 19th verse of Second Kings IV was appropriate: 'And he said unto his father, "My head, my head," and he said to a lad, "Carry him to his mother." ' I read the burial service, and the epitaph he chose was placed over his simple grave.

Lieutenant Knox of the Royal Army Medical Corps was ordered to take four ambulance wagons to the summit of Three Tree Hill, which is on the south-east corner of Taba Nyama. It was a hazardous journey: steep, and exposed to the fighting Boers, not more than 2000 yards away. 'Had the Boers wished, they could have shot down all our mules with the greatest ease as we slowly ascended the hill, but they must have seen the Red Cross flags fluttering on our ambulances and respected them. I thought at the time their fire actually became more subdued as we passed up that road.'

It was not generally the custom to give credit to the Boers at this time, particularly with regard to their humanity, but the brave lieutenant was a careful and accurate historian. His memories of 20 January ended with an extraordinary event on Three Tree Hill, at the height of the battle. He was supervising the loading of the wounded, when:

Somebody put up a hare, which ran right through the infantry. This was trying 'Tommy' too far; he could sit and shelter for most things, but a chase he could not resist. Nearly a hundred men jumped up and went after that hare, hallooing, throwing sticks, bully beef tins, and even their helmets after it, regardless of all danger. As it passed within 12 feet of where I was standing beside my pony, I knew it was safe, and felt glad when I saw it disappear from view down the hill.

Lieutenant Knox turned around.

I saw a sergeant walk up with a canteen of tea in his hand: while standing up there, open to the aim of hostile marksmen, not 2000 yards away, he was shot through his stomach when in the act of finishing his drink. This unfortunate man died that evening.

21 January was a Sunday, but even in this 'Last of the Gentlemen's Wars', the fighting had to continue on Taba Nyama. Lieutenant-Colonel Grant philosophized about their fighting leader – and the led:

There is nothing apologetic or doubtful about General Hart to start with, gallant fiery Irishman, too hot with the *ignis sacer* of fighting to see anything ridiculous in a sword angrily brandished at an enemy a thousand yards away . . . Where will British privates not rush at the word of command? and, in the name of pity, why are such commands given?

Then the Colonel, who had a musical ear, made an interesting discovery:

I became aware that the note permeating a battle is one endless E flat. How it sings and drones throughout the long days, audible, or rather sensible, amid the many-toned hubbubs around, dropping occasionally a third of a tone, but always re-ascending to its endless semibreve.

Winston Churchill, ever curious about the human predicament, clambered up to Hart's Irishmen, pinned down on the southern side of Taba Nyama. He reached the Dublin Fusiliers, and close to a wooden box referred to as the 'Officers' Mess', spoke to their 'begrimed', 'unshaven' colonel, and reported his words.

'Very few of us left now', said the colonel, surveying his regiment with pride.

'How many?'

'About four hundred and fifty.'

'Out of a thousand?'

'Well, out of about nine hundred.'

General Coke dwelt more on the Establishment line of thought when he wrote: 'January 21st. Sunday. Church parade at 7.15 a.m. [The General, of course, was not on top of Taba Nyama.] A good Sermon from the Bishop of Natal, taking as the text the Parable of the Improvident Son, and proving how necessary it is after driving out the evil spirit to garrison the heart with Christ's presence.'

On 22 January, General Warren had a meeting with his commander-in-chief, Redvers Buller, who at this time seemed to be standing hazily in the background. Buller has claimed that he was getting very worried about Warren's lethal fumblings at this time – but he certainly did nothing to stop them. Warren now began to talk about the necessity to capture Spion Kop, if the Fair View–Rosalie route was to be taken. These discussions must have been a bit like *Alice in Wonderland*. This route had already been decided on by Warren; that was why British soldiers – and a few Boers – were dying on Taba Nyama. Anyway, now it was Spion Kop as well. General Warren then called his senior officers together and after a council of war, decided on a night attack. The British would rush the Boer trenches with the bayonet, entrench during the night, enfilade the Boer position during the day, and drag up heavy guns the following night. I expect that some wiser soldier present also muttered, 'And keep our fingers crossed.' The British generals present did not know if their soldiers could hold out for a day – would they be overlooked? They did not know if deep entrenching was possible, and they did not know whether heavy guns could be got to the top and, once there, used.

The attack on Spion Kop was to be made by two columns. Initially, General Clery was to command the western part (the left), and General Coke the eastern (the right). Coke, on the right, was to lead the attack that very night (22 January). But the final order from Warren was not given until

5 p.m., and General Coke objected to this late decision. He pointed out that there was no time to reconnoitre his proposed route up Spion Kop, and that there was no guide available. Not until 7 p.m., when it was getting dark was this order countermanded. The assault on Spion Kop would now begin on the following day, the 23rd.

The Bishop of Natal wrote in his diary: 'Monday, Jan. 22 . . . I am afraid I really must go back [to Pietermaritzburg] this week. I did want to get to Ladysmith with the troops, but at the present rate of progress it does not look as if there were much chance of that this week.'

Major-General Talbot Coke's detailed diary reads:

January 23rd. Tuesday. Up at 4.0 a.m. Met Sir C. Warren at 5.0 a.m. and rode many miles, at a great pace, observing Spion Kop from various points. I do not like the operation of taking it, and do not see to what it will lead . . . About 2.30 p.m orders received for the attack on Spion Kop tonight. General Woodgate to command. The Battalions selected by him being 2/Royal Lancaster Regt. and 2/Royal Lancashire Fusiliers. My Division to support him.

So plans had been changed. The left would attack first; the right were to hold back ready to support. Now it begins to emerge, from the selection of those particular regiments, why tall grandstands in Lancashire are called 'The Kop' to this day. Lancashire men were about to climb to their fate.

It was Buller who had suggested to Warren that General Woodgate should command the attacking force. The precise composition was the Royal Lancaster Regiment (6 companies), 2nd Lancashire Fusiliers, Thorney-croft's Mounted Infantry (180 men, dismounted, of course!), and a half company of 37th Company Royal Engineers.

At the same time, Buller complained about Warren's indecisiveness on Taba Nyama. Sir Redvers stated:

. . . for four days he had kept his men continually exposed to shell and rifle fire, perched on the edge of an almost precipitous hill, that the position admitted of no second line, and the support were massed close behind the firing-line in indefensible formations, and that a panic or sudden charge might send the whole lot in disorder down the hill at any moment.

All this was true; but why did Buller allow it to happen? He was in charge and was on the spot. Buller made a good critic, but a dangerous General. Was it some lunatic military etiquette or fear of his own theories?

At about 7 p.m. the soldiers assembled on a rocky ravine north of White's Farm, just north of Trichardt's Drift. Here officers told their men that during the ascent of Spion Kop they must not talk or show any light, and if the Boers did attack them, only bayonets were to be used; there must be no thought of rifle fire. Then there was a debate as to who should actually lead the assault. Surely a bit late in that awful day to make the decision. Colonel Thorneycroft became the obvious choice; he was the only man present who knew anything about either the western or eastern side of the mountain; not that he knew much. With Thorneycroft was Colonel à Court, one of Buller's staff, and especially selected by the commander-in-chief to go up Spion Kop.

The column moved towards Spion Kop shortly after 10.30 p.m. The night was very dark and there was an intermittent drizzle of rain. Occasionally the southern stars appeared, which gave a minimum of light. At about midnight the African kraals at the base of the mountain were reached, and the ascent began. To add to the hazardous climb, a night mist was clinging to Spion Kop. I have climbed this southern spur up which those 1700 soldiers toiled, but I did it in shining African sunlight and with fair confidence that no Boer would oppose my progress. It is a dangerous route, called 'an ill-marked sheep-path' by one of those long-dead soldiers. Dangerous precipices lie to left and particularly to right. Colonel Thorneycroft, at the head, was an enormous man – some six feet two inches tall, and barrel chested with it. Indeed, someone asked him, in awe, how much he weighed. The Colonel replied: 'With my wire-cutters and map and pencil, not an ounce under twenty stone.' And upwards he climbed. The soldiers following behaved splendidly, but nothing could prevent the disconcerting noise of their nailed boots on the hard rock. They say it was an eerie climb, and I believe it. Through the damp, thick mist, they could see the vague glow of the British camp fires far below, and sometimes the twinkle of a signaller's lamp over on Three Tree Hill. They reached a line of small trees and the ascent was less steep, and here Thorneycroft's men extended as far as the easier ground would allow; the idea was to 'net' any Boer pickets that might be thrown out towards the southern side of Spion Kop. The Lancashire Fusiliers also spread out in four successive lines behind them. Through the mist they slowly advanced; ahead was the apparent crest of Spion Kop. This could be the moment of conflict. At that critical time, to the shock of those that saw it, a large white spaniel dog came bounding to the head of the column. If it barked, all could be lost. A soldier managed to grab the animal and it has been said that a young bugler-boy was ordered to lead the dog back to the base of the hill. I like to think it was a compassionate choice; certainly he was a lucky lad. Spion Kop was about to become a place not fit for children – or men or dogs, for that matter.

When the British were about twenty yards from the skyline, to their left front there came 'a hoarse guttural' shout, '*Wie kom daar?*' It was repeated 'with startling emphasis'. Every British soldier, remembering the details of his orders before setting off, threw himself to the ground. It proved a sound piece of advice, because immediately there came a blast from about seventeen mausers. Then there was a momentary silence and the British forward line could actually hear the clicking of bolts as the enemy reloaded. That was the time – and the order was shouted, 'Charge!' Bayonets at the ready crashed forward, and the seventeen Boers of the Vryheid Commando broke from their cover and ran northward. Two were killed with bayonets and the survivors must have made a very hurried retreat, because many boots were left behind, and Spion Kop is not kind to unprotected feet.

It had been arranged that if the British force succeeded in reaching the top, a lantern was to signal back to the camp below. This was impossible because the mist was so thick; so three resounding cheers were given, and they were heard by comrades far below. The time was 4 a.m. and the date was 24 January 1900.

Immediately the British artillery on Three Tree Hill, over to the west, opened fire on the presumed Boer positions.

Dawn was about to break, and now problems began to emerge. The mist that had hidden the British advance prevented them from seeing where they were or where the Boers might be. The Royal Engineers made a guess and began to try to entrench. But the ground was hard and rocky; the protection was going to be inadequate if an attack came. Dawn broke at 4.40 a.m. and by that time the shallow trench was 220 yards long. General Woodgate made the best use that he could of this defence, placing the Royal Lancasters and South Lancashires on the left (the west), Thorneycroft's Mounted Infantry in the centre, and the Lancashire Fusiliers on the right (the east).

At dawn, a mounted Boer rode towards the British trench – though some have said that he was a black African. The British fired and missed him. Now all must be discovered. General Botha moved very swiftly collecting men and concentrating them to face the British, under cover of the mist. He also rushed guns from the Acton Homes area, over to the west, and they were quickly heaved on to Green Hill, which is the eastern extremity of Taba Nyama. Botha's reflexes were in splendid shape.

At 7.15 a.m. Colonel à Court, Buller's staff officer, had a cup of tea with General Woodgate, and afterwards Woodgate sent him back down Spion Kop with a letter for Warren; a signal could still not be sent because of the mist, which this letter mentions. 'I pushed [Woodgate wrote] on a bit quicker than I perhaps should otherwise have done, lest it should lift before we got here. We have entrenched a position, and are, I hope, secure; but fog is too thick to see, so I retain Thorneycroft's men and Royal Engineers for a bit longer. Thorneycroft's men attacked in fine style.'

Colonel à Court saw Bennet Burleigh of the London *Daily Telegraph*, and airily remarked that Spion Kop could be 'held till Doomsday against all comers'.

British scouts edged forward and made an uneasy discovery: though the highest part of Spion Kop's plateau had been achieved, they did not in any way command the western, northern or eastern sides of the mountain, where the Boers must be assembling. That crest lay some 180 yards around them. And so, well forward of the main trench, these scouts with some Royal Engineers began to construct meagre forward protections. At 7.30 a.m., the mist lifted and the British were exposed, and what an exposure it was! The British found themselves spread in the centre of a plateau some 900 yards broad by 500 yards long (west to east). Eight hundred yards north of them was Conical Hill. Over to the east were the Twin Peaks, which were higher than the plateau of Spion Kop and, being at right angles to it, enfiladed it; much nearer, in the same direction, was a hill called Aloe Knoll. Over to the west, was Green Hill. All these positions were occupied by Boers, already planning their worst for the unfortunate men of Lancashire. Also, so steep were the Boer-held sides of Spion Kop that the commandos could creep within fifty yards of the new British forward positions unobserved. And as that mist lifted at 7.30 a.m. the Boers confessed their close proximity by blasting with their mausers, and the forward working party had to take what scant cover it could. Also from the direction of Green Hill, three Boer artillery guns and a pom-pom began to plaster the top of Spion Kop, from a range of not more than 3000 yards. And then another pom-pom opened fire on the British from the north-east.

Amongst the attacking Boers was a Mr Michael Davitt, an Irishman fighting with the Volunteer Irish Brigade, and he has described those first minutes:

So close were the opposing forces to each other when the sun rolled up the curtain of mist from the crown of Spion Kop for the war tragedy to commence, that the Carolina men [a Transvaal Commando] sprang at the nearest British troops and actually wrested the rifles from them before they had recovered from the surprise which the unexpected presence of the Boers created. The English were driven back at once from that point of the crest thus taken by the burghers, and the fight for the possession of the plateau began.

General Botha wrote about the immediate effect his artillery had on the situation – and also of the effect the British guns had:

Our salvation . . . was the astounding inefficiency of Buller's artillery. Our few guns, on the contrary, were splendidly served . . . Our Krupp and pom-poms told with terrible effect upon the unfortunate massed Tommies on the narrow ledge of the hill. The English guns, on the contrary, were responsible for a large number of casualties on their side; shell after shell missing the mark and falling among the men who were fighting bravely against us; some of them at one part of the fight actually ran across to our positions to save themselves from the badly directed fire from their own guns!

It was this heavy shell fire, lambasting an area the size of a decent English field, together with heavy mauser fire from Aloe Knoll on the British right flank, that was doing the terrible damage. General Woodgate had placed no sort of entrenchments or sangars facing eastwards. British soldiers were being knocked over by bullets coming into them from the east, and were being flung high into the air by shells coming from the west, north, east and, God help them, from their own south.

An effort was made to move British soldiers to the pathetic forward 'trench'. Some of Thorneycroft's Mounted Infantry went to the left of it; a few companies of the Lancashire Fusiliers to the right front, and more companies of the Royal Lancaster Regiment to the right. The carnage was now awful to contemplate. General Woodgate was one of the senior officers who was responsible for this murderous blunder, but unlike Warren and Buller, he was, at least, moving amongst his poor men with consummate bravery. Here, there and everywhere; but there was nothing he could do to stem the dreadful slaughter. What he did was to ask his signallers to make a dash for the comparative safety of the south-eastern side of the spur, up which his force had climbed, and there transmit a signal to Buller on Mount Alice, which loomed to the south in front of Spearman's Farm. The message duly arrived and it read, 'Am exposed to terrible cross-fire, especially near first dressing station. Can barely hold our own. Water badly needed. Help us. Woodgate.'

While the signaller was sending the above message his heliograph was smashed by a shell, and, to the credit of his extraordinary nerves, he completed the message with flags.

And then, at 8.30 a.m., General Woodgate shared the fate of so many of of his men: he was mortally wounded in the head, above his right eye. He simply said, 'I'm hit', as he fell to the earth. Immediately the command on

Spion Kop devolved on Colonel Crofton of the Royal Lancaster Regiment, the Colonel being the senior officer present.

At 9.50 a.m. General Warren, at the southern foot of Spion Kop, received a message from Colonel Crofton: 'Reinforce at once or all lost. General dead.' Warren replied: 'I am sending two battalions, and the Imperial Light Infantry are on their way up. You must hold on to the last. No surrender.'

In fairness to Colonel Crofton's memory, he later stated that his actual choice of words was different from the above. His phrasing was: 'General Woodgate dead; reinforcements urgently required.' Perhaps the unhappy signaller, with death flying all round, decided on his own initiative to liven up the urgency a bit; and his instinct could have been right.

And now the fighting on Spion Kop became very jumbled and difficult to follow in an overall picture. Isolated, unrelated events were happening everywhere. About 10 a.m. a group of twenty soldiers of Thorneycroft's Mounted Infantry charged to the north-eastern ridge, which was unoccupied by the British at that time. One of them, Private Bradford, stuck his rifle over the rock in front of him and it poked a soft object. The gun went off and Private Bradford discovered that the object was a Boer's chest and that he had killed him. These men of Thorneycroft's Mounted Infantry then found themselves being encircled closely on their right and before they could withdraw, half of them were dead.

John Atkins of the *Manchester Guardian* saw the bloody shambles for himself:

I shall always have it in my memory – that acre of massacre, that complete shambles, at the top of a rich green gully . . . To me it seemed that our men were all in a small patch . . . I saw three shells strike a certain trench within a minute; each struck it full in the face, and the brown dust rose and drifted away with the white smoke. The trench was toothed against the sky like a saw – made, I supposed, of sharp rocks built into a rampart. Another shell struck it, and then – Heavens! The trench rose up and moved forward. The trench was men; the teeth against the sky were men. They ran forward bending their bodies into a curve, as men do when they run under a heavy fire; they looked like a cornfield with a heavy wind sweeping over it from behind.

On the Boer side, even under these terrible conditions, very old men and children were in the firing line. One old Boer of seventy years was there with his grandson, aged fourteen years. Every time the grandfather knocked over a British soldier, the child would say, 'One more Rooinek down, Oupa.' Both of these white Africans were found amongst the dead, on the following day.

Young Deneys Reitz joined a formidable Boer counter-attack. Eight or nine hundred riflemen were clambering up the steep northern side of Spion Kop to join the firing line. The boy reached his comrades of the Pretoria Commando.

Dead and dying men lay all along the way, and there was proof that the Pretoria men had gone by for I soon came on the body of John Malherbe, our Corporal's brother, with a bullet between his eyes; a few paces further lay two more dead men of our commando. Further on I found my tent-mate, poor Robert Reinecke, shot through the head, and not far off L. de Villiers of our corporalship lay dead. Yet higher up was Krige, another of Isaac's men, with a bullet through both lungs, still alive, and beyond him Walter de Vos of my tent shot through the chest, but smiling cheerfully as we passed. Apart from the Pretoria men there were many other dead and wounded, mostly Carolina burghers from the eastern Transvaal, who formed the bulk of the assaulting column . . . The English troops lay so near that one could have tossed a biscuit among them, and whilst the losses which they were causing us were only too evident, we, on our side, did not know that we were inflicting even greater damage upon them.

Twenty-stone Colonel Thorneycroft was much in evidence wherever a fighter was needed. Some time after 10 a.m., he saw that the Boers were on top of Spion Kop at the eastern end of the ridge, and were enfilading the whole British forward line. The enormous colonel gathered around him about twenty of his own Mounted Infantry and another twenty of the Lancashire Fusiliers and charged them forward. They raced and stumbled and passed close to three officers fighting alone, with unaccustomed rifles. They were Captain Knox-Gore, and Lieutenants Flower Ellis and Newnham. Lieutenant Newnham had been wounded in two places and was bleeding to death, though he continued to fire his rifle. As the charging men passed, a third bullet mercifully killed him. All around were dead and dying. Thorneycroft saw Captain Knox-Gore suddenly stand up and point to the enfilading Boers; he shouted something inaudible into the roar of the battle, and went down dead. And the third officer Lieutenant Ellis, was never seen alive again. The charging soldiers went down one after the other, and finally Colonel Thorneycroft was down amongst the rocks and those who saw it feared the worst, but incredibly the large target had not been hit; he had sprained his ankle.

The British reinforcements that were now scrambling up the southern side of Spion Kop were commanded by General Coke and they were the 2nd Middlesex Regiment and the 2nd Dorset Regiment. General Warren had also ordered General Coke to take overall command on the mountain's top.

General Coke's diary reads:

... about 9.30 a.m. Sir Charles Warren rode up to me, and said that General Woodgate had been killed and that Colonel Crofton had reported to the effect that if he was not speedily reinforced 'all is lost'. The 2/Middlesex Regt. (which with 2/Dorset Regt.) was drawn up close to me ... the Imperial Light Infantry were ordered ... to move forward and endeavour to creep round the right of the mountain so as to bring an enfilade fire on the attacking Boers. About 11.10 a.m., with the concurrence of Sir C. Warren, I personally proceeded to the mountain, to assume command. The climb up was a severe trial of strength, the ground being covered with big slippery boulders, and very rocky. It took me nearly 4 hours to reach the summit; the narrow path was much congested by wounded being carried down and men going up. The wounded were being carried down as quickly as stretcher bearers could be found for them; one of the first I passed was General Woodgate, not then dead. It was a trial for young troops having to pass *close* by all the wounded, there being only one road (a narrow path made by the troops) for use of those both going up and down. Many of the losses had been caused by shell fire, and the wounds were of a terrible nature. I formed an opinion that too many men were being pushed into the firing line owing to urgent requests for reinforcements made from time to time by various Commanding Officers. At 12.50 p.m. I sent off the following Helio message to Sir C. Warren: 'I am now on the Plateau of Spion Kop slopes. The top of the Hill is reported crowded with men and as these are exposed to shell fire and suffering, but holding on well, I have stopped further reinforcements beyond this point, but the troops engaged know that help is close at hand. Ammunition is being pushed up. – J. Talbot Coke, M. Genl.

Earl de la Warr had arrived on the plateau with the reinforcements.

... There we halted, more or less under shelter, lying down the steep side, hanging on to rocks, bullets flying over us, killing three men of the Imperial Light Infantry, who were resting within a few feet of us, another bullet striking in the neck one of Colonel Bethune's officers who was lying by my side at the time ...

Eventually quite 4000 men were on the scene, consisting of Thorneycroft's Imperial Light Infantry, the Dorsets, Lancashire Fusiliers, Scottish Rifles, Middlesex and Rifle Brigade, with Bethune's in reserve. It was a heart-breaking sight watching the two processions filing up and down the hill – one consisting of hearty, jolly men going up full of dash and eagerness, the other chiefly consisting of dead and wounded, carried down under the greatest difficulties on stretchers, which were often in a perpendicular position. Every few yards doctors were in readiness to attend to these suffering men ...

Why were we here? Why have we come up this murderous mountain to be shot down?

While General Coke and his soldiers were about halfway to the top of

Spion Kop – and remember that Warren had just appointed Coke to the overall command – General Buller, away to the south on Mount Alice, received Colonel Crofton's urgent appeal, carried to him by his staff officer, Colonel à Court. The Colonel probably repeated his belief that Spion Kop 'could be held till Doomsday', and he suggested that Colonel Crofton must have lost his nerve. The result was that Buller immediately telegraphed to Warren, at the southern foot of Spion Kop: 'Unless you put some really good hard fighting man in command on the top, you will lose the hill. I suggest Thorneycroft.'

Well, as we know, Thorneycroft was a good hard fighting man, and General Warren heliographed to the top of Spion Kop: 'With the approval of the commander-in-chief, I place Lieutenant-Colonel Thorneycroft in command of the summit with the local rank of Brigadier-General.'

Unfortunately, no one thought of informing General Coke that he had been superseded, and he and his reinforcements were moving a little eastward of the main body of fighting soldiers. Consider the implication of what had happened. Buller had been standing well back from the action, and giving the whole responsibility to Warren, of whom he had a low opinion, but he now interfered to the extent of appointing, albeit through Warren, a new commander in the battle area. And Warren confirmed it, without informing the man he had previously appointed. Soon there would be two commanders on Spion Kop, each ignorant of the other's status. To the carnage, through Buller's and Warren's disgraceful blunder, chaos was to be added. And chaos to chaos by the countermanding of orders in the battle area. No one had a clear idea of the overall situation.

At about 11.45 a.m. Colonel Thorneycroft was painfully lying down, because of his sprained ankle, amongst his soldiers, who were firing at the Boers, on their left front and only 150 yards away. A soldier ran to him with a message, opened his mouth to deliver it, and fell dead across the Colonel; a bullet had gone through his head. A few minutes elapsed when Lieutenant Rose, of Thorneycroft's Mounted Infantry, crept towards him, and from the cover of a rock, shouted above the crash of gun fire, 'Sir Charles Warren has heliographed to say you are in command. You are a General!' Lieutenant Rose also shouted that the British right flank, if such a precise military expression can be used for the shambles, was hard pressed.

At midday the deafening noise created by the heavy guns of both sides completely drowned the firing of the massed rifles. Colonel Crofton of the Royal Lancaster Regiment shouted the order to advance; few heard it, but one who did was a bugler-boy of the 'King's Own', and in the hail of bullets, he stood up and sounded the advance. The whole company rose from relative shelter and charged the blazing crest.

The first of General Coke's reinforcements to reach the top were the 2nd Middlesex Regiment, and amongst them was Mr Packer, whom I met at the Royal Hospital, Chelsea. Mr Packer said:

We [he was a private soldier at the time] didn't know the name of the place, we didn't know where we were, we didn't know if it was Spion Kop, or what it was, until after . . . It was a very high mountain, you know, very high, must have took us nearly an hour to get up there, and some places were sheer rock, you know. You had to bump one another up . . . It was very bad up there. It was the Boer pom-pom gun that was doing all the damage. One officer wanted us to charge, and we all got up to charge with fixed bayonets, and of course he went down. He only just stood up and he went down with about five or six bullets in him. Of course, that stopped the charge.

A lot of chaps got killed putting their heads over the top of the rocks. I expect I would have done the same, only this Natal fellow, in the Imperial Light Infantry, told me, 'Don't put your head over the top – I know these buggers – fire round the rock, never over the top!'

There is a report about the Middlesex Regiment in *The Times* of London:

Wednesday, October 31, 1900.

In all the lurid tale of battle and sudden death of Spion Kop, as told by Mr Winston Churchill, nothing was more moving than the touching incident of the gallant young lieutenant of the Middlesex Regiment whose name unhappily is not known [the lieutenant's name was H. A. C. Wilson, and he was the son of the Rev. A. Wilson, Vicar of St Michael and All Angels, Chiswick], though the manner of his heroic death will long be remembered. His troops were young and excited the derision of some of the veterans of Thorneycroft's Mounted Infantry. Their officer was indignant at the slight put upon them, and to encourage them, though the Boer riflemen were barely 200 yards away, he walked up and down along the trench, speaking to the men and seeing to the sighting of their rifles; wounded, yet he would not take shelter, but continued to draw the enemy's fire until he was shot dead.

I wonder if Lieutenant Wilson was the same officer that my friend Mr Packer remembered? But I can't ask him because he has now died, some seventy years later. Rest in peace.

At about 1.30 p.m., some thirty British soldiers had had enough. They put their rifles on the ground and moved towards the Boer firing line. Armed Boers rose, waving white flags, and advanced to the surrendering British. At that point, thirty yards to the rear, 'a soldier whose stature made him everywhere conspicuous, rushed forth, limping on a stick'. It was of course Thorneycroft, who pounced on the leading Boer, a Transvaaler named de Koch. Mr de Koch has described the encounter: 'The English were about to surrender, and we were all coming up, when a great big, angry, red-faced soldier ran out of the trench on our right and shouted, "I'm the Commandant here; take your men back to hell, sir! I allow no surrenders." '

Then Thorneycroft turned his back on the astonished, but greatly impressed Boers, hobbled to the thirty disconcerted British soldiers and ordered them to follow him, adding, 'Not to hesitate a second.' He led them back, unmolested by the Boers, to the newly arrived Middlesex Regiment. He then gave orders that the whole company should rush the plateau and reoccupy the trench and crest beyond – which they promptly did, with the new General Thorneycroft limping with them as best he could.

At 2.30 p.m. General Thorneycroft wrote the following message to General Warren:

From Col. Thorneycroft. Spion Kop.
To Sir C. Warren 2.30 p.m., 24.1.00.

Hung on till last extremity with old force. Some of the Middlesex here now and I hear Dorsets coming up, but force really inadequate to hold such large perimeter. The enemy's guns on N.W. sweep the whole of the top of the Hill. They also have guns E. – cannot you bring heavy Artillery fire to bear on N.W. Guns. What reinforcements can you send to hold the hill tonight? We are badly in need of water. There are many killed and wounded. (Signed) A. Thorneycroft.

If you wish to really make a certainty of hill for night you must send more Infantry and attack enemy's guns.

Of course, both Coke and Thorneycroft were unanimous and right in wanting more effective British artillery fire. They were not going to get it.

At 3.30 p.m., General Coke sent another report to General Warren: 'We are suffering much from Shrapnel fire from our left front. Bearing magnetic north apparently from Three Tree Hill. The Hill is being cleared of Boers, the necessary reinforcements have been ordered up. Scottish Rifles just reached top of hill. Casualties heavy. More Doctors, food, and especially water, wanted. – J. Talbot Coke, M. Genl.'

At 3.05 p.m. General Coke had telegraphed to the officer commanding on the 'Upper Plateau': 'Stop any men advancing further from plateau. J.T.C.' Of course, General Coke was not aware that he was ordering about his military boss, the new General Thorneycroft!

Some time around 3 p.m. the awful farce as to who was in command reached ludicrous proportions. The Scottish Rifles arrived on Spion Kop with their Colonel Cooke. Now Colonel Cooke was senior to 'Colonel' Thorneycroft, who was now a General, and the two of them had a bit of an argument amid the shot and shell, and Colonel Cooke stumped off to ask General Coke to adjudicate. Coke, however, believed that he himself was over-all boss man, but stipulated that the new actor on the scene, Colonel Hill of the Middlesex Regiment, was senior soldier on the summit. Dear reader, try to sort it out for yourself in the peace of your study. Those soldiers were trying to sort it out, with far less information, in the middle of a very bloody battle.

Of course, a question which many military tacticians have asked was why Spion Kop was being attacked in isolation, when the great majority of the British soldiers available were doing nothing more active than watching the annihilation of their comrades from afar. General Coke was surely correct in objecting to more and more men being pushed on to the small slaughter area. The question is why dreadful Buller or incompetent Warren didn't throw in battalions at points west or east of Spion Kop. They might have guessed that General Botha was already frantically searching for Boers to hold down the British on Spion Kop. After all, Buller had calculated to Warren a few days earlier that there were only about 7000 Boers for Botha to command. Why did they not think of piercing elsewhere?

General Lyttelton down below thought of it, and observing the murderous fire that was coming at the British from the Twin Peaks a mile east of Spion Kop, he ordered the 60th King's Royal Rifles to march and capture those two elevations. The battalion split into two parts; the left half under Major Bewicke-Copley and the right half under their Colonel Buchanan-Riddell. At 1 p.m. they were across the Tugela river and soon advanced into Boer fire. The 60th Rifles advanced towards their objectives throughout the afternoon. The left Peak was attacked by the left column. It was precipitous, and amongst the mausers defending it was a machine gun. The left column began to turn the Boer defence, and the attacks on both Peaks were co-operating well. At 4.45 p.m. the left column was near enough to the top to receive the order, 'Fix swords', and they charged.

In command of the Boers at the Twin Peaks, was General Schalk Burger, who later in the war was to become the Acting President of the Transvaal. He found himself so desperately pressed that he sent a Boer galloping to General Botha for reinforcements. Botha could not really spare any men from Spion Kop, but realizing his terrible danger if the Twin Peaks were captured by the British, sent primarily the Utrecht Commando, together with his chief-of-staff, Commandant Edwards, whom I like to think of as a fellow Welshman. These Boer reinforcements were able to hold Major Bewicke-Copley's soldiers from outflanking the Boer left, but all hung critically in the balance. Then Commandant Edwards was wounded and had to return to General Botha's headquarters at Coventry's Farm.

The predicament of the British on Spion Kop had got even worse during the course of the afternoon of 24 January 1900. The only glimmer of hope for them, though few of the poor bloody soldiers knew it, was the 60th Rifles biting away at the Boer left flank, on Twin Peaks.

General Coke crept along his front line from left to right and then, at 5.50 p.m., sought the shelter of a rock and wrote a full report to Sir Charles Warren:

The original troops are still in position, have suffered severely, and the dead and wounded are still in the trenches. The shell fire is, and has been, very severe. If I hold on to the position all night is there any guarantee that our Artillery can silence the enemy's guns, otherwise today's experience will be repeated, and the men will not stand another complete day's shelling. I have in hand Bethune's Mounted Infantry and the Dorset Regt. intact to cover a withdrawal. If I remain I will endeavour to utilize these units to carry food and water up to the firing line. The situation is extremely critical. If I charge and take the Kopje in front, the advance is several hundred yards in the face of the entrenched enemy in strength, and my position as regards the Q.F. [quick-firing] guns (pom-poms) is much worse. Please give orders, and should you wish me to withdraw cover retirement from Connaught's Hill.

Top of Spion Kop. 5.50 p.m. 24. Jany. 1900 – J. Talbot Coke M. Genl.

Communications were now in a shocking state; the tracks were crammed with wounded, and with darkness coming, the heliograph was of no use. It was to be a long time before Coke got a reply from Warren.

At 6.30 p.m. General Warren asked General Coke if he could manage to keep two battalions on the summit and pull the rest away from death. General Buller had asked Warren to ask this question. Who on earth was asking whom?

Again at 6.30 p.m., General Thorneycroft began firmly to put his cards on the table. He wrote a message to Warren, stating that the men who had come up Spion Kop with him the night before (the Lancashire Fusiliers, the Royal Lancaster Regiment and Thorneycroft's Mounted Infantry) were 'quite done up', and that they had no water and ammunition was running short. He also stated that infantry reinforcements were now useless unless the Boer artillery could be properly checked. He calculated that the Boers had been bombarding those 900 yards by 500 yards, with three long-range guns, three short-range guns and several pom-poms, continuously since 8 a.m. His casualties were very heavy, and he wanted water and more stretcher-bearers. He stated, 'The situation is critical.' Once again no reply came from Warren. God Almighty!

Now the great British hope was the Twin Peaks; unfortunately there was incredible Buller to take into account. From the moment that General Lyttelton had reported his initiative to the General Officer Commanding, the old Devonian was hopping mad. He demanded to know why Lyttelton had allowed the 60th Rifles to go so far unsupported and why he had allowed them to split into two parts. The short answer to that was because there were two Peaks, but unfortunately I doubt whether Lyttelton replied quite like that. Buller went on nagging and blustering, and while the fighting soldiers of the 60th were succeeding, Lyttelton lost confidence in his military scheme and ordered the withdrawal. But Colonel Buchanan-Riddell and Major Bewicke-Copley were made of sterner stuff and ignored these shameful orders. At 6 p.m. Colonel Buchanan-Riddell was killed and though the 60th Rifles had brilliantly consolidated their victory – General Lyttelton informed them that they would get no active support from the thousands of idle British soldiers – Major Bewicke-Copley began to withdraw them at 8 p.m. They angrily retreated in excellent order towards the bonfire on the banks of the Tugela river, which guided them to their pontoon bridge. Buller had saved Botha from potential defeat. It must be noted here that not only did the Boers produce some great farmer generals, but in all fairness they received tremendous military assistance from Generals Buller and Warren and a few other Englishmen.

As darkness settled on Spion Kop, the volume of fire on the British decreased considerably. The living soldiers lay amongst their smashed comrades and prepared for an awful night and probable death at dawn. Over at Mount Alice, Buller was not feeling too bad; indeed he was planning a few more moves of his own. He had arranged that on the morrow a mountain battery and two naval guns would go up on to Spion Kop, and he had taken particular interest in details of the epaulements to be constructed by Royal Engineers. Yes, they must be eight feet thick. And General Warren was busying himself; amongst other things he had suddenly decided that a balloon might be useful. If any of these plans could have been useful, which I doubt, why not think of them on 23 January, at the very latest? Mark you, Warren had heard nothing from the top of Spion Kop since 4 p.m. At 7.30 p.m. he was handed General Coke's letter, written over an hour and a half before. General Thorneycroft's urgent message was given to General Warren the following morning.

In the meantime, Winston Churchill, as inevitable as a mauser bullet, had climbed to the top of Spion Kop. He passed amongst bloodied soldiers – and it is interesting to consider that in the vicinity was Gandhi who had volunteered to become a stretcher-bearer. What did the mature Winston Churchill call the even more mature Mahatma later in their lives – 'that half-naked Fakir'? Well, there they were, both young men, one going about the Empire's work and the other about God's. Anyway, Winston Churchill paused and looked at the battered soldiers. 'One lad of about nineteen was munching a biscuit. His right trouser leg was soaked with blood. I asked whether he was wounded. "No, sir; It's only blood from an officer's head," he answered, and went on – eating his biscuit.'

Winston Churchill also discovered a chum from Harrow School on top of the Kop:

. . . a smart, clean-looking young gentleman . . . had been found leaning forward on his rifle, dead. A broken pair of field glasses, shattered by the same shell that had killed their owner, bore the name 'M Corquodale'. The name and the face flew together in my mind. It was the last joined subaltern of Thorneycroft's Mounted Infantry – joined in the evening, shot at dawn.

Poor gallant young Englishman! . . . The great sacrifice had been required of the Queen's latest recruit.

And then Winston Churchill hurried back down the spur of Spion Kop, to Warren's headquarters at the base of the mountain. Full of emotion he hurried up to one of Warren's staff officers, Captain Levita, and spoke the famous jingo threat, 'Don't let Spion Kop be a second Majuba.' Captain Levita was probably having a bit of fun with Winston when he explained that he was busy, and that if Churchill had any ideas, he should put them to General Warren direct. Of course, Winston Churchill thought that this was a sensible idea, and got stuck into Warren. The old blimp exploded and roared, 'Who is this man? Take him away. Put him under arrest.'

Captain Levita hurriedly leapt into the breach, explaining Churchill's distinguished ancestry, etc. That bit of snobbery cooled the General down, and Winston was given the job of going back on to the top of Spion Kop, with a message for Thorneycroft, assuring him that artillery would be up with him by the next day. Winston hurried off and began to climb Spion Kop for the second time, on 24 January 1900.

General Thorneycroft did not like his first day as a General, and I don't blame him. The responsibility had been thrust upon him in the middle of carnage by stupid men, and communications were almost non-existent. Unlike his appointers, he made up his mind what he thought to be best, and acted upon it with conviction. As early as 6.30 p.m. the Royal Lancaster Regiment, or rather what was left of it, were paraded near the forward dressing-station preparatory to retirement. As dusk began, General Thorneycroft consulted with Colonel Cooke of the Scottish Rifles and with Colonel Crofton of the Lancashire Fusiliers. It was about 7.30 p.m. and the three officers talked quietly for a few minutes in a hollow, close to the dressing station. Their decision would be a matter of life or death for the remaining British soldiers on top of Spion Kop. General Thorneycroft stated that they 'were both of the opinion that the hill was untenable. I entirely agreed with their view, and so I gave the order for the troops to withdraw on to the neck and ridge where the hospital was.'

At 8.20 p.m. General Coke received a reply to the report that he had written at 5.50 p.m. – two and a half hours earlier. It was very brief and short on information: 'Report yourself immediately to General Warren. Time 8.20 p.m.' Another message arrived afterwards which would have added to the confusion but was not delivered to General Coke until the following morning. That one read: 'General Talbot Coke is to report in person as early tomorrow as possible to GOC Colonel Thorneycroft to command in his absence. Has Thorneycroft seen note from GOC. – AAG.'

The above missive was sent off at 10.10 p.m. on 24 January. Unbelievable! The GOC, who was presumably General Warren, had appointed Thorneycroft to the command on Spion Kop many hours before.

It was difficult to argue with the lunatic orders that did reach the top of Spion Kop. General Coke described his predicament in his diary:

As the Boer fire at once did for any Signallers on summit, I had to leave that place, and opened communications by Lamp Light with Sir C. Warren from above the Plateau. I had a long talk with Col. Hill (Middlesex Regt.) who I regarded as being second in command, and he concurred in my message drafted at 5.50 p.m. ... It was pitch dark before I reached the Plateau, and the walking was most difficult. It was 9.0 p.m. before I received the message ... and I tried to signal back.

'To General Warren: Night so dark and country so rough that the whole night would be taken up in journey. It is not possible to give orders without my presence. – J. Talbot Coke. M. Genl.'

But the Signallers' Lamps had run short of oil, and I could not get the message through, and there remained nothing for it but for me to obey my orders and go to see Sir C. Warren. I thus gave up all idea of evacuating the summit under cover of darkness. It took me till near 2.30 a.m. to reach his Camp. I hold that he should not have taken me away from my command at such a critical moment. It turns out that about 9.0 p.m. Col. Thorneycroft personally gave orders to Commanding Officers for a withdrawal of the whole force. Capt. Phillips, my Brigade Major, on becoming aware of the retirement, issued the following Memo which he sent to all Commanding Officers:

'11.30 p.m. 24/1/1900. This withdrawal is absolutely without the authority of Major General Coke or Sir C. Warren. The former was called away by the latter a little before 10.0 p.m. Major General Coke left the summit [as against the plateau of Spion Kop] about 6.0 p.m. Our men were holding their own, and he left the situation as such and reported that he could hold on. Someone without authority has given orders to withdraw, and has incurred a grave responsibility. Were the General here he would order an instant re-occupation of the heights.'

But nothing could now change General Thorneycroft's mind. He was determined to get the British soldiers out of their death trap; particularly the soldiers that had originally come up with him. The withdrawal from Spion Kop began to operate, and Winston Churchill met the retreating soldiers on his way upwards:

Stragglers and weaklings there were in plenty. [Winston hadn't been on that horrid plot all day.] But the mass of soldiers were determined men. One man I found dragging down a box of ammunition quite by himself; 'To do something,' he said. A sergeant with twenty men formed up was inquiring what troops were to hold the position. Regimental officers everywhere cool and cheery, each with a little group of men around him, all full of fight and energy. But the darkness and the broken ground paralysed everyone.

I found Colonel Thorneycroft at the top of the mountain. Everyone seemed to know, even in the confusion, where he was. He was sitting on the ground surrounded by the remnants of the regiment he had raised, who had fought for him like lions and followed him like dogs. I explained the situation as I had been told and as I thought. Naval guns were prepared to try, sappers and working parties were already on the road with thousands of sandbags. [The sandbags had been prepared for General Woodgate's original column, but like almost everything else had been forgotten.] What did he think? But the decision had already been taken. He had never received any messages from the general, had not had time to write any. Messages had been sent him, he had wanted to send others himself. The fight had been too hot, too close, too interlaced for him to attend to anything, but to support this company, clear those rocks, or line that trench. So having heard nothing and expecting no guns, he had decided to retire. As he put it tersely: 'Better six good battalions safely down the hill than a mop up in the morning.'

General Talbot Coke's soldiers had finally to give up, in spite of the remonstrances of his Brigade Major, Captain Phillips. General Coke wrote in his diary:

Fortunately before leaving the summit I had issued orders for the Dorset Regt. to cover the withdrawal (and to form the rear guard) should such be ordered, and these orders prevented anything like a panic. The conduct of all the Regular troops throughout the day was exemplary – they were cool and determined; the wounded were cheery, and made as light as possible of their pain, though the difficulty of carrying them on stretchers down the mountain added greatly to their sufferings. The ghastly sight of Officers one had seen full of life so lately being carried to the rear so terribly disfigured by shell fire, is not one easily to forget. Personally I was never in favour of the occupation of Spion Kop, and when Sir C. Warren first spoke to me about it, I replied 'We must be careful not to have another Majuba.'

My friend, Mr Packer, was amongst General Coke's soldiers who clambered back down the southern side of Spion Kop. Mr Packer described to me his memories of that night:

. . . it got dark and somebody says we've got to retire. We said: 'Who said so?' and he said: 'I don't know, they're all retiring.' They were all going down, see, and of course, we retired as well. There was about ten of us altogether there; I didn't know what regiment they were; I didn't know if they were my regiment or who they was. It was pitch dark, see, and there were blokes lying there wounded and couldn't get a stretcher bearer. They offered any money to get a stretcher bearer there. Couldn't get one; they had to stop there . . . When we got down to the bottom of the pine coppy, we stayed there the rest of the night. And one thing I know: there was a pool of water there. We thought it was good water, and of course we had a drink of it. We'd had a terrible day with no water or anything; all in the boiling sun. And somebody came up and said: 'Have you been drinking that water?' And we said: 'Yes'. And he said: 'They've been washing their wounds in that.' Well, we was glad to get it anyway – yes.

I asked Mr Packer if he had lost many personal friends, and he replied:

Well, there was six of us, that had chummed up on the boat going out, and five of them was killed. There was three shot in the head on Spion Kop – killed. And there was one got killed at Laing's Nek [some months later, when Buller's Natal Field Force was entering the Transvaal] – chap named Charlie Davis – yes, he got killed at Laing's Nek. And another little fellow got killed at Fort Itala [much later in the war].

Another soldier, of the Lancaster Regiment, recounted how the volunteer stretcher-bearers helped the agonizing withdrawal off the top of Spion Kop:

'Umph! them stretcher-bearers worked 'ard . . . too – they may be civilians, and mayn't look over and above smart, but we of the King's Own won't fergit all as they did for our men in a 'urry. . . . Carrying men down a place as steep as a 'ouse, and under 'eavy fire too. 'Body-snatchers' some calls 'em, and thinks they's being funny. But I says a man wot does that don't know 'is friends; and wot's more, 'e ought'er be shot. They chaps of the Volunteer Stretcher Bearers worked like 'eroes, and no mistake about it. In one company alone thirty out of a 'undred was bowled over.

At about 2.30 a.m., a message was handed to General Sir Charles Warren: 'Regret to report that I have been obliged to abandon Spion Kop, as the position became untenable. I have withdrawn the troops in regular order, and will come to report as soon as possible. – Alec Thorneycroft, Lieut.-Colonel.'

And I think 'General' Thorneycroft was right. He had been given the dreadful responsibility, and had received no proper support from his superiors, and because of failure, his soldiers were getting butchered. As he said, 'Better six good battalions safely down the hill than a mop up in the morning.'

From a contemporary Dutch paper

Lieutenant-Colonel Grant looked as the grey-faced men stole down from the summit, gaunt, dirty, utterly weary, but undefeated. . . . And he also looked, in his mind's eye, at General Sir Redvers Buller:

The attempt and its execution must stand for ever as that which in a commander is worse than a crime – a blunder. The army knows well enough who is to blame for that; but it is as well that the rest of the world should remain in ignorance, even if it should mean the prolongation of the pitiable discussion, for the burden of the responsibility for such a tragedy is too heavy for one man to bear in public.

And how were the Boers faring that night? Deneys Reitz was there:

The hours went by; we kept watch, peering over and firing whenever a helmet showed itself, and in reply the soldiers volleyed unremittingly. We were hungry, thirsty and tired; around us were the dead men covered with swarms of flies attracted by the smell of blood. We did not know the cruel losses that the English were suffering, and we believed that they were easily holding their own, so discouragement spread as the shadows lengthened . . .

Darkness fell swiftly; the firing died away, and there was silence, save for a rare shot and the moans of the wounded. For a long time I remained at my post, staring into the night to where the enemy lay, so close that I could hear the cries of their wounded and the murmur of voices from behind their breastwork.

Afterwards my nerve began to go and I thought I saw figures with bayonets stealing forward. When I tried to find the men who earlier in the evening had been beside me, they were gone. Almost in panic I left my place and hastened along the fringe of rocks in search of company, and to my immense relief, heard a gruff '*werda*'. It was Commandant Opperman, still in his place with about two dozen men. He told me to stay beside him, and we remained here until after ten o'clock, listening to the enemy who were talking and stumbling about in the darkness beyond.

At last Opperman decided to retreat, and we descended the hill by the way which he had climbed up nearly sixteen hours before, our feet striking sickeningly at times against the dead bodies in our path. When we reached the bottom most of the horses were gone, the men who had retired having taken their mounts and ridden away, but our own animals and those belonging to the dead or wounded, were still standing without food or water where they had been left at daybreak . . .

The wagons were being hurriedly packed, and the entire Carolina Commando was making ready to retire. They had borne the brunt of the day's battle and had fought bravely, but, now that the struggle was over, a reaction had set in and there was panic in the camp. Fortunately, just as the foremost wagons moved away and the horsemen were getting ready to follow, there came the sound of galloping hoofs, and a man rode into our midst who shouted to them to halt. I could not see his face in the dark, but word went round that it was Louis Botha, the new Commandant General . . .

The truth was that when the 60th Rifles had driven General Schalk Burger's Boers, together with their artillery, away from the Twin Peaks, Botha sensed that all might be lost. Not only did this British tactical victory prevent the Boers from overwhelmingly enfilading the British from the east – but now the British were in a position to do precisely the same to the Boers. At 3 a.m. on 25 January 1900, Botha held a council of war with his senior officers, and it was generally agreed that the Boer position was 'hopeless'. And then miracles began to happen. News began to seep through to Botha that for some reason the British had thrown away certain victory by withdrawing from the Twin Peaks. And then Commandant Edwards, Botha's chief-of-staff, arrived and said that he had heard that the British could not remain on top of Spion Kop because they could not get water there, and because General Woodgate was dead. For a man like General Botha, a little hope spelt certainty.

Deneys Reitz caught the mood of Botha's vigorous optimism:

He addressed the men from the saddle, telling them of the shame that would be theirs if they deserted their posts in this hour of danger; and so eloquent was his appeal that in a few minutes the men were filing off into the dark to re-occupy their positions on either side of the Spion Kop gap. I believe that he spent the rest of the night riding from commando to commando exhorting and threatening, until he persuaded the men to return to the line, thus averting a great disaster.

Sometime after 3.30 a.m. on 25 January, Botha ordered his Boers to reoccupy the evacuated Twin Peaks. To complete Botha's happiness, two of his men bravely climbed to the top of Spion Kop to search for a missing friend. These two Boers crept southward, expecting to be fired on by the British at any moment. Then, to their utter astonishment, it began to dawn on them that the only soldiers on Spion Kop were either dead or badly wounded.

Deneys Reitz related:

Gradually the dawn came and still there was no movement. Then to our utter surprise we saw two men on the top triumphantly waving their hats and holding their rifles aloft. They were Boers, and their presence there was proof that, almost unbelievably, defeat had turned to victory – the English were gone and the hill was still ours.

From the British side, to the south of Spion Kop, Lieutenant-Colonel Grant watched the new turn of events:

Looking up to the clear-cut hog's back of the summit, one could see single figures moving leisurely about where yesterday a shell-riven crowd of hundreds had swayed and shifted. These slow-moving figures were those of the Boers wandering amongst the dead, who lay in serried packs behind many of the paltry sangars. A few shots rang out from odd corners of the vast mass, and then there was silence. An armistice had been arranged, to allow of the ghastly heaps left from the threshing of the day before being swept up and hidden. All day the work went on, doctors came and went, men could be seen digging against the clear sky, and every now and then a stretcher, black with blood, containing something alive but not to be looked on, would be carried past the foot of the hill.

Lieutenant E. Blake Knox of the Royal Army Medical Corps was one of the first British to climb on to Spion Kop at dawn on 25 January:

A death-like silence reigned. Terrible indeed was our work here. In the still, obscure morning light we set to work in the trenches; wounded, dying and dead lay intermingled, and as we sorted them some unwounded men were found in a state of utter collapse and exhaustion from their ordeal on the previous day.

Lieutenant Knox was taken prisoner, because he had lost his brassard from his sleeve – his Red Cross insignia – and was only released when Botha arrived.

General Louis Botha and his staff now arrived; the former was pointed out to me – a good-looking man, with closely clipped beard and moustache, dressed in a brownish suit and wearing smart top-boots and spurs. He was unarmed, but a handsomely carved rifle, carried by a Kaffir, who also bore three bandoliers, was understood to be his. I explained my object on the hill to the General, and showed him the crested buttons on my tunic and some letters I had in my pocket, which satisfied him as to my identity. He immediately ordered my release – on parole not to leave the hill without his permission; he then very kindly gave me a cigarette, and sent to his camp close by for some coffee . . .

By 6.0 a.m. on the 25th some 500 Boers had collected on the plateau; they were all well dressed and clean. Most of them wore tweed suits, leggings and spurs, and soft hats with the Transvaal colours round the brim; each had three or four well-stocked bandoliers containing some sixty cartridges apiece. Most of them spoke English, and entered readily into conversation with our men. Their occupations were varied; one, an old burgher with a long beard, got on a rock and preached a sermon for our benefit on the horrors of war . . .

Deneys Reitz climbed on to the top of Spion Kop:

On our side of the fighting-line there had been many casualties, but a worse sight met our eyes behind the English schanses.

In the shallow trenches where they had fought the soldiers lay dead in swathes, and in places they were piled three deep.

The Boer guns in particular had wrought terrible havoc and some of the bodies were shockingly mutilated. There must have been six hundred dead men on this strip of earth, and there cannot have been many battlefields where there was such an accumulation of horrors within so small a compass.

My friend Mr Dommisse of Pretoria in the Transvaal went on top of Spion Kop, on that very day. He, of course, was a young Boer fighter, and I asked him what he felt when he looked at the dreadful scene.

I really took it in the ordinary way; one must remember that you saw dead lying about, and the wounded crying for water and help – and you look upon them as strangers. You don't know them. You know that they also have a mother, or sisters, or a father – and a certain wave of sympathy – and in a way you try to do whatever you can for them. You make them comfortable where they lie. You give them a drop of water. But that is about as far as human feeling goes. But, after all, what are they fighting for? They are not fighting for an ideal. Just a soldier; just trying to do his duty, to Queen and Country, to Queen and Empire. But what were they really fighting for? Trying to take away from a freedom, liberty loving people, their liberty and their independence. Now why are you doing it? . . . You ask them that question and they can give you no answer. They simply tell you: 'We are soldiers, and we have got to fight, that's all.' They don't know what they are fighting for; that is your British soldier, in general. It may be otherwise with the British officers, who were taken mainly from the aristocracy at that time. They were really very proud, exceedingly proud. 'I am a British officer,' and they shouted at their men; I am afraid it is true. But they should be admired for their bravery. I never saw a British officer, who didn't show, on the battlefield, under severe circumstances, that he was brave.

Mr John Atkins, of the *Manchester Guardian*, reported how 'a Boer doctor looked at the dead bodies . . . the burnt grass where shells had set fire to it, at the whole sad and splendid scene where the finest infantry in the world had suffered; "No!" he said, with double truth, "we Boers would not, could not suffer like that." '

But the last word about that day on Spion Kop must come from General Ben Viljoen:

'What made them leave so suddenly last night?' was the question we asked each other then, and which remains unanswered to this day.

General Warren has stated that the cause of his departure was the want of water, but I can hardly credit that statement, as water could be obtained all the way to the top of Spion Kop; and even had it been wanting it is not likely that after a sacrifice of 1200 to 1300 lives the position would have been abandoned on this account alone. Our victory was undoubtedly a fluke.

The surgeon, Sir Frederick Treves, has described the arrival of over a thousand wounded British soldiers at Number 4 'Stationary' Field Hospital, at Spearman's Farm. 'They [the ambulance wagons] emerged one by one out of the darkness and drew up in the open space between the two central lines of tents, and between the few uplifted lanterns held by the sergeants and the men on duty. After they had deposited their load they moved away, and vanished again into the night.'

To guide these wagons into the hospital at night, two white lights were suspended from the flagstaff, which stood at the entrance. Sir Frederick, who was always an interested man, and watched and listened very carefully, wrote about the arrival of one of these wagons:

A wagon had reached the hospital lines, and was waiting to be unloaded. A man with a shattered arm in a sling was sitting up, and at his feet a comrade was lying who had been very hard hit, and who had evidently become weaker and less conscious as the wagon had rolled along. The apparently sleeping man moved, and lifting his head to look at his pal, who was sitting above him, asked wearily, for probably the fiftieth time, 'Don't you see nothing yet, Bill, of the two white lights?'

One wounded British soldier must personify all of those indomitables who were carried off Spion Kop. Sir Frederick Treves was again the witness to this story:

A private in the King's Royal Rifles, of the name of Goodman, was brought from Spion Kop to No. 4 Field Hospital in an ambulance with many others. He was in a lamentable plight when he arrived. He had been lying on the hill all night. He had not had his clothes off for six days. Rations had been scanty, and he had been sleeping in the open since he left the camp. He had been struck in the face by a fragment of shell which had carried away his right eye, the right upper jaw, the corresponding part of the cheek and mouth, and had left a hideous cavity at the bottom of which his tongue was exposed. The rest of his face was streaked with blood, which was now dried and black – so black that it looked as if tar had been poured on his head and had streamed down his cheek and neck. Eight hours had been occupied on the journey to the hospital, and eight hours is considered to be long even for a railway journey in a Pullman car.

He was unable to speak, and as soon as he was settled in a tent he made signs that he wanted to write. A little memorandum book and a pencil were handed to him, and it was supposed that his inquiry would be as to whether he would die – what chance he had? Could he have something to drink? Could anything be done for his pain? After going through the form of wetting his pencil at what had once been a mouth, he simply wrote: 'Did we win?' No one had the heart to tell him the truth.

The British soldiers who died on top of Spion Kop were buried there, and while considering the following Boer telegram perhaps it is only fair to remember that there is little earth on that mountain before a spade meets hard rock.

T.D. ZAR 30.1.1900. From Wolmaraans, Member of Executive Council, Colenso To President, Pretoria, begins:

... Yesterday in company with General Cronje I visited the Spionkop [*sic*] battlefield, and it was most plain to me that Providence was here at work since, had the enemy held Spionkop as they did on Wednesday, they would already be in Ladysmith. Everyone of us should recognize this fact. Those burghers who scaled the heights on Wednesday behaved most gallantly. Parts of the bodies of the enemy dead, interred on the summit, still stick out of the ground. Three are quite unburied.

It is high time that the famous cultured English nation were told that their way of burying the dead is worse than that of barbaric savages. In short there is a stench on Spionkop; while vultures wheel over a battlefield extending from Upper Tugela right to Pontsdrift where they have retired. It is possible – I consider – that they are massing there to attempt Pontsdrift. All is quiet here at Colenso – ends.

As a matter of passing fact, when I was last on top of Spion Kop, about eight years ago, I carefully buried a few British bones, and the earth still contained British .303 bullet cases.

Earl de la Warr wrote: 'Although we are naturally depressed we are as determined as when the war started; and although the date may be still far distant we are confident that the survivors of this war will see the British flag hoisted over Bloemfontein and Pretoria, never, so long as our Empire lasts, to be hauled down again.'

British losses on and around Spion Kop were 32 officers and 290 men killed or died of wounds; and 33 officers and some 530 men wounded. In addition, nearly 300 men were made prisoner. The Boers suffered about 300 casualties, but only one of them was an officer, a Field-Cornet Badenhorst, from Vryheid – and he was killed.

Amazingly Winston Churchill was a great fan of General Buller, and he wrote in the London *Morning Post* a piece about the British Army's retreat from Spion Kop which included:

Buller! So it was no longer Warren! The commander-in-chief had arrived, in the hour of misfortune, to take all responsibility for what had befallen the army, to extricate it, if possible, from its position of peril, to encourage the soldiers, now a second time defeated without being beaten, to bear the disappointment. Everyone knows how all this, that looked so difficult, was successfully accomplished . . .

Buller took personal command. He arrived on the field calm, cheerful, inscrutable as ever, rode hither and thither with a weary staff and a huge notebook, gripped the whole business in his strong hands, and so shook it into shape that we crossed the river in safety, comfort and good order, with most remarkable mechanical precision, and without the loss of a single man or a pound of stores.

I do find that piece of journalism an unhealthy load of rubbish. But it is true that Buller had taken over full responsibility now. If there was to be another blunder, he could not so easily hide behind one or more of his Generals.

Incidentally, there is a story about a private who walked straight up to Buller and told him that he wasn't capable of leading ducks across a village pond. This stylish private was court-martialled but the details seem to have disappeared. But one letter from a Rochdale soldier struck even more deeply at the wretched truth: 'Poor old Joe [Chamberlain]! How he does catch it. The soldiers curse him from morning to night.'

On 25 January 1900, Buller reported his withdrawal south of the Tugela river to both Lord Roberts and Sir George White. Lord Roberts replied on 26 January, asking, 'Unless you feel fairly confident of being able to relieve Ladysmith from Potgieter's Drift, would it not be better to postpone the attempt until I am in Orange Free State?' Lord Roberts, together with most Englishmen thoughout the Empire, was getting very nervous about what Sir Redvers might do next. Lord Roberts' theory was that once he invaded the Orange Free State, the Free State Boers would leave the investment of Ladysmith and their positions on the Tugela Heights to defend their home-land. On 28 January, Buller sent a message to Lord Roberts: 'No. 178 ... De-lay is objectionable: I feel fairly confident of success this time; one can never safely attempt to prophesy, but, so far as my exertions can, humanly speaking, conduce to the desired end, I think I can promise you that I shall in no case compromise my force.'

What had Sir Redvers got up his sleeve? Lord Roberts desper-ately countered – on behalf of the shell-shocked War Office in London – with another question: was any position in Natal impregnable enough to be held by 10000 men? I presume that Lord Roberts was hinting that he would like some of Buller's thousands in his proposed march into the Orange Free State. Well, Buller wouldn't have that! Buller banged the ball back

'*The Lilliputian Boers and the British Gulliver*' – *from* Puck, *a New York magazine*

over the net with 'No. 180 . . . 16000 men would be wanted, besides a strong force of artillery, but I cannot advocate the policy indicated by the question.'

Whatever Buller's next point of attack would be, he cancelled it for the time being, and sent his message, No. 182, to Lord Roberts, explaining that the postponement was due 'to difficulties of weather'. Lord Roberts replied that this suited him, as he also was going to be delayed. And that brings us to the end of the awful month of January 1900.

12

THE SIEGE OF LADYSMITH
February 1900

How do you like horse-meat?
BOER HELIOGRAPH TO LADYSMITH

BACK inside besieged Ladysmith, H. W. Nevinson of the London *Daily Chronicle* reported for his newspaper:

February 1, 1900. – How we should have laughed in November at the thought of being shut up here till February! But here we are, and the outlook grows more hopeless. People are miserably depressed. It would be impossible to get up sports or concerts now. Too many sick, too many dead. The laughter has gone out of the siege, or remains only as bitter laughter when the word relief is spoken. We are allowed to know nothing for certain, but the conviction grows that we are to be left to our fate for another three weeks at least, while the men slowly rot. A Natal paper has come in with an account of Buller's defeat at Taba Nyama [culminating with the battle of Spion Kop] on the 25th. We read with astonishment the loud praises of a masterly retreat over the Tugela without the loss of a single man. When shall we hear of a masterly advance to our aid? Do we lose no men?

Of course the Natal *Mercury* dwelt on the successful withdrawal and played down the fact that before the final withdrawal from the whole Taba Nyama–Spion Kop fiasco, a total of 36 officers and 338 men had died, with 47 officers and 1008 men wounded and 4 officers and 307 men missing or prisoners of war. And the newspaper wasn't harping on the comparable 400 Boer casualties either. Mr Nevinson had no way of learning that the attempts to relieve Ladysmith to the south-west were no joke; and that soldiers had fought very hard for them.

On the afternoon of 1 February 1900, the sun suddenly broke through the clouds and an official message blinked into Ladysmith from Buller's force. Ladysmith gasped for a shred of good news. All they got was, 'German specialist landed Delagoa Bay [Portuguese East Africa] pledges himself to dam up Klip river and flood Ladysmith out.'

That day brought to Ladysmith one significant breakthrough: the inhabitants would eat their horses. Now, for non-English people to comprehend exactly why this was such an awful moment of truth, they must dwell on one strange phenomenon of the people called English; particularly in those sections where privilege held any sway. To eat your horse is almost as horrific as to eat your child. Henry Pearse of the London *Daily News* wrote: 'It has come at last. Horseflesh is to be served out for food, instead of being buried or cremated.'

Colonel E. W. D. Ward, the supply officer in Ladysmith, made the fateful but lifesaving decision. Incidentally, General Sir George White called Colonel Ward 'the best supply officer since Moses'. A factory was organized in the engine-shed at the railway station, to process and make maximum use of the butchered horses. The particular genius behind the details of the enterprise was probably Lieutenant McNalty of the Army Service Corps. Inside the engine-shed, only one locomotive remained, which served as a bomb-shelter – the 'horse-meat' workers scuttled into it whenever they were warned of an approaching missile. The unused engine-pits were converted into enormous cauldrons, and into these the horse-parts were thrown. War-correspondent Nevinson visited the place and remarked, 'Farewell, my Arab steed!' Then, after a primitive chemical ritual, which I will not examine

'Gentleman in Kharki' – the famous
bronze statue by Caton Woodville,
which was inspired by Rudyard
Kipling's poem and became the symbol
of the British troops during the war

South African War
Medals with bar awarded after the
Relief of Ladysmith

The Queen's chocolate box, given to
every soldier fighting for Her Majesty in the war

'Bobs' – a Boer War game

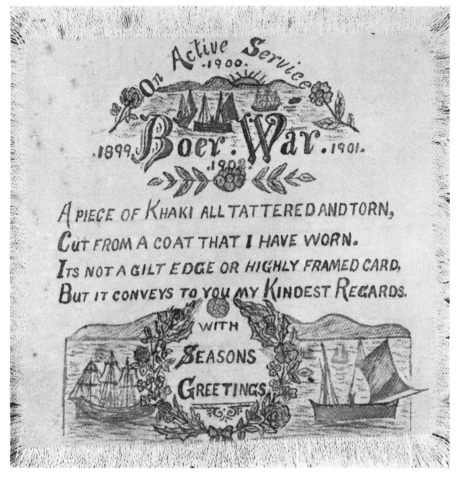

A valentine from a British soldier, inscribed on part of his khaki uniform

A handkerchief from the Boer War

Generals Buller and White on contemporary jugs

A china money-box
caricaturing President Kruger

Warren bathes on Hussar Hill – a contemporary French cartoon
(see page 326)

Queen Victoria is spanked by Kruger – a contemporary French cartoon

Three contemporary anti-British postcards, dealing with the Natal campaign

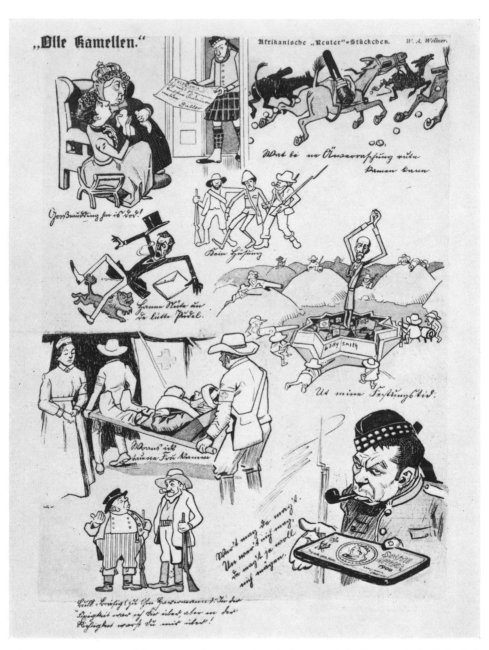

A cartoon panorama of the war emphasizing the tribulations of the Siege and the Relief of Ladysmith – from a German paper

here, an extract of horse was produced which, after careful thought, and in particular a discussion about the dangers of contravening the libel law – they wanted to imply the famous name of Bovril – they called the result **Chevril**. Even a label was printed: the only part which is not self-explanatory is 'Aduncus Bea and Co'. This, signallers explained to interested people in Ladysmith, was the official title of Colonel Ward. Every part of the horse was utilized. Chevril was meant especially for the sick, and one pint of horse soup was issued to each soldier per day. Reactions to actually swallowing Chevril were very varied. Henry Pearse of the London *Daily News*, found a young man of the Imperial Light Horse – 'scarcely more than a boy' – sitting on a doorstep, 'apparently too weak to move'. The boy was holding a spray of jasmine, and confessed that he had been wounded at Elandslaagte and at Wagon Hill, but though starving, he could not swallow horse. Mr Pearce helped the boy into his house, gave him what food he had, and his last so-precious dram of whisky.

'An old Scottish journalist and Natal correspondent', whom I cannot identify by name, had remonstrated loud and long at the barbarities of eating 'man's best friend', but finally, ravenously hungry, capitulated. 'Tell me it's beef and send it in. I'm not inquisitive.' But poor bloody Tommy Atkins, from the slums of London, Glasgow, Cardiff and Dublin, had been conditioned to a cruder philosophy. Henry Nevinson heard the joke: 'Mind that stuff; it kicks!'

2 February began with misty rain, and then the sun burst through. The British heliograph from Swaartz Kop, beyond the Tugela river, was sending another official message. Drooping hopes in Ladysmith desperately focused on the message from the Queen's Empire. What comfort could the great Power send? The words that were so important for Ladysmith spelt themselves out: 'Sir Stafford Northcote, Governor of Bombay, had been made a peer.'

Then the Boers heliographed into Ladysmith, from Umbulwana Hill, 'How do you like horse-meat?' But such a jibe could not pass without a rejoinder. As miserable as the defenders of Ladysmith now felt, they spiritedly heliographed back, presumably trying hard not to sick their Chevril: 'Fine. When the horses are finished we're going to eat Boer.'

Sickness in the small town of Ladysmith was now reaching appalling proportions. On Saturday, 3 February 1900, there were over 2300 patients in the hospital at Intombi Camp. Of these, 1240 were suffering from enteric fever and dysentery. The death rate was often about thirty a day. The cemetery close by was a melancholy and disturbing place. Medicine and vital milk was in very short supply. The saving grace of Intombi was those blessed women of vocation, the nurses. The Reverend Owen Watkins wrote about them in Intombi Camp:

Of the Nursing Sisters I cannot write as I should like; for no words could describe all that they did and all that they endured. It was a marvel of heroic endurance for gentle women to live in a camp exposed to wind and rain, heat and cold, almost perpetual duty, each with some sixty patients under her care, and most of them in a dying condition; whilst their food was unpalatable and barely sufficient to satisfy the cravings of hunger . . . in their noble devotion, cheerfully they sacrificed years out of their lives in order that they might add to the comfort of 'Tommy'. To my certain knowledge, the Sisters continued at their duty with their temperature at 103°, and with their own hands tried to concoct dainty dishes out of the small material at their command in order to tempt their patients' appetites, whilst they themselves were faint and dizzy from lack of the food which their weariness caused them to turn from with nausea. Truly, without exception, they were heroines deserving of the Royal Red Cross.

4 February was a Sunday, and the sun shone, and women and children came out on to the streets of Ladysmith and walked with as gay an air as they could manage. Straw boaters and parasols and pretty white dresses. But many observant people in the town felt that this could be the last day of relative peace before the place was overwhelmed. The Boers were concentrating to the north-west of Ladysmith. The day before, a new gun was moved towards Thornhill's Kopje, and there was much activity during the night. The military authorities believed that the attack would come on the line from Observation Hill to Range Post. Every soldier was put on the alert. Soldiers in the 'glass house' were released and sent to the perimeter. The outposts were pushed forward and doubly manned. A code of rocket signals was organized to try to keep Buller informed as to how the incipient battle might go. It was felt that this was to be the Boers' final assault on Ladysmith, and the garrison was not what it had been on 6 January. However, every effort was made to stand fast. The first hint of a possible Boer attack had reached Ladysmith in a most curious way. Apparently a Frenchman serving with the Boers learnt of the impending attack, and, believing that it would be successful, decided to invest on the Paris Stock Exchange. If Ladysmith fell, it would certainly shift the balance of finance in Europe. In Paris, an English stockbroker purchased the information, and then wired it to his partner in London, who informed the War Office, who cabled Buller, who then heliographed the warning to Sir George. How many thousands of miles to communicate an event which was being planned a few miles distant?

At 3 a.m. on 5 February every fighting man was under arms. But the Boer attack did not come; instead Ladysmith heard the boom of Buller's distant guns. They started early in the morning, reaching a crescendo at 7.30 a.m., and again at 3 p.m. The artillery continued until after nightfall. Speculation bubbled through Ladysmith. Again on the 6th the gunfire continued. Lieutenant-Colonel St John Gore of the 5th Dragoon Guards, wrote in his diary:

Firing from Buller and some Boer guns began about 5.0 a.m. Today from our camp we could see the white puff of smoke as a Boer gun fired, and the answering column of brown dust as a lyddite shell burst on the same ridge. This appeared to go on all day long. One knows nothing of what is going on, and one's attention wanders away from this distant yet visible sign of fighting, in spite of the intense personal interest every individual man among us is bound to be feeling in it!

Mr Henry Pearse of the London *Daily News* saw the great clouds of dust which always heralded a move from the Boers north of the Tugela. Hopes rose and fell and rose . . .

While all that action was going on between Buller and Botha, Sir George White held a Field General Court Martial and the most interesting charge was against a 'contractor' named Foss, who was the champion swimmer of South Africa. He was accused of 'using words calculated to create despondency', by using 'most improper language to NCOs and men of the Devon Regiment'. Now this didn't mean rude four-letter words – the Devons were no doubt accomplished at that themselves; no, what Foss had done was to exaggerate British losses at the battle of Colenso, and to suggest to the soldiers that there were 'worse things to come'. He was found guilty and sentenced to one year's imprisonment. At one time in Ladysmith everyone could shoot their mouths off about doom, as they did in the comic newspapers the *Bombshell* and the *Ladysmith Lyre*, but not now. Things were grim. It was a holding-on time. Colonel Park had put Mr Foss under arrest.

On 7 February, Lieutenant-Colonel St John Gore, wrote: 'Buller's guns again began early, and a great battle apparently raged all day; now we have almost given up speculating on what is happening, or what *has* happened.'

Well, whatever it was, it *had* happened. Buller signalled to White:

The enemy is too strong for me here, and though I could force the position, it would be a great loss . . . My plan is to slip back to Chieveley, take Hlangwane, the Boer position south of the Tugela and east of Colenso, and the next night try and take Bulwana Hill from the south. Can you think of anything better? I find I cannot take my guns and trains through these mountains. I hope to be at Hlang-wane on Saturday. Keep it dark.

How frightening that message must have been to Sir George White, and how desperate to his soldiers. Buller was abandoning his good idea, which he had failed to insist upon, of outflanking the Boer right wing, and was now planning to outflank their left wing. The taking of Hlangwane was a good idea. It would have been a good idea before or during the battle of Colenso. And what was this militarily immature question, 'Can you think of anything better?' Poor White in Ladysmith. Buller, with his well-fed South Natal Field Force was in a much better position to think of something better – if there was something better. Sir George White replied to Sir Redvers Buller: 'Cannot offer suggestions, as do not know country, or where you propose to cross Tugela. I could help at Bulwana. The closer to Ladysmith you can establish yourself the better chance we shall have here.'

It is an indictment of the British military of the period that General White did not know the country. British soldiers had been in Natal for decades. General Hunter was frank about it. He said: 'There was not a single officer in Ladysmith who could tell you anything.' Harsh that, and I must insist, inaccurate. After all, General Hunter himself was in the siege of Ladysmith, as chief-of-staff.

A rumour – one of many, many – began to circulate Ladysmith that General White was practising the Hundredth Psalm, in preparation for the approaching hundredth day of the siege.

Anyway, Buller had not successfully crossed the Tugela, and therefore Lieutenant-Colonel Gore told his 5th Dragoon Guards, who still had horses, that they would not be required for a flying column to co-operate with Buller. That night the Boers celebrated their new victory by waving searchlights over poor old Ladysmith.

8 February 1900 was the hundredth day of the siege. At about 1.30 a.m. the Boer howitzer gun on Surprise began to fire into Ladysmith. Later in the day, the cavalry were ordered to send more of their horses for slaughter, and processing into Chevril. For the mounted military man in Ladysmith there were not many Chevril jokes.

On 9 February, rations were again reduced. This was always the seal in Ladysmith that Buller was still failing. Acute observers in the town, who for security reasons heard no hard news, always cheered up when gentle Sir George White was observed to pat a child on the head, and say, 'You'll soon get some lollies.'

The Boer heliograph on Umbulwana winked a bit of repartee to the British signallers on Caesar's Camp. The Boer was a potential cricketing Springbok; his message was humorously relevant and brief: '101 not out.' The Manchester Regiment – Lancashire after all – were quick to their reply: 'Ladysmith still batting.'

A Boer artilleryman, after shelling the town for hours, wearily turned from his gun saying, 'What is the use of shelling them; they just go on playing cricket.' Then the Boers opened fire on Caesar's Camp with their Long Tom gun, and his first shot just missed the gun-trail of one of the British 12-pounder naval guns. A young naval gunnery lieutenant turned away, laconically remarking, 'They've put on a new bowler.'

On 10 February, the Volunteer soldiers of Ladysmith were ordered to begin slaughtering their horses. This was probably even more painful for these men than for the regular cavalry. The Volunteers owned their horses; the bond could be very deep. Mr Watkins-Pitchford, with the Natal Carabineers, wrote to his wife about his horse, named after Lord Roberts:

'Bobs' has not been sent that mournful road this time, but it is but a matter of time before we must part, I fear, unless Buller takes compassion upon him and saves him from the pot. After all, the 'goodbye' is but a matter of time, with men as with horses, and the depth of affection subsisting between dear ones avails nothing with the Fury who 'clips the thin-spun thread'.

Lieutenant-Colonel St John Gore, 5th Dragoon Guards, inscribed in his diary:

Feb. 11, Sunday. – Church parade service, for the dismounted regiment at 6.30 a.m., at the Naval Brigade camp (near ours), and in company with our gallant friends the Blue-jackets. The Rev. A. V. C. Hordern officiated, and gave a short service, as we stood in a nullah out of sight of Bulwana for fear the gunner there might forget it was the sabbath, as he has done before!

Colonel Gore did not mention in his diary that the day was close and sultry, with a temperature of 107°F in the shade!

Major Doveton, of the Imperial Light Horse, had been badly wounded during the battle of Wagon Hill, on 6 January. Now, Major Doveton was a well-known British imperialist, and was also known to the Boers as a prominent member of the Reform Committee, who had tried to overthrow the Transvaal Government by quisling activities in Johannesburg, in conjunction with the notorious Jameson Raid of 1896. If the Boers had reason to hate anyone, it was the English arrogance personified by the Major. But now, on 12 February 1900 he was seriously ill in Intombi hospital.

His wife, Mrs Doveton, was living on British-held territory, south of the Tugela. Nevertheless, when General Botha heard of Major Doveton's condition, he supplied an ambulance cart and a Boer escort, to drive Mrs Doveton through the Boer positions, and into Intombi Camp. These Boers demonstrated 'every mark of respectful sympathy' towards Mrs Doveton. The lady arrived as a surgeon was amputating her husband's arm. In his weak state of health, the Major could not withstand the shock of surgery, and he died that day. But his loving wife was with him at the end.

On this day that Major Doveton died through malnutrition as much as shock, an official notice went up in Ladysmith:

Eggs For Hospital. Ladysmith, 12th February, 1900.

In a letter from Colonel Ward AAG, Natal Field Force, he refers to the great number of soldiers who are now suffering from enteric fever and other diseases of a similar character, and Colonel Exham, the Principal Medical Officer, informs him that if 200 eggs could be procured a day the greatest benefit would ensue to these sick men: in fact, in the majority of cases, material assistance would be rendered towards a satisfactory recovery.

At the request of Lieut.-General Sir G. White, Colonel Ward has written me upon the subject, and it is suggested that if only a certain number of the inhabitants would give a few eggs, the required number could be obtained.

I shall be pleased to know from you at the earliest date possible, whether you will kindly assist by giving a few daily; and upon hearing from you to the effect, I shall be pleased to receive and forward same in accordance with the wishes of the Military Authorities herein expressed. – J. Farquhar, Mayor.

On 13 February, the military in Ladysmith observed that the Boers were moving eastward, to the north of the Tugela Heights, obviously parallel to Buller's laborious movement in that direction. General White signalled to General Buller, warning him of the Boers' tactical moves, and adding: 'We anxiously await news from you.' There was no immediate reply to this, but Buller did forward to Ladysmith a happy message from Lord Roberts, far over to the west of South Africa: 'I have entered Orange Free State with a large force, especially strong in Cavalry, Artillery and Mounted Infantry. Inform your troops of this, and tell them from me I hope the result of next few days may lead to pressure on Ladysmith being materially lessened.'

Well, it did that; if not obviously in the physical sense, certainly in the psychological sense. Surely many Orange Free State Boers in Natal must hurry to defend their homeland? And, indeed, over the next few days, Boer wagons were observed trekking north and north-westwards, towards the Drakensberg Mountain passes, which led to the Orange Free State. It was calculated that not less than 2000 Boer soldiers left; a desperate depletion of General Louis Botha's small army. Lieutenant-Colonel Sir Henry Rawlinson, the AAG on Sir George White's staff, now looked coldly at the facts of the matter and announced: 'We can hold out till mid-March if we eat *all* the horses.'

Mr Henry Pearse of the London *Daily News* found that the siege of Ladysmith and the attempts to relieve it were becoming an increasingly personal matter. Writing on 13 February he said:

For me the strain is tightened by news heliographed this morning that another son has come round from Bulawayo and joined the relieving force as a lieutenant of Thorneycroft's Mounted Infantry. I don't know whether pride or anxiety is paramount when I think of these two boys fighting their way towards me. Both are with Lord Dundonald's Irregular Horse, of which we have heard much from Kaffirs who tell us that Thorneycroft's Rifles and the 'Sakkabulu boys', who are now identified as the South African Light Horse, have been in the front of every fight. It may seem egotistical to let this personal note stand, but I take the incident to be an illustration of the spirit that animates English youth at this moment.

Two sons fighting for the freeing of their father! Which only goes to prove that Victorian melodrama never exaggerated!

Humour kept popping up through the grimness, though now always carrying a cutting edge. The Reverend Owen Watkins heard one soldier ask another, 'Have you heard the latest news?'

'No, what is it?'

'Why, Stanley, the chap who found Livingstone, has sailed for Natal.'

'Stanley! What's *he* coming for?'

'Why, to look for Buller, of course.'

And the soldier, so the Reverend reported, went 'off chuckling bitterly to himself'.

That German who had arrived in Portuguese East Africa was now hard at work damming the Klip river with the intention of flooding Ladysmith. No one in the town seemed capable of having a go at him; the people inside the perimeter just waited, with mild interest, to see if the flood theory would work. And on 14 February, Buller telegraphed that according to his information 300 Germans had joined the Boers around Ladysmith, and that Ladysmith was to be attacked again before 26 February. General White replied: 'I think another attack here quite possible. Have strengthened defences, and will try to give good account of ourselves, but men are on very short rations, and are consequently very weak.'

Buller had also mentioned in his message that he himself expected to be attacked. Could he really have believed this? It does seem to me unlikely that General Botha, with his depleted force, would venture from his stronghold and attack Buller's now formidable army, on open land – well suited to the battle theories of Waterloo in 1815. But, on the other hand, the garrison of Ladysmith could hear Buller's artillery banging away, far, far to the south, it is true, but nevertheless, banging away. Buller signalled again on 16 February, explaining the distant noise: 'I am engaged in trying to turn the enemy out of the position he holds south of the Tugela river and east of Colenso.'

This could only mean the significant Hlangwane Hill, and over to the east a spur of hills south of the Tugela river called Cingolo, and immediately north of Cingolo and closer to the river, Monte Cristo (see map, page 345).

On 17 February shells – and they were British – could be seen bursting over Cingolo and Monte Cristo. And then, on the 18th, discerning soldiers in Ladysmith, peering south-eastwards, could definitely identify Buller's attacking lines rolling up and over the Cingolo and Monte Cristo Heights. This was an advance. This was definitely a tactical success by the British. The Boers were being driven off their important commanding outposts south of the Tugela river. What did it portend? Mr Watkins-Pitchford, Volunteer soldier in Ladysmith, could not now be confident of anything Buller did. In a letter to his wife he confessed: '. . . My text for publication is "Buller can do no wrong", but in my innards I harbour a less comfortable creed, I fear. Still, we cannot afford to look into the future unless it promises well for we are drawing heavily upon our stock of latent hopefulness, and bankruptcy stares us in the face.'

Mr Watkins-Pitchford also noted in the letter that 'The clouds have at last burst and the rain is falling fast. This is in the nick of time as our tanks and cisterns are just exhausted and our typhoid percentage is in direct proportion to our water supply.'

On 19 February, Sir George White knew definitely about Buller's success south of the Tugela. He signalled his congratulations 'on your important success', and went on, 'Let me know when you intend attacking position north of Tugela, and whether you will come via Bulwana or Colenso road, and I will try and co-operate.' Poor, lame Sir George White and his tottering garrison. But no; the spirit was not beaten!

On 21 February, Buller replied to White's congratulations, and pathetic offer of help. He stated that he was pushing through to Ladysmith by the easterly Pieter's Road. 'I think there is only a rearguard in front of me. The large Boer laager under Bulwana was removed last night. I hope to be with you tomorrow night. You might help by working north and stopping some of the enemy getting away.'

So now Buller was swinging right round to the Boers' left flank, and he was also sweeping round to extreme optimism. But General White, like every human soul in Ladysmith, had learnt to believe nothing until it was seen to be done. Also he knew that ahead of Buller, over to the east, was a complicated jumble of hills. It could not be easy for Buller's soldiers to get through; even through a rear-guard. And Sir George White had noted railway trains in the vicinity, full of Boer reinforcements from the Transvaal, and these Boers were now hurrying in the general direction of Buller. White sent a message to Buller: 'We can detect no signs of enemy retreating; all indications point the other way.' And the Boers began to bombard Ladysmith with renewed ardour.

On 22 February, Mr Pearse of the London *Daily News*, noted how the 'trivialities' of eating preoccupied everyone's mind in Ladysmith. And if Buller were winning, what did that mean? Mr Pearse noted the weak but cheery greetings: ''Ave you 'eard the noos? They say there'll be full rations today.' Then the news came, and the full ration was postponed. Buller to White: 'I find I was premature in fixing actual date of my entry into Ladysmith, as I am meeting with more opposition than I expected, but I am progressing.'

The black African scouts employed by Sir George White confirmed what was feared. It was true that the Orange Free State Boers had left to defend their country from Lord Roberts' invasion, but the Transvaalers under the redoubtable Louis Botha were standing steadfast and determined. Gravely outnumbered they might be, but they would take some shifting. Horatio holding the bridge. And Buller was back in low key, writing: 'Can hold Monte Cristo temporarily. Shall endeavour to open communication with you further on.' Monte Cristo was on the southern, *British* side of the Tugela river. How could he fail to hold it? God help Buller!

On 24 February, it became clear in Ladysmith that the townspeople had not been very forthcoming over that appeal for eggs for dying soldiers. The Mayor issued a second official statement on the matter:

Eggs For the Sick and Wounded.
Notice is hereby given that by request of the General Officer Commanding, owners of fowls within the Borough must hand over all eggs to the Municipal Authorities for the use of the sick and wounded.
Upon intimation being given to the Town Clerk, at the office of Messrs Walton and Tatham, arrangements will be made daily to collect and receive the same, or

they can be forwarded to him direct at the office in question, between the hours of 9.0 a.m. and 1.0 p.m. (Sundays excepted).

Failing this notice being fully observed by 12 o'clock noon on Monday, the 26th inst., the Military Authorities intimate through the undersigned, that owners, with no exception, will be compelled to hand over their fowls for the purpose of supplying the eggs now so urgently required. – J. Farquhar, Mayor.

On the 25th, the inhabitants of Ladysmith were shocked to hear Buller's artillery fire gradually die away altogether. It is reported that people became very quiet, stunned by the realization that rescue might still be a long time off. Mr H. W. Nevinson of the London *Daily Chronicle*, visited Intombi Camp hospital: '. . . the patients . . . lie absolutely quiet, sleeping, or staring into vacancy. They hardly ever speak a word, though the beds are only a foot apart . . .'

Lieutenant-Colonel St John Gore, 5th Dragoon Guards, investigated and found that 'if they have bad, or no news at all, the death rate is certain to be heavier on that day . . .'

There was, however, at least one exception in Intombi, and that was Sergeant Boseley, the gunner of the 53rd Battery, Royal Field Artillery, who had lost his left arm and left leg on 6 January. That Irishman had been carried from the field of battle under fire still barking at his hard-pressed gunners, 'Buck up!' It was claimed in Ladysmith that he had broken a record by surviving a double amputation on one day. As soon as he had 'recovered', his first wish was to visit his 53rd Battery. Four men hoisted him into a cart and Mr Nevinson gently drove him to his comrades on duty. Sergeant-Gunner Boseley had a good look round, 'where the greetings of his mates were brief, emphatic and devoid of all romance'. Mr Nevinson then gave him a drive round Ladysmith but feared that the sergeant was bored. Not a bit of it; Mr Boseley said that he had enjoyed it 'immensely', and that he had never 'seen Ladysmith by daylight before!' And now, on 25 February, he was in Intombi hospital and Mr Nevinson visited him. The sergeant treated his appalling misfortunes with 'cheerful indifference', and only seemed to show regret about where 'the shell cut in half a marvellous little Burmese lady, whose robes once swept down his arm in glorious blues and reds, but are now lapped over the bone as "flaps".' Sergeant-Gunner Boseley was a red-haired Irishman; though unhappily born in Maidstone, England.

25 February was a Sunday, and Lieutenant-Colonel St John Gore went to the Anglican church, where the vicar preached a sermon on Noah and the Flood. Some may have thought that the subject was irrelevant to Ladysmith's

pressing problems, but Colonel Gore couldn't get out of his mind that German, named Krantz, who was reaching the climax of his preparations to flood Ladysmith. (Incidentally, this scheme was a monumental flop. The Klip didn't rise and virtually nothing untoward happened.) Some thinkers in Ladysmith regarded Krantz as a great blessing; they believed that the German's enthusiasm for his devilish hopes gave an excuse to the Boers not to try another hand-to-hand assault. As Colonel Gore sang hymns, as only English people can sing hymns, 'the hoarse boom of our guns on the far side of Caesar's Camp intruded itself upon us'.

Monday was cloudy and no signals reached Ladysmith. Buller's guns were heard, but at a seemingly great distance, and on that day, rations were reduced to quarter scale. It seemed clear to many people in Ladysmith that Buller was somehow retreating to the sea at Durban. As Lieutenant-Colonel St John Gore put it, 'The Englishman is always said to be peculiarly susceptible to attacks on his "food".' But they were wrong. Came the 27th and Buller's guns were still firing, rising to 'an incessant and tremendous uproar'. And this was a very significant date on the calendar for both Boer and Briton; it was 'Majuba Day'. It was the anniversary of the final Boer victory over the British in the First Boer War, over nineteen years before. The British Army had, for all those years, carried in their mentality the slogan of 'wiping something off a slate', and that 'something' was their defeat on Majuba Hill in 1881. The Boers, on the other hand, were vehemently proud of the day. During the evening of the 27th, Buller signalled to Ladysmith by lamp: 'Doing well.' He also signalled: 'I think you will be able to help me, but I am not close enough to you yet. I shall communicate with you later on.'

The inhabitants of Ladysmith could in no way feel confident; they had observed Boer ladies in pretty dresses on Umbulwana Hill, and there, for their special benefit, the Boer gunners had fired shells at Caesar's Camp and Wagon Hill. But then in the evening came another signal: Lord Roberts had captured the famous old Boer General, Cronje, together with almost his entire force of some 4000 fighting burghers. This had been achieved over on the other side of South Africa, at a place called Paardeberg, close to the Cape–Orange Free State border. Around the British fighting perimeter at Ladysmith, the weak soldiers cheered and cheered. Colonel Gore wrote in his diary: 'In the name of the British Army, we all say, "Thank God!" ' For the Boers, the news was too terrible to contemplate, so at midnight they took unusual action; they simply aimed their massed mausers at Ladysmith and blazed away in defiance.

UNION POSTALE UNIVERSELLE
NATAL

POST CARD

SUBJECT TO LETTER RATES
STAMPS UNOBTAINABLE DURING THE SIEGE
ADDRESS ONLY TO BE WRITTEN ON THIS SIDE

Piet

LONG TOM

M'Bulwana

LADYSMITH
FE 27
1900
NATAL

Mr H Smith
Berea
Durban

growing louder, and intensified by glad and willing messengers, resound the delicious words 'a HELL of a licking!' The C.O's servant Harper bursts into his master's tent shouting out, 'Buller's given the Boers a – (pause) – *devil* of a licking!'

At noon Buller signalled to Ladysmith: 'Have thoroughly beaten enemy; believe them to be in full retreat. Have sent cavalry to ascertain which way they have gone.'

13

THE RELIEVING FORCE
February 1900

*The Boer grew up with the gun, and he had to
think for himself ... And we shoot birds and
wild buck. Each man thinks for himself; each
man is his own officer.*

MACHIEL BOTHMA

ALMOST a month earlier, on 4 February 1900, Buller had received a letter
from Lord Roberts, dated '27th January', in which he repeated his earlier
warning: '... You will now know from my telegram of today that if you are
not confident of forcing your way to Ladysmith, it would, in my opinion,
be better you should abandon the attempt until I am in the Orange Free
State.'

Buller immediately replied, and after underlining his transport difficulties,
went on with the brave statement:

Ladysmith is in a bad way; White keeps a stiff upper lip, but some of those
under him are despondent; he calculates that he has now 7000 effectives; his men
are dying about eight or ten per day, and when he last gave me a statement he had
2400 in hospital; they are eating their horses, and have very little else. He expects
to be attacked in force this week, and though he affects to be confident, I doubt if he
really is. He has begged me to keep the enemy off him as much as I can, and I can
only do this by pegging away. I am going to have a try and get through the mountains
here tomorrow. The men are keen, and most of the officers, when I was explaining
my plans last night, seemed to think that we ought to succeed. I hope we may. If
I get through I get on to the plain; it is about 4 miles broad and 10 miles long; the
enemy will be in possession of the hills on each side, and holding a strong position
at the end, and I shall have great difficulty about water. Such is the position. I do
not think a move into the Free State will much affect our position here. So far as I
can make out, the Transvaalers will not go into the Free State, and they are our

main opponents. You ask me how you can help me. The only help you could give me would be another Division, and that I know you cannot spare.

Two questions seem worth asking about this missive to Lord Roberts. How exactly did Buller plan to 'get through the mountains here tomorrow? And why was he disturbing Lord Roberts by mentioning that he could not fulfil Lord Roberts' only request for 'another Division' – particularly when Buller had about 30000 fighting soldiers as against Botha's 5000, at the most? Well, Buller's battle plans we shall come to; but already, now that he, Buller, was in command, his mind was beginning to multiply the number of Boers in front of him. Buller was a long painful series of excuses.

Buller selected a hill called Vaal Krantz for his next, personally conducted, effort to relieve Ladysmith. A vital part of his strategy was the assumption that the Vaal Krantz area was the left flank of General Botha's main force, and that Vaal Krantz was capable of receiving British artillery on its top, from where the British could enfilade the Boer trenches on the hills to the west – not least of them being the Boer-held Spion Kop. On the eastern side of Vaal Krantz was a road which crossed the Tugela river at Skiet Drift, and led northward through the Tugela Heights to the plain beyond, which then led east-north-east to Ladysmith. To the immediate east of this road, opposite Vaal Krantz, was Green Hill, and behind it, to the east, a greater mass of high land called Doorn Kop. The basic idea that Buller had conceived was, through military action, to make it possible to get his army through the Tugela Heights by this road. As regards the vital question of whether artillery could be got on to the top of Vaal Krantz once it was won by the infantry, the only information that Buller had was from an English farmer, who had been in the habit of passing below the hill every time he went to Ladysmith! And this factor was vital to Buller's hopes. The actual order of battle is detailed and complicated, but one vital order was strangely missing, and that was the obvious necessity to capture Green Hill, immediately to the east of the roadway, and, indeed, the necessity to capture and occupy Doorn Kop, to the east, behind it. This order, though a bit vague and half-hearted, was finally given after the order of battle was issued. Again it is impossible for me to fathom Buller's strange mentality; plentiful detail, but missing the life-or-death essentials. Here is the order of battle which General Buller issued to his commanding officers on 3 February 1900:

1. It is the intention of the General Commanding to attack the extreme left of the enemy's positions and to endeavour to take the hill Vaal Krantz.

2. The attempt will commence by a demonstration against the Brakfontein

position [to the west of Vaal Krantz]. This will be carried out by the two Brigade Divisions RFA and the 61st Battery, covered by the 11th Brigade 5th Division.

3. During this demonstration the 4th Brigade, supported by the 2nd Division, the whole under the command of General Clery, will be formed in a suitable position E. of No. 2 Pontoon Bridge, the general idea being to cause the enemy to think that these troops are about to move from east to west across the bridge. The four guns 64th Battery are placed under General Clery's orders.

4. After a certain bombardment sufficient to cause the enemy to enter their trenches the left Battery of the Field Artillery will limber up and retire by No. 2 Pontoon Bridge to its new position, covering the throwing of the Pontoon Bridge No. 3 at Munger's Drift.

Simultaneously with this movement the 4th Brigade will move out to cover the movement, and the battery of 14 guns on Swaartz Kop [immediately south of the Tugela river] and the two 5-inch guns under it will open on Vaal Krantz and bombard the few trenches there.

5. As soon as the Pontoon No. 3 is completed the rest of the six batteries will follow each other, passing from left to right at ten minutes interval, the whole taking up positions to support the attack at Vaal Krantz, under the orders of Colonel Parsons RA, who will report to General Clery.

6. After a sufficient bombardment the 4th Brigade, supported by the 2nd Division will, under General Clery's orders, attack Vaal Krantz.

7. As soon as the hill is occupied the artillery will ascend it and shell the trenches on Brakfontein, doing all they can to enfilade any that admit of it. Colonel Parsons will arrange that two batteries always watch the hills on the right.

8. The 1st Brigade Cavalry will, when feasible, pass Vaal Krantz, and getting into the plain bring the Battery RHA into action on any convenient target.

9. The 2nd Brigade Cavalry will watch the right and rear throughout the operations.

13. The G.O.C. 10th Brigade will be responsible for the camp at Spearman's Hill and the kopjes at Potgieter's.

[Other paragraphs give instructions for the gunners, signallers and observation balloonists.]

One other point must be underlined. If General Buller had assumed correctly that the Vaal Krantz area was the extreme left of the main Boer position, it was essential that his army should move swiftly and with total surprise. The Boers might be very thin on top of the Tugela Heights, but they would move like lightning once they got a hint of Buller's plans. Buller, of course, thought that he could deceive the Boers with his feint to the west, at the Brakfontein Hills, and the delayed construction of Pontoon Bridge Number 3. But the idea that the main attack at Vaal Krantz would not commence until that feint attack was finished, and until the visible removal of

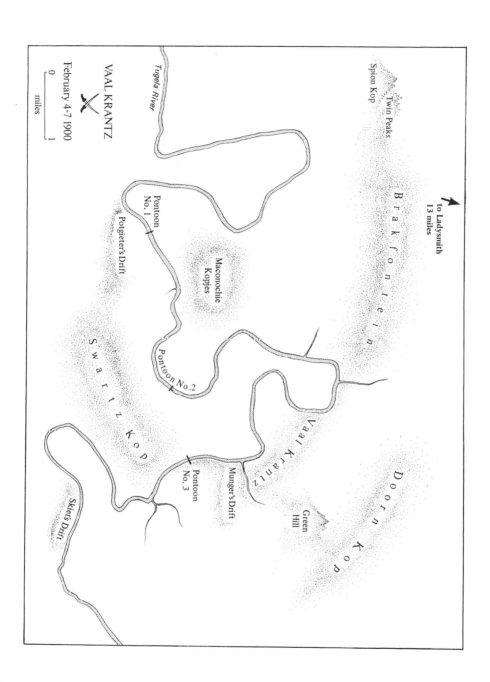

VAAL KRANTZ
February 4-7 1900

0 _____ 1
miles

to Ladysmith
13 miles

Spion Kop
Twin Peaks
Tugela River
Brakfontein
Pontoon No. 1
Potgieter's Drift
Maconochie Kopjes
Swartz Kop
Pontoon No.2
Vaal Krantz
Pontoon No. 3
Munger's Drift
Green Hill
Skiet's Drift
Doorn Kop

the Royal Field Artillery batteries to their new eastward positions south of the Tugela river and around Swaartz Kop, was completed – well, that was much too cumbersome an operation to deceive a man like General Botha. Anyway, that was Buller's very own plan, and he was leaving himself nakedly exposed; there was no one else, on this occasion, who could accept either praise or blame.

General Buller had decided on the Skiet's Drift road to Ladysmith very soon after his withdrawal from Spion Kop. As early as 27 January, he had commenced building a one-and-a-half-mile road in that direction, to move artillery. On 29 January, he spoke to his army at Spearman's Camp. He told the massed soldiers that though their efforts at Taba Nyama and Spion Kop had been unsuccessful, they had found for him the key of the road to Ladysmith. He said that he had also 'learned . . . the full value of the extraordinary tenacity of British infantry, and the manoeuvring power that tenacity gave him . . . ' Mr W. Dickson, still with his Biograph film-unit, was also present, and wrote in his diary that General Buller 'harangued the regiments on the subject of how to take advantage of the rocky, natural cover so as not to expose themselves unnecessarily to the fire of the enemy . . .' Fortunately for my friend Mr Packer of the 2nd Middlesex Regiment, he had already been warned, *before* the battle of Spion Kop, by a soldier of the Imperial Light Infantry. Lieutenant-Colonel Grant was also present, and has described the scene: ' . . . the brigades swung into hollow squares to hear Sir Redvers' speeches as smartly as ever they had done on Laffan's Plain before royalty.'

Colonel Grant was fascinated by the extreme mystery of General Buller's personality.

Laveter would have been puzzled by that square impassive face, as the General thanked his men for what they had done, and for having shown him what to do. Never a soul of the thousands there, nor, it appears, of the millions at home, understood his abrupt, cryptic sayings; but they, nevertheless, lifted a weight from hearts unconsciously heavy . . .

Sir Redvers Buller is fortunate in at least one of the attributes proper to a general, a good presence and appearance. Huge, heavy, solid and reliable to look upon, he conveys to the imagination something of that comfort derivable from the sight of a big gun or a strong intrenchment. Most difficult of men to describe: impassive as Helvellyn, yet notoriously tender, with heart bleeding for his falling soldiers; determined as fate, yet faltering before the blows of what seemed to be fate; bravest of the brave, yet a very woman in the face of certain losses . . . Such a man could do anything with soldiers, if he could but invent anything to do . . . it must be admitted that a man who could by a short unintelligible address send his defeated and diminished army merry and confident back to camp, as he did on that Monday afternoon, is an anomaly of no small military value. Such a man can always banish the despair his desperate ventures have earned, and the generals with like powers in history are to be counted upon the fingers on one hand.

It was, perhaps, imperative that Buller should hypnotically raise the spirits of his soldiers. On the day before, Sunday 28 January, a huge Christian service had been held for the military at Spearman's Camp, and Winston Churchill had reported on that:

> I attended a church parade this morning. What a chance this was for a man of great soul who feared God. On every side were drawn up deep masses of soldiery, rank behind rank – perhaps, in all, 5000. In the hollow square stood the general, the man on whom everything depended. All round were the men who within the week had been face to face with Death, and were going to face him again in a few hours. Life seemed very precarious, in spite of the sunlit landscape. What was it all for? What was the good of human effort? How should it befall a man who died in a quarrel he did not understand? All the anxious questionings of weak spirits. It was one of those occasions when a fine preacher might have given comfort and strength where both were sorely needed, and have printed on many minds a permanent impression. The bridegroom opportunity had come. But the Church had her lamp untrimmed. A chaplain with a raucous voice discoursed on the details of 'The siege and surrender of Jericho'. The soldiers froze into apathy, and after a while the formal perfunctory service reached its welcome conclusion.
>
> As I marched home an officer said to me: 'Why is it, when the Church spends so much on missionary work among heathens, she does not take the trouble to send good men to preach in time of war?'

Even an ardent fan of Buller's, Bennet Burleigh of the London *Daily Telegraph*, was not confident about his strategic arrangements. Bennet Burleigh was putting more faith in Tommy Atkins than in Buller when he reported an imaginary command he had heard: 'Fall out, today, lads, but be sure and fall in tomorrow afternoon at Ladysmith'; and this married with the theory that Tommy Atkins would be there, somehow, on time.

On 2 February 1900, the British could see that the Boers had already got wind of Buller's general intention. The Boers were busy digging trenches along the Tugela Heights, from Spion Kop in the west to Vaal Krantz in the east. Also they were digging up the road to Ladysmith, which meandered between Spion Kop and the Brakfontein Hills. Well, to that latter extent they were deceived. You will remember it was the road west of Vaal Krantz which Buller had in mind. At 5 a.m. on 3 February, General

Wynne's 11th Brigade, which had been commanded by Major-General Woodgate until his death, moved from its bivouac near Spearman's Camp and marched towards Potgieter's Drift. This brigade, comprising the South Lancashires, the York and Lancasters, the Royal Lancasters, with the Lancashire Fusiliers in support, began crossing the Tugela river once again at 9.30 a.m. They bivouacked on the northern side of the river that night. Lieutenant Colonel Grant, ever a watchful and philosophic man, glanced up at awful Spion Kop and saw Boers wandering about, 'and once or twice the figure of a woman appeared, gay in a white piqué frock and red parasol, seated complacently on the very spot at which the dead must have lain thickest'. The British soldiers could hear the gun fire around Ladysmith and some felt 'an intolerable incentive'.

4 February was a Sunday, but apart from the chaplains holding what church parades they could, the rest of General Wynne's brigade came north of the river and so relieved General Lyttelton's brigade, which had been holding those southern kopjes of the Brakfontein Height. General Botha was not present to assess this suspicious British action; after Spion Kop, he had hurried to visit his family in Pretoria. General Schalk Burger was in temporary command of all commandos from Acton Homes in the west to Munger's Drift south-east of Vaal Krantz. His combat generals were Tobias Smuts of Ermelo, Ben Viljoen and Andries Cronje (not to be confused with General Cronje over near the Cape–Free State border). Holding the Boer fort over to the far east at Colenso was General Lucas Meyer. An urgent telegram was sent to Louis Botha asking him to hurry back to Natal. W. Dickson, of Biograph fame, inscribed in his diary:

> February 4th. – The battle was to have been fought today, but the General has promised that it shall take place tomorrow instead. All are jubilant. It makes me proud to hear the plucky chaps swearing, with flashing eyes, to 'raise hell with the brutes', and to punish them for their lost comrades. Not a thought of self and the horrors with which they are about to deal. The only thing which seems to depress them is the invisibility of the enemy, while they are for ever in the open field getting murdered with shell and rifle from above.

Earl de la Warr gave himself over completely to his English aristocratic conditioning when he wrote on 4 February: 'For the sake of England and the future settlement of this country's affairs, it is most desirable that the Boers should place themselves in our hands as soon as possible.' This piece was duly printed in the *Globe*.

The Boer area upon which Buller's army focused was held by Combat-

General Tobias Smuts and his burghers. Smuts watched the British assembling in their thousands and sent urgent appeals for help to his comrades in other sectors of the long Boer line; but Botha was away and Schalk Burger seems to have been weak in authority. And, as always, the stubborn character of the Boer predominated; they would decide for themselves whether they would support Tobias Smuts' sector and they decided not to. Smuts sent a telegram to Louis Botha in Pretoria:

T.D. ZAR 4.2.1900 Secret. From General Smuts, Viljoens laager

To General Botha, Pretoria, begins:

Urgent. Situation unchanged. Attack expected early tomorrow. My position as you know precarious. Cannot get reinforcements. Commandant-General [Joubert] seems to think requests for help due to lack of faith or cowardice, shall not persist further. We shall do our duty and God help us. Glad you are coming. Enemy at Molensdrift continually drawing nearer – ends.

And then in the evening he sent a fatalistic telegram to General Lucas Meyer miles away to the east at Colenso; Lucas Meyer who was refusing to budge:

T.D. ZAR 4.2.1900 Confidential. From Combat-General Smuts, Viljoens laager

To General Meyer, Colenso, begins:

Enemy moving now in mass formation towards river. They are even coming over the Platrand behind the Boschrand and Commandant Hattingh has again evacuated a position, so that now I am bled of all help for Commandant Kelly. How we will guard our ground tonight, Heaven only knows – ends.

As day broke on 5 February 1900, the two British cavalry brigades left their bivouacs at Spearman's Farm and moved to their allotted places, which were initially to stand back in readiness to guard the flanks and rear of the army. The 1st Cavalry Brigade, under Colonel Burn-Murdoch, was also ordered to work behind the Brakfontein Heights, to the north-west of the operation, 'when able to do so'. The 2nd Cavalry Brigade's orders were 'to strongly protect the right by the ford called Skiet's Drift, also the left by Potgieter's Drift, also the rear of the force'. Which was just about the entire breadth of the attack. At 7 a.m. the first heavy gun fired; it was a naval 4·7-inch on Spearman's Hill, and it aimed at Brakfontein Height. Immediately seven batteries of the Royal Field Artillery followed suit, and the feint towards Brakfontein had begun. As the battle started, Commandant Ben Viljoen felt extremely lonely. Botha had still not returned from Pretoria, and Viljoen was at that time looking towards 30000 British soldiers, with about 400

Boers at his command, to defend about one and a half miles of the Tugela Heights. Viljoen wrote:

> Early in the morning of the 5th February, 1900, my position was heavily bombarded, and before the sun had risen four of my burghers had been put hors de combat. The enemy had placed their naval guns on the outskirts of the wood known as 'Zwartkop' [south of the Tugela river, and central to the whole operation] so as to be able to command our position from an elevation of about 400 feet. I happened to be on the right flank with ninety-five burghers and a pom-pom; my assistant, Commandant Jaapie du Preez, commanding the left flank.

At this time, General Wynne's 11th Brigade, his men of Lancashire and Yorkshire, went forward in skirmishing order towards Brakfontein. Before they reached the foothills of Brakfontein, they halted, and poured upwards a heavy fire, which remained unanswered by the few but shrewd Boers. British artillery was well in advance of Swaartz Kop; it had crossed the Tugela river at Number 1 Pontoon, and was firing north of Maconochie Kopjes. The bombardment of Brakfontein was extreme. Commandant Viljoen, a young newspaper editor during peacetime, wrote:

> The number of my fighting men was rapidly diminishing. I may say this was the heaviest bombardment I witnessed during the whole of the campaign. It seemed to me as if all the guns of the British army were being fired at us.
> Their big lyddite guns sent over huge shells, which mowed down all the trees on the kopje, while about fifty field pieces were incessantly barking away from a shorter range . . .
> On looking about me to see how my burghers were getting on I found that many around me had been killed and others were wounded. The clothes of the latter were burnt and they cried out for help in great agony.

At 9.30 a.m., the 63rd Battery Royal Field Artillery was the first to withdraw from this Brakfontein feint attack. The Battery crossed to the southern side of the Tugela river by Pontoon Number 2, and hastened to cover the construction of another pontoon, a mile south of Vaal Krantz itself. This was called Pontoon Number 3, and Royal Engineers were constructing it under a heavy fire from Boers, particularly on nearby Vaal Krantz. Meanwhile the Yorkshire men and the Lancashire men fired away at apparently nothing. Lieutenant E. Blake Knox, Royal Army Medical Corps, waiting with his stretcher-bearers, overheard the following conversation:

'Got a match, chum?'

'Where's the bloke?'

'Loose off a few rounds, chum, just to let 'im know we ain't dead!'

'Wot's we to fire at?'

'I dunno.'

'The bloke said the 'ill top; maybe Krooger's behind.'

Well, they don't sound like Northcountrymen to me; maybe they'd come under the influence of the 2nd Middlesex Regiment or some such. But this Boer silence was a dangerous trial for the British soldiers; already the 11th Brigade was further forward than Buller had planned. The silence was like a bait; the British advance line stood up, and it was feared, from Buller's distant vantage point, that they were about to move forward again. Lieutenant-Colonel Grant wrote graphically about this particular episode: 'One can imagine nothing more gloomy and terrible than this deathly silence of crowded trenches and frowning gun-pits. Even on the imperturbable British private it is not altogether without its effect, and one may notice a corresponding silence – a bad sign with our soldiers in action – and uneasy glances at the hill-tops and ridges . . .'

The worst danger was not, of course, psychological, but that the soldiers would advance too close to an impregnable position; they would not be strong enough in numbers to rush it, and too exposed to retreat. Fortunately, on this occasion, indeed exactly as it had happened at Colenso, while all was silent and tense, a single mauser was fired. There was a momentary silence and then every Boer who was there blazed away. The ordinary British soldier was not to know that there were pitifully few Boers in front of them. At the same time, the Boers fired what artillery they had; ironically, the most effective Boer fire came from Spion Kop. A question that was much debated by British soldiers at the time was who fired those single shots at Vaal Krantz and at the battle of Colenso. The Boers stated that they were signals from their generals for the burghers to attack, but the probability is that one tense nerve gave way. Considering the instinctive skill of men like Botha and Viljoen, it is unlikely that they would give a signal to fire which was premature, as it was, both at Colenso, and here at Brakfontein. But all the 11th Brigade was called upon to do on this occasion was to lie low – which they did.

Meanwhile, the Royal Engineers, who were constructing Pontoon Number 3, were having a hard time. Lieutenant-Colonel Grant wrote:

They were under a heavy rifle-fire, and suffered not a little, losing, I think, eleven men of the bridging party, and having every pontoon and plank struck by the Boer marksmen told off to harass them. If one were to sit down and think out an example of extreme discomfort and strain, requiring courage of the most real sort, I think that this job of carrying heavy weights slowly and carefully, tying elaborate knots, and adjusting unwilling timbers, all under a steady and well-aimed shower of bullets, would exceed anything that one could imagine unassisted by experience. No rush and cheering here, only the pain of battle without its antidote – excitement; only a slow, methodical and intensely responsible bit of skilled workmanship to get through, whilst the bullets whistle overhead, or thud dully into the wet planks, or more dully still into the bodies of comrades straining at the ropes and pontoon lashings.

Shortly after midday, General Wynne, having carried out his feint attack, ordered his 11th Brigade to retire. The Boers initially thought that they had beaten the British back, but the 'cunning' of Buller's plan was so laborious, and plain for all to see, that the Boers, after giving the 11th Brigade what hurried fire they could, hastened their attention to Vaal Krantz and the Doorn Kop area, where, painfully obviously, the British were moving. The feint attack was totally and inevitably useless to the British. Built into it, through Buller's stupidity, was its own defeat – and worse to come. Pontoon Bridge Number 3 was now constructed. Shortly before 1 p.m., the British artillery in front of Maconochie Kopjes were ordered to withdraw and take up their new positions, close to and south-west of Vaal Krantz. A child could have guessed what the British planned to do next – and, of course, there were children fighting with the Boers. The withdrawal of the British artillery was a hair-raising affair. Each battery had to get away at ten-minute intervals. The Boer artillery on Spion Kop and a Vickers-Maxim pom-pom, east of Brakfontein, concentrated on their withdrawal. Lieutenant Knox, Royal Army Medical Corps, could hear the calm orders given, while the shells exploded around: 'Stand to your horses! Prepare to mount! Mount! Walk! March! Trot!' As each battery left this field of action, the others kept up their fire, and had to wait patiently. John Atkins of the *Manchester Guardian*, observed an artillery officer waiting for his battery's turn. 'He sat stock-still on his horse. His hand went continually up to his mouth and dropped away again. He might have been taking snuff or pulling his moustache. Perhaps it was the action of nervousness; but nothing ever looked cooler.'

Soon all the batteries were moving. Lieutenant-Colonel Grant wrote:

For pure wild excitement the next quarter of an hour must have exceeded anything in the annals of warfare. It seemed impossible that those guns could get away: over them, between them, right upon them, burst a storm of projectiles, dashing up the earth in dun clouds, hiding guns, gunners and horses; the guns were surely lost, and something like a groan burst from all the waiting and watching thousands away on the right. But it was quickly changed to a roar of applause, as out from that tornado, quietly and in order, every man and officer in his place, trotted those incredible gunners . . .

The British artillery had a lucky escape; they suffered two officers and eight men wounded.

At 2 p.m., General Lyttelton led his brigade across Pontoon Bridge Number 3. His troops were the 1st Rifle Brigade, the 1st Durham Light Infantry, the 3rd King's Royal Rifles, the 2nd Scottish Rifles, and the 2nd Devons. As they crossed they were exposed to every scrap of fire the Boers could pour on them. Small wonder that the British soldiers were under the misapprehension that a large Boer force stood in front of them. As the British infantry raced over the river Tugela, it was noted that the Royal Engineers were still busy on the bridge that they had just constructed: '. . . the gallant sappers, methodical to the last, cleared up the debris, collected spare stores, and then retired up the bank . . .'

A Boer friend of mine, Mr Prinsloo, who now lives on a farm east of Pretoria, saw the Royal Engineers working. Mr Prinsloo was then seventeen years old. Seventy years later I asked the old gentleman to describe those hours to me, and he replied: 'Now then, I must go slowly, so that I don't cry. So that I don't cry. That was a very sad business: a cruel affair.'

The young Prinsloo looked down at the British beyond the Tugela:

They were like ants – where the soldiers came from you could not know – not us – but they came. My friends and I . . . climbed on our knees to look. You just couldn't talk above the sound of the bullets and bombs that were flying over the river. Have you ever had bullets pass you? Well, be thankful. We came to the highest point and looked. Oom van Jaarsveld, Oom Jochem, Koos Nel – we were all together. I saw how they were making the bridge; I saw two poles standing in the river and I saw them pushing planks over. The British soldiers were being shot at. Then I looked up towards Spion Kop and I saw the [Transvaal] flag waving. The British guns were directed at it . . . My friend said: 'Now the flag is gone' – but when the dust settled, the flag was waving there. The British soldiers ran two by two on to the bridge, and all the time they were being shot at by us. There wasn't a second without shells bursting. Then we heard the British bugle, and a group would spring up – some fifteen or twenty and they ran towards us. As they ran, our people said: 'Here they come!' And as they came we shot at them. We had a maxim gun. As they sprang up, we saw them fall. But when the British bugle sounded again, up they sprang, across the bridge. And there was a lot of them.

Commandant Ben Viljoen wrote: 'Our pom-pom had long since been silenced by the enemy, and thirty of my burghers had been put out of the fight. The enemy's infantry was advancing nearer and nearer and there was not much time left to think. I knelt down behind a kopje, along with some of the men, and we kept firing away at 400 paces . . .'

Another Boer friend of mine, Mr Machiel F. Bothma, now living in Pretoria, was at the battle of Vaal Krantz. He was also seventeen years old at the time, and was stationed in the vicinity of Spion Kop, under General Schalk Burger, when the order came to reinforce Commandant Ben Viljoen. When he arrived in the fighting area, he told me:

. . . a few of the burghers ran out to meet us, and others were dead. We naturally took up a position there. I am embarrassed to say how many of us there were – thirty-eight. We spread ourselves out; one here, and two there, and there one, and there two, there three, over a distance of at least a mile. And when we started shooting, the enemy thought there was a thousand people. Behind us was a stone ridge – and the British cannons thought we were there . . . and shot into that ridge. Yes, you see, it was a decoy. We said it was an Act of Providence. There were Scots there; they also didn't know where we were; they also shot over us . . . As for me, I was in a big fight for the first time, and I didn't think about anything; I only thought about shooting.

I asked Mr Bothma if he was close enough to the British soldiers to aim at individuals. He looked at me in astonishment, and then, I sensed, had to explain to me because I was a Rooinek: 'Yes. That time it was eight hundred yards. You can't miss.'

I looked at him in reciprocal astonishment. 'At what? Eight hundred yards?'

He repeated: 'You can't miss!'

Mr Bothma then stood up and said: 'Yes, yes! Even as old as I am today, with one eye blind, and the other one is not good, I would do something at eight hundred yards. Put up a piece of paper as big as a man, and I am sure I could shoot right through him, today! I will bet a pound a shot!'

I didn't take up the challenge. I was convinced that Oom Machiel could do it, and anyway, it was impractical; we were in the middle of Pretoria. I asked my old friend to explain to me the Boers' particular success with the rifle.

'The Boer,' he said, 'grew up with the gun, and he had to think always for himself. He didn't have an officer who said, "Shoot six hundred yards" and "Load! Fire!" He must do everything himself. And we shoot birds and wild buck. Each man learns for himself; each man is his own officer.'

I asked Mr Bothma if he remembered what he felt when he shot those British soldiers and he answered: 'How can I say it? You feel a little sorry for the man, for the soldier. You feel sorry for him. But the name "English";

you don't feel sorry for that. The name, the name "English", that you shoot – but not the man.'

General Lyttelton's brigade pushed forward about 600 yards north of the Tugela river, towards Vaal Krantz. The British artillery on Swaartz Kop, south of the Tugela, and the heavier guns back on Mount Alice, together with batteries of Royal Field Artillery, right up forward, all poured their concerted fire-power on to the summit of Yaal Krantz. There were sixty-six British heavy guns firing at this time – all at one small area. So far, the battle was going according to Buller's clumsy plan. The Boers had received plenty of warning, but there were too few of them to blast the British back across the Tugela river. This was General Hildyard's prearranged cue to send across No. 3 Pontoon Bridge the rest of the selected battalions. They were to branch off to the east and take Green Hill on the eastern side of the road, which pointed north and led on to the plain and Ladysmith beyond. Across went the Devons, on their way to rescue their brother regiment in Ladysmith; two companies of the East Surreys were across, and the cavalry under Colonel Burn-Murdoch were poised to charge and clear that life-line road, as soon as the right and left of it were cleared of Boers. This looked like potential success. And at that precise piece of timing, Buller announced that the attack was off. I find it difficult, indeed impossible, to describe his dreadful behaviour as other than a loss of nerve. Apparently he had been disconcerted by the strength of Boer fire from the east – though it should have been much stronger if there had been half the number of Boers that Buller imagined to be available. Buller's decision was disastrous to the whole operation. Without taking Green Hill, there was no road through to Ladysmith for the British. But it was too late now for Buller to halt the swing of Lyttelton's assault on Vaal Krantz itself. The Rifle Brigade battled their way up the eastern side of Vaal Krantz, and the Durhams fixed bayonets and charged the southern side. Commandant Ben Viljoen faced the overwhelming onslaught and my friend, Oom Machiel Bothma, was there with him. Ben Viljoen wrote:

A lyddite shell suddenly burst over our very heads. Four burghers with me were blown to pieces and my rifle was smashed. It seemed to me as if a huge cauldron of boiling fat had burst over us and for some minutes I must have lost consciousness. A mouthful of brandy and water (which I always carried with me) was given me and restored me somewhat, and when I opened my eyes I saw the enemy climbing the kopje on three sides of us, some of them only a hundred paces away from me.

I ordered my men to fall back and took charge of the pom-pom, and we then retired under a heavy rifle and gun fire. Some English writers have made much ado about the way in which our pom-pom was saved, but it was nothing out of the ordinary. Of the 95 burghers with me 20 had been killed, 24 wounded.

Oom Machiel Bothma said to me: 'Then the ridge was no longer green; the Scots with their dark dress made it black. We laid our officer out on the ground and we carried him, me and another man . . . to the ambulance . . . it was only a cart . . . and they took him away.'

At 4 p.m. precisely General Lyttelton saw one of his Durham officers, named Lascelles, waving his coat on the crest of Vaal Krantz. The Durhams were racing across the top, their bayonets glinting in the very hot sun. Not surprisingly, young Lascelles was soon mortally wounded. Winston Churchill made an unexpected claim, and I quote his journalism for whatever it is worth: 'Among those [the Boers] who remained to fight to the last were five or six armed Kaffirs, one of whom shot an officer of the Durhams. To these no quarter was given.'

It was customary for the Boers to take black Africans with them, even into the fighting line. The Boers often carried spare rifles and ammunition bandoliers. I suspect that the men Churchill mentions were carrying out this duty.

On the Boer side Combat-General Tobias Smuts was still sending desperate appeals for help:

T.D. ZAR 5.2.1900 Secret. From General Smuts, Viljoens laager

To General Meyer, Colenso, begins:

The round koppie in Standerton sector captured by enemy. Reinforcements arrived too late. Do not know if I can regain it. General Burger's cannon do nothing as far as I can discover. The entire might of the enemy is falling on me and I get no help. I shall do my duty brother but God help me. If I have losses it is not my fault. Think upon what I have said – ends.

With characteristic stubbornness, Lucas Meyer failed to take action:

T.D. ZAR 5.2.1900 Confidential. From General Meyer, Colenso

To Combat-General Smuts, Viljoens laager, begins:

Troops also advancing on Boschrand and upon Emmett's position, where Ermelo Commando formerly stood. I was all set to rush you help, but now it appears my presence is urgently required here – ends.

However the British on Vaal Krantz were getting a fair pounding from Boer guns over Spion Kop way, and also the Boers were holding the northern crest of Vaal Krantz, apart from a tenacious grip on Doorn Kop and

Green Hill. The situation was beginning to look uncomfortably like the Spion Kop disaster all over again. Then the Naval Brigade, way back on Mount Alice, did quite a bit to hush up the Boer artillery. But the whole situation was fast becoming a ghastly farce for the British. The purpose of the fighting operation, to relieve Ladysmith, was now totally ruined by the influence of Buller, and British soldiers found themselves stuck up on a hill called Vaal Krantz with nothing to do except die or, at some time, escape. About 6.30 p.m. the Boers reinforced their left flank, particularly with artillery and naturally directed their fire on to the pinned-down British; with that, night came. Lieutenant-Colonel Grant, peering closely around him for human information, recorded the following episode:

> . . . many fell; amongst whom a gallant officer of the Rifle Brigade has supplied the only gleam of fun recorded in connection with this joyless battle. Hit in the leg, the officer in question rolled over, and no doubt, as wounded men will, gave vent to the sort of sentiments which made Kipling's Highland sergeant so greatly dread a battle: 'It does make the men sweer awfu'!' Whereupon the colour-sergeant of his company rushed to his assistance, and commenced feeling for the wound in the neighbourhood of the stomach. On being somewhat sharply put right about this by the sufferer, the non-commissioned officer made the following deathless reply: 'Beg pardin, sir; from yer langwidge I concluded you was 'it in the habdomen!'

Before dawn on 6 February 1900, the British artillery, from all possible vantage points, banged away at the Boers, particularly on the northern rim of Vaal Krantz; there was a vague idea of somehow moving forward, but as far as I can fathom, this move forward would simply have been into deeper trouble. But it never came to that; the Boers could not be shifted in this crude way. Buller now didn't want to withdraw Lyttelton's brigade from their curious lodgement. Buller asked Lyttelton to hold on until the next sundown, when he, Buller, would 'watch developments'. What developments? Did he really hope that the Boers might make an actively stupid mistake? Stuck in the dust, as it were, Buller telegraphed his plight to Lord Roberts, over in the Cape, who was himself about to embark on a tricky, though highly professional, military venture.

> After fighting all day yesterday, though with but small loss, I have pierced the enemy's line and hold a hill which divides their position, and will, if I can advance, give me access to the Ladysmith plain, when I should be 10 miles from White, with but one place for an enemy to stand between us. But to get my artillery and supplies on to the plain I must drive back the enemy either on my right or on my left. It is an operation which will cost from 2000 to 3000 men, and I am not confident,

though hopeful, I can do it. The question is, how would such a loss affect your plans and do you think the chance of the relief of Ladysmith worth the risk? It is the only possible way to relieve White; if I give up this chance, I know no other.

A few points from the above document should be underlined. First, no one, least of all Buller, had 'pierced the enemy's line', thin as it was, and no Britisher held 'a hill which divides their position'. Dented, yes – but it was patently an unbroken line. Secondly, as far as driving 'back the enemy either on my right or on my left', he had the previous day created a disgraceful military joke when he had changed his own plan of taking the right (Green Hill) and had withdrawn from his left (the Brakfontein Hills) as part of his clumsy, death-inviting feint. Thirdly, what a wretched threat to throw at Lord Roberts; an estimated casualty list of between two and three thousand men. The onus of ultimate responsibility was once again pushed elsewhere, and on this occasion towards a man whose plate was more than full at that very time. Fourthly, 'not confident, though hopeful' is worthy of the Wurzel Gummidge Machiavelli that he was. Again, was such a risk worth the relief of Ladysmith? Had all of his self-respect sweated away? And lastly, there was the final Tower-of-London indictment, 'if I give up this chance, I know no other'. That was little less than a petulant lie. The Boers were a small nation, and along the Tugela Heights they were incredibly few in number. What about an intelligent military go at the far west flank, Taba Nyama, or the far east flank, beyond Colenso? Both had been tried, but both had been patently bungled by incompetent English generals. (The suggestion that some of them were Irish has always been, since the time of Wellington, a slander on the name of Ireland.) Lord Roberts replied, very properly, in his telegram, C 73, that Ladysmith must be relieved at any cost, and went on: 'Tell your troops that the honour of the Empire is in their hands and that I have no possible doubt of their being successful.'

Buller afterwards bumbled on about his surprise at getting this lead-in-your-pencil rejoinder. With a clumsy effort at irony he reminded interested parties about Lord Roberts' previous exhortation to stay on the defensive unless he, Buller, saw a reasonable prospect of success. Of course, Lord Roberts never meant any British soldier to stay on the defensive if Ladysmith was clearly going to capitulate.

On that morning of 6 February 1900, one of Buller's staff officers must have swallowed hard before asking the Blimp-personified: 'Now that you have got the left of the Boer position, why don't you roll them up, attacking with your whole force?' This was, of course, something of an exaggeration; the

British had not yet 'got the left of the Boer position', but they were at least halfway to it. Anyway, Buller didn't question the veracity of the words, but replied, 'Yes I might do that, but it is very doubtful if I could get through, for I could not support the infantry with artillery, and I would be certain to lose about three thousand men plus the chance of a defeat.'

Buller could have supported the infantry with artillery, if he had taken Green Hill and then pushed his men up on to Doorn Kop, immediately to the east of it. As it was, General Lyttelton's soldiers were pinned, and not only that, during the afternoon the Boers actually counter-attacked on Vaal Krantz. Immediately up came British reserves – as always there were plenty of reserves – and the Boers were driven back with a British bayonet charge by the King's Royal Rifles and the Durham Light Infantry. Lieutenant E. Blake Knox, Royal Army Medical Corps, was waiting for the next batch of casualties to come in, and looking around him, registered '... the dhoolie-bearers, their dark skins, lightly built frames, and many-coloured raiment, such as Indians love to wear, impressing the spectator with the thought that here again were representatives of the mighty British Empire. Let not the public forget what Great Britain owes to her colonies.'

Then the British discovered that they couldn't even get one artillery piece on to the top of Vaal Krantz, as Buller had rashly planned, because the sides were too steep, and in any case, the Boer rifle fire was too fierce for any gunners to survive, if they could have got there. Finally, to add to the humiliating out-smarting of Buller above all, the Boers had moved a Creusot 'Long Tom' gun from Ladysmith during the night and now it was platformed high towards the southern end of Doorn Kop, and it began firing its 94-pound shells, with a range of 12000 yards. The reason for so much Boer aggression at this time was that General Louis Botha had arrived on the scene at about noon, and was bustling Boer reinforcements into their battle places. As evening came, General Hildyard's 2nd Brigade relieved General Lyttelton's 11th Brigade on Vaal Krantz. Now the hill was held by the Queen's, the East Surreys and the West Yorks, with the Devons on the reverse slopes, acting as immediate reserves. As soon as General Lyttelton was released from Vaal Krantz, he hurried to General Buller; he was angry because his soldiers had not been supported and, therefore, their suffering had been worse than useless. Buller was sitting under a tree, where he had been 'throughout these two days', Churchill assures us, eating his dinner. Buller asked Lyttelton what sort of a time he had had. Lyttelton replied, 'Very bad; shot at day and night from nearly all sides!'

Buller said, 'Wait a bit!' and disappeared into his tent, reappearing with a 'large jorum' of good champagne. Whatever else General Lyttelton thought, he confessed that it was the most refreshing drink that he had ever tasted. Of course Buller was no democrat. Lieutenant E. B. Knox RAMC, noting every human nuance within range, saw that '. . . some energetic canteen-owner has erected a tent, and is doing a brisk trade, as for many it is a half-way house for a drink of temperance ale: no other beverage is allowed by General Buller to be sold to . . . the weary foot-sloggers . . .'

But Buller briefly got his come-uppance over his preoccupation with champagne. The stock of his favourite brand began to get low, so he telegraphed to his wine-merchant in England to hurry out a supply to South Africa. He ordered fifty cases and gave the strictest instructions that they were to be clearly labelled 'Castor Oil'. The time passed when the champagne should have arrived and Buller anxiously signalled his military base office for the fifty cases of expected castor oil. The officer-in-charge replied, 'Regret exceedingly no cases as described have yet reached us, but this day we have procured all the castor oil possible (twenty cases), and have despatched it without delay, as you desired. We trust this unavoidable delay has caused no serious inconvenience.'

About this time soldiers of the 10th Brigade were doing their best to bury the dead. One of these soldiers described what happened:

Some of 'Ours' 'ad been killed, and we went for to bury them, and pretty big funeral party too, and all the time the big guns were a-firing over our 'eads. Well, whether the Boers knew wot we was up to or not I dunno. Like as not they didn't; for the chaplain 'e 'adn't got on no surplice, so looked just like a commanding officer addressing of 'is men. Any'ow we 'ad 'ardly got well started when – phew-u-u-u, wang! fut! bust! – they were firing shell at us. So the parson, 'e just says quiet like, 'Lie down, men,' and went on reading out of 'is book just as if nothing wos a-'appening. It were a rum go, to be sure! There were we all a-lying flat out on the ground, shells a-plunking all around, and the parson not 'urrying of 'isself one little bit. That knocked the bottom out of any kind of service I 'ad ever been to before, and I dunno as I'm particular anxious to go to another like it either.

For Hildyard's 2nd Brigade, that night of the 6th passed with little more activity than digging-in even deeper into Vaal Krantz. Then, with 7 February, several Generals began to look closely at the terrain ahead of the British positions, and I cannot help wondering why this was such a late curiosity. General Hildyard went forward personally and felt that some progress could be made forward, under cover of dusk, but come the dawn, what would be the use? Then General Warren's two brigades were ordered round to Swaartz Kop to prepare for some vague possible piece of aggression, and

General Warren volunteered to have a look; it was his sixtieth birthday. Buller agreed to this and bade him goodbye, adding, 'Be sure you don't get killed.' Warren wriggled to the British advanced position on Vaal Krantz. 'I pulled a sleeping man out of the schanze by his heels, and crawled into his place. Then by lifting up my head fitfully, as the least movement caused a patter of bullets, I looked out and reconnoitred the country, and made little sketches and notes.'

Warren got back safely, and then he and Buller 'inspected the position'. And finally 'Captain Phillips RE, the daring aeronaut,' went up in his balloon very high, and 'reported that ridge after ridge commanded Vaal Krantz'. That put the pith-helmet on it! Buller held a council of war at 4 p.m. on 7 February, and proposed breaking off the attempt to relieve Ladysmith, and falling right back on Chieveley, where they had all started from, so many murderous days before; the army would then make the next attempt to relieve Ladysmith by taking Hlangwane, and outflanking the Boers well east of that hill and Colenso. Buller had rejected this idea back in December, but now, at painful last, perhaps he was stumbling on to a good thing. The decision to give up or not to give up Vaal Krantz was put to a vote, and Lyttelton, Wynne and Clery and, of course, Buller, were for a withdrawal; and Hart and Warren were for staying. During the early night, the 2nd Brigade withdrew from Vaal Krantz, and before midnight, the entire British force was once again south of the Tugela river, having crossed at the newly constructed Pontoon Bridge Number 4. And what did the British people think of Buller now? Lord Dundonald expressed a curious attitude: 'Both officers and men were rather annoyed at this third failure to relieve Ladysmith, but still there was no depression of spirits, in fact some looked upon our third repulse as a joke.'

Earl de la Warr was now mystified. He wrote: '. . . it is difficult to understand the use of an immense force here if only two brigades are to be used in each battle.' And Lieutenant George Salt, Royal Welch Fusiliers, wrote in a letter dated 11 February: 'I am afraid that many will have lost their confidence in Buller. I think his tactics so far have been too simple and evident for the wily Boer, and also too slow . . . I passed General Buller on the way. He does not look very cheerful.'

Buller's brighter generals were calling him 'Sir Reverse' – behind his back; and the commander-in-chief of the British Army, sharp-tongued Lord Wolseley, raised a few bitter laughs when he referred to him as the 'Ferryman'. Bennet Burleigh of the London *Daily Telegraph*, overheard 'General Debility' and 'General Paralysis'. But Winston Churchill, the loyal fan, spoke for most of the ordinary soldiers, and people back home: 'A great deal is incomprehensible, but it may be safely said that if Sir Redvers Buller cannot relieve Ladysmith with his present force we do not know of any other officer in the British Service who would be likely to succeed.'

Through Buller's timidity the British casualties at the battle of Vaal Krantz were relatively light: twenty killed and 333 wounded. Unfortunately, they all suffered in vain. General Botha wrote to his wife: 'Our loss up to last night was 30 killed and 15 wounded. Again we must thank God that the powerful British enemy has had to retreat in front of our small number.'

On 7 February 1900, Buller telegraphed the Secretary of State in London and Lord Roberts in the Cape:

No. 189: I found the Boer positions on my right and left so superior to mine, and I was so outclassed by their big guns, which I could not silence, that I have decided that it would be useless waste of life to try and force a passage which, when forced, would not leave me a free road to Ladysmith. I propose to try by a forced march to get back east of Colenso and to seize the Boer position south of the Tugela river, whence I mean to make a desperate effort to take Bulwana Hill, the garrison of which has been much weakened, at least so my information says. My view is that I have a forlorn-hope chance at both places, but if I get through here I am not at Ladysmith by a long way: while if I get through there I relieve the place.

Well, that message was depressing enough – but the manic bit was not clear until Sir Redvers arrived at Chieveley on 9 February, when he sent poor Lord Roberts a second dose of neurotic reaction:

No. 193: The operations of the past three weeks have borne in upon me the fact that I had seriously miscalculated the retentive power of the Ladysmith garrison. I now find the enemy practically neglect that, and turn their whole force upon me; I am not, consequently, strong enough to relieve Ladysmith. If you can send me reinforcements, and if White can hold out till they arrive, I think it might be done; but with a single column I believe it to be almost an impossibility. I shall continue attacking, as it keeps the enemy off Ladysmith, but I think the prospects of success are very small.

Later in the day, Buller sent another telegram to Roberts; they follow the graph of his sickness, ever blacker and again passing the responsibility and blame to someone else.

No. 195: It is right that you should know that in my opinion the fate of Lady-smith is only a question of days, unless I am very considerably reinforced. Wherever I go the enemy can anticipate me in superior force. I turned yesterday from Vaal Krantz and am moving towards Colenso. The enemy have left Vaal Krantz, and are now at Colenso; they do in six hours and 7 miles what takes me three days and 26 miles. When I said I would try and save Ladysmith, the 5th Division had arrived at the Cape, and the 6th and 7th were likely shortly to be at my disposal; but two days after you were appointed, and directed that all troops arriving after that date were to be kept at the Cape.

I understand from you that you expect to occupy Bloemfontein by the end of February, and so relieve the pressure on Ladysmith. I hope the forecast will prove correct, but I cannot help feeling that to leave Ladysmith as it is for such a chance is a great risk, and it is right I should say so.

As for myself, I am doing all I can, and certainly have reason to think that I retain the confidence of this force, who knows my difficulties, but if it is thought anyone else can do better I would far rather be sacrificed than run the risk of losing Ladysmith.

Why wasn't Buller quietly taken away? His words vary from pathological lies ('in superior force'), to the blabberings of an immature schoolboy – which would be funny, if there weren't so many mangled men in the vicinity – ('Wherever I go the enemy can anticipate me . . . they do in six hours and 7 miles what takes me three days and 26 miles').

Lord Roberts kept a grip on himself, and replied to telegrams 193 and 195, on 10 February. After summarizing their contents, he stated:

It will be seen that from date of my assuming chief command until yesterday I have had no reason to suppose that you considered reinforcements necessary for the relief of Ladysmith. To send you large reinforcements now would entail abandonment of plan of operations. . . . I must therefore request that, while maintaining bold front, you will act strictly on the defensive until I have time to see whether operations I am undertaking will produce effect I hope for. The repeated loss of men on Tugela river without satisfactory results is that which our small army cannot afford.

Sir Redvers replied on 12 February:

No. 198: . . . Pray do not think I wish to lay my troubles on you. I quite admit that I miscalculated the retentive power of Sir George White's force. I thought he would hold at least 10 000 off me. I doubt if he keeps 2000, and I underrated the difficulties of the country. I don't know our plan or where your troops are, and the last thing I wish to do is to involve your plans in confusion. I merely state the fact that I think Ladysmith is in danger, and that I find myself too weak to relieve it. But as you value the safety of Ladysmith do not tell me to remain on the defensive. To do that means to leave the whole Boer force free to attack Ladysmith. Sir George White has repeatedly telegraphed: 'I trust to you preventing them throwing their strength on me.' And again: 'The closer to Ladysmith you can establish yourself, the better chance we shall have.' I feel sure this is the right policy, and I hope you will not say I am to rest supine and leave Ladysmith alone. During the late operations I am confident the Boer force has been reduced by two men to every one I have lost, and for three weeks our operations have practically caused the cessation of the bombardment of Ladysmith. As I have said, I will do all I can, and you may rely that I will not compromise my force.

Of course, Lord Roberts in his telegram had requested a 'bold front', which did imply holding General Botha's close attention. And Lord Roberts would not have suggested that Buller should act 'strictly on the defensive', if he had thought that Ladysmith was going to fall before his planned victory over in the Cape by the end of February. Sir George White didn't expect Ladysmith to fall during that period. And since Buller had moaned 'that I find myself too weak to relieve it' – well, Lord Roberts was giving firm advice to a man who was cracking up. But Buller's arrogance couldn't accept that rationally – and he twisted it clumsily. Buller's last telegram, No. 198, crossed another one from Lord Roberts, sent on 11 February, and this betrays a rare quality of exasperation in Lord Roberts:

No. 93: I should like to have the view of your second in command on this question, which is one of such urgent importance to our position in South Africa that it is very necessary I should know whether Sir Charles Warren shares your views. Show him all your and my telegrams on this subject, also White's telegram of 28th January to me, in which he stated he could hold out until the middle of March. I wish, also, to know why, as stated in your telegram, No. 169, of 25th January, you considered it necessary to take command of operations which resulted in withdrawal from Spion Kop.

This looked optimistically like the overture of an investigation of Buller. But, unfortunately, General Warren was also going round the bend, and Lord Roberts was going to have no joy in that direction. However, Warren wasn't at Chieveley that day, so Buller replied:

No. 199: Warren comes in tomorrow, and shall send you his opinion after having read all the telegrams. My report of operations west of Spion Kop was posted to you 30th January, and should reach you before this, so I will only say that I was not in command of the operations which resulted in withdrawal from Spion Kop. During these operations I had gradually, at Warren's request, reinforced him until he practically had with him my entire force, except the, as I thought, too weak garrison of Spearman's. After he reported the abandonment of Spion Kop I decided that we had lost our chance, and took command. His whole division was there; one of his brigades had no commander, and I thought, in the circumstances, his presence with his division was essential.

I feel forced to remind the reader of at least one vital point about the above (No. 199): Buller makes no reference to his earlier act of 'calling rank', when he, personally, ordered the retirement of General Lyttelton's 3rd King's Royal Rifles from the Twin Peaks; the one positive military move during the battle of Spion Kop that would probably have destroyed Botha's desperate defence.

General Warren arrived back in Chieveley during the evening of 12 February, and Buller duly gave him all the telegrams. Of course it must have been tricky for Warren to express his honest thoughts about what Buller had been responsible for, with Buller, as it were, watching over his shoulder. The best he could manage, at the same time keeping all his options open, was in his reply which Buller forwarded for him. 'The matter involves an immense number of considerations and innumerable details, on which I may or may not share your views; but on the main and important subjects I think that my views closely coincide with yours.' That statement is worth printing and selling to unhappy Public Relations Officers, to hang above their uneasy desks.

Lord Lansdowne, the Secretary of State for War, and Lord Wolseley, both in England, received copies of those telegrams, and both, understandably, became very jumpy. Lord Wolseley confided most of his often spiteful feelings in letters to his wife: 'I have been thoroughly disappointed in him [Buller] for he has not shown any one of the characteristics I had attributed to him; no military genius, no firmness, and not even the obstinacy which I thought he possessed when I discovered he had no firmness. He seems dazed and dumbfounded when he loses men.'

Now on 7 February, Buller had informed Sir George White in Ladysmith that he was going to 'slip back' to Chieveley, drive the Boers off Hlangwane on the 10th, and the next night would attempt to take Umbulwana from the south. It seemed that Buller had at last learnt one lesson, and that on this occasion the Boers would not have time to 'anticipate' his strategy. But Buller's own brand of rot set in on the following day, when he signalled to Sir George White that he would be taking two days longer to do it.

Since the battle of Colenso, the Boers had improved their military commitment south of the Tugela river (see map, page 345). During that famous battle they only held Hlangwane Hill, a mile and three-quarters north-east of Colenso village; now their forward positions extended several miles eastward, through Green Hill (not to be confused with the Green Hill of the Vaal Krantz area), to Cingolo Mountain, and then back north-north-west along the hog's back of Monte Cristo Mountain, to the Tugela river. And east of Colenso was Buller's new choice for assault. Where exactly? That was the ever-terrible question. General Barton, perhaps bearing in mind Buller's promise to Sir George White, suggested that the British Army should strike directly at the Boers' left flank on Monte Cristo. But already Buller was sinking back into a military torpor. By 12 February his entire force, with the exception of Burn-Murdoch's cavalry brigade, and two battalions of rearguard infantry and artillery, were concentrated at Chieveley. As the British lumbered back eastward, on the night of 11 February, a Boer searchlight played on them. Whatever Buller's words had been to White in Ladysmith, implying speed and secrecy of movement, the Boers were in no way being deceived. Botha moved what burghers he could back to Colenso and east of that place. He mustered between 5000 and 6000 fighting men, and placed between 2000 and 2500 of them on his new positions south of the Tugela river. On 11 February Buller decided on his first, very timid, move. He wanted to look at Hlangwane Hill, personally, through a telescope. He therefore ordered Lord Dundonald to clear Hussar Hill, which lies south of and midway between Hlangwane Hill and Green Hill to the east. And early on the morning of 12 February, Lord Dundonald drove a few Boers away with this 2nd Cavalry Brigade, the Royal Welch Fusiliers and a battery of Field Artillery. Then Sir Redvers presented himself and peered through his telescope and decided that before he could take Hlangwane, he must take Hussar Hill – which he was standing on – and withdrew Dundonald's force, issuing orders on the following day: 'It is intended to seize Hussar Hill tomorrow, and the spurs to the east of it north of Moord Kraal and to occupy this position with artillery.'

As Dundonald withdrew from his occupation of Hussar Hill on 12 February, the Boers crept back and fired at his retreating soldiers. Ladysmith already knew that Buller was not capable of hurrying, even if he had promised. Winston Churchill was present and suffered a strange experience while retreating:

I happened to pass along the line on some duty or other when I noticed my younger brother, whose keen desire to take some part in the public quarrel had led me, in spite of misgivings, to procure him a lieutenancy, lying on the ground, with his troop. As I approached I saw him start in the quick peculiar manner of a stricken man. I asked him at once whether he was hurt, and he said something – he thought it must be a bullet – had hit him on the gaiter and numbed his leg. He was quite sure it had not gone in, but when we had carried him away we found – as I expected – that he was shot through the leg . . . It was his baptism of fire, and I have since wondered at the strange caprice which strikes down one man in his first skirmish and protects another time after time. But I suppose all pitchers will get broken in the end.

13 February began a very hot spell of weather and for that African reason, no forward movement was made. At dawn next day, Buller's entire force, with the exception of General Hart's brigade, which was ordered to hold old Gun Hill facing Colenso, silently stood to arms, and then marched out from Chieveley Camp. Their objective was Hussar Hill, five miles to the north; the hill that had been taken by Dundonald forty hours before. By 8.30 a.m. Dundonald's brigade had taken Hussar Hill a second time – though its capture this time was an unusual affair, here described by Mr John Atkins of the *Manchester Guardian*: 'The Boers raced him [Dundonald] for the hill. He won by about five minutes. The Boers were three-quarters of the way through the donga which runs from Hussar Hill to Hlangwane . . . From this they fired on the hill, and we ground back our answer from the Colt machines and tossed shrapnel down on the places where the gunners thought the Boers were likely to be.'

Meanwhile, General Lyttelton's 2nd Division had moved round to the east of the hill and General Warren's 5th Division moved to left of it, and advanced in front. The British force then halted 'in close proximity to the Boer position', and set about entrenching itself. Lieutenant E. Blake Knox, Royal Army Medical Corps, noticed 'General Buller a few hundred yards away on the top of a kopje; he was resting against a withered tree, and scanning the Boer position through his telescope'.

About midday the British opened fire with their formidable artillery and the Boers replied 'with several guns'. From Ladysmith came a signal: 'The Boer camp at Taba Nyama has broken up.' Obviously the Boers had already received all the warning that they could ever require as to where Buller would next have a go; they were leaving the Taba Nyama–Spion Kop area. Lyttelton was one general who had a feeling of urgency towards Ladysmith, and he moved his formidable 2nd Division two miles east of Dundonald, which disconcerted the Boers, Cingolo way. However, the Boers need not have worried, because Buller commanded Lyttelton to return without more ado. General Warren, on the other hand, was bent on supplying a good laugh to anyone who shared his sense of humour. He discovered that a commander on Hussar Hill had allowed his soldiers to shelter from the African sun, while leaving their arms exposed on the open hill. General Warren was close by with his staff and, approaching the poor officer, told him that he, Warren, would enact the role of sentinel over the guns, and would not release them until the unhappy officer spoke the password: 'Allow no Boer to touch any of the arms.' Warren was disappointed when he found that the soldier was too embarrassed to play the charade. But Warren was never put down and he then ordered that his mackintosh bath should be filled with hot water, and there, in front of his sweltering men, he stripped off and stepped in for a quick rub down. At that moment up rode Sir Redvers Buller and his distinguished staff. Warren was delighted, but did put a towel over his private parts while he discussed military problems with the commander-in-chief. Warren remarked cheerfully: 'I felt that I had done what I could for the day to amuse the men.' And I am not going to gainsay him – at least on that matter.

Lyttelton was still probing around to the east on 15 February, but individual initiative was not the best way; what was required was agile general strategy. Lyttelton received a message from Buller: 'If you consider enterprise too difficult do not attempt it. We are holding a large number of Boers off Ladysmith, which is, after all, all we can expect to do.'

Isn't that what he rather highmindedly rebuked Lord Roberts for suggesting? But young Major Hubert Gough – later to be known in the 1914–18 War as 'Bloody Gough' – agreed with neither. He asked himself: 'Is it really all we can expect to do?' His brother, John Gough of the Rifle Brigade, was amongst those who were starving in Ladysmith. On 15 and 16 February, the sun blazed down, and that was sufficient reason for Buller to keep his infantry stationary. British soldiers could move in the hot sun; they had been learning to do it in India for a long while. Artillery exchanges continued, and significantly, the Boers intensified theirs as they gained more and more time to reinforce. And then on the afternoon of 16 February, Buller made up his mind to lunge eastward; orders for a general advance were issued at dawn on the 17th. The objective was Cingolo Mountain, and Lyttelton's 2nd Division and Dundonald's 2nd Cavalry Brigade were to make the attempt. Dundonald's orders were to hang in the rear of the infantry and guard the flanks against a rush attack. Dundonald, as usual, exercised his commonsense, and took the Composite Regiment and the South African Light Horse round towards the rear of Cingolo, that is, the southeast corner. His soldiers dismounted and quietly made their way up the difficult terrain. It is assumed that the Boers in their trenches, facing westward, were so preoccupied by the approach of Lyttelton's thousands, that they were unaware of Dundonald's men until it was too late, and as Winston Churchill put it – he was with Dundonald – 'The Boers doubtless reflected, "No one will ever try to get through such ground as that." ' The attack came from the rear and flank of the Boer trenches, and the short of it is, the Boers were rolled north-westward along and off the top of Cingolo. Of Lyttelton's division, only the Queen's Regiment had to tackle the south-western corner of Cingolo before the Boers had fled. The Boers had been waiting in well-constructed trenches, facing the oncoming infantry; what would have happened to those British soldiers if Dundonald had not acted as he did, is unpleasant to surmise. That western side is rough with under-growth, and steep; the Queen's panted and sweated their way upwards into virtually no opposition – just as the BBC director, Lawrence Gordon Clark, and I once clambered up Cingolo, Mr Clark as far as I remember, wearing an elegant suit.

All was over by 4 p.m., with the incredibly small British loss of one officer wounded, four men killed, and thirty-one wounded. General Lyttel-ton made his report at about 5 p.m.: 'Queen's have now reached north-west corner of Cingolo and Devons are about to advance on Nek and Monte Cristo; it will take the whole Division for this. I think C-in-C should come here to see the position so that he may direct General Warren to attack Green Hill simultaneously if he thinks of it.'

Sir Redvers decided to stop further operations for the day; Monte Cristo and Cingolo Nek would be attacked on the morrow. Dundonald and his victorious soldiers bivouacked that night on the north-eastern side of Cingolo, as near to the Boers as possible. Dundonald made his report to Buller, suggesting guns should be brought on top of the mountain; he also sent Buller sketches of what he could see ahead. Buller replied: 'Thanks for sketch and information. Glad to hear you have found water. I propose trying to establish a force on the top of Monte Cristo, and to get guns up there, but it will take a bit of road-making on this side.'

The Boer General Lucas Meyer had wired to Pretoria: '... heavy fighting is proceeding ... the British being in overwhelming numbers ...'

Lieutenant-Colonel Grant wrote: 'It may be that our previous stupidity was here our salvation. Botha could not believe that so astute a movement could be our real attack, and looked for it as before from some obvious and foolish direction.'

18 February was a Sunday, and the fighting began at dawn when the Boers shelled the British on Cingolo Mountain. At 8 a.m., General Hild-yard's 2nd Brigade crossed Cingolo Nek and fought their way to the southern end of Monte Cristo; the West Yorkshire Regiment led the way, with the Queen's and East Surreys supporting. The first British soldier to get on top of Monte Cristo was Captain T. H. Berney of the West Yorks – but he was

promptly shot through the head. However, the Boers had seen the glint of Yorkshire bayonets, and they were off northward along the top of Monte Cristo, and towards the Tugela river. The British gained the craggy summit of Monte Cristo, and then the Boers fired shrapnel at them from far-off Hlangwane Hill, now on the British left flank as they advanced northward. British artillery replied and while the long-distance duel was going on, Mr John Atkins of the *Manchester Guardian* visited the British guns and noted that the Royal Artillery gunners, unlike the Royal Navy gunners, were unprotected by sandbag works. He also noted that the Royal Artillery officer, Major Caldwell, was seated in a deck-chair, as the shells fell around him, and from this comfort, he gave his orders. Mr Atkins did not ask about the deck-chair, but did ask why there was no protection.

'It's not our way!' And then, from his deck chair, 'Number one gun, fire! Number two gun, fire!'

Anyway, in a short while the Boer guns were silenced, and General Lyttelton ordered General Norcott's 4th Brigade to attack Monte Cristo. The Rifle Brigade worked northward along the western slopes, and the Royal Welsh Fusiliers, supported by General Barton's brigade, assailed the Boers' eastern flank. They were fighting to get round the Boers' rear, to the north. Dundonald's brigade watched for Boers who failed to retreat in a northern direction. The operation was very like a shepherd with his sheepdog and a difficult flock of sheep. Before midday, the Royal Scots Fusiliers of Barton's brigade charged the northern end of Monte Cristo, and those Boers who could fled. Amongst the prisoners taken was a Colonel Constantine von Braun of the Prussian Army. Everyone was fascinated by the fact that he wore 'an oilskin coat with steel netting'.

Buller recognized that Monte Cristo enfiladed and commanded Green Hill, to the south-west, and he ordered a frontal advance on it. Irish Fusiliers went first, tightly followed by the Scots Fusiliers; the pipes were playing, and an officer led on his horse. The Boers decided to beat a hasty retreat, and there was no action to write of. Could it have been the fearsome bagpipes? No, not primarily, anyway: the Boers liked to have ready horses in their rear, and not a fast-flowing Tugela river. This, to a great extent, is the reason for their weak resistance south of the Tugela. Almost every Boer seems to have carried a mental picture of how he could get away, if the going got impossible. Now, south of the Tugela river, there only remained Hlangwane in Boer hands. The British had done well, and Buller called it a day.

The Ladysmith garrison had watched the distant operations on Cingolo

Mountain and Monte Cristo and were guessing the outcome. On Monte Cristo, young Winston Churchill stood. 'From the captured ridge we could look right down into Ladysmith, and at the first opportunity I climbed up to see it for myself. Only eight miles away stood the poor little persecuted town, with whose fate there is wrapt up the honour of the Empire, and for whose sake so many hundred good soldiers have given life or limb – a twenty acre patch of tin houses and blue gum trees but famous to the uttermost ends of the earth.'

General Buller reported the following casualties between 15 and 18 February: one officer killed and eight wounded; thirteen men killed and 155 wounded – also two men missing. On 19 February, the 2nd and 5th Divisions moved westward along the southern bank of the Tugela; their objective was, of course, Hlangwane Hill. The movement of this vast array of British soldiers was really sufficient – the Boers were not going to have that lot between them and the river, and they hastened to the northern bank, and at the same time the Boers evacuated Colenso. There was now not one single fighting Boer south of the Tugela river. The British saw a great cloud of dust, rising from the direction of the Colenso–Ladysmith road. Certainly there was formidable movement on it. The question everyone was asking was whether the dust represented a general Boer retreat, or the arrival of substantial reinforcements. Buller was a man who was either up or down – though his stolid appearance suggested that he was ever-level and well-balanced. This was his disturbing delusion. At this moment in his attempt to relieve Ladysmith, he soared upwards in spirit. It must have been these relatively easy victories. Suddenly all was optimism for him. He began to believe strongly that the Boers were finished, and that belief was to suck him into yet another fatal error. The truth is that the Boers, with Louis Botha's highly intelligent assessment of the situation, were deeply disturbed by the British occupation of Cingolo and particularly Monte Cristo. Once the British had Monte Cristo, both Green Hill and Hlangwane were untenable for Boer occupation. Once the British commanded Hlangwane, both Colenso and the hills above it could not be held by the Boers. But much, much more important than those important strategical points was the fact that from Monte Cristo the British were poised to outflank the Boer left wing. Botha knew that if the British pressed across the river in that easterly direction, all, for the Boers, was probably lost. Old President Kruger, back in Pretoria, sensed even Botha's gloom, and despatched to him the stiffening prophecy for all of his burghers: 'Even if they have no earthly rock behind which to seek cover, they shall win on the open plain!'

As has been said, the Boers found for themselves some great leaders; but those great leaders were tremendously assisted by some British generals – and none would ever come second to Sir Redvers Buller in this direction. But Buller was not alone in the new, fatal, error that was on the tip of his commanding tongue. British Intelligence was suavely telling him that the Boers were on the run – which of course was true, until they realized that Buller had not finished blundering. And again, his Chief Lieutenant, his Ancient, General Warren, was busy giving him the appalling advice to cross the Tugela river just north-east of Colenso, and 'advance along the railroad'. The fact that no rolling stock at all was available, and that every inch of that way was overlooked by Boer-held hill after Boer-held hill, was somehow not understood. The overriding euphoric factor was that the Boers were busy running away from those hills. Of course, the moment the Boers sensed what Buller was going to do, they rushed back to those hills, with even more speed.

On the afternoon of 20 February, Buller went to the northern end of Monte Cristo, and through his telescope studied the northern banks of the Tugela river, from faraway Colenso to the bank due north of his telescope and very close to him. He wrote, in the evidence he later had to present to a Royal Commission:

It was clear that I must occupy Colenso, and, attacking from there, take a hill between Onderbrook and Langewacht Spruits [both pretty well north of Colenso] before any farther advance in the direction of Bulwana Hill would be possible. It also appeared to me that certainly one-half, if not the whole, of the enemy's main fortified position on the north side of the Tugela was vulnerable only to attack from the south-west, or, in other words, from Colenso; for the nature of the ground about the bank of the river forbade any attempt to force its passage from the south.

Therefore, on 21 February, the Rifle Reserve Battalion, with the Royal Lancaster Regiment in support, marched from their bivouac to occupy Colenso; this they succeeded in doing by daybreak. While they were taking their breakfast they saw the famous but decimated Irish Brigade marching towards them. At their head rode an officer 'with polished straps and sword glittering in the morning sun'; this was their very own general, Fitzroy Hart – now known to all on the British side as No-Bobs Hart because he refused point-blank to duck or bob while under fire. An order came, carried by the Irishmen, that they were to take over the occupation of Colenso, and were to remain there poised for whatever lay ahead – as if they hadn't gone through enough. By midday a pontoon bridge had been built across the

Tugela river about a mile and a half north-east of Colenso. Buller was almost committed. Major-General Talbot Coke's 10th Brigade went across it and pushed north-west, until they were checked by heavy fire from the overlooking hills. Now Buller was committed. At 3 p.m. Major-General Wynne's 11th Brigade went across, but did not fight. At nightfall, General Coke withdrew his soldiers to within 1100 yards of the river.

Then, on this day, Buller got two contradictory pieces of information. From Lord Roberts: '. . . lots of special trains are running from Natal with strong reinforcements to offer determined opposition to my advance.' That is, the Boers were leaving Natal to return to the Orange Free State–Cape Colony area. But from General White, in Ladysmith, came: 'We can detect no sign of enemy retreating; all indications point the other way.'

Well, Sir George could *see*, with his very own eyes. It would have been advisable to believe him, I would have thought. But Buller was committed! Indeed, on this day, he signalled to Sir George: 'I hope to be with you tomorrow night. I think there is only a rearguard in front of me.'

His wild optimism was as dangerous as his loose pessimism. Colonel à Court, the Intelligence officer on Buller's staff, said to Winston Churchill: 'I don't like the situation; there are more of them than we expected. We have come down off our high ground. We have taken all the big guns off the big hills. We are getting ourselves cramped up among these kopjes in the valley of the Tugela. It will be like being in the Coliseum and shot at by every row of seats.'

Colonel à Court said that *before* it happened. Buller rejected his advice, and leaned more towards General Warren's opinion that crossing the Tugela river, just north of Colenso, and straight into a deep saucer, rimmed on high by Boers, was a masterly tactical stroke. By dawn on 22 February, almost all of Buller's army was across the Tugela river, and there during the whole morning they suffered a heavy Boer bombardment, which came mainly from Grobellar's Hill to the north-west (see map, page 345). An advance was to be made that day in a generally northward direction, towards what was soon to be named Wynne Hill, which lies at the corner of the Tugela before that tortuous river begins to flow eastward again. The 11th Brigade was allotted to lead the advance, but was to be supported on its left by two battalions of the 4th Brigade. By 2 p.m. the 4th Brigade had not put in an appearance, so General Wynne, rashly perhaps, decided to order his 11th Brigade forward without support or protection on the left flank. General Wynne, incidentally, did point out to Buller that unless the Boers were driven off Grobellar's Hill, overlooking them all from the north-west, his soldiers would be enfiladed on their left; particulary if they succeeded in taking Wynne Hill. But Grobellar's was left alone, apart from a shelling, and so a potential diaster, similar to Spion Kop and Vaal Krantz, was again contrived by the commander-in-chief. The South Lancashire Regiment and the Royal Lancasters led the way, with the Rifle Reserve Battalion close behind. The soldiers went forward in wide skirmishing order. They came under heavy fire from Grobellar's Hill to the north-west, as Wynne had predicted. On that hill were three heavy Boer guns plus a mass of mauser fire; but the British progress was notable for the apparent casualness of the Tommies. General Coke had already written in his diary about this problem: 'It is curious how utterly regardless of fire all ranks became after a bit, in spite of all preaching.'

Then the Boers opened fire from Wynne Hill itself and from what would soon be called Inniskilling Hill, over to the British north-east front. British casualties began to occur at an alarming rate; soon after 2 p.m. General Wynne himself was badly wounded in the thigh and was hurried back to the rear. Colonel Crofton, of the Royal Lancaster Regiment, took over command as he had done on Spion Kop. First the men of Lancashire got on the top of Wynne Hill and battled forward. General Lyttelton's 2nd Division came up in support; but that enfilading fire on the British left was too much, and, suffering heavy casualties, the Boers drove them back to the southern end of Wynne Hill, and there Lancashire stubbornness could not be budged. The situation at dusk was a brutal impasse; but the British, as usual, were exposed and the Boers were not. And then, in the growing darkness, the Boers made a formidable counter-attack. Out on the British left, the 3rd King's Royal Rifles were actually rushed by the Boers; the British regiment retaliated with their bayonets (a weapon never used by the Boers), pursuing the Boers to a dangerously exposed position. The East Surreys came to their assistance, and then they themselves got off, and had to be extricated by the Devon Regiment. And with that sort of murderous turmoil, the day ended, to the sound of nonstop blasting. British casualties were over 500 men. The Boer opposition came mainly from the Middelburg and Ermelo Commandos.

Buller ordered his headquarters to be moved across the Tugela river, and it was placed in a hollow just under a mile south of Wynne Hill. There it came under Boer fire, which, apparently, did not disturb the old boy at all – but when his tents were hit (and presumably his champagne was disturbed) he became very angry. His fighting-spirit had not slipped. The order was 'Push for Ladysmith today, horse, foot and artillery . . . Both cavalry brigades to cross the river at once.' Winston Churchill rode a horse to headquarters.

I found Sir Redvers Buller and his Staff in a somewhat exposed position, whence an excellent view could be obtained. The General displayed his customary composure, asked me how my brother's wound was getting on, and told me that he had just ordered Hart's Brigade, supported by two battalions from Lyttelton's Division, to assault the hill . . . hereinafter called Inniskilling Hill. 'I have told Hart to follow the railway. I think he can get round to their left flank under cover of the river bank,' he said, 'but we must be prepared for a counter-attack on our left as soon as they see what I'm up to.'

Yes, it was to be 'No-Bobs' Hart's Irishmen once again. But the first infantry action of the day was a bayonet charge by men of the East Surrey Regiment, to drive back some Boers who had crept close to the British outposts during the night. The officer who led them was wounded, and before he could be dragged to safety, he received ten separate wounds. That gives some idea of what the Irish Brigade was about to face. The objective on the 23rd, as Churchill stated, was to be Inniskilling Hill. Buller decided that since his soldiers had failed to break the Boers on Wynne Hill – well, have a go at the next. At 12.30 p.m., General Hart ordered his brigade forward. The Irishmen hugged close to the bank of the Tugela river and came to the railway bridge which to this day is called Pom-pom Bridge, which was under a constant and heavy fire. Lieutenant E. Blake Knox had set up his advanced field hospital very close by, and was an eye-witness to the scene:

Every man of the brigade had therefore to run the gauntlet of the Boer marksmen, and members dropped on the bridge, where the enemy's bullets were falling thick. Some fifty men were put out of action in the race over the bridge to the rendezvous further on notwithstanding that some of the Royal Engineers had already begun to put sandbags on the sides of the ironwork as a protection from the rifle-fire . . . Until the bridge was sand-bagged only one man was allowed to cross at a time.

General Hart's plan was to attack with his whole brigade, but at 5 p.m. only two of his battalions were assembled, and rashly, as was his custom, he sent these soldiers unsupported at this frowning hill. Hart ordered a bugler to sound the 'Double', and then the 'Charge', and led them, personally, up the steep side. The Boers had ignored the obvious crest of Inniskilling Hill; they understood the geographical contours of these kopjes. Almost always there is a crest which is not the top of the hill; the Boers wisely chose to hold the more elevated position, and wait for the enemy to cross from the false crest across a glacis towards them. Such a slaughter area the Boers liked to select. On this occasion the Inniskilling Fusiliers led the way, with the Connaught Rangers close behind. All went pretty well as far as the false crest; British artillery was lambasting the Boers on the top and a good deal of protection for the Irishmen was gained from this southern rim of Inniskilling Hill. But once they reached that, the British heavy guns had to cease their fire, for fear of hitting their own men, and when the Irishmen appeared over the edge, the Boers had a clear, lengthy field of fire, downwards at them. It was about 400 yards range. Winston Churchill witnessed the moment: 'I turned my telescope on the Dutch defences. They were no longer deserted. All along the rim of the trenches, clear cut and jet black, against the sky stood a crowded line of slouch-hatted men, visible as far as their shoulders, and wielding what looked like thin sticks.'

Then let John Atkins of the *Manchester Guardian*, recount what he saw next:

The Inniskillings advanced; it was time for the Boers to fire; it was now or never, shells or no shells. The Boers drew themselves up in the trenches, their heads bobbed against the sky. They watched the flashes on the Hlangwana [*sic*] spur and ducked to the shells. Still the Inniskillings, the Dublins, and the Connaughts came on. And now followed the most frantic battle-piece that I have ever seen. Night soon snatched it away, but for the time it lasted it was a frenzy, a nightmare. Boer heads and elbows shot up and down, up and down; the defenders were aiming, firing, and ducking; and all the trenches danced madly against the sky. The first few thin lines of the Inniskillings sank down like cut grass. Their places refilled; still the attackers came on. Two or three Boers stood up on the trenches; and now all forgot to duck. Someone in the trenches appeared to be handing up loaded rifles. Still the attackers hurried on and fell or staggered forward over the stony ground, and the dusk received them on the brown hillside long before the trenches on the sky were blotted out.

Lieutenant Knox, waiting for the casualties that must soon be brought to him, was also watching, and wrote:

There was not, however, the slightest wavering, and as we watched them with straining eyes through our glasses against the dim sky-line, for the light was now fading, we could see the gallant Inniskillings pass swiftly forward with a dash and enthusiasm almost cruel to watch, for at the moment a roar of musketry loud as a thunder-clap echoed on our ears, the whole Boer position blazed into one continuous stream of fire, and the figures of the front line of that gallant regiment fell like corn in front of a mowing-machine. They had been exposed to what was, perhaps, the heaviest frontal and enfilade rifle-fire from each flank that had fallen to the lot of

British troops in the campaign. Never faltering at the sight of the fate of the first line, the second rushed headlong on. A cheer that reached the ears of the army below noted the fact that the first trench had been reached and carried at point of the bayonet.

I WERE THE IRISH WHO WIN EVRY'TIME

From An Active Army Alphabet

The surviving Boers in this forward trench fled back and upwards to their main position; the surviving Irishmen followed as well they could. The Boers above held their fire until their comrades tumbled into the trench with them, and then 'there came another swish of Mauser bullets, and another line of our officers and men went down, and what was left of that gallant band, which had done all that human courage and endurance could do, lay on that bullet-swept glacis, and emptied their magazines as best they could at the dark slouch hats momentarily exposed on the battlements above.'

The Irish had lost about 450, killed and wounded; more than half of these were Inniskilling Fusiliers. When old Queen Victoria was told, she wept, and sobbed, 'Oh, my poor Irish!' And it has been said that this massacre of Hart's Irish Brigade prompted Her Majesty to visit Ireland and to order the establishment of the Irish Guards. On Inniskilling Hill, in the colony of Natal, those Irishmen who could crawled back and built crude sangars for themselves. Less frenzied fighting continued throughout the night.

When dawn came on 24 February, it was found that the main firing-lines were about 300 yards apart. In between there lay many badly wounded Irishmen. The Boers, knowing how badly smashed these 'British' soldiers were, concentrated their fire on the forward makeshift sangars. Relief for Hart's brigade had been promised; by 8 a.m. none had arrived, and Colonels Brooke and Sitwell decided that enough was enough and gave orders for the poor soldiers to retire. During this retirement more men were killed, including Colonel Sitwell. One company of Inniskillings, out on the left, did not receive this order, and remained where they were. At about 10 a.m. help did arrive when the Durham Light Infantry came up and took over the unpleasant forward position. Those Irishmen who could gave the Geordies a 'ringing cheer'. It is difficult even to guess what the survivors of Inniskilling Hill felt that day, except for their leader, General Hart, and he was simply keen to get back to the fray. He had been sent replacement troops: the East Surrey Regiment, half a battalion of the West Yorkshire Regiment and half a battalion of the Scottish Rifles. General Hart just wanted to attack Inniskilling Hill again, and if necessary (I am sure) again and again. It was a mentality that would become very famous in the First World War. But Buller had another idea; not more subtle, but a different idea. As usual, the commander-in-chief was inwardly very upset by the casualties, but still he had not arrived at the particular psychological corner at which he would suddenly give up. He was still displaying the stubbornness which Lord Wolseley had hoped for as a last resort. Buller's new idea was to press on blindly to the next obstacle in the eastward chain, Railway Hill (see map, page 345). And since Buller felt that he couldn't relinquish the part hold the British had on Inniskilling Hill, he felt that the operation was perhaps too complicated for Hart and he therefore asked his deputy, Warren, to take over.

Even under these terrible circumstances, this General did not lose his peculiar sense of humour. He went forward with Buller and his staff to have a close look at the situation. After a while, Buller noticed that Warren was shaking with laughter and called to him over the banging of the guns to ask what was so funny. 'Come over and see,' shouted Warren, and portly Sir Redvers crawled under shot and shell towards his delighted colleague. 'Look at your staff,' roared Warren, and pointed out that as each shell passed over their heads, they all ducked and the lower the rank, the lower the head appeared to go down. Buller was very cross as he puffed back, and ordered his officers to keep their heads steady under fire; Warren was very pleased with himself, and confided, 'A good laugh does one's inside so much good.' Finally it was decided by Warren that Hart could have a go at Railway Hill, which lay to the north-east of Wynne Hill, and around which the railway line wound, on its track to Ladysmith. By the time this was settled it was 4 p.m., and it was generally decided to postpone this now monotonous but frightening routine until the morrow.

At this point a significant and mysterious change came over Buller. A new positive germ of an idea began to move in his head. Perhaps it began with the thought of holding Inniskilling Hill while attacking Railway Hill. It had echoes of holding Spion Kop while attacking the Twin Peaks. Did it turn in Buller's mind that perhaps if he did this, it might be more than the Boers could hold? Anyway, that night he began to move his artillery back across the Tugela river; he said he wanted to place them high up on Monte Cristo Mountain, which faced the Boers' extreme left flank. And then one of his Intelligence officers, Colonel Sandbach, reported to him that he had found a bridgeable place over the Tugela river, due south of Inniskilling and Railway Hills, and, it was reported, the high northern banks of the Tugela would give ample cover to soldiers if they had to move eastward. This was a plan and a route to outflank to the east General Botha's Boer army.

Buller gave orders to get all of his artillery back on to the southern side of the Tugela, where they were to be arrayed on the high ground facing Wynne Hill, Inniskilling Hill, Railway Hill and east of them, Pieter's Hill. And then with startling, quiet authority he ordered most of his army to march back over that pontoon bridge north-east of Colenso; when they had done so, the bridge was to be dismantled and reassembled at the place that Colonel Sandbach had discovered – disgracefully, it was the only pontoon bridge available. When General Lyttelton had first heard about Buller's idea to push eastwards towards Monte Cristo, he had rather unkindly stated that these ideas 'appeared so sound that I doubted if they were his own . . .'

Came Sunday, 25 February, and General Buller ordered forward a flag of truce to the Boer commandants, Louis Botha and Lucas Meyer, requesting an armistice to enable the British to collect their wounded and bury their dead. The Boer leaders refused to grant a formal armistice, but agreed to an informal arrangement that if the British undertook not to attack the Boer positions during that day, the Boers would allow the wounded to be collected and the dead buried. The plight of these wounded was now terrible; many had lain out on these African hillsides for as long as forty hours, under the African sun and teeming rain, without food and water. Some British soldiers in the advanced trench had thrown water bottles and food into the no-man's-land, in the hope that some poor soul could reach it. On the previous day, the 24th, the order had been given to the British artillery to continue bombarding Inniskilling Hill, which would have added to the agony of the wounded Irishmen. But Hart countermanded that order. Now the British tentatively raised their heads above the sangars and clambered over into the area of dreadful suffering. Lieutenant-Colonel Grant described the scene:

Colonel Hamilton of the Queen's, with his white flag, is the central figure . . . Behind him a group of perhaps a dozen officers of the line . . . and behind them again the advanced guard of a trenchful of curious private soldiers, all rather self-conscious, but glancing with steady eyes around at the poor dead with which the rocky ground was covered. Oh, those dead! How still and uncouth they lay, all dreadful and discoloured by three days of tropical sun, and three damp, oppressive nights. Who can say that there is beauty in death? Certainly there is none in violent death though in rare instances the body, so swiftly robbed of life, does fall into lines of dignity and nobility. But mostly the awesomely immobile form looks what it is – stricken, and, one would swear, shocked at its fate. There is little mistaking a dead man at any distance. Be the pose never so lifelike, there is an angularity, an utter nonchalance, an irresponsibility about the prone figure that fixes the attention at once.

But all this is a digression. For a few moments – rather anxious ones it may be said – Colonel Hamilton and his little following stood motionless among the motionless dead, every eye fixed on the Boer trench, and a lively wonder in every mind as to what sort of entity would presently emerge therefrom. Behind, on our crest-line, all was silent as the grave; ahead, the same uncanny stillness. Suddenly a blunt-looking head emerged, apparently from the earth itself, followed by another and another . . . Then two or three figures showed openly on the parapet, their uprising reminding one of nothing so much as that of a gamekeeper straightening his back from the cramp of setting his traps in a weasel run.

But there was nothing of the gamekeeper about the man who first strode forward to meet us. Seldom have I set eyes on a more magnificent specimen of male humanity than the commandant of the trenchful of Boers, Pristorius [*sic*] by name, a son of Anak by descent, and a gallant, golden-bearded fighting man by present occupation; for in far-away Middelburg those mighty limbs – he told it us without any of the stupid deprecation which would probably have characterised a similar confession on the part of an Englishman – were wont to stretch themselves beneath a lawyer's desk. Close on his heels came what a person who had never seen Boers before would have thought the strangest band of warriors in the world: old men with flowing, tobacco-stained, white beards; middle-aged men with beards burnt black with the sun and sweat of their forty years; young men, mostly clean shaven, exhibiting strongly the heavy Dutch moulding of the broad nose and chin; big boys in small suits; suits of all kinds and colours, tweed, velveteen, homespun, and 'shoddy', all untidy in the extreme, but mostly as serviceable as their wearers. The only sign of a uniform was the turn-out of Pristorius himself, a suit of well-made khaki, studded with silver buttons and silver stars wherever there was room for button or star. A gentleman, and a dandy, this Pristorius, who bewailed comically the loss of his boots and hair-brushes in the scurry from Monte Cristo. 'Monte Cristo, you call it!' laughed he; 'I call it a small Hell!' ...

It was much more difficult for them to conceal the natural discomposure which all men feel in the presence of the silent dead than for their more artificial opponents. From the airy and easy demeanour of the uniformed British officers, that dreadful plateau might have been the lobby of a London club. A Briton is at all time prone to conceal his emotions, and certainly, in this instance, the idiosyncrasy gave him a great social advantage over the superstitious Burghers, with their sidelong glances and uneasy shiftings.

Colonel Grant decided to try a chat with an archetypical Boer:

'Good morning!' quoth I. 'Gumorghen,' rumbled the oak-tree sourly. 'Surely we can be friends for five minutes,' I ventured, after a pause. The rugged countenance was suddenly, not to say startlingly, illumined with a beaming smile. '*Why* not, indeed! *Why* not, officer! Have you any tobacco?' Out came my pouch, luckily filled to bursting that very morning, and the oak-tree proceeded to stuff a huge pipe to the very brim ... Was I guilty of 'aiding and abetting the Queen's enemies' by thus easing their torments for a while?

By this time the plateau was presenting quite an animated scene. Parties of Boer and British officers were strolling about in all directions, never approaching *too* near their respective defences. Here stood a little group of Dutchmen around a Briton, there a like number of Britons around an interesting Boer. A young officer of the Devons was busily engaged in preparing to take a snap-shot of the scene ...

Colonel Grant made the most of his opportunity to communicate with the Boers on Inniskilling Hill, and while talking to another Boer, asked the big question: ' "Aren't you fellows sick of this? How much longer do you intend to keep us out here, and yourselves from your farms and families?" The reply was more frank than I had expected. "Of course we don't like it any more than you do; but, three years, yes! three years we will stay out and fight!" '

Well, that Boer was something of a prophet. After nearly three years, and having faced getting on for half a million British soldiers, there were Boers still fighting on the veldt; half-starved and in rags. Those men are known in South Africa to this day as the 'bitter-enders'. General Lyttelton himself came up to this 'no-man's-land', and talked to Commandant Pretorius and other Boers. The questions and attitudes seemed always to be similar. The Boers were astonished that Lyttelton seemed to accept the heavy British casualties coolly. One of them challenged him that the British had had a 'rough time'. 'A rough time?' repeated Lyttelton. 'I suppose so. But for us, of course, it is nothing. We are used to it, and we are all well paid for it. This is what we are paid for. This is the life we always lead – you understand?'

The Boers were heard to say, 'Great God,' as they looked around at the obscenity of the battlefield. Lyttelton's dead and dying soldiers were paid a shilling a day *before* stoppages.

During this time, of course, the wounded were being removed to the field hospitals, and the dead were being buried, and, in addition, Buller was getting on with moving his guns and soldiers back across the Tugela river. It was a great advantage to him when the Boers refused to grant an official armistice; if that had happened, he could not legally have continued his military plans. On the other hand, the Boers continued working on that Sunday to improve their trenches and sangars; that was probably the reason that they refused to grant an armistice. As the dead British soldiers were buried, friends took letters, some regimental buttons, and medal ribbons from their uniforms, to send to relatives back in Britain. Of recent years, the South African Government has permitted some of these bodies to be dug up for reburial elsewhere. I have therefore been a witness to the fact that though these mementoes were often removed, money was left in the pockets. By 6 p.m. the last dead British soldier was buried in the African earth. Colonel Grant wrote:

> The wearied and saddened chaplain had said the last solemn words over the huge grave containing the husks of so many brave departed spirits. The truce was at an end, though the influence of it lingered for a while even after Briton and Boer had parted with a wave of the hand or a ceremonious salute, or, as in more than one case, a curiously inscrutable *auf wiedersehen*.

That atmosphere that Colonel Grant described, of a reluctance to start killing each other again, extended itself strangely for four silent hours. It was a mute statement to Colonial Secretary Chamberlain and the Tory Government in London, and to wretched Milner in Cape Town, and finally to businessman Cecil Rhodes, already released from the siege of Kimberley, that the men who had to carry out their murderous political and economic plans soared above them in quality of spirit. However, these hours of the dove did not last, and at about 10 p.m. one isolated Boer fired his gun, and from that moment, the mausers and the Lee-Enfields took up the challenge and were soon followed by the heavy guns on both sides. Once started those massed guns did not stop again through night and day, and night and day.

From a very early hour on the morning of 26 February, Buller's entire army was very busy taking up new specific positions. Every one of his heavy guns was now south of the Tugela river, with the exception of the 73rd Battery, Royal Field Artillery. The mass of guns had been placed in a long regular line, facing the Tugela or more significantly pointing across that river at Wynne Hill, Inniskilling Hill, Railway Hill and the next one east-wards, Pieter's Hill. Behind these guns, heavier ones were on Hlangwane Hill and on the hills eastwards, and finally were ranged along the heights of Monte Cristo; there were seventy of these guns in all, but not including the long-range guns at Chieveley.

The infantry were also methodically and judiciously placed, covering all potential eventualities, but nevertheless, they were beginning to look like an efficient piece of aggression. On the western flank, General Coke's 10th Brigade held Colenso and the kopjes west and north of that place. Then came General Hildyard's English Brigade holding the low hills facing Wynne Hill, and what remained of General Hart's Irishmen, reinforced by two battalions of Colonel Norcott's brigade, holding what they could of Inniskilling Hill. General Barton's Fusilier Brigade, Colonel Kitchener's Lancashire Brigade, and the two remaining battalions of Norcott's brigade had recrossed the Tugela river and were placed ready and waiting on Hlang-wane Hill; also the 1st Border Regiment had joined them from Chieveley. The Irregular cavalry brigade under Lord Dundonald were out on the British extreme right flank, on the Nek between Cingolo Mountain and Monte Cristo: they were there to watch the Boer left flank. Also, as daylight came, the Rifle Reserve Battalion received orders to join their brigade on Hlang-wane. This regiment was the last to cross the pontoon bridge north-east of Colenso, before it was removed to its new site, due south of Railway Hill. Incidentally, the previous brigade organization had been completely disrupted by the haphazard fighting over the past five days, so this new arrangement was a sensible improvisation, and all this complicated operation was Buller's.

The change that had been discernible in him forty hours before was continuing and growing. His staff officer, Colonel à Court, rode with him along the whole line of the British force, and was taken aback by Buller's metamorphosis. 'He had suddenly become the old War Office Buller, and dictated so rapidly that I could scarcely keep pace with him, but as he went on

I saw that he had a complete grasp of the operation, and that everything that I had hoped would be done was in the orders.' This feeling had been transmitted to his fighting men. Lieutenant-Colonel Grant witnessed it, and wrote:

No member of Buller's army will ever forget the tense feeling which pervaded the air . . . A tiger crouching before it springs is a limp, nerveless creature compared to a host of 25000 desperate men preparing, perhaps unconsciously, for the onslaught that is to decide once and for ever the bloody quarrel of months. It is not too much to say that the relief of the 10 000 Britons beleaguered in Ladysmith overshadowed all else, even the ultimate issue of the whole campaign, in the minds of men and officers. Pretoria could wait, but comrades perishing of fever, starving on starved horseflesh, driven to hide like conies in holes and burrows from the pitiless shells, every one of which was a fresh insult to battalions who had helped to overthrow Napoleon himself, they could *not* wait, and no words of mine can describe the fulness of that pause before the final casting of the die.

And then, on that keyed-up, waiting day, General Buller received a telegram from Her Majesty Queen Victoria: 'I have heard with the deepest concern of the heavy losses sustained by my brave Irish soldiers. I desire to express my sympathy and my admiration of the splendid fighting qualities which they have exhibited throughout these trying operations.' Buller replied: 'Sir Redvers Buller has, on the part of the Irish Brigade, to thank the Queen for her gracious telegram of sympathy and encouragement.'

It is not easy for us in the 1970s to understand all these sentiments. But the fact is that the Queen's message stiffened the army's sense of purpose even more. They were at least reminded that everyone was waiting back in the 'Old Country'. And there was another reason why the British soldiers in South Africa thought of their Queen and their homeland on that day. Victoria had spent her own money on buying every single soldier a tin containing chocolate. The tin was specially designed, and the manufacturers of the chocolate, being Quakers, refused to make a profit. It was on this very significant day that the thousands of gifts arrived. General Coke wrote in his diary:

February 26th. Monday . . . The Queen's Chocolate is issued to the Brigade – the tins are nicely got up, and the present of our Gracious Sovereign will be greatly appreciated. It is rather unfortunate that the men are not in a position to take more care of the gift, but Her Majesty's desire was that the men should receive the present in the field. I have opened our Post Office so that the cases can be sent home by the men.

Many of the soldiers refused to eat such an astonishing gift, and promptly returned the tins unopened to their families. These tins were then often framed and hung as a precious decoration on the living-room wall. The Boers and most European countries made a great joke of this chocolate and the anti-British cartoons that resulted usually contrasted the chocolate with cruel death. Private Ernest Shepton, however, wrote from Natal to his mother in Cheltenham:

I am sending you a tin of chocolate, a present which all the troops have received from the Queen. I could not resist opening it and having a taste before I sent it away. You can all have a taste of it or make a cup of cocoa, whichever you prefer; but keep enough for us to have a drink together with when I come home. Please keep the tin for me, because I value it more than I shall the medal which I shall get when the war is over, because it is a present from the Queen. And if I get knocked over – please keep it in remembrance of me.

Over in the Boer trenches, high up on those famous hills, all was not well. The news had reached the burghers that Kimberley, way over in the Cape, had been relieved by Lord Roberts' cavalry, and now they knew that General Cronje's 4000 Boers, who had been up to this time all-victorious, were

Queen Victoria dispenses chocolate in a contemporary Dutch cartoon. Hostile cartoonists frequently assumed that the Queen's chocolate was supplied in liquid form

surrounded and were being blasted at a place called Paardeberg. The Orange Free State Boers had left General Botha and had fled westward to try to prevent this impending disaster. And on top of all of his other troubles, Botha, for the first time, was suffering self-deception – or rather blind optimism. He watched the British assembling south of the Tugela river, and wrote a letter on the afternoon of the 26th to Commandant-General Joubert, who was ill in Pretoria; in this letter he stated that it was quite possible that the British were retiring because of their heavy losses. But in his own clever mind he must have felt darkly uneasy, as those massed British heavy guns methodically pounded the Boer positions. Were they, perhaps, working out a murderous fine range? And if so, for what purpose?

Light relief for the day came from young Winston Churchill. Lord Dundonald was patrolling his cavalry over on the British eastern flank, but as the evening came on, Dundonald relaxed sufficiently to walk over to the bivouac of the South African Light Horse, where he found Colonel Byng laughing. 'I must tell you what Winston said this evening,' Colonel Byng went on: 'Winston said he wanted to get the D.S.O., as it would look so nice on the robes of the Chancellor of the Exchequer.' He added: 'I told him he must first get into Parliament, if he could get any constituency to have him!' Of course, it was a fine joke on that evening of 26 February 1900!

27 February was the anniversary of the British defeat on Majuba Hill in 1881 during the First Boer War. The British Army had longed for revenge ever since. Rudyard Kipling had expressed the feeling by writing the words 'wiping something off a slate', and now was this a mystical coincidence that the British Army was marshalling itself so formidably on this very day? Many men who were present wrote about the curious elation. John Atkins, of the *Manchester Guardian*: 'I never saw infantry strain at the leash as they strained this day. The renascence of confidence and power and spirit and dash was complete. It was Majuba Day; the attack had been planned dramatically.'

The dawn was cloudy, and with it came a barrage from the big guns that was unlike anything heard in southern Africa before; they pounded the Boer positions on Wynne Hill, Inniskilling Hill, Railway Hill and Pieter's Hill with lyddite and shrapnel.

Buller's battle plan was basically simple. The troops that had remained north of the Tugela river were holding the area north of Colenso, and were also pressing towards Wynne Hill and Inniskilling Hill to increase that pressure and thereby persuade the Boers that any further attack

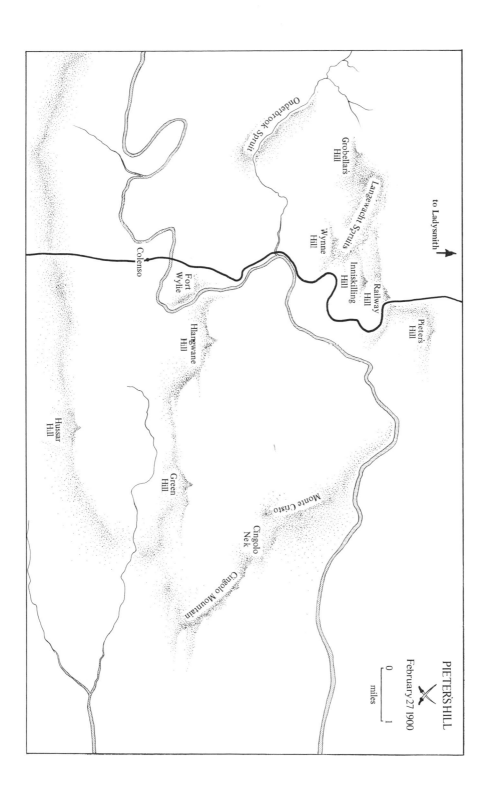

PIETER'S HILL

February 27 1900

Onderbrook Spruit

Grobelar's Hill

Langewacht Spruits

Wynne Hill

Inniskilling Hill

Railway

Pieter's Hill

to Ladysmith

Colenso

Fort Wylie

Hlangwane Hill

Husar Hill

Green Hill

Monte Cristo

Cingolo Nek

Cingolo Mountain

0   1

miles

that might come would probably be from that direction. This would encourage the Boers to concentrate about those hills, and thereby tend to make this area the Boers' left flank. Meanwhile, the whole range of hills would be bombarded from east to west with intense concentration, and the British soldiers south of the Tugela river would cross over the newly constructed pontoon bridge, south of Railway Hill. Some of these troops would then move eastward under the shelter of the northern riverbank, until they were in a position to assault Pieter's Hill. From that point every British soldier along the whole front would attack the Boers, though in succession, starting at Pieter's Hill, then Railway Hill, then Inniskilling Hill and finally Wynne Hill. All this was sound military theory, because Pieter's Hill was dominated by the British guns on captured Monte Cristo, and therefore was not as formidable as it had been. And if Pieter's Hill were taken by the British, the position of the Boers on Railway Hill to the west would become untenable, and so on westward. And, of course, those British attacking Pieter's Hill might very well find themselves outflanking the Boers' left, at the very outset.

At 10.30 a.m. the new pontoon bridge across the Tugela was ready. The soldiers who were to cross it were under General Warren, and as they were poised for the move, General Buller received a 'Clear the line' telegram from Lord Roberts, announcing the surrender of General Cronje's force of 4000 Boers at Paardeberg. The British regiments were already on the move towards the pontoon bridge, and as the news of Lord Roberts' victory reached them, regiment by regiment, they cheered on this morning of Majuba Day. Did the Boers in their disintegrating trenches know what those cheers signified? Certainly the news of Cronje's terrible defeat had reached them, and before they had come to personal grips with the British, disaster had already been heralded. I doubt that they could have heard the cheering because of those massed British guns. Young Deneys Reitz had just arrived on the scene:

A bombardment more violent than that of yesterday broke out ahead of us, and, when we came to the rear of Pieter's Heights, we saw the ridge on which lay the Bethal men (and our own) going up in smoke and flame. It was an alarming sight. The English batteries were so concentrating on the crest that it was almost invisible under the clouds of flying earth and fumes, while the volume of sound was beyond anything that I have ever heard. At intervals the curtain lifted, letting us catch a glimpse of the trenches above, but we could see no sign of movement, nor could we hear whether the men up there were still firing for the din of the guns drowned all lesser sounds.

The first British soldiers to cross the pontoon bridge were the 1st Royal Irish Fusiliers, the 2nd Royal Scots Fusiliers and the 2nd Royal Dublin Fusiliers, all under General Barton. Once across, these troops turned right and moved eastward under the shelter of the high northern banks of the Tugela, and towards the foot of Pieter's Hill. Then came the 2nd Royal Lancasters, the 2nd West Yorks, the 1st South Lancashires and the 1st York and Lancaster Regiment, under Brigadier Kitchener; they moved directly northward in preparation to attack Railway Hill. Finally, across the bridge went the 1st Durham Light Infantry, the 1st Rifle Brigade, the 2nd East Surreys, and a half battalion of the 2nd Scottish Rifles, under Brigadier Norcott, and these soldiers were again to move north to attack Inniskilling Hill, together with the Connaught Rangers, the Royal Inniskillings, and the Imperial Light Infantry, under (of course) General 'No-Bobs' Hart.

When Barton's soldiers reached the northern end of the pontoon bridge, they were confronted by a signpost, erected by the Royal Engineers, and claiming 'To Ladysmith'. It is reported by Lieutenant Knox, Royal Army Medical Corps, that this gave rise to 'much cheerful comment' from 'the men as they passed by'. It should not be imagined that this was anything like a sylvan scene. Lord Dundonald described it: 'The din of musketry in the gorge through which the Tugela flowed was past belief – it was one continuous roar . . .' And that was *before* the actual assault!

At 12.30 p.m. Barton's battalions were in place and were steeling themselves to attack. On the left were the Irish Fusiliers and on the right were the Scots Fusiliers and in support were the Dublin Fusiliers. Five hundred very steep feet confronted them, and up they went. The Boers poured in a heavy enfilading fire of pom-pom and Creusot shells from the east, and rifle fire from their positions on Railway Hill, to the immediate west. The summit of Pieter's Hill consists of three distinct kopjes, stretching northward. The Irish Fusiliers rushed the first with 'admirable precision', and took it. Then the entire brigade joined forces to attack the second kopje, and in crossing the open ground, the poor old Irish lost two officers and fourteen men killed, and six officers and seventy men wounded, 'out of a total of three companies'. But, dauntless to the end, they pushed the Boers back; the time was 2.30 p.m. Now there only remained the third, northern kopje, on Pieter's Hill, and General Barton selected three companies of the Dublins and one company of the Scots for the purpose. These troops, led by Captain McBean, worked round to the right of the hill, but were met by a formidable Boer fusillade, and finally they were pinned down in a donga, with every one of their officers hit except one.

At about this time, 3 p.m., Brigadier Kitchener ordered his brigade to attack Railway Hill, and up from the riverbed went the men from Lancashire and Yorkshire. The first 400 feet were almost precipitous, but so hard was the fighting on Pieter's Hill to the east that they reached the crest unnoticed and in comparative safety. Then they had to cross open ground and be fully exposed to Boer fire from the summit. The brigade extended over a wide front, with the Royal Lancasters on the left, the West Yorks and South Lancashires on the right, and the York and Lancaster Regiment in support. A direct assault was ordered, and the West Yorks were off in deadly style, diverting slightly to their left, where Boers were strongly holding the railway cutting – the line to Ladysmith. The Royal Lancaster Regiment were supposed to go straight for the nek, or high land, which joined Railway Hill to Inniskilling Hill, and which was lined by Boer trenches. But as they charged, they suffered a heavy fire from Boers on Inniskilling Hill, and suddenly, because of this, they veered half-left and went straight at these Boers with the bayonet. Brigadier Kitchener seeing that a gap was thereby growing in his attack, quickly ordered the South Lancashires to fill it. These men led by Colonel McCarthy O'Leary – a good Lancashire man if ever there was one – went at the strongly fortified nek, and took it with the bayonet; Colonel McCarthy O'Leary was shot at the moment of victory. However, the very top of Railway Hill was still held by the Boers, and British shell fire was plastering it. The British were facing Not only the Boers but a dreadful British barrage directly in front of them as well. The time was shortly after 4 p.m.

Lieutenant Blake Knox, Royal Army Medical Corps, wrote: 'What were our men to do? To stay where they were without cover and in the open was foolhardy; to retreat was disgrace; to proceed was exposure, not only to the enemy's fire, but to that of our own guns. The question was soon answered. A general advance with fixed bayonets was ordered.'

Captain Limpus, of HMS *Terrible*, was with the great naval guns that were firing at the Boer trenches, and yet so close to the British. He wrote in his diary:

Then the guns redoubled their efforts. The shell bursts seemed almost continuous, lyddite and shrapnel throwing up earth and stones at each trench. One could now see the Boers as they rose up to fire and the way in which they managed to keep their fire going won our admiration, but we felt that they must be crushed down by shell fire and that our men must be helped all we knew. The bombardment was now terrible . . .

Winston Churchill viewed the outcome:

The Lancashire Brigade advanced on a wide front. Norcott's Riflemen were already prolonging their line to the right. The Boer fire was dispersed along the whole front of attack, instead of converging on one narrow column. The assault was going to succeed. We stood up on our rocks. Bayonets began to glitter on the distant slope. The moving lines increased their pace. The heads of the Boers bobbing up and down in their trenches grew fewer and fewer. They knew the tide was running too strongly. Death and flight were thinning their ranks. Then the sky-line of Railway Hill bristled with men who dropped on their knees forthwith and fired in particular haste at something that was running away down the other side. There was the sound of cheering. Railway Hill was ours.

Lieutenant Knox remarked: 'If the attack was superb, the defence was heroic.'

If the military theory was to prove practical, Inniskilling Hill must now be the next objective. General Norcott's brigade and what was left of General Hart's Irishmen were still holding those costly lodgements on the south-west of Inniskilling Hill. Now the Royal Lancasters were coming at the Boers from the south-east with murder in their hearts and bayonets fixed. Simultaneously up got Hart's men and Norcott's men, with the Durham Light Infantry taking the lead. It was 5 p.m. Captain Knox wrote:

Assaulted on three sides by three separate bodies of troops, supported by an artillery fire of seventy guns, was it any wonder that some of the Boers, about sixty in number, ran like hunted rats from their trenches? A tall man, a huge fellow in a dark jersey was seen to go out boldly and try to rally them. Returning, he sprang on the top of a sangar, and while in the act of emptying his magazine into the advancing infantry, a 50-pound lyddite shell burst right upon him. Thus vanished the last defender of Hart's [Inniskilling] Hill!

Already a great hole had been torn across General Louis Botha's line. Only the northern kopje on Pieter's Hill seemed to stand between the entire Natal Field Force and poor old Ladysmith. It is certainly true that some 25 000 British soldiers, together with their massed heavy guns, were already beginning to point in that direction.

At 5.30 p.m. Sir Redvers Buller gave new orders to Lord Dundonald: 'I am sending the cavalry and a strong force of artillery to pursue the Boers who I think are leaving their positions.' Lord Dundonald and his cavalry brigade were delighted, and hastily saddled up and rode for the pontoon bridge; but as they reached it, Sir Redvers was there in person to prevent their crossing. His explanation was that the Boers were still firing in the hills behind the Tugela Heights and would prove a danger. The cavalry returned dejectedly pondering that to chase the Boer rearguard was the very best thing they could have done. Was Buller veering into another manic doubt? Anyway, the Boers were definitely off the Tugela Heights. Surely not even Buller could now delay the relief of Ladysmith.

At 6 p.m., General Barton withdrew three companies of the ubiquitous Irishmen from his left, and ordered them to go for the last, northern kopje on Pieter's Hill. These Irish Fusiliers went forward and upwards into very heavy fire from the Boer bitter-enders. The Irish Fusiliers were given covering fire from the Dublins, but this did not prevent their losing a third of their number, with every one of their officers either killed or wounded, before they reached the southern end of the last kopje. During this Irish charge, our eyewitness, Lieutenant Blake Knox, was wounded in the thigh, and he lay amongst the rocks on the side of Pieter's Hill:

> Some of the Dublins were now rushing by. I recognised their accents as they came up. They were charging along with fixed bayonets on their way to reinforce the Scots Fusiliers. What they took me for I do not know, but one huge, hulking fellow evidently suspected me to be a crouching Boer, and drew back for a lunge. I shouted at him, and, with the observation, 'Right! be aisy, now!' he passed on and disappeared.

There were now few Boers left to oppose the onslaught; it was virtually the last ditch stand. Amongst the few fighting survivors was young Deneys Reitz:

> ... and for a space we caught the fierce rattle of Mauser rifles followed by British infantry swarming over the skyline, their bayonets flashing in the sun. Shouts and cries reached us, and we could see men desperately thrusting and clubbing. Then a rout of burghers broke back from the hill, streaming towards us in disorderly flight. The soldiers fired into them, bringing many down as they made blindly past us, not looking to right or left. We went too, for the troops cheering loudly, came shooting and running down the slope.
>
> Of our Pretoria men who had been on the ridge not one came back. They had been holding an advanced position to the right of the Bethal section, and had been overwhelmed there. They stood their ground until the enemy was on them, and they were bayoneted or taken to the last man. Thus our corporalship was wiped out, with its leader, Isaac Malherbe, the bravest of them all, and their going at this calamitous time was scarcely noticed.

The Boer General, Ben Viljoen, even managed a flicker of humour at this tragic time: 'It must have been a race for the Distinguished Service Order or the Victoria Cross to be won by the one who was first to enter Ladysmith ... I noticed the Irish Fusiliers on this occasion, as always, in the van.' Another Boer, Dietlof van Warmelo, wrote with the heroic style of a proud and honest soldier: 'Our fall was great. For the first time there was a general panic. The two Republics, being forced to venture on war against a powerful kingdom, felt themselves staggering under the heavy blow.'

Incidentally there were at least two Boer women fighting on the Tugela Heights, Mrs Otto Krantz and Mrs Helena Herbst. It has also been stated that two of the last burghers to leave the elevated battlefield were Generals Lucas Meyer and Louis Botha.

On the British side 'a boy of a south-country regiment' described his experience of victory to a Wesleyan chaplain:

Just as we got to the top, the Colonel he give the command, 'Charge!' and then it was bay'n'ts down, a big yell, and we went straight for them trenches. But did the Boers run as they ginerily does when they sees cold steel? No' a bit on it; they knew a game worth two o' that; they just sat tight, and kept on potting away, a-picking off the orfficers and non-coms. Fust a capting got 'it, then I see the colour-sergint knocked over, then the colonel 'e wint down; then my dander riz – for 'e were a good colonel, sir, and a real gintleman – and I says, says I to myself, 'Mr Boer, you'll 'av to pay fer this yer', and I think as 'ow thim were the sentiments of the whole rigimint. But just as we were on top on 'em not five yards away, down goes their bundooks [rifles], up goes their arms, and they shouted, 'We surrender!' 'Surrender, do yer,' sez I; 'bit late, ain't it? 'Ere's a bay'n't just fer to 'elp you to remember our colonel.' But' (this in a tone of deep regret) 'it wer'n't no go, sir. The adjutant 'e clips in and knocks up our bay'n'ts. 'They've surrendered,' sez 'e, 'leave them alone.' But the rigimint didn't like it, sir, and small wonder; fer I don't call that there playing the game, do you?

It seemed that Ladysmith was on the edge of rescue. John Atkins, of the *Manchester Guardian*, saw the moment of realization:

On every part of the hill troops climbed up into the sun and a golden, splendid property. On all the hills in front of me British troops bristled. A sudden realization of victory swept over the field; there was a cessation, almost a silence; guns no longer crashed; and then from some part of the field there came a little unaided cheer, that asked assistance. Assistance came; cheer answered cheer, backwards and forwards across the river, till all the cheers became the same cheer, and staff officers forgot that they were not as ordinary officers and threw up their helmets and shook hands with one another. No one minded that the Boer gunners were throwing a dying flare of shells on to our hills. The night was on us, and that is the time to build entrenchments. Never was an attack better timed.

A British soldier spoke to John Atkins:

'I bayonet that man' [he] said, pointing to a prisoner, and here he rehearsed the appropriate action.

'Did you hurt him much?' some one asked.

'Oh, no,' was the answer, 'I bayoneted him as gently as I could. And I gave him water, too; he had more than I did. Ah, I told him he was a lucky man to fall across *me*.'

Winston Churchill went prowling round the debris of battle, and observed a group of Boer prisoners. 'Looking at these very ordinary people, who grinned and chattered without dignity, and who might, from their appearance, have been a knot of loafers round a public-house, it was difficult to understand what qualities made them such a terrible foe.' Winston Churchill spoke to the private soldier guarding these Boer prisoners and asked him how many there were under his bayonet:

'Only forty-eight, sir . . . and there wouldn't have been so many as that if the officers hadn't stopped us from giving them the bayonet. I never saw such cowards in my life. Shoot at you till you come up to them, and then beg for mercy. I'd teach 'em.' With which remark he turned to the prisoners, who had been issued rations of beef and biscuit, but who were also very thirsty, and began giving them water to drink from his own canteen, and so left me wondering at the opposite and contradictory sides of human nature as shown by Briton as well as Boer.

Lieutenant Knox had managed to get away from the immediate carnage and was having his wound dressed, close to another group of Boer prisoners:

One haggard, middle-aged burgher who was near me was waiting his turn to get a wound in his thigh dressed. A long, ragged splinter of shell, partly covered with khaki-coloured paint, protruded from his wound through his breeches. His face, hands and clothes were stained a canary yellow from a lyddite shell which had burst near him. Small, dry, hard droplets of the half-burnt explosive hung from the threads of his torn garments and from his singed hair. I brought him a tin of bovril, and asked if I could dress his wound. He was rather silent and surly at first, but soon thawed, and entered into conversation with me. 'Such a day,' he said, 'and such a slaughter! Our cause is lost; let me die.'

During the afternoon, General Lucas Meyer's staff surgeon, Dr Krieger, came through the British lines to collect wounded Boers. He was confronted by a glowering General Warren who significantly showed him a dum-dum bullet which had been found on the body of a dead Boer. Now a dum-dum was a soft-nosed expansive bullet which inflicted a terrible wound, and which had therefore been condemned by 'civilized' countries. Mr H. C. Hillegas, who was with the Boers, has described the encounter:

General Warren . . . asked him [Dr Krieger] why the Boers used a variety of cartridge which was not sanctioned by the rules of civilized warfare. Dr Krieger took the cartridge in his hand, and, after examining it, returned it to Sir Charles, with the remark that it was a British Lee-Melford dum-dum. General Warren seemed to be greatly nonplussed when several of his officers confirmed the physician's statement and informed him that a large stock of dum-dum cartridges had been acquired by the Boers at Dundee. It is an undeniable fact that the Boers captured thousands of rounds of dum-dum bullets which bore the broad arrow of the British Army, and used them in subsequent battles.

Late on that ominous 27 February 1900, Lord Dundonald received another order for his cavalry brigade: 'To cross the pontoon tomorrow morning and reconnoitre the enemy.' This very act Buller had prevented Dundonald from carrying out earlier in the day. It seemed that Buller wanted to give the defeated Boers enough time to escape total retribution. That night, General Louis Botha lay down under a tree, covering himself with blankets and coats, as the warm Natal rain poured on him. I am sure he was quietly pondering how he would go on fighting the British for years, if necessary.

This final battle of the Tugela Heights lasted for six hours, and the British suffered 500 casualties. The total British casualties for the entire two weeks' fighting were 26 officers and 347 men killed or died of wounds, and 99 officers and 1710 men wounded. The Boer casualties are more difficult to calculate because they always took pains to conceal their losses. On 27 February they lost between 150 and 200 burghers. And over the whole fortnight the Red Cross Identification Department stated that 81 were killed and 343 wounded – though it has been estimated that the total figure was around the 500 mark.

14

THE RELIEF OF LADYSMITH

I thank God we have kept the flag flying.
SIR GEORGE WHITE

In Ladysmith, the populace and military sensed that tribulation was beginning to end. The news had come through from Buller suggesting a decisive victory, and though his words were now taken with a wagon load of salt, this time it all seemed different. Buller's message had ended, 'I believe the enemy to be in full retreat.' The Reverend Owen Watkins, the Wesleyan military chaplain beleaguered in Ladysmith throughout the siege, was one of those who went to look for themselves.

Eagerly we scrambled to the top of the kopjes which had for so long been our homes, and with field-glasses and telescopes scanned the country round us. As we did so exclamations burst simultaneously from all lips – every road was black with our enemy in full flight, every drift was choked with wagons and guns. On all sides it was the same – in thousands they fled, in deadly fear, as we afterwards learned, that our cavalry, with lances and swords, would be upon and amongst them. At the sight our hearts leaped within us, for we began to realise what all this meant to us – we saw our deliverance at hand. But as we rejoiced, our dismounted cavalry fumed and chafed like dogs held in leash, longing to be at them, but powerless – their horses were all eaten. 'Look at them!' I heard a cavalry officer exclaim, almost crying with vexation as he spoke. 'Look at them! Completely at our mercy! The chance of a lifetime, and we haven't got a horse!'

At daybreak on 28 February, Buller's cavalry moved to reconnoitre the Boers. There were the two brigades: the 1st under Brigadier-General Burn-Murdoch comprising the Royal Dragoons, the 13th Hussars, and 'A' Battery, Royal Horse Artillery; and the 2nd Brigade, under Lord Dundonald, comprising mainly the Irregulars: Thorneycroft's Mounted Infantry, the South African Light Horse, and the Composite Mounted Infantry, which was made up of units of the Natal Carabineers, the Natal Police and odds and ends of the King's Royal Rifles, the Dublin Fusiliers and the Imperial Light Horse. First, Dundonald sent a patrol of Thorneycroft's Mounted Infantry forward in a northerly direction alongside the railway; they contacted the Boers around Pieter's Station. Dundonald then brought up the rest of his brigade, and the forward patrol suffered a few casualties. The infantry came forward; General Lyttelton's division occupied Pieter's railway station. Once this was accomplished, Dundonald moved northward again, and coming to a hill-crest, discovered a Boer laager immediately behind it. The Boers, without hesitation, mounted and came straight at the British, but were met by machine-gun fire which emptied 'many saddles' and scattered the Boers to both flanks.

Meanwhile General Burn-Murdoch's regulars had broken out eastward into the open ground and towards Umbulwana Mountain. Here they were met by three Boer heavy guns which shelled, particularly, the 13th Hussars. Again Dundonald's soldiers advanced and occupied kopjes in front of them. It was at this point that a bit of military wheeling and dealing occurred. Lord Dundonald was approached by Captain Bottomley, commanding a squadron of the Imperial Light Horse, and the Captain reminded his lordship of a promise which he had made 'weeks before', that if possible, Captain Bottomley's squadron 'should lead the advance on Ladysmith'. Now, on that day, Colonel Thorneycroft was leading the advance, and it was Dundonald's normal policy not to make fundamental changes of this nature on any day. However, a promise was a promise, and Dundonald sent for Major Hubert Gough and told him that his composite regiment was to do the scouting for the brigade on that day, thereby relieving Thorneycroft's Mounted Infantry. Gough was leading the Imperial Light Horse and the Natal Carabineers.

Then Dundonald, having made these delicate rearrangements took his brigade in a more eastward direction towards Umbulwana, but there came under the Boer heavy-gun fire and turned his brigade northward again. At 3 p.m. Dundonald received a message from Major Gough, stating that the ridge in front of him was unoccupied and asking what he should do. Dundonald replied, 'Take your regiment on the hill and I will support.' Major Hubert Gough, as he then was, wrote:

... my main body were crossing a flat, open space towards this ridge when the Boers fired one shell from the big gun on Umbulwana Mountain ... They had not got our range very accurately, and this one shell went plump into the ground about three hundred yards to my right. I had an uneasy feeling that there were more to follow, with perhaps the range more accurately fixed, but nevertheless I determined to take a chance and continue our advance . . .

I had just reached the ridge in front of me when an orderly galloped up and thrust a note into my hand. It was an order from Dundonald 'to retire at once'. This last shell fired by the Boers shook him, and it might have succeeded in bringing our entry into Ladysmith that day to an abrupt conclusion! . . .

From where I now was I could look across the plain of Ladysmith and see the tin roofs of its houses about three miles away. I had not the slightest intention of obeying the order to retire. I just crumpled the note up and threw it to the ground, telling the orderly to return to Dundonald and report that he had delivered the message.

Well, Hubert Gough was ever a difficult man, but timidity was never one of his faults, and, inevitably, forward he went. They rode into Intombi hospital. Hubert Gough related:

As we rode into this camp we were greeted with cheers, shouts and tears of surprise and delight – but they were tears of happiness and relief. Doctors, nurses, orderlies and every convalescent who could get off his bed, swarmed round us, shaking us by the hand and patting our knees as we sat on our horses. It was the first scene in what was the most moving drama in the lives of the 120 or so British soldiers who made up my two squadrons.

I now made up my mind to proceed straight on into Ladysmith, but two things had to be done first. I sent a message back to Dundonald, and, ignoring his order to retire, wrote that I was already within the Ladysmith perimeter, and was going on into the town at once. The second matter which had to be attended to was to arrange our entry into the town. It had to be conducted with dignity and in order! A strong feeling of emulation and rivalry existed between these two proud and grand squadrons [Imperial Light Horse and Natal Carabineers]. They felt that this was an historic moment for them. Who was to be the first to enter the beleaguered town? I think I came to a solution worthy of Solomon! All scouts were recalled and the squadrons were to ride in side by side, each in double file, so we still presented a front of fours. Bottomley and Bridges [afterwards Sir Tom Bridges – a Governor of one of the Australian States] rode at the head of the little column of Imperial Light Horsemen, Mackenzie and one of his officers rode at the head of the column of Natal Carabineers. I rode at the head of the whole column. Honour was thus satisfied.

At this point one of Major Gough's troopers broke ranks, and galloped to the side of his commanding officer; this, from a military point of view, would seem to be reprehensible behaviour, till one learns that this trooper had been at Eton College with Gough. The trooper simply said to the Major: 'An Eton boy must be first into Ladysmith.' Whether he was allowed to stay up front and so overrule Gough's 'solution worthy of Solomon', I don't know. Anyway, Gough continued his story:

Personally I think it was the most moving moment of my life, up to that moment anyhow. After four months, while we had struggled to save the honour and safety of our country's arms, and had watched its fading fortunes with agony, and had thought of our many relations and friends gradually coming nearer and nearer to a surrender – a surrender which would have covered us with shame and certainly have shaken the Empire – suddenly to realise that all was saved – at long last. Victory naturally lifted a tremendous weight off every heart and filled us with elation, due to immense revulsion of feeling! But the relieving force maintained a dignified calm.

We advanced across the open plain at a walk towards the town – still nearly three miles distant. The steep and rugged heights of Caesar's Camp and Wagon Hill were passed close on our left and we could see some of our men in the sangars (stone defences) standing up to gaze at us, and to make sure that this was the head of Buller's relieving army at last. Then they stood up and waved their helmets and cheered. The plain seemed empty. We crossed the small Fourie's Spruit. A few poor, thin, starving horses were to be seen trying to pick up what grazing there was, and one or two men herded and guarded them. These were men of the main body of the Natal Carabineers, who had been shut up in the siege. They looked up and saw us coming!

Within the Ladysmith perimeter the Reverend Owen Watkins was on top of Observation Hill with some soldiers; they were watching the Boer exodus.

One who was sweeping the country with his glasses suddenly stopped with an exclamation: 'British Cavalry, by Jove! or I'm a Dutchman!' At first we would not believe, but at last we were convinced, for coming down the hill to the right of the Intombi Camp our incredulous eyes beheld three squadrons of British horse in a formation which never yet have Boers made.

Major Gough continued the story as he remembered it:

Suddenly one of them jumped up, climbed bare-backed on to a wretched worn-out horse and with nothing but a halter round its neck, kicked it, with a considerable display of energy, into a weak and lumbering canter, and advanced to meet us. He was so speechless with excitement that he could say nothing, but, taking off his slouch hat and waving it, he thrust it into my face as he passed shouting 'What ho!' He then galloped down the length of our column shouting 'What ho!' He never said another word till he found old friends in the column and joined them. After this preliminary but warm welcome we continued our advance till we arrived at the 'drift' (or ford) across the Klip River on which the town stands. As we entered the drift groups of some dozen horsemen were to be seen sitting on the high bank opposite, waiting to greet us. One of them dashed into the stream to meet us and shake me frantically by the hand. It was Captain Clive Dixon of my own regiment (16th Lancers) [the artist who compiled the famous 'Leaguer of Ladysmith' set of water-colour drawings] – a very old and dear friend. He was ADC to Sir George White, the commander of the Ladysmith garrison.

One of the horsemen who rode out from Ladysmith to meet Major Gough's patrol was Mr Watkins-Pitchford of the Natal Carabineers.

. . . across the plain we pelted as hard as we could gallop drawing nearer and nearer each moment to the dark mass of horsemen rapidly advancing towards us. At the end it was like a hostile cavalry charge rather than the meeting of two friendly bodies of men. As we drew within shouting range we yelled and howled like packs of wild dogs. Caps and helmets were waved, guns frantically brandished, horses plunged and bucked with fright, and in a moment the two columns were merged into a struggling mass of horsemen, besieged and deliverers mixed inextricably in one disorderly mass of cheering, laughing, gesticulating, hand-shaking, back-slapping men. All showed wear and tear. Tattered and lean and brown, the one side with privation and exposure and long anxiety, and the other with hard fighting and desperate derring-do.

As we plunged and slip down the steep drift to the river the scene was beyond description, the slipping, splashing horses and the excited shouting people on the banks above, mad with delight. It was a picture I would not have missed for anything. Ones heart was in ones throat all the time to see so much unalloyed human joy. Never this side of heaven can I hope to see such a scene of happiness, and it was all impromptu.

Hubert Gough continued his account of the first soldiers into Ladysmith:

As we climbed up the steep bank out of the stream, I was greeted by Sir George White himself. With him were Generals Ian Hamilton, Archie Hunter and Colonel Beauchamp-Duff and (I think) Brocklehurst, with his Brigade Major, Major Guy Wyndham, also of my own regiment. Sir George White only said: 'Hallo, Hubert, how are you?' – all very quiet and unemotional. I had known him very well when he was Commander-in-Chief in India, and had often dined at his house Snowden in Simla.

Mr Nevinson of the London *Daily Chronicle* witnessed Hubert Gough and his men enter the town itself:

About six [p.m.] I had driven out (being still enfeebled with fever) to King's Post, to see the tail-end of the Boer wagons disappear. On returning I found all the world running for all they were worth to the lower end of the High-Street and shouting wildly. The cause was soon evident. Riding up past the Anglican Church came a squadron of mounted infantry. They were not our own. Their horses were much too good, and they looked strange. Behind them came another and another. They had crossed the drift that leads to the road along the foot of Caesar's Camp past Intombi to Pieter's and Colenso. There was no mistake about it. They were the advance of the relief column, and more were coming behind. It was Lord Dundonald's Irregulars – Imperial Light Horse, Natal Carabineers, Natal Police, and Border Mounted Rifles.

Mr Donald Macdonald, of Australia's newspaper the *Morning Argus*, left his horseflesh dinner, and hurried, as best he could, into Ladysmith's High Street:

All the colours and all the nations of earth seemed blended together in a con-fused throng, all its tongues raised in one exultant din. It was worth having lived and suffered through the siege for that supreme hour. In the rush to the river were the red fezes of the Malays, for once roused from their Oriental stoicism. Mixed up with them were the parti coloured turbans of the coolies and dhoolie-bearers, their white clothing flapping in the wind over their spindle shanks, bare from the knees. The Zulus and Kaffirs were delirious. They leaped into the air and sang and shouted, their white teeth and white eyeballs gleaming. The hospitals had poured out their sick and wounded; all rushed to join in the paean of welcome. There were soldiers with white and shrunken faces; men wounded in the legs, who shuffled slowly down the road. One poor young infantry officer had stopped at a deep street channel – he had not strength to step over it. I lifted him to the other side but it was no trouble, he was light as a child. Two other officers drove down in a pony trap, and the ghastliness of their faces impressed one, even in that time of wild excitement. They were, in plain and painful truth, living skeletons. An old Kaffir woman tottered along the footpath, her tears streaming down her face. 'Listen to her; listen to her,' said a Natal farmer. 'That's good, isn't it?' I could listen, but not understand, so he interpreted. The words the Kaffir woman spoke were really the sentiment of that time of triumph. 'The English can conquer everything but death; why can't they conquer death?'

There has been some difference of opinion as to when, exactly, Lord Dundonald entered Ladysmith. Major Hubert Gough, who was not short of spleen, records that he was actually dining with Sir George White and his staff that evening, when:

. . . the door suddenly opened and Dundonald and Winston Churchill burst in, considerably heated, and somewhat excited after their long gallop of about six miles – for Dundonald must have been in or near Nelthorpe when my message reached him, telling him that I was already inside the Ladysmith defences, and was going straight into the town. He and Churchill at once decided they must come in too; and leaving his brigade without any orders, Dundonald started, accompanied by Churchill, to gallop after me in the hope of being present at my meeting with Sir George White. It must have taken them a good hour to get into Ladysmith, galloping on indifferent ponies over what was, at times, pretty rough going, and a good deal of scrub and almost in the dark.

Mr Watkins-Pitchford, writing to his wife from Ladysmith, corroborates Major Gough's version of who got into Ladysmith and when. He inscribed, in sudden capital letters 'DUNDONALD HAD NO MORE HAND IN THE RELIEF OF LADYSMITH THAN I HAD! And all reports as to his brilliant action in being first into the place are false.'

What is certain is that Lord Dundonald was about six miles south of Ladysmith when he received Major Gough's peremptory announcement that he was taking his patrol straight into the town. It is also true that Dundonald decided to go forward himself without his brigade. He argued that since the area ahead had not been properly scouted, he could not be sure how many Boers might still be capable of attacking his brigade's flanks; so he sent it back under the command of Colonel Thorneycroft. Dundonald then selected 'Major Birdwood, Lieutenant Clowes, Lieutenant Winston Churchill, and some orderlies' to gallop with him to Ladysmith. Winston Churchill takes up the story:

Never shall I forget that ride. The evening was deliciously cool. My horse was strong and fresh, [not the 'indifferent ponies' of Gough's imagination] for I had changed him at midday. The ground was rough with many stones, but we cared little for that. Beyond the next ridge, or the rise beyond that, or around the corner of the hill, Ladysmith – the goal of all our hopes and ambitions during weeks of almost ceaseless fighting. Ladysmith – the centre of the world's attention, the scene of famous deeds, the cause of mighty efforts – Ladysmith was within our reach at last. We were going to be inside the town within an hour. The excitement of the moment was increased by the exhilaration of the gallop. Onward wildly, recklessly, up and down hill, over the boulders, through the scrub, Hubert Gough with his two squadrons, Mackenzie's Natal Carabineers and the Imperial Light Horse, were clear of the ridges already. We turned the shoulder of a hill, and there before us lay the tin houses and dark trees we had come so far to see and save.

Suddenly there was a challenge. 'Halt, who goes there?' 'The Ladysmith Relief Column', and thereat from out of trenches and rifle pits artfully concealed in the scrub a score of tattered men came running, cheering feebly, and some were crying. In the half light they looked ghastly pale and thin. A poor, white-faced officer waved his helmet to and fro, and laughed foolishly, and the tall, strong colonial horsemen, standing up in their stirrups, raised a loud resounding cheer, for then we knew we had reached the Ladysmith picket line.

Presently we arranged ourselves in military order, Natal Carabineers and Imperial Light Horse riding two and two and two abreast so that there might be no question about precedence, and with Gough, the youngest regimental commander in the army, and one of the best, at the head of the column, we forded the Klip River and rode into the town.

Now, either Gough or Churchill was a bloody liar. Perhaps Lord Dundonald clears up the matter to some extent. Dundonald wrote: 'We then continued our gallop and reached Ladysmith some few minutes after the Natal Carabineers and Imperial Light Horse had passed across the river into the town.'

Australian war-correspondent Donald Macdonald, however, confuses the issue by writing:

Then they formed up their detachments side by side and so came in together, with Dundonald . . . They swung into the main street, marching through a living avenue of cheering men and women, whom they had placed under a life-long obligation, while the little ones were hoisted on shoulders for a look at the long-looked-for relief column. And in the half-light of moon and twilight Sir George White and his Staff galloped round the corner, and the leaders shook hands.

Then the long-pent-up excitement and enthusiasm burst forth in a very tumult of joy, and none who were privileged to see and hear it will ever forget. Men were no longer ashamed of their emotions. They cheered and laughed and even cried, for there was a catch in the voice and tears streaming down many a face, and women, more deeply moved, caught up their little ones and kissed them, and thanked God for their preservation and deliverance. Surely it was the greatest sight, that little gathering of mud-stained, battle-worn riflemen, that the eye of man ever looked upon. So we, who were so deeply concerned, thought it.

Cheers for the relief column, cheers for Buller, but loudest, and most heartfelt, cheers for Sir George White. There was something of filial affection in the ovation that the garrison gave its General. Long before there had been impatience, sometimes irritation, born of the feeling that it was not right for ten thousand of the pick of Britain's soldiers to sit down there and endure insult and aggression. All that had long since died away, and, repentant that they had, in their ignorance, wronged this grand old soldier, they made it up to him now in the fulness of their hearts, in their hour of succour and exultation. They gathered about him, caught his bridle-rein and stirrup-leathers, hung around his horse, and cheered until the flying rear-guard of the Boer army must have heard them over the ridges . . . The bowed back of the old fighter straightened, his sunken cheeks flushed, and his eyes shone. He had borne disappointment after disappointment – a responsibility the weight of which few could share, and this, too, was his reward. More than once he tried to speak and failed. Fifty years of soldiering and the subjugation of the weaker man were not equal to that great occasion.

Because the people of Ladysmith crowded round old Sir George White VC so closely, in a bond of fellowship that was born of their shared suffering, he could get no further than the vicinity of the gaol. Here the Boer prisoners were kept and from a wire-enclosed balcony they could view the strange spectacle below them – with very mixed feelings. Suddenly there was a lull in the celebratory noise, and Sir George White spoke 'in a voice trembling with emotion, but clear and soldierly for all that'. Sir George White said:

I thank you men, one and all, from the bottom of my heart, for the help and support you have given to me, and I shall always acknowledge it to the end of my life. It grieved me to have to cut your rations, but I promise you that I will not do it again. I thank God we have kept the flag flying.

And that last sentence became the famous slogan of the siege of Ladysmith: 'I thank God we have kept the flag flying.' Three cheers were given for Sir George White – and for Sir Redvers Buller. Then the people stood in the streets of Ladysmith and sang 'God Save the Queen', 'in every possible key and pitch'. And they say the cheering went on and on. Immediately after this, Sir George White ordered a roll-call of the number of men in the garrison of Ladysmith who were fit enough to pursue the Boers. The result was found to be very small. Many of the soldiers volunteered, but after a hurried medical check, only 2000 out of the entire force were found fit enough to go. They were ordered to prepare themselves to move northward along the Newcastle road on the following morning. Colonel W. G. Knox would command them, and men from the 1st Liverpools, the 1st Devons, the 2nd Gordons, the 5th Dragoons, the 19th Hussars and the 53rd and 67th Batteries of the Royal Field Artillery, were represented.

That evening of 28 February 1900, the evening that Ladysmith was relieved, Sir George White gave a small celebratory dinner party in his residence, up on Convent Hill. At 7 p.m. the guests assembled. Dundonald was there – having first sent a message to Buller, 'Am in Ladysmith. Dundonald' – Major Hubert Gough was present and so, of course, was Winston Churchill. The officers in charge of Sir George White's mess had kept a few luxuries aside for this very occasion – whenever it might come – and now, two bottles of champagne and 'a tin or two of sardines' were shared around. Sir George was at the head of the table, and Major Gough reports that he was at his right side with General Hunter on his other side. Winston Churchill wrote of the occasion:

That night I dined with Sir George White, who had held the town for four months against all comers, and was placed next to Hamilton, who won the fight at

Elandslaagte and beat the Boers off Wagon Hill, and next but one to Hunter, whom everyone said was the finest man in the world. Never before had I sat in such brave company nor stood so close to a great event. As the war drives slowly to its close more substantial triumphs, larger battles, wherein the enemy suffers heavier loss, the capture of towns, and the surrender of armies may mark its progress. But whatever victories the future may have in store, the defence and relief of Ladysmith, because they afford, perhaps, the most remarkable examples of national tenacity and perseverance which our history contains, will not be soon forgotten by the British people, whether at home or in the Colonies.

Meanwhile, out on Pieter's Hill and Railway Hill, on Inniskilling Hill, and Wynne Hill, and in the area north of Colenso, thousands of Buller's soldiers lay down to sleep, while a sub-tropical rain storm poured down on them. From this time onwards, Buller was going to be more cautious and bumbling than he had ever been before.

At 4.30 a.m. on 1 March, Lord Dundonald had a breakfast of sausages in Ladysmith. At 5 a.m. he joined Major Hubert Gough and his composite regiment on parade, and then they all rode back south to join Dundonald's Irregular Brigade; with them went Colonel Sir Henry Rawlinson, one of Sir George White's staff, to report to General Buller the known situation around Ladysmith . . . On the ride south, Lord Dundonald suddenly realized what was in the sausages, and he was nearly sick.

When Buller received White's message from the hands of Rawlinson, it made no difference to his timid tortoise plans whatsoever. Two thousand half-starved soldiers from Ladysmith could totter northwards as far as they could manage, but Buller's men would not be permitted to co-operate. Buller's orders to his army and the seventy-five wagons of medical supplies and food for Ladysmith, was to 'move in the direction of Ladysmith'. It must be remembered that on that very day, hordes of Boers were fleeing northward, but still were close in to the west and east of Ladysmith. And it must also be remembered that those supplies were desperately needed by the starving and dying.

Buller's most positive contribution for the day was his order issued to his cavalry: 'The Force will move in the direction of Ladysmith; 1st Cavalry Brigade [Burn-Murdoch] covering the right front and right flank of the advance; 2nd Cavalry Brigade [Dundonald] the left front and left flank. Each Brigade will detach a squadron as rear-guard to the whole Force.'

Dundonald took his brigade as far as Nelthorpe and there bivouacked. Burn-Murdoch pushed his brigade across the swollen Klip river and actually got to the foot of Umbulwana Mountain and there heard firing close by. But Burn-Murdoch made the monstrous error of sending a galloper back to Buller, to secure permission to attack, and received for his bureaucratic pains a strong order from Buller not to move an inch. In actual fact a patrol of the Imperial Light Horse under Major Karri Davies, acting on their own initiative and therefore with no inhibitions from Buller, rode up one side of Umbulwana while the Boers were loading their notorious 'Long Tom' gun on the other side, for transport to Modder Spruit station, just north of Ladysmith. That last Boer train left Modder Spruit for the north at 11 a.m. If Buller had attacked the Boers during their chaotic withdrawal, the Second Boer War would have been of shorter duration than it was. The Boer General Ben Viljoen wrote: 'The British must have been so overjoyed at the relief of Ladysmith that Generals Buller and White did not think it necessary to pursue us, at any rate for some time, a consideration for which we were profoundly grateful.'

My old Boer friend, Mr Dommisse of Pretoria, was present during the Boer retreat, and he said to me:

The Commandos were falling back across the Klip river, and it really was, to a certain extent – well, the Commandos were really disorganized – they were not fleeing, but they were retreating in a more or less disorganized way. It was a great trek and at the Sunday's river there was only one bridge. We were ordered to cross that bridge. It took days and days before all the Commandos had crossed the Sunday's river. I saw General Joubert standing on the bridge of Sunday's river, trying to stop the burghers – trying to stop them – trying to organize them again, and show defence. But he couldn't succeed. They pushed him aside; they really pushed him aside, and I remember the words he said, 'May the heavens fall upon you.'

Generals Louis Botha and Lucas Meyer had persuaded some Boers to hold a rear-guard position north and east of Modder Spruit, which is a few miles north of Ladysmith. In this direction the Ladysmith detachment of 2000 starving men marched; there were some 'skeleton horses'. This force advanced to Long Hill, north-east of Ladysmith, and then moved west and occupied Pepworth Hill without any opposition. They then moved their artillery down to Limit Hill, and from there were actually able to shell several Boer ox-wagons. And finally, Major Abdy was able to move his 53rd Battery, Royal Field Artillery, to a hill spur overlooking Modder Spruit Station; from there they fired on Boers who were loading several trains, and on to a large Boer camp in the vicinity. Ladysmith's infantry also joined in with long-range rifle fire and the Boers replied with vigour. The last Boer train moved out of Modder Spruit station, crossed the Modder Spruit bridge and stopped. A Boer got out of the train and ran to the bridge and back to the train again. Suddenly the bridge exploded into the air and the train puffed northward. The Ladysmith soldiers could do nothing further; they rested where they were, cruelly exhausted. They had suffered very light casualties: two officers and six men wounded; but they had done all they were physically capable of doing. Buller was preparing to make his personal entry into Ladysmith while his formidable army waited on those Tugela hills. General Lyttelton was the most articulate senior officer present, and he said about Buller's failure to pursue the Boers: '... dispirited by defeat, encumbered by a huge train of wagons, the Sunday river in blood behind them with only one bridge, they were at our mercy. Few commanders have so wantonly thrown away so great an opportunity.'

Buller first called at Intombi hospital; there is no denying his concern for suffering. At midday he entered Ladysmith and the townspeople went out to meet him, headed by Sir George White and his staff. Though even on this occasion Buller appears to have made a hash of it. W. Dickson arrived with his film-unit and wrote in his diary: 'General Buller made an unofficial entrance into the town from the opposite side, the people all having congregated at the Iron Bridge entrance.' However, the generals repaired to the convent, on Convent Hill, for a discussion.

To the credit of the Royal Engineers' Telegraph Department, one hour after this meeting the wires had been completed to the south and the war-correspondents were able to telegraph their stories. But the first message that went was to Her Majesty Queen Victoria, officially announcing the relief of Ladysmith. A reply came back to Sir Redvers Buller: 'Thank God for news you have telegraphed to me; congratulate you and all under you with all my heart. – V.R.I.' And Buller replied to this: 'Troops much appreciate your Majesty's kind telegram. Your Majesty cannot know how much your sympathy has helped to inspire them.'

Also on 1 March, a number of the Naval Brigade, who had been blasting their way for many weeks to the relief of Ladysmith, decided to travel the ten miles to visit in particular their fellow seafarers belonging to HMS *Powerful*. Captain Jones RN wrote in his despatch: '... before leaving crammed our holsters with whisky, tobacco, and cigarettes for the *Powerfuls*, but our route lying through the neutral camp and hospital of Itombi [*sic*], we were pretty well plundered before we ever saw them.'

And on that day Colonel Ian Hamilton wrote to his wife 'on half a sheet of foolscap':

Buller has just come in, and one of his staff tells me that if I write a line just now whilst he is drinking some beer he will get it in time for the English mail tonight . . . Well, darling, I have had a hard time there's no doubt about it. For more than 100 days always the chance of being bowled over by night just as much as by day. It is impossible that such close association with death should not in some way change one's views and it has made me personally think a good deal more seriously about religion and many other sides of life. It may be a case of 'when the devil was sick, etc.' but I do not aim quite so high as the devil did on that occasion and so the fall may not be so great either. I have been in fine health lately, until about a week ago when my poor inside began to revolt against the diet of horseflesh and biscuits provided for it, and I am a bit fine-drawn . . . I need not tell you, darling, how much you have been in my thoughts all this trying time. I think you know it . . .

On 3 March 1900, Buller's army made its formal entry into the town of Ladysmith. Lieutenant-Colonel Grant wrote:

Like all the really pregnant things of the earth, it is beyond the art of the word-painters, who have tried their skill upon it and often spoilt it, painting cheering, dancing figures, tears and antics of joy, embracings. There was none of this: the garrison were but just able to stand, much less dance; hundreds could not stand, but crouched or sat in the ranks, a piteous guard of honour.

Winston Churchill, on this occasion, stood on Ladysmith's High Street, amongst the waiting garrison:

At eleven o'clock precisely the relieving army began to march into the town. First of all rode Sir Redvers Buller with his headquarters staff and an escort of the Royal Dragoons. The infantry and artillery followed by brigades, but in front of all, as a special recognition of their devoted valour, marched the Dublin Fusiliers, few, but proud.

Many of the soldiers, remembering their emerald island, had fastened sprigs of green to their helmets, and all marched with a swing that was wonderful to watch.

Sir Redvers Buller, riding at the head of his army, noted the soldiers of Ladysmith lining his route. 'I was shocked to see how attenuated the men were, and I perceived that they were very much weaker than I had been led to expect.'

Colonel Grant continued his account:

The bronzed sweating thousands passed through that army of shrunken ghosts in all but absolute silence, more eloquent than volleys of hurras. The only approach to cheering I heard was a long murmur, more like a sigh than a cheer, which rippled along the lines as the vanguard of Dublins swung in sight, and a subdued shout as the Devons and Rifle Brigade swept through their brother ranks at four miles an hour, glancing from side to side, with a rough hail here and there as old pals caught each other's eyes, but mostly in silence.

Two old friends of mine were in Ladysmith on that day. Mr Packer of the 2nd Middlesex Regiment marched through with the relieving force, and he described to me that after emptying his pockets which were 'full of rain' from the preceding night, they entered Ladysmith.

. . . the first thing I noticed when I went in was the clock tower of the Town Hall; it had a shell right through it. We met a lot of those sailors from the *Powerful* – and they was all asking about different places in London, and how things were getting on. Of course they looked a bit starved like; they looked a bit white, you know.

I asked Mr Packer if the relieving force got a good reception as they marched along Ladysmith's High Street, and he replied, 'Well, they cheered and all that, but they didn't make much fuss of us – though they was glad to see us like; to relieve them like.'

My other friend, Mr George Hall, the Royal Engineer from Newcastle, was one of the garrison who lined the streets, and he told me of his memories:

. . . we were lined up on the roadside. And a thing I never seen before – was a unit coming up the road. Our old major, an old tyrant – he bawled at us: 'Slope arms!' 'Present arms!' What the hell's the matter here, we asked ourselves. And then the salute: 'Eyes right!' Then of course we tumbled it when we saw a sergeant wearing the Yellow Badge. The danger badge of the Royal Engineers – what do they call it now – Explosives? They were big, bronze, dirty looking fellows; we were standing weak-kneed, starving. It was a sight!

The Reverend Owen Watkins, Wesleyan Chaplain, stood and watched Buller and his soldiers coming in:

One regiment I noted was commanded by a captain; his seniors were all either wounded or killed; many companies were commanded by mere boys fresh from Sandhurst, and in nearly all half the officers were missing.

The heroes looked dirty and war-worn, but were proud and happy, and as they passed they threw to us, their comrades, treasured plugs of tobacco, which had long been laid by for 'the poor beggars in Ladysmith'. The contrast between the robust and bearded veterans of a dozen battles, and the pale, emaciated defenders of Ladysmith was great – till then we had not realised how wasted and weak we were.

Sir George White, Victoria Cross, was quiet and unostentatious to the end. Colonel Grant wrote: 'Not one man in a thousand perceived Sir George White sitting upon his horse in front of the Town Hall, with that on his handsome face which would have been worth 500 guineas on canvas.' And finally, as the last of Buller's army passed, the Mayor of Ladysmith, Mr Joseph Farquhar, advanced towards Sir George and asked him to receive an address of thanks which the townspeople of Ladysmith had prepared and were anxious to present to him. The general dismounted slowly from his horse and stood on the steps of the Town Hall for the simple ceremony. General White replied, complimenting the people on their behaviour during the siege, and thanking them for the way they had borne so many hardships – and he said that he rejoiced with them that because of their devotion and the bravery of the soldiers, they had all kept the Queen's flag flying over Ladysmith. There were cheers, and all the tired people went back to their homes.

That day General Buller published an address to the Natal Field Force, in his army orders:

Soldiers of Natal,

The relief of Ladysmith unites two forces, both of which have, during the last four months, striven with conspicuous gallantry and splendid determination to maintain the honour of their Queen and country.

The garrison of Ladysmith have during four months held their position against every attack with complete success and endured many privations with admirable fortitude.

The relieving force has had to force its way through an unknown country across an unfordable river and over almost inaccessible heights, in the face of a fully prepared, well-armed and tenacious enemy. By the exhibition of the truest courage, the courage which burns steadily as well as flashes brilliantly, it has accomplished its object and added a glorious page to the history of the British Empire.

Ladysmith has been relieved. Sailors and soldiers, colonials and homebreds, have done this, united by the one desire, inspired by one patriotism.

The GOC congratulates both forces on the martial qualities which they have shown; he thanks them for their determined efforts, and desires to offer his sincere sympathy to the relations and friends of those good soldiers and gallant comrades who have fallen in the fight. – (Signed) Redvers Buller, General.

Z WAS OUR **Z**EAL

SINGING

"GOD SAVE

THE QUEEN."

EPILOGUE

AND so Ladysmith, the Aldershot of South Africa, was relieved. The rejoicing that rang around the British Empire was a psychological response to the end of a series of astonishing and embarrassing defeats. Remember we were – as Colonel Lang, an old British veteran of the war, once said to me – 'God's Almighty'. The relief was not only for Ladysmith; it was for every far flung corner of the British Empire. The British – particularly the English – went potty with joy. Canon Rawnsley wrote:

The Relief of Ladysmith

To General Sir Redvers Buller, February 28, 1900.

LADYSMITH ours?
Now praised be the powers!
    Here's to you, Buller, my heart and my hand!
Bells rouse the people,
And flags from each steeple
    Flutter to utter the joy of the land.

[Four more verses followed.]

And to add to Britain's euphoria, on the day before Hubert Gough and Winston and the other tearaways entered Ladysmith, that is, on 27 February 1900, Lord Roberts' army had inflicted a terrible defeat on General Cronje's army of Boers, over at Paardeberg on the Cape–Orange Free State front.

On 18 February the British trapped and surrounded these Boers who were over-encumbered with wagons, women and children. It was assumed that they must immediately capitulate, but old Cronje was specific: 'I will never surrender. If you wish to bombard, fire away.' Kitchener was in charge because Lord Roberts was ill, and with uncalled-for brutality he ordered the most callous assault. Particularly brutal and stupid for his own British soldiers. Kitchener ordered units of the mounted infantry to charge the Boer position. He arrogantly stated: 'We'll be in the laager by half past ten!' Colonel Hannay, commanding the 1st Mounted Infantry Brigade, recognizing the dangerous idiocy of Kitchener's order, but not being able to disobey, rode alone on horseback to a suicidal death, to demonstrate that no others must follow him.

The Boers fought back on 18 February, on the 19th, 20th, 21st, 22nd, 23rd, 24th, 25th, 26th and then, on the 27th, from positions where the stench and suffering were unbearable, they surrendered. Four thousand of them. This Boer disaster over to the west and the British advance to the relief of Ladysmith was decisive in one way. It became clear to the Boers that they could no longer face the great British armies in set-piece battles.

My old friend, Mr Dommisse of Pretoria, described to me the day of decision:

The commandos then fell back on Kroonstad [in the Orange Free State] . . . there was President Steyn, there was General de Wet, there was General de la Rey, General Botha, and Paul Kruger, the president. Paul Kruger came up trying to stop the burghers, the commandos, from falling back. Well, he did not succeed. Even Paul Kruger. He was there with a carriage drawn by four mules, with a detachment of ZARPS, South African Mounted Police. The bombs were falling near Paul Kruger and General de Wet came up to him and begged him to retreat – 'for God's sake because I can't protect you and I don't want to see you killed here'. The commanders called a council-of-war and they decided that they would defend the country to the last man. Their decision was taken with President Steyn, de la Rey and the others which I have just mentioned. The way of fighting was awkward at that time – to defend a position against an army of sixty thousand men was regarded as useless. So to my mind, the guerilla war was started at that date, at Kroonstad.

Incidentally, by a cruel or a splendid coincidence, depending upon whose side you are on, 27 February was the anniversary of the British defeat on Majuba Mountain in 1881. 27 February is Majuba Day.

Back in Ladysmith, Buller wrote to his family in England:

Here I am at last. I thought I was never going to get through here. We have had a hard busy time and I have not been able to write to you for the last three mails. I really have not had time to eat and sleep, much less write. However, it is all over and well over, thank God . . .

I must say the men were grand: they meant to do it, and it was a real pleasure to command them. It has all seemed to me like a dream. Every day some new complication to meet, and every day the same roar of guns and rattle of musketry, with, alas, every day the long list of killed and wounded, which is what I cannot bear. However, I thought if I got in it would cost me 3000 men, and I hope I have done it under 2000, which is something. Congratulatory telegrams of all sorts are pouring in upon me, and I feel that the great British public will like it none the less because there has been a butcher's bill . . .

Two days after the relief of Ladysmith, Sir George White's failing health seriously declined. He pencilled a note to his wife: 'Struck down by severe attack of fever. Cannot write more – have wired. Don't be anxious, dear.'

Sir George was invalided home to England. He voyaged in the *Dunvegan Castle* and arrived at Southampton on 14 April 1900. His health improved and he was appointed Governor of Gibraltar. This duty continued until 1905 when he was offered the Governorship of the Royal Hospital, Chelsea. He remained there until he died on 24 June, 1912. He was a quiet, much respected man.

Buller held his ground in Natal. Lord Roberts was planning his massive advance across the two Boer republics. The two distinguished soldiers exchanged a remarkable number of messages. The basic trouble was that Lord Roberts was in command but General Buller didn't enjoy being commanded and no one was keen to remove him from his control of the Natal Field Force. In Ladysmith Buller's generals who had fought with him to cross the Tugela river, learnt for the first time about his telegram to Sir George White, suggesting the surrender of Ladysmith. Amongst the British officers, confidence in Buller was now very low. General Ian Hamilton wrote to the war-correspondent Spencer Wilkinson: 'Buller is no use . . . It is a question of life or death of ourselves here as well as of the empire in general, and I write to beg you to use all your influence to get the man recalled before he does more mischief . . .'

Well, Buller wasn't recalled. But his most lethal 'mischief' was behind him. From now on he would be extremely careful.

Lord Roberts moved and entered Bloemfontein, the capital of the Orange Free State, on 13 March 1900. On 30 May the British were in Johannesburg, and Lord Roberts' army entered the capital of the Transvaal, Pretoria, on 5 June 1900. President Kruger and his Government were moving eastward on a railway train towards Portuguese East Africa.

Buller and his army had crawled northward and on 6 August broke away from the railway between Volkrust and Standerton, both places in the Transvaal, and moved northward to co-operate directly at long last with Lord Roberts' army which was now advancing eastward. The two British armies were fighting together at the battle of Bergendal on 26 August 1900.

The British reached the eastern extremity of the Transvaal border. The country was apparently conquered and so on 6 October General Buller bade farewell to his men. Whatever the officers thought of him, Tommy Atkins held him in high regard; they stood along his route out of the Transvaal and cheered him. My old veteran friend, Mr George Hall of Newcastle, England, thought well of him seventy years later: 'We didn't like the way he was sent home. Among the rank and file we put it down as Lord Roberts' son being killed . . . Poor old fellow [Buller]; made a scapegoat.'

Another soldier wrote to England from South Africa, after Buller had left: 'There is no General now who comes round to see how we are getting on.' Well, that must be the sum of it: he loved them in his funny awkward way, so they returned love. The 'butcher's bill' was another matter altogether; and in Tommy Atkins' mind, quite beside the point.

And there were a few big-wigs on Buller's side. He was given a farewell banquet before he left South Africa and after receiving a sword of honour, Sir William Peace made a speech: 'Sir Redvers Buller had saved Natal, South Africa, and the British Empire.'

His ship arrived at Southampton on 9 November 1900 and enthusiasm for him seemed to be unreserved. Southampton gave him the Freedom of the Borough, Lord Wolseley met him personally, and the Queen sent for him. But the news of that surrender telegram and the handling and squabbles about Spion Kop were beginning to permeate the country, and a number of formidable enemies waited for retribution.

Buller was restored to his old appointment as General Officer Commanding at Aldershot. All seemed reasonably well for a short while. But then the criticisms began in earnest, culminating in a devastating attack in *The Times* which stated that he was not fit to be in command of the First Army Corps. That did it! Buller attended a luncheon given by the Queen's Westminster Volunteers and he fumbled his dangerous cards on the table. He said: 'I assert that there is no one in England junior to me who is as fit as I am!' He then put the rope around his own neck by trying to talk his way out of the surrender telegram issue. The powerful lads had had enough of him. He wasn't playing the Establishment's game and he was making an awful mess of his own. Lord Roberts turned against him, the new Secretary for War, St John Brodrick, turned nastily against him, and that wretched man Edward the Seventh turned against him. On 23 October 1901 poor old Buller was relieved of his command at Aldershot and was retired on England's *half* pay. Of course, if I have to choose between King Edward the Seventh and

Mr George Hall, I'll choose Mr Hall every day. 'Poor old fellow; made a scapegoat.'

On 2 June 1908 General the Right Honourable Sir Redvers Buller VC, GCB, GCMG died. His last words were: 'I am dying. Well, I think it is about time to go to bed now.'

So sure were the British that the war in South Africa was virtually over that on 1 September 1900 Lord Roberts proclaimed the annexation of the Transvaal Republic to the Queen's Empire. This, to unperceptive minds, seemed confirmed when President Paul Kruger left Portuguese East Africa on the Dutch cruiser *Gelderland* on 19 October 1900. The very old man was bound for exile in Europe where he died. At the end of November, Lord Roberts handed over his supreme command in South Africa to Lord Kitchener and returned to England. But before Bobs left he instituted the dreadful scorched-earth policy and the inevitable concentration camps. Inevitable, that is, if you decide on a scorched earth. Lord Roberts voyaged away from the cruel tragedy to a gigantic and loving reception in England. The Queen, of course, received him and he replaced Lord Wolseley as commander-in-chief of the British Army. Lord Roberts died in France in 1914 while visiting his half-frozen Indian soldiers, with whom he had served for forty-one years – but in warmer eastern climes.

The war in South Africa was not over. What was it that Kruger had said as the conflict became inevitable? 'The republics are determined, if they must belong to England, that a price will have to be paid which will stagger humanity.' Well, the Boers were now going to fulfil the old man's prophecy. They began to hit back at Kitchener's vast army with an awesome will. They instructed the world in the art of guerilla warfare. They lived off their burning land and fought at the gallop. Kitchener retaliated with great lines of barbed wire and block-houses stretching across and across southern Africa, and with massive sweeps by mounted soldiers. The Boers were never finally defeated in the field. They went on fighting until the end of May 1902. They had been fighting the weight of the British Empire for nearly three years. Now most of the fighting burghers were in rags and very hungry. Their women and children were in British concentration camps and in these camps something over twenty thousand women and children and old men had died, out of a very small – numerically, that is – nation. The breaking point of Boer determination to fight to the point of national extermination was close. It is not for me in this book to discuss the agonized debates that took place between the great Boer leaders: de la Rey, Louis Botha, President Steyn, Christian de Wet, Hertzog, Olivier, Smuts and President Schalk

Burger. They agonized over the humiliation of joining the British Empire. But two of them were young and knew that their starving burghers could not win by force of arms before extinction, and they looked at the brighter side of the potential British Commonwealth. These two, of course, were Jan Smuts and Louis Botha, and both in the years to come did more than anyone else, perhaps, to try and make the British Commonwealth a better ideal than it ever became.

At 11.05 p.m. on Saturday, 31 May 1902, the peace treaty was signed. During the negotiations Kitchener had astonishingly shown compassion for the Boer delegates; Milner, none.

Hertzog and Smuts had composed a statement which underlined their philosophy. I will give it in full:

We, the national representatives of both the South African Republic and the Orange Free State, at the meeting held at Vereeniging from the 15th of May till the 31st of May, 1902, have with grief considered the proposal made by His Majesty's Government [Queen Victoria had died] in connexion with the conclusion of the existing hostilities, and their communication that this proposal had to be accepted, or rejected, unaltered. We are sorry that His Majesty's Government has absolutely declined to negotiate with the Government of the Republics on the basis of their independence, or to allow our Government to enter into communication with our deputations in Europe. Our people, however, have always been under the impression that not only on the grounds of justice, but also taking into consideration the great material and personal sacrifices made for their independence, that they had a well-founded claim for that independence.

We have gravely considered the future of our country, and have specially observed the following facts:

Firstly, that the military policy pursued by the British military authorities has led to the general devastation of the territory of both Republics by the burning down of farms and towns, by the destruction of all means of existence, and by the exhausting of all resources required for the maintenance of our families, the existence of our armies, and the continuation of the war.

Secondly, that the placing of our families in the concentration camps has brought on an unheard-of condition of suffering and sickness, so that in a comparatively short time about twenty thousand of our beloved ones have died there, and that the horrid probability has arisen that, by continuing the war, our whole nation may die out in this way.

Thirdly, that the Kaffir tribes within and without the frontiers of the territory of the two Republics, are mostly armed and are taking part in the war against us, and through the committing of murders and all sorts of cruelties have caused an unbearable condition of affairs in many districts of both Republics. An instance of this happened not long ago in the district of Vryheid, where fifty-six burghers on one occasion were murdered and mutilated in a fearful manner.

Fourthly, that by the proclamations of the enemy the burghers still fighting are threatened with the loss of all their movable and landed property – and thus with utter ruin – which proclamations have already been enforced.

Fifthly, that it has already, through the circumstances of the war, become quite impossible for us to keep the many thousand prisoners of war taken by our forces, and that we have thus been unable to inflict much damage on the British forces (whereas the burghers who are taken prisoners by the British armies are sent out of the country), and that, after war has raged for nearly three years, there only remains an insignificant part of the fighting forces with which we began.

Sixthly, that this fighting remainder, which is only a small minority of our whole nation, has to fight against an overpowering force of the enemy, and besides is reduced to a condition of starvation, and is destitute of all necessaries, and that notwithstanding our utmost efforts, and the sacrifices of everything that is dear and precious to us, we cannot foresee an eventual Victory.

We are therefore of opinion that there is no justifiable ground for expecting that by continuing the war the nation will retain its independence, and that, under these circumstances, the nation is not justified in continuing the war, because this can only lead to social and material ruin, not for us alone, but also for our posterity. Compelled by the above named circumstances and motives, we commission both Governments to accept the proposal of His Majesty's Government, and to sign it in the name of the people of both Republics.

We, the representative delegates, express our confidence that the present circumstances will, by our accepting the proposal of His Majesty's Government, be speedily ameliorated in such a way that our nation will be placed in a position to enjoy the privileges to which they think they have a just claim, on the ground not only of their past sacrifices, but also of those made in this war.

We have with great satisfaction taken note of the decision of His Majesty's Government to grant a large measure of amnesty to the British subjects who have taken up arms on our behalf, and to whom we are united by bonds of love and honour; and express our wish that it may please His Majesty to still further this amnesty.

There were still about 22 000 Boers fighting on the veldt. They are known in the Republic of South Africa as 'the bitter-enders'. One of those bitter-enders is my friend Mr Dommisse of Pretoria, and he has related to me the arrival of the cruel news of peace:

... then we received a message that peace was declared and we went to a place near Heidelberg. The commandos, about six hundred men, gathered there and General Botha came riding up – that was about the 5th of June – and he told us all about peace; the terms of peace and so on. That we had to surrender arms – officers could retain their rifles. So the commando rode into Heidelberg and threw down their arms. But most of the men there – there was a little kopje – said: 'Surrender my rifle – never!' So they smashed them to pieces with rocks – threw them away. One old Oomie, as we called him, said: 'Oh no! I've taken this rifle from the khakis and I'm not going to hand it back to them!'

Well, that is the end of my story – but there is a question you may ask. How was it possible for the Boer commandos to keep on fighting till practically the last day of the war? How was it possible that twenty thousand Boers, with insufficient ammunition, and food, and clothing, and no doctors or heavy guns or ambulances, or anything like that, could hold back the British army of five hundred thousand men? How is it possible? That is a question worth answering – but I'm not going to give you that answer now.

BIBLIOGRAPHY

AMERY, L. S. (Editor), *The Times History of the War in South Africa 1899–1900*, vols 1, 2 & 3, Sampson Low, Marston & Co. Ltd, 1900–5.

ATKINS, JOHN BLACK, *The Relief of Ladysmith*, Methuen & Co., 1900.

BILLINGTON, ROLAND CECIL, *A Mule-Driver at the Front*, Chapman & Hall Ltd, 1901.

BULLER, GENERAL THE RT. HON. SIR REDVERS, *Evidence of General the Rt. Hon. Sir Redvers Buller, V.C., G.C.B., G.C.M.G., taken before the Royal Commissions on the War in South Africa*, Longmans, Green & Co., 1904.

BURLEIGH, BENNETT, *The Natal Campaign*, Chapman & Hall Ltd, 1900.

BURNE, LIEUTENANT, RN, *With the Naval Brigade in Natal*, Edward Arnold & Co., 1902.

CHURCHILL, WINSTON SPENCER, *London to Ladysmith via Pretoria*, Longmans, Green & Co., 1900. New York: Harcourt Brace Jovanovich (abridged, Harvest Books).

COLVIN, IAN, *The Life of Jameson*, vol 2, Edward Arnold & Co., 1922.

CONAN DOYLE, A., *The Great Boer War*, Smith, Elder & Co., 1900.

CROWE, GEORGE, *The Commission of H.M.S. Terrible*, George Newnes Ltd, 1903.

DAVIS, RICHARD HARDING, *With Both Armies in South Africa*, Charles Scribners & Son, 1900.

DAVIS, WEBSTER, *John Bull's Crime or Assaults on Republics*, Abbey Press, 1901.

DAVITT, MICHAEL, *The Boer Fight for Freedom*, Funk & Wagnalls Co., 1902. New York: Gordon Press.

DE LA WARR, THE EARL, *Some Reminiscences of the War in South Africa*, Hurst & Blackett Ltd, 1900.

DE VILLEBOIS-MAREUIL, COLONEL, *War Notes. The Diary of Colonel de Villebois-Mareuil*, Methuen & Co., 1902.

DICKSON, W. K.-L., *The Biograph in Battle*, T. Fisher Unwin, 1901.

DUNDONALD, LT.-GENERAL THE EARL OF, *My Army Life*, Edward Arnold & Co., 1926.

DURAND, SIR MORTIMER, *Field-Marshal Sir George White, O.M., V.C., G.C.B., G.C.S.I., G.C.M.G., G.C.I.E., D.C.L., LL.D.*, William Blackwood & Sons, Edinburgh & London, 1915.

ENGELENBURG, DR F. V., *General Louis Botha*, George G. Harrap & Co. Ltd, 1929.

FRENCH, MAJOR THE HON. GERALD, *The Life of Field-Marshal Sir John French*, Cassell & Co. Ltd, 1931.

GARDYNE, LT.-COLONEL A. D. GREENHILL, *The Life of a Regiment: a history of the Gordon Highlanders*, The Medici Society Ltd, 1939.

GARVIN, J. L., *The Life of Joseph Chamberlain*, Macmillan & Co. Ltd, 1934.

GIBBS, PETER, *Death of the Last Republic*, Frederick Muller Ltd, 1957.

GOUGH, GENERAL SIR HUBERT, *Soldiering On*, Arthur Baker Ltd, 1954. New York: Robert Speller and Sons.

HALDANE, GENERAL SIR AYLMER, *A Soldier's Saga*, William Blackwood & Sons Ltd, 1948.

HAMILTON, IAN, *The Happy Warrior: General Sir Ian Hamilton by his Nephew*, Cassell & Co. Ltd, 1966.

HAMILTON-BAYNES, THE RT. REV. ARTHUR, DD, BISHOP OF NATAL, *My Diocese During the War*, George Bell & Sons, 1900.

HART-SYNNOT, B. M. (Editor), *Letters of Major General Fitʒ Roy Hart-Synnot*, Edward Arnold, 1912.

HOLMES WILSON, CAPTAIN C., *The Relief of Ladysmith. The Artillery in Natal*, William Clowes & Son Ltd, 1901.

HOLT, EDGAR, *The Boer War*, Putnam, 1958.

HUTCHINSON, G. T., *Frank Rhodes*, Private, 1908.

JACSON, COLONEL M., *The Record of a Regiment of the Line*, Hutchinson & Co., 1908.

JEANS, SURGEON, T. T., RN (Editor), *Naval Brigades in the South African War*, Sampson Low, Marston & Co. Ltd, 1902.

JUTA, MARJORIE, *The Pace of the Ox*, Constable & Co. Ltd, 1936.

KNOX, E. BLAKE, *Buller's Campaign*, R. Brimley Johnson, 1902.

KRUGER, PAUL, *The Memoirs of Paul Kruger told by Himself*, 2 vols. T. Fisher Unwin, 1902. Port Washington, N.Y.: Kennikat Press, 1970.

KRUGER, RAYNE, *Good-Bye Dolly Gray*, Cassell, 1959.

LINES, G. W., *The Ladysmith Siege 2nd November 1899–1st March 1900*, Wilson's Music & General Printing Co. Ltd, n.d.

MACDONALD, DONALD, *How We Kept the Flag Flying*, Ward, Lock & Co. Ltd, n.d.

MCHUGH, R. J., *The Siege of Ladysmith*, Chapman & Hall, 1900.

MCKENZIE, FREDERICK A., *Paul Kruger*, James Bowden, n.d.

MAHAN, CAPTAIN A. T., USN, *The Story of the War in South Africa*, Sampson Low, Marston & Co., 1900. Westport, Connecticut: Greenwood Press.

MALLET, VICTOR, *Life With Queen Victoria*, John Murray, 1968.

MARAIS, J. S., *The Fall of Kruger's Republic*, Oxford, Clarendon Press, 1961. New York: Oxford University Press, 1961.

MARLING, COLONEL SIR PERCIVAL, *Rifleman and Hussar*, John Murray, 1931.

MEINTJES, JOHANNES, *De la Rey: Lion of the West*, Hugh Keartland Publishers, 1966.

MEINTJES, JOHANNES, *General Louis Botha*, Cassell, 1970.

MELVILLE, COLONEL SIR C. H., CMG, *Life of General the Right Hon. Redvers Buller, V.C., G.C.B., G.C.M.G.*, 2 vols, Edward Arnold & Co., 1923.

NEVINSON, H. W., *Ladysmith: Diary of a Siege*, Methuen & Co., 1900.

O'MOORE, MACCARTHY, *The Romance of the Boer War*, Elliot Stock, 1901.

PEARSE, H. H. S., *Four Months Besieged: The Story of Ladysmith. Unpublished Letters from the Special Correspondent of the Daily News*, Macmillan & Co. Ltd, 1900.

PRIOR, MELTON, *Campaigns of a War Correspondent*, Edward Arnold, 1912.

RALPH, JULIAN, *Towards Pretoria*, C. Arthur Pearson Ltd, 1900.

RANSFORD, OLIVER, *The Battle of Spion Kop*, John Murray, 1969. New York: International Publications Service, 1969.

REITZ, DENYS, *Commando*, Faber & Faber Ltd, 1929. Mystic, Connecticut: Lawrence Verry, 1968.

ROMER, MAJOR C. F. & MAINWARING, MAJOR A. E. *The Second Battalion Royal Dublin Fusiliers in the South African War*, A. L. Humphreys, 1908.

ST JOHN GORE, LT.-COLONEL (Editor), *The Green Horse in Ladysmith*, Sampson Low, Marston & Co. Ltd, 1901.

SALT, LIEUTENANT GEORGE, *Letters and Diary of George Salt during the War in South Africa 1899–1900*, John Murray, 1902.

SMYTH, MAJOR B., *A History of the Lancashire Fusiliers*, vol 2, Sackville Press, 1904.

STERNBERG, COUNT, *My Experiences of the Boer War*, Longmans, Green & Co., 1901.

STIRLING, JOHN, *Our Regiments in South Africa*, William Blackwood & Sons, 1903.

STIRLING, JOHN, *The Colonials in South Africa*, William Blackwood & Sons, 1907.

SYKES, JESSICA, *Side Lights on the War*. T. Fisher Unwin, 1900.

SYMONS, JULIAN, *Buller's Campaign*, The Cresset Press, 1963. Chester Springs, Pennsylvania: Dufour Editions, 1963.

THOROLD, ALGAR LABOUCHERE, *The Life of Henry Labouchere*, Constable & Co. Ltd, 1913.

TREVES, FREDERICK, *The Tale of a Field Hospital*, Cassell & Co. Ltd, 1900.

VAN WARMELO, DIETLOF, *On Commando*, Methuen & Co., 1902.

VERNER, LT.-COLONEL WILLOUGHBY, (Editor), *The Rifle Brigade Chronicle for 1900*, John Bale, Sons & Danielsson Ltd, 1901.

VILJOEN, GENERAL BEN, *My Reminiscences of the Anglo-Boer War*, Hood, Douglas & Howard, 1902. Mystic, Connecticut: Lawrence Verry, 1973.

WATKINS, OWEN S., *Chaplains at the Front: by One of Them*, S. W. Partridge & Co., 1901.

WATKINS-PITCHFORD, H., *Besieged in Ladysmith*, Pietermaritzburg, Shuter & Shooter, 1964.

WRENCH, JOHN EVELYN, *Alfred Lord Milner*, Eyre & Spottiswoode Ltd, 1958.

WYLLY, COLONEL H. C., *History of the Manchester Regiment*, Forester Groom & Co. Ltd, 1925.

Anonymous
Pen Pictures of the War, Horace Marshall & Son, 1900.
'Defender', *Sir Charles Warren and Spion Kopf*, Smith, Elder & Co., 1902.
'Linesman', *Words by an Eyewitness*, William Blackwood & Sons, 1902.
'An Average Observer', *The Burden of Proof*, Grant, Richards, 1902.
Who's Who at the War, Adam & Charles Black, 1900.

And many unpublished diaries and letters.

INDEX

Compiled by Gordon Robinson

à Court, Colonel, 259, 260, 261, 266, 331, 341–2
Abadie, Lieutenant, 298
Abdy, Major, 81, 218, 364
accidents due to mistaken identity: East Surreys fire on West Yorks, 137
Acton Homes, 208, 230, 245, 248, 250, 260
Addison, Major, 151
Adye, Major, 83, 91
Albert, 94
Albrecht, Trooper, 220
Allen, Private, 60
Aloe Knoll, 261, 262
Altham, Major, 109–10
Amajuba (Majuba), 234
Amery, L. S., 140
armoured train: expeditions, 126, 127–8; attack by Boers, 129–35
Ashby, Mr, 153
Atkins, J. B., 254, 263, 280, 310 325, 328, 334, 344, 351
atrocities: stories from Elandslaagte, 50–1, 52–5; from Ladysmith, 120, 121; from Frere station, 135; by Kaffirs against Boers, 376–7
Australasia, 26
Ava, Lord, 161, 169
Avoca, 28

Babtie VC, Major, 191
baby, first of the siege, 108
Baden-Powell, 1st Baron, 124, 163, 175
Badenhorst, Field-Cornet, 282
Ball, Private W., 61
Barker, Archdeacon, 96, 101, 104, 226

Barton, Major-General, 125, 136, 180, 181, 192, 241, 324, 328, 341, 347, 350
Bastion Hill, 255
Bateson, Major, 100
Baynes, Right Reverend Arthur Hamilton (Bishop of Natal), 5, 14, 20, 40, 75, 201–2, 242, 246, 247, 249, 257, 258
Bearcroft, E. J., 195
Beasley, Lieutenant, 87
Beauchamp-Butt, Colonel, 358
Bell's Kopje, 154
Belmount, 148
Bergendal, battle of, 374
Berney, Captain, 327
Bester's Valley, 213, 215
Bethune, Colonel, 265
Bethune's Mounted Infantry, 270
Bewicke-Copley, Major, 269, 270, 271
Bezuidenhout, G., 111
Biggarsberg Mountains, 18, 30
Billing, Trooper, 188–9
Biograph in Battle – its Story in the South African War, 25
Birdwood, Major, 360
birthday celebrations (Prince of Wales), 105–6
Blaaukrantz river, 126
Blake, Colonel, 38
Blewitt, Major, 122
Bloemfontein, ideas about capturing, 94, 107, 321; Roberts enters, 373
Bloemfontein Conference (1899), xiv, 1
'Bloody Mary' naval gun, 82
Blueback Ridge, 115
Border Mounted Rifles, 150
Border Regiment, 183, 184, 186, 341
Boschrand, 307, 314

Boseley, Sergeant, 218, 296

Botha, General Louis (Boer commander): takes command from Meyer, 78; victory at battle of Ladysmith, 88; devastator of British, 118; youthful inventiveness, 126; dominates Mooi river, 136; stands fast at Brynbella Hill, 137–8; strengthening Colenso position, 132, 177, 200; battle despatch after brilliant victory at Colenso, 193, 200, 201; praise for Colonel Long's impetuosity, 196–7; on bravery of British Irish Brigade, 200, 201; Spion Kop: defeat turns to victory, 260, 262, 269, 277–8, 279; compassion for the enemy, 292; depletion of army on invasion of Orange Free State, 293, 294, 295; absence in Natal, 306, 307, returns to front, 317; writes of British retreat at Vaal Krantz, 320; intelligent assessment, 329; refuses armistice, 337; blind optimism, 344; hole torn across his line, 349; among last to retreat from Tugela Heights, 351; persuades men to hold rearguard, 364; at Kroonstad withdrawal, 372; agonizing debates, 375; supports British Commonwealth, 376; surrender at Heidelberg, 377–8

Bothma, Machiel F., 300, 312–13, 314

Bottomley, Captain, 355

Bowen, Major Robert, 102, 108, 114, 116, 145, 146–7, 158–9, 164, 170–1, 217, 225

Brabant's Horse, 125

Brackenbury, General, 119

Bradford, Private, 263

Brakfontein Hills, 301–2, 305, 306, 307, 308, 316

bravery: of Irish Brigade at Colenso, 200, 201; of Devons at Wagon Hill, 221–3, 225; of Imperial Light Horse at Wagon Hill, 225–6

Bridges, Tom, 356

Bridle Drift, 178, 183, 200

British Ambulance Corps, 195

Brocklehurst, General, 99, 152, 358

Brodrick, St John, 374

Bronkhorst Spruit, xiii

Brooke, Colonel, 336

brutality: of British at Elandslaagte, 52–5; of Boers shelling Ladysmith hospital, 120, 121

Brynbella Hill, 123, 136–8

Buchanan-Riddell, Colonel, 269, 271

Buller VC, General Sir Redvers (C.-in-C. South Africa): doubts his ability to command, 9–10; gazetted C.-in-C., 12; excluded from War Office conferences 13–14; difficult relationship with Lansdowne, 14; audience with Queen, 22; philosophical musings, 22–3; fearlessness described by Earl de la Warr, 24–5; tentative advice to White, 93–4; thinks about capturing Bloemfontein, 94; lands at Cape Town, 123; impassiveness, 124; telegraphs for extra division, 125; splits his army corps, 126; criticized for leaving staff at Cape, 140; goes to Natal, 140; organizing in Pietermaritzburg, 141; solicitous about care of troops, 141; loyalty of troops, 141; organizes Intelligence Department, 141; suggests surrender to White, 161–2, 196; asks Lansdowne for blockade of Delagoa Bay, 174; frontal attack and defeat at Colenso, 176–202; wounded after extraordinary ride through enemy's fire, 188–9; 'I ought to let Ladysmith go', 195–6; growing weakness as commander, 196; superseded by Roberts, 203, 204; relationship with Roberts, 207–8; announces second attempt at relief, 210–11; fails to help White, 219; marking time, 227; crosses Tugela river, 229–30; stands by whilst Caesar's Camp is attacked, 238–9; directs his army to outflank Boers, 239–42; at Mount Alice, 245, 246; 'secret' orders to Warren, 247–8; 'no turning back' appeal, 249; defeat at Taba Nyama, 254–7, 258, 285; complains about Warren's indecisiveness, 258; Spion Kop defeat, 258–82, 285; blunders save Botha from defeat, 271; praise from Churchill, 282, 319–20; withdraws south of Tugela river, 283, 285; drives Boers off Cingolo and Monte Cristo Heights, 294, 329; asks

Roberts for reinforcements, 301, 320; outclassed at battle of Vaal Krantz, 301–20; mystery of personality, 304–5; asks Roberts if Ladysmith is worth the risk, 315–16; fondness for champagne, 318; third failure to relieve, 319; occupies Colenso, 330; his metamorphosis to decisiveness, 341–2; cheered at relief of Ladysmith, 316, 362; more cautious and bumbling than ever after relief, 363; failure to attack Boers after their withdrawal, 364; personal entry into Ladysmith, 365, 366, 367; congratulations from Queen, 365; moves north at last to co-operate with Roberts at battle of Bergendal, 373–4; sent home to be GOC Aldershot, 374; consequences of surrender telegram, 374; criticized and retired on half pay, 374; death, 375

Buller, Lady, 22
Bullock, Colonel, 192–3
Bulwana Hill, 289, 291, 294, 320, 330
Burger, General Schalk, 269, 277, 306, 307, 375–6
Burleigh, Bennet, 4, 47, 49, 56, 74, 88, 97, 182–3, 261, 305, 319
Burn-Murdoch, Colonel, 183–4, 307, 313, 324, 354, 355, 363–4
Burne RN, Lieutenant C. R. N., 237
Burton, Major-General, 178
Butler, Lieutenant-General Sir William, 1–2
Byng, Lieutenant-Colonel the Honourable Julian, 244–5, 344

Caesar's Camp, 97, 103, 105, 106, 119, 159, 160; Boer attack on, 212–19 *passim*; 223, 224, 291, 297, 357, 359
Caldwell, Major, 328
Cambridge, Duke of, 22
Cape Colony: fears of rebellion, 93
Cape Town: Buller's arrival, 123
Carisbrooke Castle, 143
Carleton, Lieutenant-Colonel F. R. C., 76, 77, 82–3, 87
Carlisle, Lieutenant, 245
Carolina Commando, 261, 264, 277
cattle raiding by Boers, 115, 136
celebratory dinner party, 362–3

Cemetery Hill, 103
censorship, press, 109–10
Chamberlain, Joseph (Colonial Secretary), xiv, 1, 2, 5, 9, 19, 66, 113, 120, 203, 283, 340
Chieveley, 128, 160, 201, 202, 207, 239, 240, 241, 243, 289, 319, 323, 324, 325, 341
Childe, Major, 255
chocolate from the Queen, 342–3
Christian Victor, Prince, 97, 202
Christmas Day (1899), 167–71
Christopher House, 215, 218
church parade, 305
Churchill, Winston: at sea *en route* for Cape Town, 23–4, 25, 26; unsolicited advice to Buller, 97; describes debarkation, 123; views Colenso, 126–7; a new hero, but captured during armoured car expedition, 127–33, 134, 181; at Gun Hill after escape from Pretoria, 237; hears attack on Caesar's Camp, 238, 239; on army's excess baggage, 242–3; takes messages, 244, 255; present at ambush of Boers, 252; climbs Taba Nyama, 257; tales of Spion Kop, 267, 272, 274; in praise of Buller, 282, 319–20; attends church parade, 305; at battle of Vaal Krantz, 314, 317; with wounded younger brother, 324–5; with Dundonald on Cingolo Mountain, 326; on captured Monte Cristo, 329; with Buller, 333; at Inniskilling Hill, 334; provides light relief, 344; views action at Railway Hill, 348–9; and Boer prisoners, 352 galloping to relieve Ladysmith, 359–61; witnesses entry of Buller's army, 366
Cincinnati Enquirer, 52
cinematography, 25, 242
Cingolo hills, 294, 325, 326–9, 328–9, 341
Clark, Lawrence Gordon, 243, 244, 327
Clery, General Sir Francis: occupies Frere and makes it forward British base, 117, 141; commanding in Natal, 126, 140; lays groundwork for organization of Natal Field Force, 140–1; relinquishes command to Buller, 141; orders put out in his name at battle

Clery, General Sir Francis—*cont.*
of Colenso, 180; accompanies Buller
under fire at Colenso, 180; at funeral
of Lieutenant Roberts, 202; ordered
to make demonstration in front of
Colenso, 238; camped at Pretorius
Farm, 239–40, 241, 243, 244; assault
on Taba Nyama, 254; attack on Spion
Kop, 257; in command at battle of
Vaal Krantz, 302, 319
Clowes, Lieutenant, 360
Cockburn, Major, 116
Codrington, Captain, 216
Coke, Major-General Talbot, 240,
246–7, 253, 257, 258, 264–6, 267, 268,
269, 270, 271, 273–5, 331, 332, 341,
342
Colenso, 92, 93, 94, 95, 96, 125, 126,
139, 142, 143, 160; British defeat at
battle of, 161, 163, 164, 175, 176–202;
map, 179; 242, 319, 321, 324, 329;
occupied by British, 330, 341
Colesburg, 125
Commonwealth ideal, 376
communication: difficulties, 107, 109–10;
heliographic, 145, 246, 287, 291; with
Boers in no-man's-land, 338–40
compassionate treatment of British
wounded by Boers, 98
Composite Regiment, 326
Conan Doyle, Sir Arthur, 40
concentration camps introduced, 375, 376
Congreve VC, Captain, 190, 191, 192–3
Conical Hill, 261
Connaught Rangers, 183, 184, 188, 334,
347
Connaught's Hill, 270
Convent Hill, 166, 215, 235, 362, 365
convent hospital evacuated after shelling,
105
Conyngham Greene (British representa-
tive in Pretoria), 19, 20, 21
Cooke, Colonel, 269, 273
Copley, Major Bewick, 202
Corps of Guides, 150
Cove Redoubt, 103, 235
Coventry's Farm, 270
cowardice: Boer, 53–4; British, 184, 186,
198
Craddock, Mr, 145–6

Crofton, Colonel, 263, 265, 266, 273, 332
Cronje, Andries, 306
Cronje, General, 68, 281, 297, 306, 343,
346, 371

Daily Chronicle, 48, 54, 71, 97, 99, 106,
120, 121, 228, 229, 285, 296
Daily Mail, 51, 84, 118, 228
Daily News, 42, 286, 289, 293, 295
Daily Telegraph, 56, 88, 112, 117, 120,
182, 305, 319
Dartnell, Colonel, 60, 61, 64, 169, 170
Davies, Major Karri, 151, 152, 169, 170,
364
Davis, Charles, 275
Davis, Webster, 212
Davitt, Michael, 261
Dawkins, Major, 81
Dawnay, H., 79
De Jager, Field-Cornet Zacharias, 219,
220
De Koch, Mr, 268
De La Rey, General, 118, 327, 375
De la Warr, Earl, 24, 265, 282, 306, 319
De Lasalle, Colonel, 142
De Lasalle, Mr, 142
De Villiers, Corporal L., 264
De Villiers, Field-Cornet Japie, 219, 220
De Villiers, General, 216, 219
De Vos, Walter, 264
De Vries, Field-Cornet, 111
De Wet, General Christian, 87, 88, 118,
372, 375
De Witt Hamer, Captain, 56
Delagoa Bay, 174, 286
Dennis, Lieutenant, 220
Denny, Major, 253–4
description of Ladysmith, 26–7
Devon Regiment, 188, 192, 220–2, 225,
239, 289, 313, 317, 327, 332, 362, 366
Devonshire Post, 150
Dick-Cunyngham VC, Colonel, 44, 121,
216
Dickson, W. K.-L., 25, 242, 304, 306,
365
Dixon, Captain Clive, 79, 358
documents, incriminating discovery at
Dundee, 66–7
Dommisse, Mr, 279–80, 364, 372, 377
Doorn Kop, 239, 301, 310, 314, 317

Dormant Commission, 206
Dorset Regiment, 264, 265, 268, 270, 275
Doveton, Major, 291–2
Doveton, Mrs, 292
Down, Private, 35
Drakensberg Mountains, 28, 292
Drummer, Sergeant, 50
Du Plessis, Charlie, 111
Du Preez, Commandant Jaapie, 308
Duff, Beauchamp, 14
dummy guns constructed, 242
Duncan, Captain, 87
Dundee: exposed position, 18; Boer spies at, 27; defence of, 28–30, 31–2; desertion by British, 60–1; discovery of incriminating documents by Boers, 66–7
Dundonald, Lieutenant-General (later Major-General) the Earl of: appointed to command of mounted troops, 142–3; departure from mother, 143; reconnaissance to Colenso village, 143, 175; attack on Colenso, 178, 180; failure to capture Hlangwane Hill, 191–2, 200, 207; at Lieutenant Roberts's funeral, 202; in vicinity of Acton Homes, 230; entrenched on Mount Alice, 243, 244–5; crosses Tugela river, 249–50; the only fast-moving British commander but handi-capped by order to send back some of his men, 250, 252; destroys fifty Boers, 253; delayed by Warren, 253, 254; captures Bastion Hill, 255; attitude on third failure to relieve Ladysmith, 319; seizes Hussar Hill, 324, 325; takes Cingolo Mountain, 326–7; watching the Boer left flank, 341, 344; at battle of Pieter's Hill, 347; prevented by Buller from pursuit of Boers, 349; ordered to reconnoitre Boers, 353, 354; orders Gough to retire, 355, 356; gallops with Churchill into Ladysmith, 359–60, 361; attends celebratory dinner, 362; bivouacs at Nelthorpe, 363
Dunn, J. G., 38, 54, 63
Dunn, J. S., 225
Dunne, Bugler John Francis, 186–7

Dunottar Castle, SS, 22, 23, 24, 26, 123
Dunvegan Castle, 373
Durban: description of atmosphere, 28; decision to hold, 125; Redvers Buller lands, 126
Durban Light Infantry, 128, 130
Durham Light Infantry, 313, 314, 317, 336, 347, 349
Dwyer, Private, 184
dysentery: British supply Boers with chlorodyne, 108; 144, 164, 227, 287

East Surrey Regiment, 137, 313, 317, 327, 332, 333, 336, 347
Easton, C., 66–7, 163
Echo, 156
Edward, Prince of Wales (later Edward VII), 22, 105, 106, 111, 374
Edwards, Commandant, 270, 277
Edwards, H., 64
Edwards, Lieutenant-Colonel A., 150, 151, 153
Egerton, Lieutenant, 96
eggs for the sick and wounded, 292, 295
Elandslaagte: Boers capture goods train, 30, 41–2; battle of, 43–57; map, 45
Elliott, T., 111
Ellis, Lieutenant Flower, 264
Emmett, Field-Cornet, 192, 314
End Hill, 104
enteric fever, 114, 144, 162–3, 164, 165–6, 228, 231, 287, 292
entry of Buller's army into Ladysmith, 366–8
epidemic during siege, 160, 172, 228, 287–8
Erasmus, Major, 153
Erasmus, General, 31, 34, 37, 58, 60, 62, 63, 68, 75, 119, 156
Ermelo Commando, 314, 332
Estcourt, 125, 126–7, 136, 138
Evening News, 53
Exham, Colonel, 292
Fair View Farm, 248
Farquhar, Joseph, Mayor of Ladysmith, 101, 165, 171, 292, 295–6, 368
Field, Lieutenant, 222
field hospitals, 194–5, 280–1
firing habits of Boers, 104, 110
Fitzgerald, Captain, 220

Flagstone Spruit, 103
flood threat by German, 286, 293, 297
Fly Kraal Post, 163
food shortage at Ladysmith, 121, 156, 165, 171; eating the horses, 235, 286–7, 290, 293
Forbes, Sergeant, 48
Ford, Father, 225
Forestier Walker, General Sir F. (GOC Cape Colony), 13, 16, 23, 123, 206
Fort Itala, 275
Fort Wylie, 180, 182, 197
Forte, HMS, 178
Foss, Mr, 289
Fowke, Captain, 151
franchise argument, xiv, 19
Freeman, Sergeant J., 34
French, Major-General John (later Field-Marshal Sir John), 41, 43, 44, 46, 56, 76, 78, 95, 97, 125
Frere, 128, 141, 143; armoured train attacked and Churchill's capture near Frere station, 129–35; 209, 210, 238, 239, 240, 241, 242
Fyffe, Captain, 87

Gale, Captain, 66
Galopaud, M., 192
Gandhi, 272
Gatacre, General, 125, 174, 175, 176, 206
Gedge, Mr, 202
Gelderland, 375
German volunteers with the Boers, 42
Gladstone, William Ewart, xiii
Glanfield, Private, 193
Glencoe: its exposed position, 13, 18; stand made by Penn-Symons, 19, 21; rail communication interrupted, 30, 41
Globe, The, 24, 306
Gloucestershire Regiment, 71, 83–4, 86, 87, 88, 90, 91, 92
gold discovery in Traansvaal precipitates war, xiii–xiv
Goldie, Captain, 182
Golding, G. J., 57
Goodman, Private, 281
Gordon, Adam Lindsay, 159
Gordon, Captain, 187

Gordon Highlanders, 47–8, 49, 50, 112, 117, 120, 163, 168, 213, 216, 218, 362
Gordon Hill, 103
Gore, Major St John C. (later Lieutenant-Colonel), 47, 166, 232, 235, 289, 290, 291, 296–7, 298–9
Gough, Major Hubert, 326, 355–61, 362, 363
Gough, John, 326
Grant, Lieutenant-Colonel, 237–9, 254–5, 256, 276, 278, 304–5, 306, 309–10, 310–11, 315, 327, 338–9, 340, 342, 366–7, 367–8
Grant, Major, 66
Graphic, 228
Graspan, 148
graves of British, 224–5
Green Hill, 261, 301, 313, 315, 316, 317
Greytown, 94
Grimwood, Colonel G. C., 76, 77, 78–9, 80, 81
Grobellar's Hill, 331–2
Groenwald, Gunner, 164
guerilla warfare, 372, 375
Gun Hill, 76, 147, 148; night sortie on Boer guns, 150–3, 164; 187, 193, 195, 237, 238, 242, 325
Gunning, Colonel Bobby, 32, 35

Haig, Major Douglas (later 1st Earl), 95
Haldane, Captain A., 127–9, 130, 132, 133
Hall, Bobbie, 47
Hall, George, 32, 213–15, 220, 221, 223, 367, 375
Hallahan, Corporal, 63–4
Hamilton, Colonel Ian (later General Sir Ian): respect for Boers, 3; accompanies White to Natal, 14; wins fight at Elandslaagte, 43, 50; commands 7th Brigade in battle of Ladysmith, 77, 79, 81; defending Ladysmith, 103; beats Boers at Wagon Hill, 212, 213, 215, 216, 217, 220, 224; praise for Imperial Light Horse, 225–6; greets relief force, 358; attends celebratory dinner, 362–3; letter to wife, 366; reports that Buller is no use, 373
Hannay, Colonel, 372
Harris, Admiral Sir R., 75
Harrismith men, 219

Hart, Major-General Fitzroy: commands 5th Brigade at Colenso, 178; decimation of his Irishmen, 183–4, 186, 187–8, 196, 200; blamed by Buller for losses, 198–9; moved to Pretorius Farm, 240, 241; cause of losses to the 11th Brigade, 254; ridiculous commands, 256; in favour of staying on Vaal Krantz, 319; holds Gun Hill, 325; refusal to duck while under fire, 330; back at Colenso, 330; assault on Inniskilling Hill, 333, 336, 338, 341, 347, 349

Hattingh, Commandant, 307

headquarters, Sir George White's, 102; hit by shells, 166; 219–20

Heidelberg surrender by Boers, 377–8

Helpmakaar Ridge, 103, 119

Hely-Hutchinson, Sir Walter (Governor of Natal), 2–3, 18, 21

Henderson, Major, 150, 152, 228

Hendry, Jack, 184, 186

Herald, Walter, 51

Herbert, Captain Kenny, 141, 181, 182, 188

Herbst, Mrs Helena, 351

Hertzog, General James, 375, 376

Highland Brigade, 176

Hildyard, General, 125, 126, 136, 138, 140, 178, 180, 181, 183, 188, 202, 239, 241, 254, 313, 317, 318, 327, 341

Hill, Colonel, 269, 273

Hillegas, H. C., 352–3

Hinton, Driver Fred, 189

History of the War in South Africa, 60

Hlangwane Hill, 177–8, 180, 191–2, 197, 200, 207, 289, 290, 294, 319, 323, 324, 328, 329, 334, 341

Hobbs, Major, 137, 138

Hockaday, Corporal, 220

Holland Volunteer Contingent, 56

Hordern, Rev. A. V. C., 219

horses' fate, 235, 286, 290, 291

hospitals shelled, 105, 120, 165

hostilities begin, 21, 26, 27

Howard, Major-General F., 103

Hughes, Captain, 189

hundredth day of siege, 290

Hunt, Colonel, 181, 182, 189, 197

Hunter, General Sir Archibald (chief-of-staff to White): commands Ladysmith, 44; with artillery at battle of Ladysmith, 81; indispensable to White, 124; question of replacing White, 140; leads assault on Gun Hill, 150–1, 152–3; frankly states that no officer in Ladysmith knows the country, 290; greets relief party, 358; Churchill says everyone calls Hunter 'the finest man in the world', 363

Hussar Hill, 324, 325

Hussars, 19th, 219, 362; 13th, 355

Illustrated London News, 48, 56, 156

Impati Hill, 30, 31, 34, 37, 58

Imperial Light Horse, 47, 48, 104, 112, 118, 150, 151, 153, 158, 167, 200, 213, 215, 216, 220, 222, 225–6, 239, 250, 355, 360, 361, 364

Imperial Light Infantry, 263, 265, 267, 347

Impressions of a War-Correspondent, The, 56

Indian contingent, 17

individuality of Boers, 3, 105

Ingogo, xiii

Inniskilling Hill, 332, 333–6, 337, 338–41, 344, 346, 347, 348, 349, 363

Intaba Nyama, see Taba Nyama

Intelligence Department: organized by Buller, 141; 330

Intintanyani, 68, 70

Intombi Camp, wounded and civilians transferred to, 101; 171; sickness and death rate, 287–8, 296; 291–2, 356, 359, 365

invasion of Natal by Boers, 27–8, 126

Irish Brigade (the 5th), slaughtered at Colenso, 183–4, 186–8, 196, 200, 254; 330, 335–6

Irish-American Brigade with the Boers, 38, 54, 63, 261

Iron Railway Bridge at Colenso, 94, 117, 138, 178, 180, 183

Irregular Horse (Dundonald's), 230, 293, 341, 363

Jameson, Leander Starr, xiv, 102, 112, 152

Jameson Raid, xiv
Jelunga, 79
jingoism, 36, 87, 101
Johannesburg, xiii; British occupy, 373
Johannesburg Commando, 47, 51, 53
Johannesburg Police, 137, 138, 192
Jomini, General, 23
Jones RN, Captain E. P., 178, 365
Jones VC, Lieutenant Digby, 153, 154, 213, 214, 215, 220
Joubert, Field-Cornet, 50
Joubert, Commandant-General Piet: invades Natal, 30–1; urges Meyer to move from Dundee, 62–3; sympathy and regrets in letter to White, 65; restraint at battle of Ladysmith, 82, 88; compassion for wounded prisoners, 98; agrees to movement of townspeople to Intombi, 100; accompanies Botha in the invasion of southern Natal, 126; orders Churchill's imprisonment for the duration, 133; injured when thrown from horse, 138; wife loads his guns, 163; orders reoccupation of Hlang-wane, 177; marital arrangements, 211–12; bombards Caesar's camp, 218; refuses help to General Smuts, 307; ill in Pretoria, 344; fails to prevent retreat, 364
Joubert, Mrs, 212, 218
journals, siege, 113–14, 118–20, 121–2, 145–6, 148–8, 157, 164–5, 116–17, 210, 225, 227–8, 289
Junction Hill, 102–3

Kaffir tribes, 376–7
Kainguba Heights, 83, 84, 87, 88, 92, 124
Kekewich, Colonel, 124
Kelly, Commandant, 307
Kempsey, Private Oliver, 4
Kimberley, besieged by Boers, 23, 123, 124, 234, 340; relieved by Lord Roberts's cavalry, 343
Kincaid, Major, 98
kindness, acts of: at Elandslaagte, 55–6; at battle of Ladysmith, 89
King's Post Hill, 80, 103, 153, 358
King's Royal Rifles, 34, 215, 216, 217, 219, 269, 270, 271, 317, 323, 332

Kipling, Rudyard, 344
Kitchener of Khartoum, Field-Marshal 1st Baron, 23; appointed chief-of-staff to Lord Roberts, 203, 204; orders callous assault on Boers at Paardeberg, 371–2; takes over command from Roberts, 375; fighting guerilla war with Boers, 375; peace treaty negotiations, 376
Kitchener, Colonel F. W. (later Brigadier), 136, 137, 341, 347, 348
Klip river, 103, 104, 121, 147, 160, 165, 286, 293, 297, 357, 361, 363, 364
Knox, Colonel W. G., 80, 102, 117, 150, 152, 160, 362
Knox, Lieutenant E. Blake, 249, 256, 278–9, 308, 310, 317, 318, 325, 333, 334, 347, 348, 349, 350, 352
Knox, Major, 37, 39
Knox-Gore, Captain, 264
Kock, General, 31, 41, 43, 44, 46, 55, 60
Krantz, Herr, 297
Krantz, Mrs Otto, 351
Krieger, Dr, 352–3
Kroonstad, Boers start guerilla war, 372
Kruger, Paul Johannes (President, Transvaal): smashes Uitlanders during Jameson Raid, xiv; makes concessions to Milner, xiv; hardens attitude, xv; God-fearing, 142, 143; dispatch from Botha at Colenso, 193, 200; reluctantly supports attack on Ladysmith, 212; stiffening prophecy for burghers, 329, 375; fails to stop retreat, 372; with-draws to Portuguese East Africa, 373; exiled to Europe, 375
Krugersdorp Commando, 137, 138, 192, 201

ladies of Ladysmith, their coolness, 80
'Lady Anne' naval gun, 82
Ladysmith, battle of: route of British, 76–92
Ladysmith Bombshell, The, 113–14, 145–6, 166–7, 210, 225, 227–8, 289
Ladysmith Lyre, The, 118–20, 121–2, 148–9, 157, 164–5, 228, 289
Lafone, Captain, 222
Laing's Nek, xiii, 275

Lambton, Captain the Honourable
Hedworth, 82, 96, 105, 107, 114, 121,
164
Lancer's Hill, 104, 160, 210–11, 230, 234
Lancers, 5th, 52–3, 54, 82, 219
Lang, Colonel, 371
Langewacht Spruit, 330
Lansdowne, 5th Marquess of (Secretary
of State for War), 9, 10, 11, 12, 13,
14, 22, 92, 125, 140, 142, 174–5, 195,
202, 203, 204, 205, 209, 323
Lascelles, Mr, 314
Leicester Mounted Infantry, 115
Leicester Post, 103
Lennox Hill, 37, 39
Levita, Captain, 272
Limit Hill, 77, 79, 82, 150, 364
Limpus RN, Captain, 348
Lindsay, Sergeant, 220
Lines, G. W., 156
Liverpool Regiment, 77, 81, 218, 362
Lombaard, Field-Cornet, 111–12
Lombard's Kop, 77, 78, 81, 96, 104, 108,
150, 152
Long, Colonel, 126, 127, 180–1, 182,
183, 188, 189, 196–8, 200
Long Hill, 75, 76, 77, 78, 104, 364
Long Valley, 159, 160
'Long Tom' Creuzot gun, 78, 79, 82,
98, 103, 104, 107, 118, 119, 120,
151, 153, 298, 317, 364
Lotter, Mr, 146
Luttig, Jan, 155
Lynch, George, 56, 81–2, 105, 156–8
Lyttelton, General: leaves Cape Town
for Durban, 125; only general with
field experience, 139; begs Buller to go
to Natal, 140; commands 4th Brigade
at Colenso, 178, 180; told by Buller to
get Hart out of a mess, 187; crosses
Tugela, 230, 250, 311; moves to
Springfield, 240; approves of prayer
before going into action, 249; orders
capture of Twin Peaks, 269; orders
withdrawal after loss of confidence,
271; on Brakfontein Height, 306; assault
on Vaal Krantz, 313, 314, 315; placated
with champagne by Buller, 317–18;
withdrawal from Peaks, 319, 323; the
one general with feeling of urgency

over Ladysmith, 325, 326; tackles
Cingolo, 327; orders attack on Monte
Cristo, 328; in support at Wynne Hill,
332; assault on Inniskilling Hill, 333;
doubts about Buller, 337; cool
acceptance of casualties, 339–40;
occupies Pieter's station, 355

McBean, Captain, 347
Macdonald, Donald, 68, 70, 71, 74, 97,
104, 109–10, 114, 218, 221, 224–5,
231, 234, 359, 361
McHugh, R. J., 112, 117, 120
Mackworth, Major, 217
MacNalty, Lieutenant, 235, 286
Maconochie Kopjes, 250, 308, 310
Macpherson, Rev. E. G. F., 88, 92
Mafeking: besieged by Boers, 23, 123,
124, 163, 174, 175
Magersfontein Hills, British losses, 163,
176
Maiden Castle, 103
Majuba Day, 297, 344, 372
Majuba Hill, battle of, xiii, 3, 297
Malan, Lieutenant, 153
Malherbe, Field-Cornet Isaac, 88, 89, 350
Malherbe, John, 264
Manchester Fort, 215
Manchester Guardian, 193, 254, 263, 280,
310, 335, 328, 334, 344, 351
Manchester Regiment, 47, 48, 49, 50, 55,
81, 97–8, 215, 217, 291
maps: South Africa, xii; northern Natal,
xviii; Tugela Heights, 16; Talana Hill,
33; battle of Elandslaagte, 45; battle of
Rietfontein, 69; battle of Colenso, 179;
Taba Nyama and Spion Kop, 251;
Vaal Krantz, 303; battle of Pieter's
Hill, 345
marksmanship, Boer, 3, 133, 312
Marling VC, Major, 3–4, 21, 27, 30, 31,
39, 58, 59, 64, 65–6, 75–6, 97, 99, 101,
106, 161, 223
Martins, Reverend, 67
Masterton, Lieutenant, 222
Mathews, Father, 86
Matin, 192
Maude, Mr, 228
Maurice, Sir Frederick, 60
Melbourne Argus, 68, 104

Melvill, Captain, 66
Mentz, Commandant, 87
Metcalfe, Colonel, 153, 154, 155
Methuen, General Lord, 125, 148, 174, 175, 176, 206
Meyer, General Lucas (Boer commander): advances on Dundee, 31; tardiness in pursuing British to Ladysmith, 62–3; occupies Pepworth Hill and Long Hill, 75; nervous collapse, and is replaced by Botha, 78; in charge at Colenso, 306; stubbornness, 314; reports heavy fighting on Monte Cristo, 327; refuses armistice, 337; among last to leave Tugela Heights, 351; persuades men to hold rearguard, 364
Meyer, Oscar, 114–15
Middle Hill, 104
Middleburg Commando, 332
Middlesex Regiment, 264, 265, 267, 268, 309
Miller-Wallnutt, Major, 220
Milner, Sir Alfred (High Commissioner), xiv–xv, 1–2, 16, 123, 125, 140, 197, 340, 376
mobility of Boers, 3, 28
mobilization by Britain, 19
Modder River, 148, 176, 206
Modder Spruit, 152, 364, 365
Mohawk, 207
Molensdrift, 307
Möller, Colonel, 37, 38, 39, 58
Monte Cristo, 294, 295, 324, 327–8, 329, 330, 337, 339, 341, 346
Mooi river: as line of defence, 27; Boer defeat, 117; 136, 138, 140
Moord Kraal, 324
Moore, Mrs, 108
Morning Argus, 359
Morning Herald, 156
Morning Leader, 85, 88
Morning Post, 102, 282
Mount Alice, 243–4, 245–6, 262, 266, 271, 313, 315
Mountain Battery No. 10, 77, 79, 84, 89, 90, 91, 92, 118, 150
Mounted Infantry Brigade, 372
Mounted Infantry Hill, 104, 218
Muggison, Miss, 165

Munger's Drift, 302
Murphy, Sergeant, 50
Murray, Sergeant George, 187
Murray, Hon. T. K., 141
Murray, Major, 64
Myers, Molly, 76

Natal: possibility of Boer invasion, 18; invasion, 27–8, 30; 126; fears of rebellion, 93; British troops move into south, 107
Natal Carabineers, 218, 252, 291, 355, 357, 360, 361
Natal Field Force, 141, 164, 174, 180, 188, 199, 237, 238, 239, 275, 290, 349, 368, 373
Natal Mounted Rifles, 70, 218
Natal Mercury, 285
Natal Volunteers, 65, 70, 96, 103, 150, 151, 160, 215
Naval Brigade with their guns at Ladysmith, 82, 95, 96, 99, 107, 147–8, 167, 178, 180, 181, 213–15, 216, 235, 242, 245, 291, 315, 328, 348, 365
Nels, Reverend, 67
Nelthorpe, 359, 363
Nevinson, H. W., 48, 54, 71, 97–8, 99, 101, 104, 106–7, 109, 117, 120, 121, 171–2, 228–9, 230–1, 232, 235, 285, 286, 287, 296, 358–9
New Year 1900, 237
New York Journalist, 66
Newcastle: Boer penetration, 30
Newnham, Lieutenant, 264
Nicholson's Nek, rout of the British at, 83–92
Nineveh, 24
Norcott, General, 328, 341, 347, 349
Norgate, Mr, 183, 186
Northcote, Sir Stafford, 287
Nurse VC, Corporal, 189, 190
nurses at Intombi Camp: their heroism, 288

Observation Hill, 103, 114, 116, 119, 155, 164, 212, 230, 288, 357
Official History of the War, The, 34–5
Ogilvy, Lieutenant RN, 181, 197

O'Hara, Major, 38

O'Leary, Colonel McCarthy, 348

Onderbrook Spruit, 160, 330

Opperman, Commandant, 277

optimism of the Boers, 4

Orange Free State: support for the Transvaal, 6, 11, 16; route for attacking the Transvaal, 11–12; battle of Rietfontein, 67–73; marksmen, 85; Roberts invades, 292; Boers flee westward, 344

Packer, Mr, 267, 275, 304, 367

Paley, Captain, 155

Paardeberg: defeat of Boers, 297, 344, 346, 371–2

Paris, H. H., 40, 61

Park, Colonel, 221, 222, 289

Park, Major, 44, 46

Parsons, Colonel, 183, 302

peace treaty negotiations, 376–7

Pearse, Henry, 102, 286, 289, 293, 295

Penelope, 57

Penn-Symons, General Sir William, 1, 2–3, 4, 6, 14, 18–19, 26, 27, 28–30, 31, 32, 34, 40, 41, 58, 65

Pepworth Hill, 75, 76, 77, 78, 79, 82, 95, 104, 111, 118, 364

Phillips, Captain, 274, 275, 319

Philomel, HMS, 178

Pienaar, Field-Cornet, 42, 43, 56

Pietermaritzburg: threatened by Boers, 29; protection, 94, 125, 126; 141; Buller organizing at, 120–1

Pieter's Hill, 337, 341, 344; map, 345; battle of, 346–53; 363

pig-sticking, human, 52–3

Pine, Sir B. C. C., 27

Platrand, 307

Platt, Gunner, 181–2

Pohlmann, Lieutenant, 201

Pollard, Captain, 38

Pom-pom Bridge, 333

population of Ladysmith, 27; deterioration under shell fire, 104–5; philosophical attitude, 116–17; dogged spirit, 145

Porrit's Drift, 241

Potgieter's Drift, 142, 159, 164, 175, 176, 208, 210, 211, 229, 230, 231, 233, 234, 241, 244, 247, 250, 302, 306, 307

Powerful, HMS, 82, 121, 167, 365, 367

preparation for war, British, 66–7

present-day Ladysmith, ix–x

Pretoria: Churchill's escape, 237; British occupation, 373

Pretoria Commando, 84, 264

Pretorius, Commandant, 338, 339–40

Pretorius, Mr and Mrs, 244

Pretorius Farm, 239, 240, 241, 243, 244, 245

Prinsloo, Chief-Commandant Marthinus, 67

Prinsloo, Mr, 311

Prior, Melton, 44, 46, 48–9, 54, 56, 88, 90, 96, 97

propaganda: anti-Boer, 51; anti-British, 66–7

psychological: problem, 114; warfare, 155

Puck magazine, 283

Queen's Regiment, 188, 317, 327

Queenstown, 175

raiding actions out of Ladysmith: on Gun Hill, 150–3; on howitzer on Surprise Hill, 153–6

Raikes, Lieutenant, 217

Railway Hill, 336, 337, 341, 344, 346, 347, 348, 349, 363

Range Post, 103, 118, 119, 288

Ration Post, 103

Rawlinson, Lieutenant-Colonel Sir Henry, 3, 293, 363

Rawnsley, Canon H. D., 186, 197–8, 371

Reed VC, Captain, 191

regiments in South Africa, British, 6; Indian, 17; British inside Ladysmith perimeter, 98–9

Reinecke, Robert, 264

Reitz, Deneys, 37–8, 39, 84, 85, 87–8, 89–90, 155, 211, 264, 276–7, 278, 279, 346, 350

Reitz, F. W., 36–7, 155

relief of Ladysmith, 354–69

relieving force: Nov. 1899, 123–44; Dec. 1899, 174–209; Jan. 1900, 237–84; Feb. 1900, 300–53

religion: Boers, 46, 67, 101–2, 115–16, 157; British, 249, 257, 305

retreat of Boers, 364–5

retreat of British to Ladysmith, 58–73

Rhodes, Cecil, xiv, 25, 124, 169, 242, 340

Rhodes, Major Frank (later Colonel), 25, 102, 112, 161, 169

Rice, Captain, 84–5, 86, 87

Richardson, Private, 189

Riddell, Colonel Buchanan, 202

Rietfontein, battle of, 67–73; map, 69

Rifle Brigade, 79, 81, 153, 154, 155, 158, 313, 315, 328, 330, 347, 366

Rifle Brigade Chronicle for 1900, 79

Rifle Reserve Battalion, 332, 341

Rifleman's Post, 103

Rifleman's Ridge, 104

Rigby, Captain, 22, 26

Roberts VC, Lieutenant the Hon. Fred S., 190–1, 201–2, 203, 204

Roberts of Kandahar and Waterford, 1st Baron, Field-Marshal, 8, 9, 190, 202; death of son at Colenso, 201, 203–4; supersedes Buller as C.-in-C. South Africa, 203, 204; relationship with Buller, 207; advises evacuation of Ladysmith, 207; cannot reinforce Buller, 234, 321; asks White to hold out, 234; proposed march into Orange Free State, 283–4; enters Orange Free State, 292, 295; captures General Cronje, 297; Buller asks him for another Division, 301; tells Buller that Ladysmith must be relieved at any cost, 316; asks for Warren's views, 322, 331; defeat of Boers at Paardeberg, 346, 371; enters Bloemfontein, 373; army takes Pretoria, 373; turns on Buller, 374; proclaims annexation of Transvaal, 375; institutes scorched-earth policy and concentration camps, 375; hands over to Kitchener, 375; replaces Wolseley as C.-in-C. British Army, 375; death in France, 375

Roberts, Lady, 202

Roestof, G., 111

Rogers, Private, 55

Rosalie Farm, 248

Rose, Lieutenant, 266

Rouillard, Dr, 146

Royal Army Medical Corps, 89

Royal Artillery: bravery at battle of Ladysmith, 81; losses at Colenso, 181–3, 188, 189–91; 215, 218, 249; inefficiency at Spion Kop, 262; 304, 307, 308, 310–11, 313, 328, 341, 362, 364

Royal Commission on the War in South Africa, 196

Royal Dragoon Guards, 168, 183, 252, 290, 362, 366

Royal Dublin Fusiliers, 34, 35, 36, 37, 77, 87, 94, 128, 183; death-trap at Colenso, 184, 187; at Taba Nyama battle, 257; 334, 347, 350, 366

Royal Engineers, 213, 215, 221, 250, 260, 261, 271, 308, 309–10, 333, 347, 365, 367

Royal Hotel: used by the élite, 102, 112

Royal Inniskilling Fusiliers, 183, 184, 188, 334–6, 347

Royal Irish Fusiliers, 35, 36, 38, 63–4, 83, 84–5, 89, 90, 91, 92, 328, 347, 350

Royal Lancashire Fusiliers, 254, 258, 259, 260, 262, 264, 270

Royal Lancaster Regiment, 258, 260, 262, 270, 273, 275, 330, 332, 347, 348, 349

Royal Red Cross, 288, 353

Royal Scots Fusiliers, 328, 347, 350

Royal Welsh Fusiliers, 241, 328

Royston, Colonel, 76, 103, 150, 159

St Andrew's Day, 120

Salisbury, 3rd Marquess of (Prime Minister), 5, 203

Salt, Lieutenant George, 197, 319

Sand River Convention, xiii

Sandbach, Colonel, 337

Schiel, Lieutenant-Colonel, 42, 44, 56

Schofield VC, Captain, 189, 190

Schreiber, Captain, 182

Schreiner (Prime Minister, Cape Colony), 123

scorched-earth policy, 375, 376

Scott, SS, 16, 17

Scott-Chisholme, Colonel, 43

Scottish Rifles, 268, 269, 336, 347

Shepton, Private Ernest, 343

Sherston, Colonel, 35
siege: Nov. 1899, 96–122; Dec. 1899, 145–72; Jan. 1900, 210–36; Feb. 1900, 285–99
Sims, Gunner, 220
Sitwell, Colonel, 336
Skiet's Drift, 247, 301, 307
Smith, Ernest, 44, 46
Smith, E. W., 85, 88, 89
Smith's Nek, 34, 39
Smuts, Jan, 19, 152, 375, 376
Smuts, Combat-General Tobias, 306, 307, 314
South African Light Horse, 125, 244, 245, 249, 255, 293, 326, 344
South Lancashire Regiment, 260, 332, 347, 348
Spearman, Mr, 244
Spearman's Camp, 304, 306
Spearman's Farm, 243, 244, 249, 262, 280, 307
Spearman's Hill, 302, 307
spies and rumours of spies, 28, 114–15, 144, 171
Spion Kop, 159, 229, 230, 231, 233, 234, 243, 245, 247, 248, 250; map, 251; 254, 257; British defeat at, 258–82, 285; 301, 304, 305, 306, 309, 310, 311, 312, 314, 322, 323
Springfield, 176, 210, 240, 241, 243, 245, 248
Springfield Bridge, 243
Standard and Diggers' News, 134, 157, 200
Standerton, 373
Star Hill, 104, 115
Starke, Dr, x, 112–13
Steevens, G. W., 51, 70, 71, 77–8, 90, 118, 147–8, 164–5, 228–9
Stephenson, Bombardier, 191
Steyn, Martinus (President, Orange Free State), 6, 16, 212, 372, 375
Stirling, Lieutenant R. G., 32, 34, 35
Stoneman, Colonel, 118, 228
Stopford, Colonel, 187
Stormberg, 163; British disaster, 175; 206
Strong, Peter, ix–x, 187
Sundays: agreement not to fight on, 101–2, 115

Sunday's River, 364
Surprise Hill, 80, 104, 115, 148; assault on Boer positions at Surprise Hill, 154–6; 290
surrender by Boers, 377–8
surrender telegram and its aftermath, 161–2; 196, 373, 374
Swaartz Kop, 287, 302, 308, 313, 318
Swaziland Commando, 200

Taba Nyama Heights, 208, 229, 231, 243, 245, 248, 250; map, 251, 252; battle on, 254–7, 258, 285, 304, 316, 325
Tabanhlope Mountains, 125–6
Talana Hill: map, 33; battle of, 32–40
Tale of a Field Hospital, The, 194
Tantallon Castle, 14, 16
Tartar, HMS, 126, 127, 128
Telegraph Hill, 115, 154
Telegraph Ridge, 104
Terrible, HMS, 178, 348
Thackeray, Colonel, 188
Thompson, Private L., 35
Thompson, Rev., 225
Thorneycroft, Lieutenant-Colonel (sometime General), 192, 259, 264, 266, 268, 269, 270–1, 272–3, 274, 276, 293, 355, 360
Thorneycroft's Mounted Infantry, 137, 192, 258, 260, 261, 262, 263, 264, 267, 270, 272, 355
Thornhill, Mr, 153
Thornhill's Kop, 104, 115, 288
Three Tree Hill, 254, 256, 259, 260, 268
Times, The, 47, 53, 139, 267, 374
Times History of the War in South Africa, The, 56, 60, 78–9, 80–1, 140, 180
Tintwa Pass: Boer invasion point, 27, 28
Tod, Lieutenant, 217
Town Hall: as hospital, 74; hit by shell, 120, 165
Transvaal: annexation, xiii; ultimatum to Britain, 19–20; Roberts proclaims annexation, 375
treachery in Ladysmith, 144
Treves, Sir Frederick, 193–5, 201, 249, 280–1
Trichardt, General, 62, 63
Trichardt's Drift, 229, 247, 249, 258

Tringham, Lieutenant, 72
Tuckey, Rev., 225
Tugela Heights, 107–8, 109, 159, 211,
    219, 229, 230, 232, 233, 234, 243, 250,
    253, 292, 301, 302, 305, 308, 316, 349,
    350, 351, 353
Tugela river: as a defensive line for the
    British, 13; difficulties of crossing, 109;
    Boer crossing to invade Natal, 125;
    Boer withdrawal to north bank, 138;
    Buller's plans and failures to cross,
    159 et seq.; first British crossings, 250
    et seq.; Buller retreats across, 283,
    285; Boers hasten to northern bank,
    329; Buller's army across, 331; Buller
    orders artillery back south of river,
    337, 341; British advance across, 346–7
Tunnel Hill, 103
Turner, Lieutenant, 151
Twin Peaks, 245, 261, 269, 271, 325
typhoid fever, 231

Uitlanders: rebellion and defeat, xiv
ultimatum from Boers to British
    Government, 19–20
Umbulwana Hill, 77, 101, 103, 104, 111,
    117, 118, 163, 165, 218, 287, 291, 297,
    323, 355, 364
Utrecht Commando, 269

Vaal Krantz, 159, 245; battle of, 301–20;
    map, 303
Van der Merwe, J. F., 111
Van der Walt, G., 111
Van Reenan's Pass, 231
Van Tonders Pass, 62, 63
Van Warmelo, Dietlof, 351
Venter's Spruit, 250, 253, 254
Ventor, Mr, 118
Vereeniging peace negotiations, 376
Victoria, Queen: support and sympathy
    for troops, 9; proclamation summon-
    ing Parliament and calling out reserves,
    19; meets Buller, 22; confidence in
    White, 92; entertains Lady White at
    Windsor, 145; presents son's VC to
    Lady Roberts, 202; receives Lord
    Roberts, 203, 375; New Year message
    to Natal Field Force, 237; grief for
    Irish troops, 335; buys each soldier
    chocolate, 342–3; messages on relief
    of Ladysmith, 365
Victoria Crosses at Colenso, 191
Viljoen, General Ben: fighting command-
    ant of Johannesburg Commando, 46;
    pleads with Kock to open fire, 46;
    faces murderous attacks at Elands-
    laagte, 49–50; escapes from battle-
    field, 53; permits for cowards, 53–4;
    on loss of padres, 67; ordered to
    upper Tugela area, 154; describes
    Spion Kop victory as a fluke, 280; at
    Vaal Krantz battle, 306, 307–8, 311–12,
    313–14; humour at relief of Ladysmith,
    350; grateful at not being pursued, 364
Volkrust, 373
Von Braun, Colonel Constantine, 328
Vryheid: murder of Boers by Kaffirs, 377
Vryheid Commando, 192, 260

Wagon Drift, 177
Wagon Hill, 103, 106, 119, 159, 160,
    170, 211, 212, 213, 215; battle of, 216–
    26, 291, 297; 357
Wagon Point, 212, 213, 215, 217, 218,
    219, 220, 221, 223
Wakkerstroom burghers, 177
Walker, Lieutenant, 222
Walker, Miss Mabel, 61
Ward, Colonel E. W. D. (supply
    officer), 14, 79, 108–9, 165, 168, 286,
    292
Warren, General Sir Charles: chosen to
    command 5th Division, 205; details of
    career, 205; eccentricity, 205; lands at
    Cape Town, 206; supersedes Methuen
    on Modder front, 206; lands at
    Durban, 209; crosses Tugela, 229, 230,
    takes Spion Kop at heavy cost, 233;
    division ready to march, 239, 240, 241,
    243; Buller's orders to cross Tugela,
    247–8; crosses river, 250; depletes
    Dundonald of cavalry, 252; indecisive-
    ness on Taba Nyama, 253–5, 258;
    Spion Kop attack, 257, 258, 264–5,
    268, 270, 271–2, 275, 276; disgraceful
    blunder, 266; incompetence, 269;
    rejects Churchill's advice, 272; lunatic
    orders, 273; departure from Spion
    Kop, 280; reconnoitres Swaartz Kop,

319; Roberts seeks his views, 322–3; amusing the men, 325–6, 336–7; appalling advice for Buller, 330, 331; and dum-dum bullets, 352–3

water supply from Klip river, polluted, 103, 147, 160

Watkins, Reverend Owen Spencer, 92, 152, 155–6, 224, 225, 288, 293, 354, 357, 367

Watkins-Pitchford, H., 61, 65, 96–7, 226–7, 235–6, 291, 294, 358, 360

Watkins-Pitchford, Mrs, 226, 236

Weenen, 126, 145

Weilback, Commandant, 153, 158

Wessels, Gert, 220

West Yorkshire Regiment, 126, 137, 138, 317, 327, 336, 347, 348

Westminster Gazette, 189

Westminster Volunteers, 374

White VC, General Sir George (Natal commander); his gammy leg, 6, 8; campaigns, 8, 17; given Natal command, 8; blames financiers in the City, 8–9; first impressions of South Africa, 16–17; arrives Ladysmith, 21, 26; decides perimeter of defence, 26, 41; vacillations, 27; success at battle of Elandslaagte, 44, 46, 57, 67–73; checks Boers at battle of Rietfontein, 67–73; routed at battle of Ladysmith, 83–92; admits blame and thinks he should be superseded, 90–1; entrenches at Ladysmith, 93–4; sends non-combatants to Intombi Camp, 101; establishes defence pattern, 102–3; on psychological problem, 114; generous nature, 121; asks Buller for reinforcements, 124; Buller doubts his capabilities, 40; complains of traitors, 144; co-operates with Buller's assault, 159–60; Buller's surrender suggestion turned down, 161–2, 163; narrow escape when HQ hit, 166; moves naval guns, 213; moves to Convent Hill, 215; describes Wagon Hill success, 217, 224, 226; appeals to Buller to act, 219; offers to break out, 233–4; describes effect to India if Ladysmith should fall, 233–4; appreciation of Dundonald's confident message, 245;

praises supply officer Colonel Ward, 286; lacks knowledge of the country, 290; greets relieving force, 358, 359, 360, 361–3; 'thank God we have kept the flag flying', 362; gives celebration dinner, 362–3; welcomes Buller, 365, 367; receives address of thanks from townspeople, 368; invalided home with fever, 373; appointed Governor of Gibraltar, 373; Governorship of Royal Hospital, Chelsea, 373; death, 373

White, Lady, 92, 223, 230, 232, 233

White's Farm, 258

Wickham, Major, 60

Wilford, Colonel E. P., 71, 72

Wilkinson, Spencer, 373

Williams, W., 53

Willow Grange, battle of, 136–8, 140

Wilson, Rev. A., 267

Wilson, Lieutenant H. A. C., 267

Winburg Commando, 216

Wing, Major, 153

Witwatersrand, xiii

Wolfe-Murray, Colonel, 125, 126

Wolley, Captain, 66

Wolmaraans, Mr, 281–2

Wolseley, 1st Viscount (C.-in-C. British Army), 5, 8, 11, 13, 22, 27, 204, 206, 319, 323, 336, 374, 375

Wood, Field-Marshal Sir Evelyn, 22

Wood, Sergeant, 184

Woodgate, Major-General, 233, 240, 258, 260–1, 262, 265, 274, 278, 306

Woodhouse, Mr, 113

Woodhouse, Sergeant, 137

Wortley, Colonel Stuart, 202

wounded: exchange of, 98; praiseworthy treatment of prisoners by Boers, 98

Wright's Farm, 250

Wyndham, Major Guy, 358

Wynne, Major-General, 306, 308, 310, 319, 331–2

Wynne Hill, 331, 332, 333, 337, 341, 344, 346, 363

York, 94

York and Lancaster Regiment, 254, 347, 348

Young, Gunner C. H., 189
Yule, Brigadier-General, 34–5, 58–60,
    61, 62, 63, 64, 65, 66, 67, 68, 72

Zeppelin, Count, 56
Zoutpansberg Commando, 200
Zulus: antipathy to whites, 18